America Now

Short Readings from Recent Periodicals

NINTH EDITION

EDITED BY

Robert Atwan

Emerson College

Series Editor, *The Best American Essays*

EXERCISES PREPARED WITH THE ASSISTANCE OF

Valerie Duff-Strautmann

Jeffrey Ousborne
Suffolk University

Gregory Atwan

Bedford/St. Martin's   Boston • New York

For Bedford/St. Martin's

Developmental Editor: Christina Gerogiannis
Production Editor: Annette Pagliaro Sweeney
Production Supervisor: Ashley Chalmers
Senior Marketing Manager: Molly Parke
Editorial Assistant: Mallory Moore
Copy Editor: Nancy Benjamin, Books By Design, Inc.
Photo Researcher: Arlin Kauffman
Permissions Manager: Kalina Ingham Hintz
Senior Art Director: Anna Palchik
Text Design: Dutton & Sherman Design
Cover Design: Billy Boardman
Cover Photo: Woman at a Newsstand © Ed Eckstein/CORBIS
Composition: Glyph International
Printing and Binding: RR Donnelley & Sons

President: Joan E. Feinberg
Editorial Director: Denise B. Wydra
Director of Marketing: Karen R. Soeltz
Director of Production: Susan W. Brown
Associate Director, Editorial Production: Elise S. Kaiser
Managing Editor: Elizabeth M. Schaaf

Library of Congress Control Number: 2010936224

Acknowledgments

Adriana Barton. "If You're Happy and You Know It, You're in Third: Bronze-Medal Winner's Joyous Reaction Reaffirms Theory That Third Place Is a More Pleasant Place to Be Than Second, Psychologists Say" from *The Globe and Mail,* February 18, 2010. Copyright CTVglobemedia Publishing Inc. All rights reserved. Used by permission.
Brent Baughman. "Growing Older in the Digital Age: An Exercise in Egotism" from *The Berkeley Beacon,* Emerson College, February 25, 2010. Reprinted by permission of the author.

Acknowledgments and copyrights continue at the back of the book on pages 367–69, which constitute an extension of the copyright page. It is a violation of the law to reproduce these selections by any means whatsoever without the written permission of the copyright holder.

At the time of publication all Internet URLs published in this text were found to accurately link to their intended Web site. If you do find a broken link, please forward the information to mmoore@ bedfordstmartins.com so that it can be corrected for the next printing.

About the Editor

Robert Atwan is the series editor of the annual *Best American Essays*, which he founded in 1985. His essays, reviews, and critical articles have appeared in the *New York Times*, the *Los Angeles Times*, the *Atlantic Monthly*, *Iowa Review*, *Denver Quarterly*, *Kenyon Review*, *River Teeth*, and many other publications. For Bedford/St. Martin's, he has also edited *Ten on Ten: Major Essayists on Recurring Themes* (1992), *Our Times*, Fifth Edition (1998), and *Convergences*, Third Edition (2009). He has coedited (with Jon Roberts) *Left, Right, and Center: Voices from Across the Political Spectrum* (1996), and is coeditor with Donald McQuade of *The Writer's Presence*, Seventh Edition (2009). He is currently a special assignments faculty member at Emerson College in their Writing, Literature and Publishing department.

Preface for Instructors

People write for many reasons, but one of the most compelling is to express their views on matters of current public interest. Browse any newsstand, library magazine rack, or Web page and you'll find an abundance of articles and opinion pieces responding to current issues and events. Too frequently, students see the writing they do in a composition class as having little connection with real-world problems and issues. *America Now*, with its provocative professional and student writing — all very current opinion essays drawn from a range of periodicals — shows students that by writing on the important issues of today, they can influence campus and public discourse and truly make a difference.

The ninth edition of *America Now* offers a generous sampling of timely and provocative material. *America Now* is designed to immerse introductory writing students in the give-and-take of public dialogue and to stimulate thinking, discussion, and composition. Its overriding instructional principle — which guides everything from the choice of readings and topics to the design of questions — is that participation in informed discussion will help generate and enrich student writing.

America Now systematically encourages its users to view reading, thinking, discussion, and writing as closely interrelated activities. It assumes that (1) attentive reading and reflection will lead to informed discussion; (2) participation in open and informed discussion will result in a broadening of viewpoints; (3) an awareness of different viewpoints will stimulate further reflection and renewed discussion; and (4) this process in turn will lead to thoughtful papers.

The book's general introduction, "The Persuasive Writer: Expressing Opinions with Clarity, Confidence, and Civility," takes the student through these interrelated processes and offers some useful guidelines for engaging in productive discussion that will lead to effective essays. Three annotated student essays serve as models of persuasive opinion writing. Instructors may also find helpful my essay "Writing and the Art of Discussion," which can be found in the instructor's manual.

New to This Edition

Following is a brief overview of the ninth edition of *America Now*. For a more in-depth description of the book, see "Using *America Now*" beginning on page ix of this preface.

53 readings and 20 visual texts — all new and *very* current. Drawn from more than 46 recent periodicals, including 12 student newspapers, each reading not only is new to this edition but also has appeared within a year or two of the book's publication. With half of its selections published in 2010, *America Now* is the most current short essay reader available. Some of the readings you will find in the ninth edition are by best-selling authors Daniel Gilbert and Walter Mosley on happiness, the popular *Freakonomics* writers Steven D. Levitt and Stephen J. Dubner on irrational fears, famed novelist John Edgar Wideman on Barack Obama's biggest challenge, and noted environmentalist Bill McKibben on saving the planet.

Eight new issues of current interest — and lively visuals. Eight of the twelve thematic chapters have been updated to reflect the changing interests of students over the past two years. Sure to spark lively discussion and writing, these new topics include names, happiness, the ethics of eating, photography, fear, and privacy. In a new "media coverage" chapter, we examine whether our increasing reliance on Twitter, Facebook, and other media is dramatically altering the ways we read and write.

New "casebook" chapter. The book's final chapter, "Immigration: Who Is an American?" contains seven selections that focus on one of today's most widely discussed issues. The expanded chapter, which also includes a debate between experts on the topic, can be used by instructors who want to set up classroom panels or forums for extended discussion and writing.

A revised, student-friendly introduction now offers students more help than ever with writing at the college level. Clear and comprehensive checklists provide at-a-glance reference tools for such skills as supporting opinions.

Using *America Now*

Professional and Student Writing from a Wide Variety of Sources

The book's selections by professional writers are drawn from recent periodicals, ranging from specialized journals such as *Chronicle of Higher Education* to influential general magazines such as the *New Yorker, Outside,* and *Parade.* As would be expected in a collection that focuses heavily on social trends and current events, *America Now* features several newspapers and news-oriented magazines: the *Boston Globe,* the *New York Times,* and the *Cleveland Plain Dealer.* With its additional emphasis on public discourse, this collection also draws on some of America's leading political magazines, including *The New Republic, Mother Jones, The Nation, The Weekly Standard, American Prospect,* and *The Progressive.* Also represented are magazines that appeal primarily to specialized audiences, such as *Orion, Wired,* and *Tikkun.* In general, the selections illustrate the variety of personal, informative, and persuasive writing encountered daily by millions of Americans. The readings are kept short (many under three pages, and some no longer than a page) to hold student interest and to serve as models for the student's own writing. To introduce a more in-depth approach to various topics, the book includes a few longer essays, especially in the final chapters.

America Now also features twelve published student selections from print and online college newspapers. These recent works reveal student writers confronting in a public forum the same topics and issues that challenge some of our leading social critics and commentators, and they show how student writers can enter into and influence public discussion. In this way, the student selections in *America Now* — complemented by Student Writer at Work interviews — encourage students to see writing as a form of personal and public empowerment. This edition includes 11 brief, inspiring interviews in which student authors in the book explain how — and why — they express their opinions in writing.

To highlight models of persuasive writing, each chapter contains an annotated section of a student paper labeled "Looking Closely." The comments point out some of the most effective strategies of the student writers in the book and offer advice for stating a main point, shaping arguments, presenting examples and evidence, using quotations, recommending a course of action, and more.

Timely Topics for Discussion and Debate

Student essays not only make up a large percentage of the readings in this book, but also shape the volume's contents. As we monitored the broad spectrum of online college newspapers — and reviewed several hundred student essays — we gradually found the most commonly discussed campus issues and topics. Issues such as those mentioned on page viii of this preface have provoked so much recent student response that they could have resulted in several single-topic collections. Many college papers do not restrict themselves to news items and editorial opinion but make room for personal essays as well. Some popular student topics are climate change, gender, food, immigration, and privacy, all of which are reflected in the book's table of contents.

To facilitate group discussion and in-class work, *America Now* features ten bite-sized units and two in-depth "casebook" chapters at the end. These focused chapters permit instructors to cover a broad range of themes and issues in a single semester. Each can be conveniently handled in one or two class periods. In general, the chapters move from accessible, personal topics (for example, names, happiness, food, and photography) to more public and controversial issues (race, environment, and immigration), thus accommodating instructors who prefer to start with personal writing and gradually progress to exposition, analysis, and argument.

Since composition courses naturally emphasize issues revolving around language and the construction of meaning, *America Now* also includes a number of selections designed to encourage students to examine the powerful influence of words and symbols.

The Visual Expression of Opinion

Reflecting the growing presence of advertising in public discussion, among the book's images are recent opinion advertisements (or "op-ads"). These pieces, which focus on racial profiling and immigration, encourage students to uncover the visual and verbal strategies of various advocacy groups trying to influence the consciousness and ideology of large audiences.

Because we live in an increasingly visual culture, the book's introduction offers a section on expressing opinions visually — with striking examples from photojournalism, cartoons, and opinion advertisements. Examples from these visual genres are also found throughout the book along with the work of such graphic artists as Garry Trudeau. Another assortment of visual selections, titled "America Then," provides students with historical perspectives on "America Now." These images show that many of the issues we deal with today have roots in the past. They include the first map that named America, fallout shelters from the Cold War era, and the photograph of a Cuban child that caused a national sensation in 2000.

The Instructional Apparatus: Before, During, and After Reading

To help promote reflection and discussion, the book includes a prereading assignment for each main selection. The questions in "Before You Read" provide students with the opportunity to explore a few of the avenues that lead to fruitful discussion and interesting papers. A full description of the advantages gained by linking reading, writing, and classroom discussion can be found in my introduction to the instructor's manual.

The apparatus of *America Now* supports both discussion-based instruction and more individualized approaches to reading and writing. Taking into account the increasing diversity of students (especially the growing number of speakers for whom English is not their first language) in today's writing programs, the apparatus offers extensive help with college-level vocabulary and features a "Words to Learn" list preceding each selection. This vocabulary list with brief definitions will allow students to spot ahead of time some of the words they may find difficult; encountering the word later in context will help lock it in memory. It's unrealistic, however, to think students will acquire a fluent knowledge of new words by memorizing a list. Therefore, the apparatus following each selection includes additional exercises under the headings "Vocabulary/Using a Dictionary" and "Responding to Words in Context." These sets of questions introduce students to prefixes, suffixes, connotations, denotations, tone, and etymology.

Along with the discussion of vocabulary, other incrementally structured questions follow individual selections. "Discussing Main Point and Meaning" and "Examining Sentences, Paragraphs, and Organization" questions help to guide students step by step through the reading process, culminating in the set of "Thinking Critically" questions. As instructors well know, beginning students can sometimes be too trusting of what they see in print, especially in textbooks. Therefore, the "Thinking Critically" questions invite students to take a more skeptical attitude toward their reading and to form the habit of challenging a selection from both analytical and experiential points of view. The selection apparatus concludes with "In-Class Writing Activities," which emphasize freewriting exercises and collaborative projects.

In addition to the selection apparatus, *America Now* contains end-of-chapter questions designed to stimulate further discussion and writing. The chapter apparatus approaches the reading material from topical and thematic angles, with an emphasis on group discussion. The introductory comments to each chapter highlight the main discussion points and the way selections are linked together. These points and linkages are then reintroduced at the end of the chapter through three sets of interlocking study questions and tasks: (1) a suggested topic for discussion,

(2) questions and ideas to help students prepare for class discussion, and (3) several writing assignments that ask students to move from discussion to composition — that is, to develop papers out of the ideas and opinions expressed in class discussion and debate. Instructors with highly diverse writing classes may find "Topics for Cross-Cultural Discussion" a convenient way to encourage an exchange of perspectives and experiences that could also generate ideas for writing. Located on the book's Web site (bedfordstmartins.com/americanow) are ESL and Developmental Quizzes that test vocabulary and comprehension skills. Electronic scoring, which can be monitored by instructors, offers immediate feedback.

You get more print and digital choices for *America Now*

America Now doesn't stop with a book. Online, you'll find both free and affordable premium resources to help students get even more out of the book and your course. You'll also find convenient instructor resources, such as downloadable sample syllabi, classroom activities, and even a nationwide community of teachers. To learn more about or order any of the products below, contact your Bedford/St. Martin's sales representative, e-mail sales support (sales_support@bfwpub.com), or visit the Web site at bedfordstmartins.com/americanow.

Companion Web site for America Now

bedfordstmartins.com/americanow
Send students to free and open resources, choose flexible premium resources to supplement your print text, or upgrade to an expanding collection of innovative digital content.

Free and open resources for *America Now* provide students with easy-to-access reference materials, visual tutorials, and support for working with sources.

- *ESL and Developmental Quizzes* for every reading in *America Now*
- Links to the periodicals — professional and student — found in *America Now*
- 5 free videos of real writers from *VideoCentral*
- 3 free tutorials from *ix visual exercises* by Cheryl Ball and Kristin Arola
- *TopLinks* and *AuthorLinks* with reliable online sources
- *Research and Documentation Online* by Diana Hacker

- *Bedford Bibliographer*: a tool for collecting source information and making a bibliography in MLA, APA, and *Chicago* styles

VideoCentral is a growing collection of videos for the writing class that captures real-world, academic, and student writers talking about how and why they write. *VideoCentral* can be packaged with *America Now* at a significant discount. An activation code is required. To order *VideoCentral* packaged with the print book, use ISBN 978-0-312-58721-5.

Re:Writing Plus gathers all of Bedford/St. Martin's premium digital content for composition into one online collection. It includes hundreds of model documents, the first ever peer-review game, and *VideoCentral*. *Re:Writing Plus* can be purchased separately or packaged with the print book at a significant discount. An activation code is required. To order *Re:Writing Plus* packaged with the print book, use ISBN 978-0-312-58719-2.

i-series on CD-ROM

Add more value to your text by choosing one of the following CD-ROMs, free when packaged with *America Now*. This popular series presents multimedia tutorials in a flexible format — because there are things you can't do in a book. To learn more about package options or any of the products below, contact your Bedford/St. Martin's sales representative or visit the Web site at bedfordstmartins.com/americanow.

ix visual exercises help students put into practice key rhetorical and visual concepts. To order *ix visual exercises* packaged with the print book, use ISBN 978-0-312-58718-5.

i-claim: visualizing argument offers a new way to see argument — with 6 tutorials, an illustrated glossary, and over 70 multimedia arguments. To order *i-claim: visualizing argument* packaged with the print book, use ISBN 978-0-312-58717-8.

i-cite: visualizing sources brings research to life through an animated introduction, four tutorials, and hands-on source practice. To order *i-claim: visualizing argument* packaged with the print book, use ISBN 978-0-312-58716-1.

Instructor Resources

You have a lot to do in your course. Bedford/St. Martin's wants to make it easy for you to find the support you need — and to get it quickly. To find everything available with *America Now*, visit bedfordstmartins.com/americanow.

The Instructor's Manual for *America Now* is bound into the Instructor's Edition and is also available in PDF that can be downloaded from the companion Web site or the Bedford/St. Martin's online catalog. In addition to chapter overviews, teaching tips, and suggested answers to every question posed in the text, the Instructor's Manual includes sample syllabi and plenty of ideas for classroom activities and discussion.

Teaching Central offers the entire list of Bedford/St. Martin's print and online professional resources in one place. You'll find landmark reference works, sourcebooks on pedagogical issues, award-winning collections, and practical advice for the classroom — all free for instructors.

Bits collects creative ideas for teaching a range of composition topics in an easily searchable blog. A community of teachers — leading scholars, authors, and editors — discuss revision, research, grammar and style, technology, peer review, and much more. Take, use, adapt, and pass the ideas around. Then, come back to the site to comment or share your own suggestion.

Content cartridges for the most common course-management systems — Blackboard, WebCT, Angel, and Desire2Learn — allow you to easily download digital materials from Bedford/St. Martin's for your course.

Acknowledgments

While putting together the ninth edition of *America Now,* I was fortunate to receive the assistance of many talented individuals. I am enormously grateful to Gregory Atwan, Valerie Duff-Strautmann, and Jeffrey Ousborne who contributed to the book's instructional apparatus. They also prepared the Instructor's Manual, bringing to the task valuable classroom experience at all levels of composition instruction. Liz deBeer of Rutgers University contributed a helpful essay in the Instructor's Manual on designing student panels ("Forming Forums"), along with advice on using the book's apparatus in both developmental and mainstream composition classes.

To revise a text is to entertain numerous questions: What kind of selections work best in class? What types of questions are most helpful? How can reading, writing, and discussion be most effectively intertwined? This edition profited immensely from the following instructors who generously took the time to respond to the eighth edition: Helane Androne, Miami University Middletown campus; LaToya W. Bogard, Mississippi State University; Tim Brotherton, Georgia Perimeter College; Noreen Lace, California State University, Northridge; Samuel Maio, San Jose State University; Mahli Xuan Mechenbier, Kent State University; Marti Miles-Rosenthfield, Collin College; Timothy Quigley, Salem State College; Julia Ruengart, Pensacola Junior College; Guy

Shebat, Youngstown State University; and Bradley Tucker, Georgia Perimeter College.

I'd also like to acknowledge instructors who have reviewed previous editions, and whose ideas and suggestions continue to inform the book: Kim M. Baker, Roger Williams University; Kevin Ball, Youngstown State University; Deborah Biorn, St. Cloud State University; Joan Blankmann, Northern Virginia Community College; Diane Bosco, Suffolk County Community College; Melanie N. Burdick, University of Missouri–Kansas City; Mikel Cole, University of Houston–Downtown; Danielle Davis, Pasadena City College; Darren DeFrain, Wichita State University; Kaye Falconer, Bakersfield College; Steven Florzcyk, the State University of New York–New Paltz; Nancy Freiman, Milwaukee Area Technical College; Andrea Germanos, Saint Augustine College; Jay L. Gordon, Youngstown State University; Kim Halpern, Pulaski Technical College; Jessica Harvey, Alexandria Technical College; Chris Hayes, University of Georgia; Sharon Jaffee, Santa Monica College; Patricia W. Julius, Michigan State University; Jessica Heather Lourey, Alexandria Technical College; Brian Ludlow, Alfred University; Sherry Manis, Foothill College; Terry Meier, Bakersfield College; Melody Nightingale, Santa Monica College; Kimme Nuckles, Baker College; Michael Orlando, Bergen Community College; Thomas W. Pittman, Youngstown State University; Marty Price, Mississippi State University; David Pryor, University of the Incarnate Word; Hubert C. Pulley, Georgia Southern University; Sherry Robertson, Pulaski Technical College; Lynn Sabas, Saint Augustine College; Vicki Lynn Samson, Western Kentucky University and Bowling Green Community College; Jennifer Satterlee, Parkland College; Wendy Scott, Buffalo State College; Andrea D. Shanklin, Howard Community College; Ann Spurlock, Mississippi State University; Linda Weiner, the University of Akron; Frances Whitney, Bakersfield College; Richard A. Williams, Youngstown State University; and Martha Anne Yeager-Tobar, Cerritos College.

Other people helped in various ways. I'm indebted to Barbara Gross of Rutgers University, Newark, for her excellent work in helping to design the Instructor's Manual for the first edition. Two good friends, Charles O'Neill and Jack Roberts, both of St. Thomas Aquinas College, went over my early plans for the book and offered many useful suggestions.

I also am grateful to Kyle Giacomozzi for his generous and skillful assistance in helping me gather material for this edition and then getting that material in electronic form for submission. As always, it was a pleasure to work with the superb staff at Bedford/St. Martin's. Jane Helms and Ellen Thibault, my editors on earlier editions, shaped the book in lasting ways and helped with the planning of the revision. I also am indebted to my developmental editor, Christina Gerogiannis. As usual, Christina provided excellent guidance and numerous suggestions, while doing her utmost best to keep a book that depends on so many moving parts and timely material on its remarkably tight schedule. Christina is also responsible for the student interviews that are such an important feature of this edition. Sophia Snyder, associate editor, and Mallory Moore, editorial assistant, contacted the students profiled in the book and worked energetically on the book's Web site and Instructor's Manual. Kalina Hintz and Martha Friedman managed text and art permissions under a tight schedule. Annette Pagliaro Sweeney guided the book through production with patience and care, staying on top of many details, and Elizabeth Schaaf managed the production process with great attentiveness. I was fortunate to receive the careful copyediting of Nancy Benjamin. In the marketing, advertising, and promotion departments, Angela Dambrowski deserves warm thanks for her work, as does marketing manager Molly Parke.

I am grateful to Charles H. Christensen, the retired president of Bedford/St. Martin's, for his generous help and thoughtful suggestions throughout the life of this book. Finally, I especially want to thank Bedford's president, Joan E. Feinberg, who conceived the idea for *America Now* and who continues to follow it closely through its various editions, for her deep and abiding interest in college composition. It is a great pleasure and privilege to work with her.

Robert Atwan

Contents

1

What's in a Name?   47

Are you the kind of person who gives your car or truck a nickname? Do names matter to you? Do you think names can have cultural, political, or social significance? Are you offended by some names? An advertisement looks at why some drivers endearingly name their pickup trucks. . . . We just completed the first decade of the twenty-first century—now *what* do we call it? asks one of the nation's most influential magazines. . . . A University of North Dakota student confronts the controversial nickname of its sports team: Is the "Fighting Sioux" an abusive stereotype or actually a tribute to Native Americans?. . . The magazine for "thinking mothers" debates a question women have been asking since the feminist movement began—whose name should the family take? . . . How did two vast continents in the Western Hemisphere wind up with the name *America*? It all starts with a map.

Happiness: Can It Be Defined?   77

Nearly everyone thinks they know what will make them happy—but do they? Do we even know what happiness is? Recently, scientists have begun to design intriguing experiments that have altered some conventional beliefs of what it means to be happy. The Harvard psychologist and best-selling author of *Stumbling on Happiness* acquaints us with some surprising research. . . . Why is it, asks an online journalist, that Olympic athletes who place third are happier than those who come in second? . . . Do you agree with a noted American novelist who suggests that our government ought to establish an agency to "monitor, propagate and ensure the happiness of our citizens"? . . . While visiting Indonesia, a University of Alaska, Fairbanks, student learns a valuable lesson about happiness. . . . A "Spotlight on Research" features a University of North Carolina professor who is one of the nation's leading researchers on the science of happiness.

3

Is There an Ethics of Eating? 99

What do our eating habits and food preferences tell us about ourselves and
our society? Do we have ethical responsibilities to eat in a way that insures
our health and the health of the planet? Should we be striving to eat only
locally grown and organic food? Is it unethical to eat meat? A Southern magazine editor worries that fresh, local food is rapidly becoming a luxury item....
Fast food chains are here to stay, claims a specialist in ethical investing, so the
most realistic thing for us to do is to improve them.... An essayist struggles
with all the personal dilemmas of responsible eating.... Our "willful ignorance" about the food we consume says much about us, argues a University of
Minnesota, Twin Cities, student.

4

Photography: Can We Believe What We See?   125

Can you trust the images you see in the news? Do photographs and video always provide objective pictures of an event? Do you see a photo in a magazine and think it's offering you an exact impression of what an event, an object, or a person actually looked like? A prominent photography editor claims that "modern photo manipulation is seriously screwing up our concept of reality and our willingness to believe what we see in magazines." . . . A noted art critic is suspicious of how both experts and the news media have interpreted the notorious torture photos taken at the Abu Ghraib prison in Iraq. . . . After losing some special photos when her computer crashed, a Bryn Mawr student puts her digital camera aside and turns to an older model that uses actual rolls of film. . . . A major news event in the spring of 2000 alerted the American public to the distortions of photography.

5

What Do We Fear?   149

The list of things Americans are afraid of seems to grow daily—terrorism, epidemics, food poisoning, violent crime, environmental hazards, and natural disasters represent only a few. Why do we live in constant anxiety? Are these fears justified or are they irrational? "We're quite bad at assessing risk," claim the authors of the best-selling book *Freakonomics*, and "get bent out of shape over things we shouldn't worry about so much." . . . A UCLA psychiatrist thinks Americans are addicted to overreaction. . . . "I'm done freaking out about touching doorknobs,"

6

How Is Today's Media Altering Our Language?   171

Are we in the midst of a literacy revolution? Are Facebook, Twitter, online chatting, and other forms of new media fundamentally changing the ways we read and write? A new-media reporter cites evidence showing that today's college students not only write more than ever but are also "pushing our literacy in bold new directions." . . . Some of that evidence is challenged in a "Spotlight on Research" summary from a noted intellectual journal. . . . The use of blogs, social-networking sites, and other Web sites is quickly changing the way we define words, claims a prominent authority on dictionaries. . . . What's happening to trusted journalism? asks a University of Central Arkansas student who worries that too many people are relying on questionable sources of information. . . . A blogger takes a satirical look at the composition of a typical blog. . . . How did Americans convey "instant messages" long before the Internet?

7

Gender Roles: Should Women Act More Like Men? 199

Are there real, biologically caused differences between the ways men and women behave, or are these differences trifling and due largely to social customs? For example, are men innately more aggressive than women, and does that trait help them succeed in the corporate world? A communications professor believes women could be more successful if they behaved more like men, that is, like "arrogant self-aggrandizing jerks." . . . In response, a political journalist doubts that behaving like men will truly help women's advancement in the workplace. . . . An opinion writer takes a provocative look at workplace stereotyping at one of the nation's most fashionable events—the Academy Awards—and asks: Why are there separate Oscars for actors and actresses? . . . Is chivalry dead? asks a Boise State University student. No, she suggests, not if it's gender neutral and permits women to behave like men and men like women. . . . A "Spotlight on Research" item investigates the titles of romance novels to answer the famous question: "What do women want?"

8

Does Our Need for Security Threaten Our Right to Privacy?   225

Does our need for security in times of terrorism outweigh our need for privacy? Can both needs be reconciled, as President Obama suggests, or must one give way to the other? A noted legal commentator believes that the new full-body scanning machines being installed in airports across the nation represent "a virtual strip search — and an outrage." . . . But a Cleveland columnist takes a lighter view of the surveillance machines, arguing that the X-ray images could be considered "pornographic" only if "your sexual fantasies steer toward cartoon characters and robots.". . . The scanning machines are necessary because profiling doesn't work, maintains a Washington State University student who was once detained by a Chicago airport official who told him, "With a name like Mohammed Farooq Ali Khan, you are going to be held everywhere." . . . A nature writer expresses her objections to government surveillance by examining the significance of our fingertips.

9

Barack Obama: What Does His Election Mean to America?   249

On November 4, 2008, American voters took an unprecedented step and elected an African American to the highest office in the land. What would this mean to a nation with a long and divisive racial history? Would we enter, as many claimed, a post-racial society, or would certain problems be so insurmountable that little progress could be made? And what did the election mean to America's black community? A prominent novelist views the new first family from a communal perspective: "Finally, the world could see what we've always known: Black families can be loving, intact, nurturing worlds that produce confident, talented children." ... Reflecting on young people, another prominent novelist thinks that urban poverty may not be solved simply by electing a president with a different skin color. ... "While Obama embodies a milestone in America's history as the first African American president," a Santa Clara University student writes, "he is not the president of only African Americans." . . . Writing for a progressive magazine, a Pulitzer Prize–winning reporter argues that Obama's image only "appears radically individualistic and new" but is actually a continuation of the same old corporate power that ruled the previous administration.

10

Social Networking—How Is It Transforming Behavior?   275

How is our new technology transforming our social lives? Are Facebook and Twitter bringing us closer to others and helping us to form communities more easily? Or is social networking an illusion and a way of avoiding real human contact? "Dad," argues a daughter in a popular comic strip, "You make it sound like social media is ruining my life. It's *not*." ... "I make a conscious decision to broadcast my life every day, and I accept the consequences," claims a journalist and blogger who admits "oversharing" can result in embarrassment. ... An Emerson College student is amazed by all the new media responses a birthday can elicit, but feels that "We're missing the point if the first thing we look forward to on our birthday is an over-flowing inbox." ... After a promising student dies, a communications professor wonders about the "new, uncharted form of grieving" that will confront us in the age of Facebook.

Saving the Planet: Is It Too Late? 299

Is the earth warming at a dangerous rate? Or is the climate crisis just a lot of hot air? Whom shall we trust: the scientists who warn us about imminent danger or the scientists who argue that the crisis is either politically motivated or wholly exaggerated? While participating in his town's recycling day, one of the nation's major environmental authors reflects on the many different kinds of "waste" that moment by moment destroy the environment. . . . *Rolling Stone* magazine reports that the Arctic is melting faster than anyone predicted. . . . But a noted conservative columnist maintains that the "myth" of global warming "is sinking with greater force than melting icebergs." . . . "If the planet could be saved based on what kind of cereal a consumer bought," writes a University of Massachusetts student, "evidently, there would be no problem." . . . One of America's most popular scientists warned against global warming in 1985.

12

Immigration: Who Is an American? 327

Is there a satisfying solution to the problem of illegal immigration? Do immigrants valuably add to the work ethic of American culture? Should the foreign-born partners of gay Americans enjoy the same rights of citizenship as heterosexual Americans? What is the impact of immigration on American identity? Two experts disagree on whether immigrants help to increase the virtues of hard work and "grit" in the United States. . . . An undocumented worker describes in vivid detail his arduous journey across the California border. . . . "Spanish is again being devalued and people who speak it discriminated against," argues a prominent author who worries about the language skills of first-generation Americans. . . . A Tulane University student urges Congress to pass existing legislation allowing the partners of lesbian, gay, bisexual, and transgender Americans a path to citizenship. . . . The enormous number of black immigrants from Africa and the Caribbean compose a vital part of our ongoing African American history and identity, maintains a leading black historian. . . . Should our growing population be slowed down by stricter immigration laws? A 1999 advertisement thinks so.

The Persuasive Writer

Expressing Opinions with Clarity, Confidence, and Civility

It is not possible to extricate yourself from the questions in which your age is involved.
— Ralph Waldo Emerson, "The Fortune of the Republic" (1878)

What Is America Now?

America Now collects very recent essays and articles that have been carefully selected to encourage reading, provoke discussion, and stimulate writing. The philosophy behind the book is that interesting, effective writing originates in public dialogue. The book's primary purpose is to help students proceed from class discussions of reading assignments to the production of complete essays that reflect an engaged participation in those discussions.

The selections in *America Now* come from two main sources — from popular, mainstream periodicals and from college newspapers available on the Internet. Written by journalists and columnists, public figures and activists, as well as by professors and students from all over the country, the selections illustrate the types of material read by millions of Americans every day. In addition to magazine and newspaper writing, the book features a number of recent opinion advertisements (what I call "op-ads" for short). These familiar forms of "social marketing" are often sponsored by corporations or nonprofit organizations and advocacy groups to promote policies, programs, and ideas such as gun control, family planning, literacy, civil rights, or conservation. Such advertising texts allow the reader to pinpoint and discuss specific techniques of verbal and visual persuasion that are critical in the formation of public opinion.

I have gathered the selections into twelve units that cover today's most widely discussed issues and topics: social media, racial identity, gender differences, consumption and marketing, environmentalism, privacy and surveillance, and so on. As you respond to the readings in your discussion and writing, you will be actively taking part in some of the major controversies of our time. Although I have tried in this new edition of *America Now* to represent as many viewpoints as possible on a variety of controversial topics, it's not possible in a collection of this scope to include under each topic either a full spectrum of opinion or a universally satisfying balance of opposing opinions. For some featured topics, an entire book would be required to represent the full range of opinion; for others, a rigid pro-con, either-or format could distort the issue and perhaps overly polarize students' responses to it. Selections within a unit usually illustrate the most commonly held opinions on a topic so that readers will get a reasonably good sense of how the issue has been framed and the public discourse and debate it has generated. But if a single opinion isn't immediately or explicitly balanced by an opposite opinion, or if a view seems unusually idiosyncratic, that in no way implies that it is somehow editorially favored or endorsed. Be assured that questions following *every* selection will encourage you to analyze and critically challenge whatever opinion or perspective is expressed in that selection.

Participation is the key to this collection. I encourage you to view reading and writing as a form of participation. I hope you will read the selections attentively, think about them carefully, be willing to discuss them in class, and use what you've learned from your reading and discussion as the basis for your papers. If you do these things, you will develop three skills necessary for successful work in college and beyond: the ability to read critically, to discuss topics intelligently, and to write persuasively. These skills are also sorely needed in our daily lives as citizens. A vital democracy depends on them. The reason democracy is hard, said the Czech author and statesman Václav Havel, is that it requires the participation of everyone.

America Now invites you to see reading, discussion, and writing as closely related activities. As you read a selection, imagine that you have entered into a discussion with the author. Take notes as you read. Question the selection. Challenge its point of view or its evidence. Compare your experience with the author's. Consider how different economic classes or other groups are likely to respond. Remember, just because something appears in a newspaper or book doesn't make it true or accurate.

Form the habit of challenging what you read. Don't be persuaded by an opinion simply because it appears in print or because you believe you should accept it. Trust your own observations and experiences. Though logicians never say so, personal experiences and keen observations often form the basis of our most convincing arguments.

Participating in Class Discussion: Six Basic Rules

Discussion is a learned activity. It requires a variety of essential skills: speaking, listening, thinking, and preparing. The following six basic rules are vital to healthy and productive discussion.

1. **Take an active speaking role.** Good discussion demands that everyone participates, not (as so often happens) just a vocal few. Many students remain detached from discussion because they are afraid to speak in a group. This fear is quite common — psychological surveys show that speaking in front of a group is one of our worst fears. It helps to remember that most people will be more interested in *what* you say than in how you say it. Once you get over the initial fear of speaking in public, your confidence will improve with practice.

2. **Listen attentively.** No one who doesn't listen attentively can participate in group discussion. Just think of how many senseless arguments you've had because either you or the person with whom you were talking completely misunderstood what was said. A good listener not only hears what someone is saying but also understands *why* he or she is saying it. Listening carefully also leads to good questions, and when interesting questions begin to emerge, you know good discussion has truly begun.

3. **Examine all sides of an issue.** Good discussion requires that we be patient with complexity. Difficult problems rarely have obvious and simple solutions, nor can they be easily summarized in popular slogans. Complex issues demand to be turned over in our minds so that we can see them from a variety of angles. Group discussion broadens our perspective and deepens our insight into difficult issues and ideas.

4. **Suspend judgment.** To fully explore ideas and issues, you need to be open-minded and tolerant of other opinions, even when they contradict your own. Remember, a discussion is not a debate. Its primary purpose is communication, not competition. The goal of group discussion should be to open up a topic so that everyone is exposed to a spectrum of attitudes. Suspending judgment does not mean you shouldn't hold a strong belief or opinion about an issue; it means that you should be receptive to rival beliefs or opinions. An opinion formed without an awareness of other points of view — one that has

continued

not been tested against contrary ideas — is not a strong opinion but merely a stubborn one.

5. **Avoid abusive or insulting language.** Free and open discussion occurs only when we respect the beliefs and opinions of others. If we speak in ways that fail to show respect for differing viewpoints — if we resort to name-calling or use demeaning and malicious expressions, for example — not only do we embarrass ourselves, but we also close off the possibility for an intelligent and productive exchange of ideas. Some popular radio and television talk shows are poor models of discussion: Shouting insults and engaging in hate speech are usually the last resort of those who have little to say.

6. **Be prepared.** Discussion is not merely random conversation. It demands a certain degree of preparation and focus. To participate in class discussion, you must consider assigned topics beforehand and read whatever is required. Develop the habit of reading with pen in hand, underlining key points, and jotting down questions, impressions, and ideas in your notebook. The notes you bring to class will be an invaluable aid.

When your class discusses a selection, be especially attentive to what others think of it. It's always surprising how two people can read the same article and reach two entirely different interpretations. Observe the range of opinion. Try to understand why and how people arrive at different conclusions. Do some seem to miss the point? Do some distort the author's ideas? Have someone's comments forced you to rethink the selection? Keep a record of the discussion in your notebook. Then, when you begin to draft your paper, consider your essay as an extension of both your imaginary conversation with the author and the actual class discussion. If you've taken detailed notes of your own and the class's opinions about the selection, you should have more than enough information to get started.

What Are Opinions?

One of the primary aims of *America Now* is to help you learn through models and instructional material how to express your opinions in a persuasive, reasonable, civil, and productive fashion. But before we look at effective ways of expressing opinion, let's first consider opinions in general: What are they? Where do they come from?

When we say we have an opinion about something, we usually mean that we have come to a conclusion that something appears true or seems to be valid. But when we express an opinion about something, we are not claiming we are 100 percent certain that something is so. Opinion does not imply certainty and, in fact, is accompanied by some degree of doubt and skepticism. As a result, opinions are most likely to be found in those areas of thought and discussion where our judgments are uncertain. Because human beings know so few things for certain, much of what we believe, or discuss and debate, falls into various realms of probability or possibility. These we call opinions.

Journalists often make a distinction between fact and opinion. Facts can be confirmed and verified and therefore do not involve opinions. We ordinarily don't have opinions about facts, but we can and often do have opinions about the interpretation of facts. For example, it makes no sense to argue whether Washington, D.C., is the capital of the United States since it's an undisputed fact that it is. It's a matter of record and can be established with certainty. Thus, we don't say we have an opinion that Washington, D.C., is the nation's capital; we know for a fact that it is. But it would be legitimate to form an opinion about whether that city is the best location for the U.S. capital and whether it should permanently remain the capital. In other words:

- *Washington, D.C., is the capital of the United States of America* is a statement of fact.
- *Washington, D.C., is too poorly located to be the capital of a vast nation* is a statement of opinion.

Further, simply not knowing whether something is a fact does not necessarily make it a matter of opinion. For example, if we don't know the capital of Brazil, that doesn't mean we are then free to form an opinion about what Brazilian city it might be. The capital of Brazil is a verifiable fact and can be identified with absolute certainty. There is no conflicting public opinion about which city is Brazil's capital. The answer is not up for grabs. These examples, however, present relatively simple, readily agreed-upon facts. In real-life disputes, a fact is not always so readily distinguished from an opinion; people argue all the time about whether something is a fact. It's therefore a good idea at the outset of any discussion or argument to try to arrive at a mutual agreement of the facts that are known or knowable and those that could be called into question. Debates over abortion, for example, often hinge on biological facts about embryonic development that are themselves disputed by medical experts.

An opinion almost always exists in the climate of other, conflicting opinions. In discourse, we refer to this overall context of competing opinions as public controversy. Every age has its controversies. At any given time, the public is divided on a great number of topics about which it holds a variety of different opinions. Often the controversy is reduced to two opposing positions; for example, we are asked whether we are pro-life or pro-choice; for or against government health care; in favor of or opposed to same-sex marriage; and so on. This book includes many such controversies and covers multiple opinions. One sure way of knowing that something is a matter of opinion is that the public is divided on the topic. We often experience these divisions firsthand as we mature and increasingly come into contact with those who disagree with our opinions.

Some opinions are deeply held — so deeply, in fact, that those who hold them refuse to see them as opinions. For some people on certain issues there can be no difference of opinion; they possess the Truth, and all who differ hold erroneous opinions. This frequently happens in some controversies, where one side in a dispute is so confident of the truth of its position that it cannot see its own point of view as one of several possible points of view. For example, someone may feel so certain that marriage can exist only between a man and a woman that he or she cannot acknowledge the possibility of another position. If one side cannot recognize the existence of a different opinion, cannot entertain or tolerate it, argues not with the correctness of another's perspective but denies the possibility that there can legitimately be another perspective, then discussion and debate become all but impossible.

To be open and productive, public discussion depends on the capacity of all involved to view their own positions, no matter how cherished, as opinions that can be subjected to opposition. There is nothing wrong with possessing a strong conviction, nor with believing our position is the better one, nor with attempting to convince others of our point of view. What is argumentatively wrong and what prevents or restricts free and open discussion is twofold: (1) the failure to recognize our own belief or position as an opinion that could be mistaken; and (2) the refusal to acknowledge the possibility that another's opinion could be correct.

Is one person's opinion as good as another's? Of course not. Although we may believe that everyone has a right to an opinion, we certainly wouldn't ask our mail carrier to diagnose the cause of persistent heartburn or determine whether a swollen gland could be a serious medical problem. In such instances, we respect the opinion of a trained physician. And even when we consult a physician, in serious matters we often seek second and even third opinions just to be sure. An auto mechanic is in a better position to evaluate a used car than someone who's never repaired a car; a lawyer's opinion on whether a contract is valid is more reliable than that belonging to someone who doesn't understand the legal nature of contracts. If an airline manufacturer wants to test a new cockpit instrument design, it solicits opinions from experienced pilots, not passengers. This seems obvious, and yet people continually are persuaded by those who can claim little expert knowledge on a subject or issue: For example, how valuable or trustworthy is the opinion of a celebrity who is paid to endorse a product?

When expressing or evaluating an opinion, we need to consider the extent of our or another person's knowledge about a particular subject. Will anyone take our opinion seriously? On what authority do we base our position? Why do we take someone else's opinion as valuable or trustworthy? What is the source of the opinion? How reliable is it? How biased? One of the first Americans to study the effects of public opinion, Walter Lippmann, wrote in 1925, "It is often very illuminating, therefore, to ask yourself how you get at the facts on which you base your opinion. Who actually saw, heard, felt, counted, named the thing, about which you have an opinion?" Is your opinion, he went on to ask, based on something you heard from someone who heard it from someone else, who in turn heard it from someone else?

How Do We Form Opinions?

How can we possibly have reasonable opinions on all the issues of the day? One of the strains of living in a democracy that encourages a diversity of perspectives is that every responsible citizen is expected to have informed opinions on practically every public question. What do you think about the death penalty? About dependency on foreign oil? About the way the media cover the news? About the extent of racial discrimination? Certainly no one person possesses inside information or access to reliable data on every topic that becomes part of public controversy. Still, many people, by the time they are able to vote, have formed numerous opinions. Where do these opinions come from?

Although social scientists and psychologists have been studying opinion formation for decades, the sources of opinion are multiple and constantly shifting, and individuals differ so widely in experience, cultural background, and temperament that efforts to identify and classify the various ways opinion is formed are bound to be tentative and incomplete. What follows is a brief, though realistic, attempt to list some of the practical ways that Americans come by the opinions they hold.

1. *Inherited opinions.* These are opinions we derive from earliest childhood — transmitted via family, culture, traditions, customs, regions, social institutions, or religion. For example, young people may identify themselves as either Democrats or Republicans because of their family affiliations. Although these opinions may change as we mature, they are often ingrained. The more traditional the culture or society, the more likely the opinions that grow out of early childhood will be retained and passed on to the next generation.

2. *Involuntary opinions.* These are opinions that we have not culturally and socially inherited or consciously adopted but that come to us through direct or indirect forms of indoctrination. They could be the customs of a cult or the propaganda of an ideology. Brainwashing is an extreme example of how one acquires opinions involuntarily. A more familiar example is the constant reiteration of advertising messages: We come to possess a favorable opinion of a product not because we've ever used it or know anything about it but because we have been "bombarded" by marketing to think positively about it.

3. *Adaptive opinions.* Many opinions grow out of our willingness — or even eagerness — to adapt to the prevailing views of particular groups, subgroups, or institutions to which we belong or desire to belong. As many learn, it's easier to follow the path of least resistance than to run counter to it. Moreover, acting out of self-interest, people often adapt their opinions to conform to the views of bosses or authority figures, or they prefer to succumb to peer pressure than to oppose it. An employee finds himself accepting or agreeing with an opinion because a job or career depends on it; a student may adapt her opinions to suit those of a professor in the hope of receiving a better grade; a professor may tailor his opinions in conformity with the prevailing beliefs of colleagues. Adaptive opinions are often weakly held and readily changed, depending on circumstances. But over time they can become habitual and turn into convictions.

4. *Concealed opinions.* In some groups in which particular opinions dominate, certain individuals may not share the prevailing attitudes, but rather than adapt or "rock the boat," they keep their opinions to themselves. They may do this merely to avoid conflict or out of much more serious concerns — such as a fear of ostracism, ridicule, retaliation, or job loss. A common example is seen in the person who by day quietly goes along with the opinions of a group of colleagues but at night freely exchanges "honest" opinions with a group of friends. Some individuals find diaries and journals to be an effective way to express concealed opinions, and many today find online chat rooms a space where they can anonymously "be themselves."

5. *Linked opinions.* Many opinions are closely linked to other opinions. Unlike adaptive opinions, which are usually stimulated by convenience and an incentive to conform, these are opinions we derive from an enthusiastic and dedicated affiliation with certain groups, institutions, or parties. For example, it's not uncommon for someone to agree with every position his or her political party endorses — this phenomenon is usually called "following a party line." Linked opinions may not be well thought out on every narrow issue: Someone may decide to be a Republican or a Democrat or a Green or a Libertarian for a few specific reasons — a position on war, cultural values, environment, civil liberties, and so forth — and then go along with, even to the point of strenuously defending, all of the other positions the party espouses because they are all part of its political platform or system of beliefs. In other words, once we accept opinions A and B, we are more likely to accept C and D, and so on down the chain. As Ralph Waldo Emerson succinctly put it, "If I know your sect, I anticipate your argument."

6. Considered opinions. These are opinions we have formed as a result of firsthand experience, reading, discussion and debate, or independent thinking and reasoning. These opinions are formed from direct knowledge and often from exposure and consideration of other opinions. Wide reading on a subject and exposure to diverse views help ensure that our opinions are based on solid information and tested against competing opinions. One simple way to judge whether your opinion is carefully thought out is to list your reasons for holding it. Some people who express opinions on a topic are not able to offer a single reason for why they have those opinions. Of course, reasons don't necessarily make an opinion correct, but people who can support their opinions with one or more reasons are more persuasive than those who cannot provide any reasons for their beliefs (see "How to Support Opinions").

This list is not exhaustive. Nor are the sources and types above mutually exclusive; the opinions of any individual may derive from all six sources or represent a mixture of several. As you learn to express your opinions effectively, you will find it useful to question yourself about the origins and development of those opinions. By tracing the process that led to the formation of our present opinions, we can better understand ourselves — our convictions, our inconsistencies, our biases, and our blind spots.

From Discussion to Writing

As this book amply demonstrates, we live in a world of conflicting opinions. Each of us over time has inherited, adopted, and gradually formed many opinions on a variety of topics. Of course, there are also a good number of public issues or questions about which we have not formed opinions or have undecided attitudes. In many public debates, members have unequal shares at stake. Eighteen-year-olds, for example, are much more likely to become impassioned over the government reviving a military draft or a state raising the legal age for driving than they would over Medicaid cuts or Social Security issues. Some public questions personally affect us more than others.

Thus, not all the issues covered in this book will at first make an equal impact on everyone. But whether you take a particular interest in a given topic or not, this book invites you to share in the spirit of public controversy. Many students, once introduced to the opposing sides of a debate or the multiple positions taken toward a public issue, will begin to take a closer look at the merits of different opinions. Once we start evaluating these opinions, once we begin stepping into the shoes of others and learning what's at stake in certain positions, we often find ourselves becoming involved with the issue and may even come to see ourselves as participants. After all, we are all part of the public, and to a certain extent all questions affect us: Ask the eighteen-year-old if he or she will be equipped to deal with the medical and financial needs of elderly parents, and an issue that appears to affect only those near retirement will seem much closer to home.

As mentioned earlier, *America Now* is designed to stimulate discussion and writing grounded in response to a variety of public issues. A key to using this book is to think about discussion and writing not as separate activities but as interrelated processes. In discussion, we hear other opinions and formulate our own; in writing, we express our opinions in the context of other opinions. Both discussion and writing require articulation and deliberation. Both require an aptitude for listening carefully to others. Discussion stimulates writing, and writing in turn stimulates further discussion.

Group discussion stimulates and enhances your writing in several important ways. First, it supplies you with ideas. Let's say that you are participating in a discussion on the importance of ethnic identity (see selections in Chapter 12). One of your classmates mentions some of the problems a mixed ethnic background can cause. But suppose you also come from a mixed background, and when you think about it, you believe that your mixed heritage has given you more advantages than disadvantages. Hearing her viewpoint may inspire you to express your differing perspective on the issue. Your perspective could lead to an interesting personal essay.

Suppose you now start writing that essay. You don't need to start from scratch and stare at a blank piece of paper or computer screen for hours. Discussion has already given you a few good leads. First, you have your classmate's opinions and attitudes to quote or summarize. You can begin your paper by explaining that some people view a divided ethnic identity as a psychological burden. You might expand on your classmate's opinion by bringing in additional information from other student comments or from your reading to show how people often focus on only the negative side of mixed identities. You can then explain your own perspective on this topic. Of course, you will need to give several examples showing *why* a mixed background has been an advantage for you. The end result can be a first-rate essay, one that takes other opinions into account and demonstrates a clearly established point of view. It is personal, and yet it takes a position that goes beyond one individual's experiences.

Whatever the topic, your writing will benefit from reading and discussion, activities that will give your essays a clear purpose or goal. In that way, your papers will resemble the selections found in this book: They will be a *response* to the opinions, attitudes, experiences, issues, ideas, and proposals that inform current public discourse. This is why most writers write; this is what most newspapers and magazines publish; this is what most people read. *America Now* consists entirely of such writing. I hope you will read the selections with enjoyment, discuss the issues with an open mind, and write about the topics with purpose and enthusiasm.

The Practice of Writing

Suppose you wanted to learn to play the guitar. What would you do first? Would you run to the library and read a lot of books on music? Would you then read some instructional books on guitar playing? Might you try to memorize all the chord positions? Then would you get sheet music for songs you liked and memorize them? After all that, if someone handed you an electric guitar, would you immediately be able to play like Jimi Hendrix or Eric Clapton?

I don't think you would begin that way. You probably would start out by strumming the guitar, getting the feel of it, trying to pick out something familiar. You probably would want to take lessons from someone who knows how to play. And you would practice, practice, practice. Every now and then your instruction book would come in handy. It would give you basic information on frets, notes, and chord positions, for example. You might need to refer to that information constantly in the beginning. But knowing the chords is not the same as knowing how to manipulate your fingers correctly to produce the right sounds. You need to be able to *play* the chords, not just know them.

Learning to read and write well is not that much different. Even though instructional books can give you a great deal of advice and information, the only way anyone really learns to read and write is through constant practice. The only problem, of course, is that nobody likes practice. If we did, we would all be good at just about everything. Most of us, however, want to acquire a skill quickly and easily. We don't want to take lesson after lesson. We want to pick up the instrument and sound like a professional in ten minutes.

Wouldn't it be a wonderful world if that could happen? Wouldn't it be great to be born with a gigantic vocabulary so that we instantly knew the meaning of every word we saw or heard? We would never have to go through the slow process of consulting a dictionary whenever we stumbled across an unfamiliar word. But, unfortunately, life is not so easy. To succeed at anything worthwhile requires patience and dedication. Watch a young figure skater trying to perfect her skills and you will see patience and dedication at work; or watch an accident victim learning how to maneuver a wheelchair so that he can begin again an independent existence; or observe a new American struggling to learn English. None of these skills are quickly or easily acquired. Like building a vocabulary, they all take time and effort. They all require practice. And they require something even more important: the willingness to make mistakes. Can someone learn to skate without taking a spill? Or learn a new language without mispronouncing a word?

What Is "Correct English"?

One part of the writing process may seem more difficult than others — correct English. Yes, nearly all of what you read will be written in relatively correct English. Or it's probably more accurate to say "corrected" English, because most published writing is revised or "corrected" several times before it appears in print. Even skilled professional writers make mistakes that require correction.

Most native speakers don't actually *talk* in "correct" English. There are numerous regional patterns and dialects. As the Chinese American novelist Amy Tan says, there are "many Englishes." What we usually consider correct English is a set of guidelines developed over time to help standardize written expression. This standardization — like any agreed-upon standards such as weights and measures — is a matter of use and convenience. Suppose you went to a vegetable stand and asked for a pound of peppers and the storekeeper gave you a half pound but charged you for a full one. When you complained, he said, "But that's what *I* call a pound." Life would be very frustrating if everyone had a different set of standards: Imagine what would happen if some states used a red light to signal "go" and a green one for "stop." Languages are not that different. In all cultures, languages — especially written languages — have gradually developed certain general rules and principles to make communication as clear and efficient as possible.

You probably already have a guidebook or handbook that systematically sets out certain rules of English grammar, punctuation, and spelling. Like our guitar instruction book, these handbooks serve a very practical purpose. Most writers — even experienced authors — need to consult them periodically. Beginning writers may need to rely on them far more regularly. But just as we don't learn how to play chords by merely memorizing finger positions, we don't learn how to write by memorizing the rules of grammar or punctuation.

Writing is an activity, a process. Learning how to do it — like learning to ride a bike or prepare a tasty stew — requires *doing* it. Correct English is not something that comes first. We don't need to know the rules perfectly before we can begin to write. As in any activity, corrections are part of the learning process. You fall off the bike and get on again, trying to "correct" your balance this time. You sample the stew and "correct" the seasoning. You draft a paper about the neighborhood you live in, and as you (or a classmate or instructor) read it over, you notice that certain words and expressions could stand some improvement. And step by step, sentence by sentence, you begin to write better.

Writing as a Public Activity

Many people have the wrong idea about writing. They view writing as a very private act. They picture the writer sitting all alone and staring into space waiting for ideas to come. They think that ideas come from "deep" within and reach expression only after they have been fully articulated inside the writer's head.

These images are part of a myth about creative writing and, like most myths, are sometimes true. A few poets, novelists, and essayists do write in total isolation and search deep inside themselves for thoughts and stories. But most writers have far more contact with public life. This is especially true of people who write regularly for magazines, newspapers, and professional journals. These writers work within a lively social atmosphere in which issues and ideas are often intensely discussed and debated. Nearly all the selections in this book illustrate this type of writing.

As you work on your own papers, remember that writing is very much a public activity. It is rarely performed alone in an "ivory tower." Writers don't always have the time, the desire, the opportunity, or the luxury to be all alone. They may be writing in a newsroom with clacking keyboards and noise all around them; they may be writing at a kitchen table, trying to feed several children at the same time; they may be texting on subways or buses. The great English novelist D. H. Lawrence (1885–1930) grew up in a small impoverished coal miner's cottage with no place for privacy. It proved to be an enabling experience. Throughout his life, he could write wherever he happened to be; it didn't matter how many people or how much commotion surrounded him.

There are more important ways in which writing is a public activity. Writing is often a response to public events. Most of the articles you encounter every day in newspapers and magazines respond directly to timely or important issues and ideas, topics that people are currently talking about. Writers report on these topics, supply information about them, and discuss and debate the differing viewpoints. The units in this book all represent topics now regularly discussed on college campuses and in the national media. In fact, all of the topics were chosen because they emerged so frequently in college newspapers.

When a columnist decides to write on a topic like airport security measures that threaten individual privacy, she willingly enters an ongoing public discussion about the issue. She hasn't just made up the topic. She knows that it is a serious issue, and she is aware that a wide variety of opinions have been expressed about it. She has not read everything on the subject but usually knows enough about the different arguments to state her own position or attitude persuasively. In fact, what helps make her writing persuasive is that she takes into account the opinions of others. Her own essay, then, becomes a part of the continuing debate and discussion, one that you in turn may want to join.

Such issues are not only matters for formal and impersonal debate. They also invite us to share our *personal* experiences. Many of the selections in this book show how writers participate in the discussion of issues by drawing on their experiences. For example, the essay by Brian Jay Stanley, "Confessions of a Carnivore," is based largely on the author's personal observations and experience, though the topic — whether people should or should not eat meat — is one widely discussed and debated by countless Americans. You will find that nearly every unit of *America Now* contains a selection that illustrates how you can use your personal experiences to discuss and debate a public issue.

Writing is public in yet another way. Practically all published writing is reviewed, edited, and re-edited by different people before it goes to press. The author of a magazine article has most likely discussed the topic at length with colleagues and publishing professionals and may have asked friends or experts in the field to look over his or her piece. By the time you see the article in a magazine, it has gone through numerous readings and probably quite a few revisions. Although the article is credited to a particular author, it was no doubt read and worked on by others who helped with suggestions and improvements. As a beginning writer, you need to remember that most of what you read in newspapers, magazines, and books has gone through a writing process that involves the collective efforts of several people besides the author. Students usually don't have that advantage and should not feel discouraged when their own writing doesn't measure up to the professionally edited materials they are reading for a course.

How to Support Opinions

In everyday life, we express many opinions, ranging from (as the chapters in this collection indicate) weighty issues such as race relations or the environment to personal matters such as our Facebook profile. In conversation, we often express our opinions as assertions. An assertion is merely an opinionated claim — usually of our likes or dislikes, agreements or disagreements — that is not supported by evidence or reasons. For example, *"Amnesty for illegal immigrants is a poor idea"* is merely an assertion about public policy — it states an opinion, but it offers no reason or reasons why anyone should accept it.

When entering public discussion and debate, we have an obligation to support our opinions. Simple assertions — *"Men are better at math than women"* — may be provocative and stimulate heated debate, but the discussion will go nowhere unless reasons and evidence are offered to support the claim. The following methods are among the most common ways you can support your opinions.

1. **Experts and authority.** You support your claim that the earth is growing warmer by citing one of the world's leading climatologists; you support your opinion that a regular diet of certain vegetables can drastically reduce the risk of colon cancer by citing medical authorities.

2. **Statistics.** You support the view that your state needs tougher drunk driving laws by citing statistics that show that fatalities from drunk driving have increased 20 percent in the past two years; you support the claim that Americans now prefer smaller, more fuel-efficient cars by citing surveys that reveal a 30 percent drop in SUV and truck sales over the past six months.

3. **Examples.** You support your opinion that magazine advertising is becoming increasingly pornographic by describing several recent instances from different periodicals; you defend your claim that women can be top-ranked chess players by identifying several women who are. Note that when using examples to prove your point, you will almost always require several; one example will seldom convince anyone.

4. **Personal experience.** Although you may not be an expert or authority in any area, your personal experience can count as evidence in support of an opinion. Suppose you claim that the campus parking

continued

facilities are inadequate for commuting students, and, a commuter yourself, you document the difficulties you have every day with parking. Such personal knowledge, assuming it is not false or exaggerated, would plausibly support your position. Many reporters back up their coverage with their eyewitness testimony.

5. **Possible consequences.** You defend an opinion that space exploration is necessary by arguing that it could lead to the discovery of much-needed new energy resources; you support an opinion that expanding the rights of gun ownership is a mistake by arguing that it will result in more crime and gun-related deaths.

These are only a few of the ways opinions can be supported, but they are among the most significant. Note that providing support for an opinion does not automatically make it true or valid; someone will invariably counter your expert with an opposing expert, discover conflicting statistical data, produce counterexamples, or offer personal testimony that contradicts your own. Still, once you've offered legitimate reasons for what you think, you have made a big leap from "mere opinion" to "informed opinion."

Writing for the Classroom: Three Annotated Student Essays

The following three student essays perfectly characterize the kind of writing that *America Now* features and examines. The essays will provide you with effective models of how to express an opinion on a public issue in a concise and convincing manner. Each essay demonstrates the way a writer responds to a public concern — in this case, the stereotyping of others. Each essay also embodies the principles of productive discussion outlined throughout this introduction. In fact, these three essays were especially commissioned from student writers to perform a double service: The essays show writers clearly expressing opinions on a timely topic that personally matters to them and, at the same time, demonstrate how arguments can be shaped to advance the possibility of further discussion instead of ending it.

These three essays also feature three different approaches to the topic of stereotyping. Each essay reflects a different use of source material: The first essay uses none; the second responds directly to a recent controversial magazine article; and the third relies on reading material that supports a thesis. Thus, students can observe three distinct and common methods of learning to write for the classroom:

1. expressing an opinion based on personal experience alone
2. expressing an opinion in response to an opposing opinion
3. expressing an opinion with reference to reading and research

Although there are many other approaches to classroom writing (too many to be fully represented in an introduction), these three should provide first-year students with accessible and effective models for the types of writing they will most likely be required to do in connection with the assignments in *America Now*.

Each essay is annotated to help you focus on some of the most effective means of expressing an opinion. First, read through each essay and consider the points the writer is making. Then return to the essay and analyze more closely the key parts highlighted for examination. This process is designed to help you see how writers construct arguments to support their opinions. It is an analytical process you should begin to put into practice on your own as you read and explore the many issues in this collection. A detailed explanation of the highlighted passages follows each selection.

Expressing an Opinion Based on Personal Experience Alone

The first essay, Kati Mather's "The Many Paths to Success — With or Without a College Education," expresses an opinion that is based almost entirely on personal experience and reflection. In her argument that Americans have grown so predisposed to a college education that they dismiss other forms of education as inferior, Mather shows how this common attitude can lead to unfair stereotypes. Her essay cites no formal evidence or outside sources — no research, studies, quotations, other opinions, or assigned readings. Instead, she relies on her own educational experience and the conclusions she draws from it to support her position.

Kati Mather wrote "The Many Paths to Success — With or Without a College Education" when she was a senior at Wheaton College in Massachusetts, majoring in English and Italian studies.

Kati Mather

The Many Paths to Success — With or Without a College Education

| 1 *Opens with personal perspective* | <u>I always knew I would go to college. When I was younger, higher education was not a particular dream of mine, but I understood that it was the expected path.</u> (1) | 1 |

Even as children, many of us are so thoroughly groomed for college that declining the opportunity is unacceptable. Although I speak as someone who could afford such an assumption, even my peers without the same economic advantages went to college. <u>Education is important, but I believe our common expectations — that everyone can and should go to college, and that a college education is necessary to succeed — and the stigmas attached to those who forgo higher education, are false and unfair.</u>

In the past, only certain fortunate people could attain a college education. But over time, America modernized its approach to education, beginning with compulsory high school attendance in most states, and then evolving into a system with numerous options for higher learning. (2) Choices for post-secondary education today are overwhelming, and — with full- and part-time programs offered by community colleges, state universities, and private institutions — accessibility is not the issue it once was. In our frenzy to adhere to the American dream, which means, among other things, that everyone is entitled to an education, the schooling system has become too focused on the social expectations that come with a college education. It is normally considered to be the gateway to higher income and an upwardly mobile career. But we would all be better served if the system were instead focused on learning, and on what learning means to the individual.

<u>It is admirable that we are committed to education in this country, but not everyone should be expected to take the college track. Vocational education, for instance, seems to be increasingly a thing of the past, which is regrettable because careers that do not require a college degree are as vital as those that do. If vocational schooling were more widely presented as an option — and one that everyone should take the time to consider — we would not be so quick to stereotype those who do not attend traditional academic institutions. Specialized labor such as construction, plumbing, and automobile repair are crucial to a healthy, functioning society.</u> (3) While a college education can be a wonderful thing to possess, we need people to aspire to other forms of education, which include both vocational schooling and learning skills on the job. Those careers (and there are many others) are as important as teaching, accounting, and medicine.

Despite the developments in our educational system that make college more accessible, financial constraints

2

2
Establishes main point early

3

3
Supports main point

4

exist for many — as do family pressures and expectations, intellectual limitations, and a host of other obstacles. Those obstacles warrant neither individual criticism nor far-reaching stereotypes. For example, a handful of students from my high school took an extra year or two to graduate, and I sadly assumed that they would not be as successful as those who graduated on time. I did not stop to consider their situations, or that they might simply be on a different path in life than I was. Looking back, it was unfair to stereotype others in this way. Many of them are hard-working and fulfilled individuals today. <u>There is no law that says everyone has to finish high school and go to college to be successful. Many famous actors, musicians, artists, and professional athletes will freely admit that they never finished high school or college, and these are people we admire, who could very well be making more money in a year than an entire graduating class combined.</u> (4) Plus, we applaud their talent and the fact that they chose their own paths. But banking on a paying career in the arts or sports is not a safe bet, which is why it is so important to open all practical avenues to young people and to respect the choices they make.

> **4**
> *Provides examples of alternatives to college*

We should focus on this diversity instead of perpetuating the belief that everyone should pursue a formal college education and that those who do not are somehow inadequate. There are, of course, essential skills learned in college that remain useful throughout life, even for those who do not pursue high-powered careers. As a student myself, I will readily admit that a college education plays an important role in a successful life. <u>The skills we have the opportunity to learn in college are important to "real" life, and some of these can be used no matter what our career path.</u> (5) Among other things, I've learned how to interact with different people, how to live on my own, how to accept rejection, how to articulate what I want to say, and how to write. Writing is one of the most useful skills taught in college because written communication is necessary in so many different aspects of life.

> **5**
> *Offers balanced view of alternatives*

I hope that my college education will lead to success and upward mobility in my career. But I can also allow that, once out of college, most students want to find a job that relates to their studies. In these hard times, however, that may not always be the case. I know from my own experience that other jobs — including those that do not require a college education — can be meaningful to anyone with the will to

5

6

work and contribute. I'm grateful for the opportunities I've had that led to my college education, and though I do think we have grown too rigid in our thinking about the role of education, I also think we have the chance to change our attitudes and approaches for everyone's benefit.

6

Closes by summarizing position

The widespread belief that everyone must go to college to be a success, and that everyone *can* go to college, is not wholly true. Of course, many people will benefit greatly from a quality education, and a quality education is more accessible today than ever before. But college is not the only option. (6) Hard-working people who do not take that path can still be enormously successful, and we should not think otherwise. We can all disprove stereotypes. There are countless accomplished people who are not formally educated.

7

This country offers many roads to success, but we must remember that embracing diversity is essential to all of us. While I will not deny that my education has helped me along my chosen path, I firmly believe that, had I taken a different one, it too would have enabled me to make a valuable contribution to our society.

8

Comments

The following comments correspond to the numbered annotations that appear in the margins of Kati Mather's essay.

1. Opens with personal perspective. Mather begins her essay with an effective opening sentence that at once identifies her background and establishes the personal tone and perspective she will take throughout. The word *always* suggests that she personally had no doubts about attending college and knew it was expected of her since childhood. Thus, she is not someone who opted to skip college, and she is writing from that perspective. As a reader, you may want to consider how this perspective affects your response to arguments against attending college; for example, would you be more persuaded if the same argument had been advanced by someone who decided against a college education?

2. Establishes main point early. Mather states the main point of her essay at the end of paragraph 1. She clearly says that the "common expectations" that everyone should attend college and that only those who do so will succeed are "false and unfair." She points out that those who don't attend college are stigmatized. These general statements allow her to introduce the issue of stereotyping in the body of her essay.

3. Supports main point. Although Mather does not offer statistical evidence supporting her assumption that a college education is today considered a necessity, she backs up that belief with a brief history of how the increasing accessibility of higher education in the United States has evolved to the point that a college degree now appears to be a universal entitlement.

4. Provides examples of alternatives to college. In paragraph 3, Mather introduces the subject of vocational education as an alternative to college. She believes that vocational training is not sufficiently presented to students as an option, even though such skills are as "vital" to society as are traditional college degrees. If more students carefully considered vocational schooling, she maintains, we would in general be less inclined to "stereotype" those who decide not to attend college. In paragraph 4, she acknowledges how she personally failed to consider the different situations and options faced by other students from her high school class.

5. Offers balanced view of alternatives. In paragraph 5, Mather shows that she is attempting to take a balanced view of various educational options. She thus avoids a common tendency when forming a comparison — to make one thing either superior or inferior to the other. At this point in the argument, some writers might have decided to put down or criticize a college education, arguing that vocational training is even better than a college degree. By stating how important college can be to those who choose to attend, Mather resists that simplistic tactic and strengthens her contention that we need to assess all of our educational options fairly, without overvaluing some and undervaluing others.

6. Closes by summarizing position. In her concluding paragraphs, Mather summarizes her position, claiming that "college is not the only option" and reminding readers that many successful careers were forged without a college degree. Her essay returns to a personal note: Had she decided not to attend college, she would still be a valuable member of society.

Expressing an Opinion in Response to an Opposing Opinion

Candace Rose Rardon's essay "Not-So-Great Expectations" tackles the difficult and sensitive question of differences in gender. Like Mather, Rardon draws from personal experience in her argument, but rather than responding to a general climate of opinion, she is writing in direct contradiction to another writer — in this case, the columnist Christopher Hitchens, whose essay "Why Women Aren't Funny" proposes a sense-of-humor gap between the sexes. This forces Rardon to structure her argument in relation to Hitchens's essay, to cite the essay verbatim, to concede points to him, and to distance herself from another writer with roughly the same position as her own. In doing so, Rardon crafts an argument — that women can be just as funny as men — that is both personal and engaged with an open dialogue.

Candace Rose Rardon graduated Phi Beta Kappa from the University of Virginia with a BA in English language and literature in 2008.

Candace Rose Rardon
Not-So-Great Expectations

We've all no doubt heard or used the idiom, "She can't take a joke," to describe that particularly sensitive soul in our circle of friends. <u>In his 2007 *Vanity Fair* article "Why Women Aren't Funny," Christopher Hitchens takes this expression two steps further in his discussion of women and humor: women often don't *get* the joke, and they certainly can't *make* one.</u> (1) As a female and thus a part of the gender of "inferior funniness," as Hitchens so graciously puts it, I was appalled by his argument and immediately went on the defensive. Although I'm no comedian and would never describe myself as "funny," I have plenty of girlfriends who make me laugh til my sides hurt; they defy the blanket statements abounding in Hitchens's article.

<u>But I wasn't the only one to question his argument. Just over a year later, Alessandra Stanley wrote a countering article for *Vanity Fair* titled, "Who Says Women Aren't Funny?"</u> (2) Stanley asserts that, not only are they funny, women — now more than ever — possess established, widely embraced careers "dishing out the jokes with a side of sexy." To me, the underlying issue stemming from this pair of articles is a question of expectations — both of *who* and *what* is funny. To near any solution in this debate of women and humor, we must begin by raising these expectations. For starters, what *is* actually expected of men and women? If, as Stanley writes, "society has different expectations for women," what are these divergent requirements? For Hitchens, there is a lot of pressure riding on a man's ability to make a woman laugh. Women don't feel this pressure, he says, because "they already appeal to men, if you catch my drift." If I'm catching Hitchens's drift, a woman's physical attractiveness is analogous to a man's sense of humor

1

1
Cites opposing view concisely

2

2
Additional response expands discourse

as a necessary component in impressing the opposite sex. According to Hitchens, it seems to be all about what one has to offer. If a woman is attractive, there is no need for her to be funny or intelligent. Moreover, Hitchens even suggests a combination of qualities actually becomes "threatening to men if [women] appear too bright."

3

Extra examples broaden scope of argument

At this point, I can't help but think <u>of the pilot episode</u> <u>of *Sex and the City*,</u> (3) in which Miranda Hobbes brings up this exact point to her date, Skipper Johnston: "Women either fall into one of two categories: beautiful and boring, or homely and interesting? Is that what you're saying to me?" Despite Skipper's resounding "no" for an answer, it's clear Miranda has a point. Society has conditioned us into this mindset. Society has set the bar low for women — in my opinion, much lower than what women are capable of offering. This is an idea reinforced by <u>Patricia Marx, an</u> <u>American humorist,</u> former writer for *Saturday Night Live*, and one of the first two women writers on *The Harvard Lampoon*. As quoted in Stanley's article, Marx speculates, "Maybe pretty women weren't funny before because they had no reason to be funny. There was no point to it — people already liked you." Thus, if women are not expected to be funny, why should they be?

3

To take the question of expectations another step further, Hitchens cites a recent study from the Stanford University School of Medicine analyzing the different ways men and women process humor based on their responses to seventy black-and-white cartoons. Dr. Allan L. Reiss, who led the research team, explains, "Women appeared to have less expectation of a reward, which in this case was the punch line of the cartoon. So when they got to the joke's punch line, they were more pleased about it." These lower expectations translate into higher standards for what's funny. <u>Can these</u> <u>women be blamed? Just because the women in the study</u> <u>submitted the cartoons to a higher level of analysis and scru-</u> <u>tiny than men, that does not qualify them as unfunny and</u> <u>even "backward in generating" humor, as Hitchens asserts.</u> (4) The study essentially points out that men and women have very different expectations when it comes to what they deem funny. Dr. Reiss continues, "The differences can help account for the fact that men gravitate more to one-liners and slapstick while women tend to use humor more in narrative form and stories." Or, as Hitchens puts it, "Men will laugh at almost anything, often precisely because it is — or they are — extremely stupid. Women aren't like that."

4

4

Challenges the meaning of statistics

So with that in mind, I have to ask: Would a woman even 5
want to make a man laugh? A brief look at TV shows geared
primarily towards a male audience answers my question.
Spike TV, a network designed for young adult males, features shows with humor that is often crude, immature, and
just childish — not exactly the qualities any woman I know
is racing to embody. Instead, women often want to make
men laugh for the same reasons they'd want to make anyone,
male or female, laugh — to reach common ground, establish
familiarity, and build friendship. Slapstick and one-liners by
their nature do not achieve those goals. Even in relationships
between the two sexes, men don't usually try to make women
laugh through slapstick; rather, such humor is culturally
perceived as a way of fostering camaraderie between males.
Essentially, Hitchens's argument is flawed here because none
of this means women aren't funny. The sense of narrative in
women's humor, as pointed out by the Stanford study, is simply a different idea of what is funny. It actually makes sense
that women are deemed "not funny" by male counterparts
such as Hitchens. If Hitchens believes women generally fall
short in the humor department, and that we do so because
women are slower to laugh at slapstick and one-liners, then
making a man laugh is a quality I wouldn't even want.

5

*Places debate in
larger context*

Whenever I'm faced with a problem, I always have to 6
ask, <u>is there a concrete solution?</u> In other words, <u>are there</u>
<u>any expectations for change? Can you indeed change your</u>
<u>sense of humor?</u> (5) A quick search through Amazon.com
reveals scores of books that seem to think so, such as Jon
Macks's *How to Be Funny* (Simon and Schuster, 2003) or
Steve Allen's *How to Be Funny: Discovering the Comic You*
(Prometheus Books, 1998) and *Make 'Em Laugh* (Prometheus Books, 1993). But where does our sense of humor
come from in the first place? Can you develop this ability
to crack a joke, or is it something we're born with? Hitchens agrees with the latter idea, writing that Mother Nature
has equipped "many fellows with very little armament for
the struggle" of impressing women. Stanley, though, seems
to feel "the nature-versus-nurture argument also extends to
humor," asserting that our sense of humor is often prede-
termined by our culture and society. I find some truth in
both of these arguments. While the Stanford study points
out the innate differences in each gender's responses to
humor, our society has also conditioned these differences
and continues to reinforce our expectations of each sex.
Changing these expectations will be no easy task.

Finally, the question of women and humor is not about whether a woman can be attractive and funny, as Stanley's point seems to be. In fact, I find the photographs that accompany her article, portraying female comedians in seductive, alluring poses, to be just as demeaning as Hitchens's generalizations. It's about looking past stereotypes and gender lines and raising our expectations for all parties involved. I've known plenty of funny females and an equal number of not-so-funny guys. And I refuse to accept low expectations — of *who* is funny and *what* is funny.   7

If Hitchens still wants to insist women aren't funny, well . . . *the joke's on him.* (6)   8

6
Ends on an appropriate punch line

Comments

The following comments correspond to the numbered annotations that appear in the margins of Candace Rose Rardon's essay.

1. Cites opposing view concisely. Rardon is obliged to quote Hitchens's essay, but instead of a long block quotation articulating his position as a whole, she begins by citing the title and the phrase "inferior funniness," which gets at the gist of her antagonist's argument without burdening the reader with too much outside material. This concision allows Rardon to move straight into her own points. Notice how this argument is immediately personal: Rardon declares that she was "appalled" by Hitchens's position when she came across it, and that her immediate reaction was that she had "plenty of girlfriends who make me laugh til my sides hurt."

2. Additional response expands discourse. Toward the middle of paragraph 2, Rardon quotes Alessandra Stanley's response to Hitchens's article. Adding another voice more or less on her side helps frame the debate and contextualizes Rardon's essay within an already existing exchange of opinions. But Rardon does not buy into Stanley's argument wholesale; she announces that she'll try to probe a larger question — "*who* and *what* is funny." Rardon sets us up to expect an essay not only about genetic differences between the sexes but also about the nature of humor itself, and what we laugh at.

3. Extra examples broaden scope of argument. In paragraph 3, Rardon brings in two other sources to back up her view that "society has set the bar low for women — in my opinion, much lower than what women are capable of offering." The first is the HBO series *Sex and the City*, and the second (also cited by Stanley) is humorist Patricia Marx.

These very divergent sources of information — a hit television show and a print humor writer — help broaden the scope of the argument beyond the simple manufacture of one-liners. The appeal to *Sex and the City* especially offers Rardon's readers a familiar voice in doubting the dichotomy between attractive women and intelligent women.

    4. Challenges the meaning of statistics. In paragraph 4, Rardon attacks what would appear to be a strong plank in Hitchens's argument: a Stanford study seeming to indicate that men are more likely than women are to appreciate the punch lines of one-line jokes. Rardon employs an interesting tactic here: Instead of casting doubt on the data or the reasoning of the study as manifested in Hitchens's piece, she challenges her opponent's very conception of humor. Rardon asserts that the sort of simpleminded jokes Hitchens alludes to aren't true humor, and asks rhetorically, "Would a woman even want to make a man laugh?" The Stanford study doesn't prove, Rardon argues, that women are less funny than men, but simply that women possess "a different idea of what is funny." In paragraph 5, Rardon sketches her own delineation of the purposes of humor: "to reach common ground, establish familiarity, and build friendship." Is this an agreed-upon definition? Or is Rardon arguing for the supremacy of this definition?

    5. Places debate in larger context. Rardon goes on to place the Hitchens-Stanley debate in the context of the age-old argument of nature versus nurture. If it's true that men and women have different senses of humor, are their genes or cultural conditioning to blame? Rardon says she sees truth in both sides but offers a strong admonition that cultural stereotypes about women are often firm and hard to crack. Even Stanley's article in defense of female funniness, Rardon points out, features photographs of female comedians in alluring poses, a reinforcement of gender roles that Rardon finds "just as demeaning as Hitchens's generalizations." By reminding us about the difficulty of overcoming preconceptions about gender, Rardon underlines the significance of an issue that might otherwise seem trivial to some readers.

    6. Ends on an appropriate punch line. Rardon ends with a punch line: "If Hitchens still wants to insist women aren't funny," she writes, "well . . . *the joke's on him.*" This isn't the only time the tone of Rardon's essay is humorous. What is the importance of a female writer making a few jokes in a piece defending the joke-making ability of women? More important, how should an author approaching this difficult topic balance the impulse to take a wry look at the subject — and even to crack a joke here and there — and the desire to afford it the seriousness and gravity it merits? How do you think Rardon achieves this balance?

Expressing an Opinion with Reference to Reading and Research

Our third example shows a student writer responding to an assignment that asks him not only to consider the issue of stereotyping from a personal perspective but also to refer to relevant readings found in the library or on the Internet. In "How to Approach a Different Culture?," Milos Kosic uses the highly popular 2006 movie *Borat* and his physical resemblance to the central character (played by Sacha Baron Cohen) as a way to make Americans aware of how easily and unfairly they can stereotype people from other cultures. Most fans of the film are unaware of its subtitle: *Cultural Learnings of America for Make Benefit Glorious Nation of Kazakhstan.*

To lend support to some of his points, Kosic quotes from two essays he found while doing research. At the end of the essay, he provides a "Works Cited" list to indicate the precise sources of his quotations.

Milos Kosic has studied journalism at Northwest Community College in Powell, Wyoming, and English at City College of New York.

Milos Kosic

How to Approach a Different Culture?

1

Opens with a specific moment

Joss said that I look like Borat the second time we met. (1) It was a hot summer morning, and a group of us were out eating breakfast when he let the comment slip. Joss, who hadn't yet bothered to remember my name, was visiting from out of town. We share a group of friends, and at that moment all of them laughed, shaking their heads up and down, yes, yes, and they turned to me to observe the similarities more closely. To make his joke complete, Joss raised his palm and enthusiastically added in a high-pitched impression of Borat, "High five!"

1

I didn't really care because, honestly, what Joss said was not far from the truth. With the exception of a few style differences between us — namely, moustache and haircut — my face pretty much resembles Borat's. In fact, it is so obvious that even one of my professors couldn't manage to keep it to himself, making the observation

2

once in front of the whole class and leaving me blushing. This time, at breakfast, I didn't blush. I was a good sport about the joke and hoped only that Joss would soon move on to a new topic of conversation.

2
Increases dramatic tensions

But he didn't. <u>He started asking me questions about Kazakhstan. He wanted to know if we sleep with our sisters there. Do we eat dogs?</u> (2) These questions were ridiculous for many reasons, not least of which is the fact that I am not from Kazakhstan. I'm from Serbia, which is not even geographically close to Kazakhstan, but for Joss it didn't make a difference. He gleefully asked, "Are all the women in Serbia fat?" He mentioned a famously large American actress and exclaimed, "She must have been from Serbia!" I stopped listening when he asked how much he could buy a Serbian girl for. I put my head down and prayed really, really hard that he hadn't seen the first season of *24*, in which a bunch of Serbian terrorists attempt to assassinate an African-American presidential candidate. The last thing I needed was to feel like my safety was compromised just because of my nationality.

It had happened once already, a year ago, while I was getting a haircut. One of the waiting customers was complaining loudly about Orthodox Christianity, the primary religion in Serbia, connecting it with Islamic terrorism. As the barber's scissors danced around my head, I suddenly remembered a friend of my mother's, who, after hearing that I was studying in the U.S., asked my parents, "Why did you send him right into enemy hands?"

Well, at that moment, I felt like I was in the enemy's hands. I felt an undeniable need to belong, to hide who I was and where I was from. In his essay, "Leave Your Name at the Border," Manuel Muñoz describes this feeling, shared by many immigrants, as the <u>"corrosive effect of assimilation . . .</u>

3
Supports idea with quotation

<u>needing and wanting to belong, . . . seeing from the outside and wondering how to get in and then, once inside, realizing there are always those still on the fringe."</u> (3) But then the barber chimed in, saying in his western, cowboy's accent, "I don't have anything against the Orthodox." I relaxed for a moment and responded, "Huh, good for me that you don't." But as I turned to the customer, I realized that I may have made a mistake.

Now that I had exposed my identity to "the enemy," I expected a couple of harsh words, or at least a dirty look, but it was not so dramatic. With a sudden change in demeanor, the customer was eager to hear more about

3

4

5

6

Serbia, telling me about his army experiences abroad. I was the first Serb that he had met. His obvious embarrassment made me uncomfortable.

4

Approaches issue with open tone of voice

<u>Both my interaction in the barbershop and the one with Joss remind me that I am always on the outside.</u> (4) Dinaw Mengestu discusses his experience as an immigrant in his essay, "Home at Last." He is "simply . . . Ethiopian, without the necessary 'from' that serves as the final assurance of [his] identity and origin." Mengestu explains his cultural dilemma as follows: It "had less to do with the idea that I was from Ethiopia and more to do with the fact that I was not from America." I can identify with Mengestu's situation.

7

Since I've come to the U.S., I've been called a Russian, a Communist, and a Texan. I have been asked all kinds of questions from "Do you eat Pez in your country?" to "Do you have electricity there?" Even though my professors and American friends usually assume that those kinds of earnest questions bother me, they don't. It's quite interesting, actually, to hear people thinking about my background as something completely different from their own, a life with candles instead of electric light and with a Chihuahua on my lunch plate.

8

I feel almost sad when I reveal that none of that is true. Many of us try to find something to identify with, but there have been so many racial and cultural mixtures throughout time that now it is almost impossible to define yourself as a member of one particular group. <u>I grew up eating at</u>

9

5

Establishes a broad identity

<u>McDonald's and watching *The Simpsons*. My shelves were overwhelmed with Harry Potter and Stephen King books, CDs of Creedence, Led Zeppelin, and The Rolling Stones. My favorite show as a kid was *Baywatch*. Yes, *Baywatch*.</u> (5) I even collected *Baywatch* sticky cards and filled a whole album. So even though I may identify myself as a reader, fast food enthusiast, or classic rock fan, others may see me as something else entirely.

I could have told Joss all of these things, but, of course, he wouldn't want to know any of this; it would mean his joke was pointless. I guess it is because of people like Joss that the cousins and friends of Manuel Muñoz felt that traditional Mexican names — or "nombres del rancho" — "were names that stood as barriers to a complete embrace of an American identity, simply because their pronunciations required a slip into Spanish, the otherness that assimilation was supposed to erase."

10

Maybe changing "Milos" would make things easier for 11
me, too, but I don't want to do that. I don't want to become
Miles or Mike so that I can chum up with someone who
judges me by my name or my nationality. My name is not
only a word but part of my identity. Rather than "redefine"
myself, as Mengestu puts it, I choose to believe that "there
is room here for us all." Aside from the obvious fact that
he should avoid using Hollywood movies — and satires,
no less — as reliable sources, Joss should try to learn about
other cultures instead of ridiculing them. I am sure he
would be surprised by the interesting things he might hear.
For example, did you know that in Mongolia it is offensive
to touch the back of someone's head? Or that Japanese people never make fun of another person? They simply don't
see a good reason for doing it, even if you happen to look
like Borat.

6

*Demonstrates
source of
quotations*

Works Cited (6)

Mengestu, Dinaw. "Home at Last." *Open City*. Winter 2008.
    Print.

Muñoz, Manuel. "Leave Your Name at the Border." *New
    York Times*. New York Times, 1 Aug. 2007. Web. 1 Aug.
    2007.

Comments

The following comments correspond to the numbered annotations
that appear in the margins of Milos Kosic's essay.

1. Opens with a specific moment. Writing often grows out of our
responses to the opinions and comments of others. Note that Kosic
begins his essay with a concrete reference to joking remarks made by
an acquaintance. The jokes deal with the writer's resemblance to the
central character of the film *Borat*, a physical resemblance that Kosic
concedes in paragraph 2 isn't "far from the truth." In his opening paragraphs, Kosic deftly lays out the scene and introduces an element of
dramatic tension. You should observe that he begins not with general
statements about cultural differences and stereotyping, but instead
with a highly specific moment.

2. Increases dramatic tensions. In paragraphs 3 and 4, Kosic
increases the dramatic tension of the scene by showing how Joss keeps
joking instead of moving on to new conversational topics. Kosic lets us
see the stereotypical views some Americans may have about other
cultures, indicating that Joss even confuses one country (Serbia) for

another (Kazakhstan). By the end of paragraph 4, we learn of the personal dangers Kosic feels as a result of stereotyping, and in paragraph 5 he expands on this feeling of danger, again using specific characters and incidents.

3. Supports idea with quotation. Note how Kosic reinforces his feeling of cultural conflict by introducing a quotation from Manuel Muñoz's "Leave Your Name at the Border." You should observe how Kosic uses ellipses (. . .) to indicate that he is citing not the entire passage but only the parts relevant to his point. The ellipses point out that some text is omitted.

4. Approaches issue with open tone of voice. Kosic ties both anecdotes together with a reference to Dinaw Mengestu's essay "Home at Last." Kosic's experiences in America — like Mengestu's — have reinforced his sense that he is an outsider — a nonnative individual in a culture unwilling to extend itself and learn more about the outside world. Note that Kosic responds not with anger toward those who frighten him or ask him silly, stereotypical questions but rather with an understanding that accepts the fact that they have no idea what his cultural background is like, that they consider it "something completely different from their own." Throughout the essay, he does not express anger, sarcasm, or disgust toward those who use stereotypes but instead is approachable and open to further discussion. As a quick exercise, try rewriting paragraph 8 in an angry tone of voice.

5. Establishes a broad identity. In paragraph 9, Kosic illustrates how much American popular culture he absorbed while growing up in Serbia: McDonald's, Stephen King, Led Zeppelin, and so on. These specific examples help persuade his readers that he cannot be defined by a single non-American identity.

6. Demonstrates source of quotations. To show his reliance on source material for his essay, Kosic adds a "Works Cited" list. This list, arranged in alphabetical order by the authors' last names (not in the order that the citations appeared in the essay), allows readers to find the works he cites.

The Visual Expression of Opinion

Public opinions are expressed in a variety of ways, not only in familiar verbal forms such as persuasive essays, magazine articles, or newspaper columns. In newspapers and magazines, opinions are often expressed through photography, political cartoons, and paid opinion advertisements (or op-ads). Let's briefly look at these three main sources of visual opinion.

Photography

At first glance, a photograph may not seem to express an opinion. Photography is often considered an "objective" medium: Isn't the photographer simply taking a picture of what is actually there? But on reflection and careful examination, we can see that photographs can express subjective views or editorial opinions in many different ways.

1. A photograph can be deliberately set up or "staged" to support a position, point of view, or cause. For example, though not exactly staged, the renowned World War II photograph of U.S. combat troops triumphantly raising the American flag at Iwo Jima on the morning of February 23, 1945, was in fact a reenactment. After a first flag-raising was photographed, the military command considered the flag too small to be symbolically effective (though other reasons are also cited), so it was replaced with a much larger one and the event reshot. The 2006 Clint Eastwood film *Flags of Our Fathers* depicts the reenactment and the photo's immediate effect on reviving a war-weary public's patriotism. The picture's meaning was also more symbolic than actual, as the fighting on the island went on for many days after the flag was raised. Three of the six

© AP Photo/Joe Rosenthal

"Flag Raising at Iwo Jima," taken by combat photographer Joe Rosenthal on February 23, 1945.

Americans who helped raise the famed second flag were killed before the fighting ended. The photograph, which was also cropped, is considered the most reproduced image in photographic history.

2. A photographer can deliberately echo or visually refer to a well-known image to produce a political or emotional effect. Observe how the now-famous photograph of firefighters raising a tattered American flag in the wreckage of 9/11 instantly calls to mind the heroism of the Iwo Jima marines.

© The Record (Bergen County, New Jersey). Photo by Thomas E. Franklin.

"Three Firefighters Raising the Flag," taken by Thomas E. Franklin, staff photographer for *The Record* (Bergen County, NJ), on September 11, 2001.

3. A photographer can shoot a picture at such an angle or from a particular perspective to dramatize a situation, to make someone look less or more important, or to suggest imminent danger. A memorable photograph taken in 2000 of Cuban refugee Elián González, for example, made it appear that the boy, who was actually in no danger whatsoever, was about to be shot (see "America Then . . . 2000," page 146).

4. A photographer can catch a prominent figure in an unflattering position or embarrassing moment, or in a flattering and lofty fashion. Newspaper or magazine editors can then decide based on their political or cultural attitudes whether to show a political figure in an awkward or a commanding light.

5. A photograph can be cropped, doctored, or digitally altered to show something that did not happen. For example, a photo of a young John Kerry was inserted into a 1972 Jane Fonda rally to show misleadingly Kerry's association with Fonda's anti-Vietnam War activism. Dartmouth College has created a Web site that features a gallery of doctored news photos. (See cs.dartmouth.edu/farid/research/digitaltampering/.)

6. A photograph can be taken out of context or captioned in a way that is misleading.

These are only some of the ways the print and online media can use photographs for editorial purposes. Although most reputable news sources go to great lengths to verify the authenticity of photographs, especially those that come from outside sources, and enforce stiff penalties on photographers who manipulate their pictures, some experts in the field maintain that doctoring is far more common in the media than the public believes.

"We can no longer afford to accept news photography as factual data," claims Adrian E. Hanft III, a graphic designer, in an August 2006 photography blog. "If we are realistic," he continues, "we will come to the conclusion that much of the photography in the news is fake — or at least touched up to better tell the story. It is relatively simple to doctor a photo and everybody knows it. The fact that the term 'Photoshop it' is a part of the English vernacular shows just how accustomed to fake photography we have become. The interesting thing is that in the face of the massive amounts of doctored photos, most people still expect photos in the news to be unaltered. I think this has something to do with a human desire for photographs to be true. We know the cover photo of Teri Hatcher (of "Desperate Housewives" fame) is touched-up but we don't question it because we *want* her to look like that. Likewise when we see news stories that confirm our beliefs we want them to be true. As photo manipulation becomes easier and easier, there is an increase in the demand for photographs that confirm what people want to believe. The market responds by flooding the world with 'fake' photography. Today people can believe almost anything they want and point to photography that 'proves' their beliefs."

Political Cartoons

The art of American political cartoons goes back to the eighteenth century; Benjamin Franklin was allegedly responsible for one of the nation's earliest cartoons. Almost from the start, political cartoonists developed what would become their favored techniques and conventions. Because cartoonists hoped to achieve an immediate intellectual and emotional impact, usually with imagery and a brief written message, they soon realized that exaggeration worked better than subtlety and that readily identified symbols were more quickly comprehended than nuanced or unusual imagery. The political cartoon is rarely ambiguous — it takes a decided position that frequently displays enemies negatively and friends positively. Rarely does a political cartoonist muddy the waters by introducing a mixed message or entertaining an opposing view. A cartoonist, unlike a columnist, cannot construct a detailed argument to support a position, so the strokes applied are often broad and obvious.

The humorous impact of most political cartoons depends on a combination of elements. Let's look at three relatively recent cartoons and examine the role of **context, iconography, exaggeration, irony, caricature, symbol**, and **caption**. Please note that the following cartoons are included for illustrative purposes only. They were not selected for their political and social opinions or for their artistic skill but primarily because they conveniently demonstrate the major elements and techniques of the political cartoon. Many other recent cartoons could just as easily have been selected.

First, a note about **context**. Chances are that if you don't know the political situation the cartoonist refers to, you won't "get" the cartoon's intended message. So it's important to remember that the cartoon's meaning depends on previously received information, usually from standard news sources. In other words, most cartoonists expect their audience to know a little something about the news story the cartoon refers to. Unlike the essayist, the cartoonist works in a tightly compressed verbal and visual medium in which it is unusually difficult to summarize the political context or the background the audience requires for full comprehension. This is one reason that cartoonists often work with material from headlining stories that readers are likely to be familiar with. In many cases, the audience needs to supply its own information to grasp the cartoon's full meaning.

"When It's Too Late to Warn Iran," by *U.S. News & World Report* cartoonist Doug Marlette, published on September 25, 2006.

Let's examine the context of the 2006 cartoon "When It's Too Late to Warn Iran." The cartoonist expects his audience to know that the United Nations has been criticized for its soft handling of Iran's nuclear weapons program by continually issuing warnings without taking more concrete action. So the spoken words in the cartoon are presumably by the head of the UN, and the cartoon's message is that even after Iran uses its nuclear weaponry, the UN will *still* be issuing ultimatums. The cartoon thus satirizes the UN as powerless and ineffectual in the face of nuclear threat. Note how much political context the audience is asked to supply and how much information it needs to infer. Ask yourself: If you knew nothing of Iran's plans and the UN's involvement, would you be able to understand the cartoon at all? Also, imagine that you saw the cartoon without the spoken comment: How would you interpret the imagery?

The image is unambiguous: The United Nations building is rocketing upward as a result of a nuclear explosion, torn away from its New York City site. Note the elements of **iconography**. Iconography is the use of shorthand images that immediately suggest an incident, idea, era, institution, and so on. Such images are intended to reflect immediately and clearly what they stand for. For example, a teenager with a pack of cigarettes rolled up inside the sleeve of his T-shirt is iconographic of the 1950s; a cap and gown indicates an academic; a briefcase represents a businessperson or a public official; a devil is traditionally represented with horns and a pitchfork. In this cartoon, the mushroom cloud represents a nuclear explosion and the building represents the institution of the United Nations, which is labeled on the side in case someone doesn't recognize its familiar architecture. The cartoonist doesn't use a caption but instead includes the conventional dialogue balloon to indicate that someone is speaking. The speaker isn't pictured or identified but is clearly inside the building.

Note, too, the cartoon's use of **exaggeration** and unrealistic depiction: Does anyone imagine that — outside of a comic strip — a nuclear blast would send an entire building skyward and totally intact, and that we could hear a single human voice? We are, of course, not expected to understand the events literally. Nor are we even to assume that Iran *will* attack the United States. The overall effect is to call attention to the weakness of the UN by showing it to be all talk and no action.

To "get" the cartoon's full meaning is to understand its clever use of **visual irony**. Although it's a large literary subject, irony can be understood simply as a contrast between what appears to be expressed and what is actually being expressed. The contrast is often humorous and could be sarcastic, as when someone says after you've done something especially dumb, "Nice work!" What appears to be expressed (verbally)

"It's Only until We End Terrorism," by syndicated cartoonist Ed Fischer.

in the cartoon is that the ineffectual United Nations is issuing yet again another "last warning." What is actually expressed (visually) is that this statement truly and literally is — now that the United Nations has been completely destroyed — the institution's "last warning."

Let's turn to another cartoon, this one of former president George W. Bush, which demonstrates a cartoonist's use of **caricature** and **symbol**. **Caricature** is the artistic rendering of someone's physical features in an exaggerated manner for quick recognition. Depending on their political perspective, cartoonists can use caricature for purposes of quick identification or as a way to demean, stereotype, or satirize someone. Throughout his presidency Bush was portrayed by political cartoonists as a goofy-looking individual with large, protruding ears.

The political context of the cartoon is readily understood: After the terrorist attacks of 9/11, President Bush advanced policies in the name of security that many Americans considered serious violations of civil rights and liberties. To visually reinforce the powers the president assumed, the cartoonist depicts him not as a president but as a king. Note the regal

"Of course it would be a different story entirely if we could extract crude oil from stem cells."

"Stem Cells," by *New Yorker* cartoonist Jack Ziegler, published on August 7–14, 2006.

symbols of throne, crown, robe, and scepter. Note, too, the dangling pair of binoculars that symbolize government spying.

Now to a third cartoon that illustrates another common feature of the cartoonist's stock-in-trade: the succinct combination of topical issues. In this case, the cartoonist's humor covers two national debates — the use of stem-cell research and the oil crisis. Like the anti–United Nations cartoon, this one also relies heavily on iconography, in the image of the instantly recognized Capitol building in Washington, D.C. The architecture dominates the cartoon and dwarfs the unidentified male figures carrying briefcases, who might be members of Congress or lobbyists.

The Capitol architecture lends the scene an aura of dignity and stateliness that is undercut by the cynical remark of the caption, which suggests that conservative pieties over the sacredness of stem cells would be easily set aside if the cells yielded crude oil. In other words, economic interests and profits would "of course" trump religious and ethical positions. The casually expressed remark suggests that the speaker would in no way protect stem cells from scientific use if they could help our oil supply.

Note that this cartoon depends almost entirely on its **caption** for its effect. There is nothing intrinsic to the overall drawing that links it to the caption. If there were no caption and you were invited to supply one, you might come up with any one of thousands of remarks on any number of topics or issues. The main function of the image is to set the remark in a political context. The remark then can be read as a satirical comment on how our current government works — on profits, not principles.

The relationship between the Capitol building and the caption does, however, suggest an ironic incongruity. The imposing image of the U.S. Capitol — like the UN in the cartoon on page 36, one of the world's most significant political buildings — would seem more in keeping with a principled rather than an unprincipled comment. Thus, the overall image adds to the satire by making us aware of the separation between how a revered political institution should perform and how it actually does. For example, consider how the level of satire would be reduced if the cartoonist used the same caption but instead portrayed two research scientists in a medical laboratory.

Opinion Ads

Most of the ads we see and hear daily try to persuade us to buy consumer goods like cars, cosmetics, and cereal. Yet advertising does more than promote consumer products. Every day we also encounter numerous ads that promote not things but opinions. These opinion advertisements (op-ads) may take a variety of forms — political commercials, direct mail from advocacy groups seeking contributions, posters and billboards, or paid newspaper and magazine announcements. Sometimes the ads are released by political parties and affiliated organizations, sometimes by large corporations hoping to influence policy, and sometimes by public advocacy groups such as Amnesty International, the National Association for the Advancement of Colored People, the National Rifle Association, or — as we see on page 41 — the American Civil Liberties Union (ACLU).

THE MAN ON THE LEFT
IS 75 TIMES MORE LIKELY TO BE STOPPED BY THE POLICE WHILE DRIVING THAN
THE MAN ON THE RIGHT.

It happens every day on America's highways. Police stop drivers based on their skin color rather than for the way they are driving. For example, in Florida 80% of those stopped and searched were black and Hispanic, while they constituted only 5% of all drivers. These humiliating and illegal searches are violations of the Constitution and must be fought. Help us defend your rights. Support the ACLU. To learn more and to send your Members of Congress a free fax go to www.aclu.org/racialprofiling.

american   civil   liberties   union
125 Broad Street, 18th Floor, NY, NY 10004 www.aclu.org

DeVito/Verdi

"The Man on the Left," an opinion advertisement that was part of the ACLU's 2000 campaign against racial profiling.

This selection represents only one of hundreds of such opinion ads readers come across regularly in newspapers and magazines. To examine carefully its verbal and visual techniques — whether you agree with its message or not — will help you better understand the essentials of rhetorical persuasion.

At the center of the ad (which appeared in many magazines in 2000), we see two photographs. The man on the left nearly everyone will recognize as Martin Luther King Jr. The other photo will be familiar to many Americans, especially older ones, but may not be recognized by all — it is the convicted California mass murderer, Charles Manson. The ad's headline refers only to "the man on the left" and "the man on the right." According to the headline, then, King, one of the nation's most outstanding leaders, "is 75 times more likely to be stopped by the police while driving" than one of the nation's most horrific murderers. The headline and photos are intended to attract our attention. The image of King also powerfully suggests that the issue of civil rights is still alive. (The ad's creators expect us to set aside the facts that King has been dead for decades and Manson has never been released from prison. So there is no possibility that the particular man on the left "is" more likely to be subjected to a police search than the particular man on the right. Thus, the ad's central statement cannot be taken as literally true.)

Why doesn't the headline say "Martin Luther King is 75 times more likely to be stopped by the police while driving than Charles Manson"? Why does the ad deliberately not identify each photo? One reason may be that the ACLU is counting on King's iconographic status; he needs no identification. But what about Manson: Did you instantly recognize him? Why doesn't the ACLU balance the photos by portraying John F. Kennedy, another American icon, on the right? The main point of the ad would not be at all affected if Kennedy were on the right because the central issue is that African American drivers are more likely to be stopped than whites. Nor would the ad's message be affected if the photo on the right were simply of an anonymous, clean-shaven, white male. So, given the message, any white male could have been used instead of Manson. Why portray Manson?

Featuring Manson drives home the point that the system of stopping drivers based on their skin color is totally indiscriminate and doesn't take status, character, or virtue into account. The ACLU wants to surprise, even shock, its audience into realizing that the U.S. criminal justice system would stop and search one of America's most honored public figures while giving a free pass to one of the nation's most reviled convicts. Analyzing the ad in this way, however, raises an uncomfortable issue. If you don't recognize Manson (who was convicted in 1971 and has rarely been seen since his sentencing) and are still surprised or shocked by the headline, is it then because of the way he looks — the long hair, full beard, and glaring eyes? Does he look suspicious? If you think so, are you also engaging in a kind of "profiling," allowing yourself to think the man on the right ought to be stopped simply because he fits some kind of stereotype — a "hippie," a homeless person, a mentally ill individual? Here's a good question to ask about a visual image presented in a way that assumes you know what or who it is: What are the unintended consequences if you don't know it? In this case, what happens to the ad's message if you don't recognize either figure from the 1960s?

Besides the visual argument outlined above, the ad also expresses in smaller print a verbal argument. In print advertising, this element usually contains the ad's central argument and is known as body copy, body text, or simply text to distinguish it from the headline, illustrations, and other visuals. The argument is essentially that "humiliating and illegal searches are violations of the Constitution and must be fought." The text does not state why or how racial profiling (a term not used in the ad) violates the Constitution. In other words, it assumes our assent and offers no reasons why we must be legally concerned about the issue. There is no mention of which part of the Constitution the police violate, nor is any relevant phrase of the Constitution quoted directly.

The argument depends wholly on statistical evidence that a disproportionate percentage of certain drivers are stopped by the police. Note that the headline and the body of the text appear to cite two different sets of statistics: The headline claims that someone like King "is 75 times more likely to be stopped" than a white person, while the text reads that "in Florida 80% of those stopped and searched were black and Hispanic, while they constituted only 5% of all drivers." These two statistics are offered with no attribution of sources (Who gathered them? Is the source reliable?) nor any dates (Are they recent?). We might also wonder why only Florida is mentioned. The ad also introduces an ambiguity by mentioning the Florida statistic because we are then led to wonder what the statistic in the headline refers to. Is it only in Florida that the man on the left "is 75 times more likely to be stopped"? Or does that number represent a national figure? And is the number also meant to represent Hispanics, or does the "75" in the headline refer only to African Americans as represented by King? To question these numbers and their manner of presentation is not to dispute their accuracy or the seriousness of the issue, but only to demonstrate the necessity of responding to statistical evidence cautiously before giving our assent to an argument.

Nearly all opinion ads (and most ads in general) are action oriented. The purpose of persuasion is to produce a change in opinion or attitude that will produce social or political action. This ad, like most opinion ads, encourages a twofold action: (1) It asks the reader to assent to an opinion (in this case, that our Constitution is being violated); and (2) it asks directly for the reader's support, which could mean both to encourage the work of the ACLU and to assist it with donations. Note the text's final words: "Help us defend your rights. Support the ACLU." Because ads must work in such a compressed verbal format, some of the words we need to pay special attention to are pronouns. A reader may wonder why the final words didn't say, "Help us defend the rights of African Americans and Hispanics" (or "people of color"), since the ad never claimed that the rights of any other group were being violated. But "your rights" is intentionally all-inclusive: It stands for you, the reader, and everyone else. In a highly abbreviated way, the ad implies that whenever anyone's constitutional rights are violated, everyone's rights are violated.

The ad contains an extra visual feature that may take a while to notice or comprehend. The ad isn't just a page in a magazine; it's designed to look like the sort of wanted poster the police and FBI display to help catch criminals or the kind often seen in pictures of the old West ("Wanted — Dead or Alive"). Note the discoloration from weather and the nails attaching it to what appears to be a wooden surface. Why did the designer do this? Why take the ad's image to another dimension? And how does imagining the ad as a wanted poster affect its overall argument and our response? The ACLU's intention, it seems, is to enforce the image of criminalization. One photo is of an actual psychopathic criminal, so the wanted poster image makes sense in its depiction of Manson (though he is already in prison). But why would King, one of the greatest Americans, appear on a wanted poster? The general effect appears to be that in the eyes of the highway police who are profiling black drivers, even someone as distinguished as King would be considered a criminal. The effect and implication of the wanted poster ramp up the visual rhetoric and contribute to the shock value of the advertisement.

Writing as Empowerment

Writing is one of the most powerful means of producing social and political change. Through their four widely disseminated gospels, the first-century evangelists helped propagate Christianity throughout the world; the writings of Adam Smith and Karl Marx determined the economic systems of many nations for well over a century; Thomas Jefferson's Declaration of Independence became a model for countless colonial liberationists; the carefully crafted speeches of Martin Luther King Jr. and the books and essays of numerous feminists altered twentieth-century consciousness. In the long run, many believe, "The pen is mightier than the sword."

Empowerment does not mean instant success. It does not mean that your opinion or point of view will suddenly prevail. It does mean, however, that you have made your voice heard, that you have given your opinions wider circulation, that you have made yourself and your position a little more visible. And sometimes you get results: A newspaper prints your letter; a university committee adopts your suggestion; people visit your Web site. Throughout this collection, you will encounter writing specifically intended to inform and influence a wide community.

Such influence is not restricted to professional authors and political experts. This collection features a large number of student writers who are actively involved with the same current topics and issues that engage the attention of professionals — the environment, racial and ethnic identity, gender differences, media bias, and so on. The student selections, all of them previously published and written for a variety of reasons, are meant to be an integral part of each unit, to be read in conjunction with the professional essays, and to be criticized and analyzed on an equal footing.

America Now urges you to voice your ideas and opinions — in your notebooks, in your papers, in your classrooms, and, most important, on your campus and in your communities. Reading, discussing, and writing will force you to clarify your observations, attitudes, and values, and as you do, you will discover more about yourself and the world. These are exciting times. Don't sit on the sidelines of controversy. Don't retreat into invisibility and silence. Jump in and confront the ideas and issues currently shaping America.

What's in a Name?

"What's in a name?/" asks Shakespeare's Juliet: "That which we call a rose / By any other word would smell as sweet." Yet not everyone has agreed with Juliet's widely quoted remark. For a large number of Americans, names are a matter of vital importance. Names can suggest family origins, social status, racial and ethnic identity, or religious affiliation. They can be a source of amusement, too. For example, many people personalize their cars and trucks with nicknames, Patrick Olsen suggests in a brief essay-advertisement that reminds us of how names can help us form close attachments to even inanimate objects.

Sometimes we have trouble coming up with appropriate names for certain objects, events, or, as Rebecca Mead writes in "What Do You Call It?" an awkward period of time. It's easy to refer to the fifties, the sixties, or the eighties, but what do we call the decade that just ended, the years 2000 through 2009: "The ohs? The double-ohs? The zeros? . . ." Mead suggests, "We still don't have a good collective name for the first decade of the twenty-first century," and she offers some interesting reasons why this failure of nomenclature may be historically significant.

In the American news cycle, it seems that every few weeks some name or another is offending some group or organization. For years a battle has been waged by the National Collegiate Athletic Association (popularly known as the NCAA) against colleges that have persisted in using what the organization since 2005 has considered hostile and stereotypical Indian names, mascots, and logos in their sports programs. For example, the sports teams at the University of North Dakota are known as the "Fighting Sioux." Does changing that name spell the end of a legacy? asks Brittany Bergstrom, a University of North Dakota psychology major, writing from the scene of the action.

Since the rise of the modern feminist movement in the early 1970s, about-to-be married women have debated the issue of last names. Should they retain their names, assume their spouse's, adopt a hyphenated name, or switch to their mother's maiden name? These are only a few of the options. And whose name should the children bear? In a debate featured in *Brain, Child: The Magazine for Thinking Mothers*, two women take opposing sides on the issue in the article, "Does a Family Need to Share a Surname?" Laura Williamson argues no, claiming that both she and her husband believe that "automatically naming a child for his or her father because the majority says so isn't necessary." Liz Breslin, on the other hand, believes, along with her partner, that "having the same name is part of the shared identity we treasure."

Finally, we take a step back some five hundred years and look at the peculiar way that we became Americans. Who named us? Answer: It's someone whose name in all probability you have never heard of.

Patrick Olsen

Does Your Pickup Truck Have a Nickname?

[*Cars.com*, September 22, 2009]

BEFORE YOU READ

When is a thing not just a thing? Have you ever loved or named an inanimate object? If you have, you're not alone. Read the article below and consider how you've fallen in love with something you own and how that love manifests itself.

WORDS TO LEARN

domestic (para. 1): pertaining to one's own country (adjective).

moniker (para. 5): a person's name, especially a nickname (noun).

hauler (para. 5): a vehicle used for hauling or trucking (noun).

respondents (para. 8): people who make a reply (noun).

priorities (para. 9): things given special attention (noun).

diehards (para. 10): people fanatically devoted to something (noun).

In a survey of U.S. truck drivers, PickupTrucks.com found that 40 percent buy only domestic nameplates, 37 percent have a nickname for their pickup truck and only 41 percent think sex is more important than their truck. 1

While the majority of truck owners—57 percent—say they "buy the truck that best fits my needs, whether it's an American company or a foreign company," 40 percent say they will only buy a U.S. nameplate. Three percent of those surveyed say they only buy foreign-made pickups. 2

The online survey of 1,068 truck owners age 18 and older was conducted in August. 3

In findings that may concern the Detroit Three automakers, the survey found that truck owners ages 18–24 had the least loyalty to U.S. brands with 30 percent saying they'll only buy American. Pickup owners 4

Patrick Olsen is editor-in-chief of Cars.com.

© Bill Pugliano/Getty Images.

Scene from the North American International Auto Show, the world's largest auto show, in Detroit, Michigan, 2008.

ages 55–64 were the most loyal with 46 percent saying they'd only buy Detroit's trucks.

There was a similar age gap when looking at those owners who create a nickname for their ride. Overall, 37 percent of drivers say they've got a moniker for their hauler, and roughly half of all owners ages 18–34 have one; two-thirds of all drivers 35 and older said they didn't name their trucks. For those older than 65, 80 percent said they didn't bother with a nickname.

Staying with the softer side of truck owners, 64 percent said that they think their truck is a reflection of their personality. Again, younger drivers were more likely to say that (73 percent for ages 25–34) than older drivers (only 55 percent of drivers 55–62 agreed with that statement).

Perhaps one of the ways owners show off that personality is to sleep in their truck beds. Overall, only 35 percent claim they've done it, but for those owners 18–24, fully 50 percent claim to have nodded off in the back. Most telling is that 45 percent of drivers in the West said they had, but in the rest of the country, no region had more than 34 percent of drivers who had slept in the back.

Finally, we know trucks are important to their drivers, but the key question is, how important. We asked, "Which of these are more important than your truck?" We let respondents choose up to three answers, but the top four stood out:

1. Spouse: 72%
2. House: 60%
3. Sex: 41%
4. Dog/pet: 39%
5. TV: 21%
6. Sports team: 10%
7. Other: 22%

It's encouraging to think that truck owners are more concerned   9
about their hubby, wife or significant other, and that they value having someplace to call home. But really, 41 percent see sex as more important than their truck? Priorities, people. It's heartening to see that Fido gets some respect, too.

> There are some real truck diehards out there.

There are some real truck diehards out there; 2 percent said — nothing! — is more important than their truck.   10

We're pretty sure those guys are our readers.   11

VOCABULARY/USING A DICTIONARY
1. How would you define a *survey* (para. 3) based on how the word is used in this article? In other contexts, what might the word *survey* mean?
2. *Hauler* (para. 5) in this context refers to a vehicle. What does it mean to *haul* something? Why might that be an appropriate term for a pickup truck?
3. What is the origin of the word *percent* (para. 1)? Why might this article deal with *percentages*?

RESPONDING TO WORDS IN CONTEXT
1. What is meant by the phrase *age gap* (para. 5)?
2. Do you know what a *truck bed* (para. 7) is? Where might you find one?
3. Olsen says there is some data that "may *concern* the Detroit Three automakers" (para. 4). Is that the same as saying the automakers will be *concerned* by the findings presented here?

DISCUSSING MAIN POINT AND MEANING
1. What does this article suggest about the relationship between pickup truck drivers and their vehicles?

2. What generalizations can be made about younger truck drivers vs. older truck drivers based on the evidence provided in this article?
3. It is "most telling" that 45 percent of drivers in the West said they've slept in their trucks (para. 7). What does that statistic tell you?

EXAMINING SENTENCES, PARAGRAPHS, AND ORGANIZATION

1. This article originally appeared on Cars.com, but a version of it also appeared in an advertising supplement in *The Boston Globe*. Does it read like an advertisement? Explain.
2. Olsen writes, "64 percent said that they think their truck is a reflection of their personality" (para. 6). What do you think that means? How do you understand the use of the word *personality* in this context?
3. What is the effect of the numbered points near the end of the article? Why does Olsen include them?

THINKING CRITICALLY

1. Did any of the information presented here about truck owners surprise you? Why or why not?
2. How was the information for this article gathered? Does it provide enough research?
3. Based on what you've read, do you think people who drive pickups have relationships with their vehicles that are similar to those of regular car drivers? Motorcycle or moped riders? Bicyclers? What are the similarities and what are the differences?

IN-CLASS WRITING ACTIVITIES

1. Take a look at advertising supplements online or in print for a local or national newspaper. What is the overall tone of the pieces you find there? Do you feel that this article is similar to or different from what you find elsewhere? Explain in writing.
2. Truck drivers are presented here as having a certain unique relationship with and loyalty to their vehicles. Can you imagine being in a similar relationship with an inanimate thing in your life? Describe what that is or what it would be. How does it or would it manifest itself?
3. How different is one pickup truck from another? Do a little research on pickups — different makes and models — and write a short essay comparing them. Do they have different "personalities" that attract different kinds of people? What are the advantages of owning one over another? Is there an overall appeal to trucks in general that you can identify from your research?

Rebecca Mead

What Do You Call It?

[*The New Yorker,* January 4, 2010]

BEFORE YOU READ

How does the "name" of a decade influence one's perception of it? Is it better to choose a name based on events taking place or on the general outlook of politicians and newsmakers of the time? In your opinion, what have been some of the defining moments of the first decade of the twenty-first century?

WORDS TO LEARN

retrospect (para. 1): looking back at the past (noun).

appellation (para. 1): name (noun).

decennial (para. 1): occurring every ten years or lasting ten years (adjective).

linguistic (para. 2): relating to language (adjective).

obsolescence (para. 2): the condition of no longer being in use (noun).

cipher (para. 2): zero; something of no value (noun).

whiff (para. 2): a slight gust of air or a slight trace of odor (noun).

resigned (para. 2): submissive (adjective).

hysteria (para. 3): behavior characterized by overwhelming fear or other emotional excess (noun).

apposite (para. 3): appropriate (adjective).

cumulative (para. 3): increasing by continuous additions (adjective).

depravities (para. 5): corrupt or wicked acts (noun).

catastrophic (para. 5): disastrous (adjective).

congenial (para. 6): agreeable (adjective).

blight (para. 6): a state of decay or deterioration (noun).

overdetermined (para. 7): excessively decided (adjective).

I n retrospect, it might be recognized as a troubling harbinger that, ten years ago, no consensus could be reached in this country on what to call the decade upon which we were about to embark. The ohs? The double-ohs? The zeros? The zips? The nadas? The naughties?   1

A New Yorker *staff writer since 1997, Rebecca Mead was born in London and holds degrees from Oxford University and New York University. A versatile writer with an ability to cover as well as discover stories about an enormous variety of topics, she is most recently the author of* One Perfect Day: The Selling of the American Wedding *(2007).*

As the reassuringly comprehensible nineties were drawing to a close, all these were suggested as possible designations for the coming era. When Madison Avenue and the collective editorial boards of the nation's newspapers failed to come up with a killer appellation in advance, there was at least confidence that, by decade's end, a majority-pleasing solution to the problem of decennial nomenclature would have presented itself.

As we near the end, however, we still don't have a good collective name 2 for the first decade of the twenty-first century — at least, not one beyond "the first decade of the twenty-first century," which is gratifyingly lacking in cuteness but may be too wordy for practicality, particularly given contemporary constraints. (Call it that on Twitter, and you've used up a third of your character allotment.) Arguably, a grudging agreement has been reached on calling the decade "the aughts," but that unfortunate term is rooted in a linguistic error. The use of "aught" to mean "nothing," "zero," or "cipher" is a nineteenth-century corruption of the word "naught," which actually does mean nothing, and which, as in the phrase "all for naught," is still in current usage. Meanwhile, the adoption of "the aughts" as the decade's name only accelerates the almost complete obsolescence of the actual English word "aught," a concise and poetic near-synonym for "anything" that has for centuries well served writers, including Shakespeare ("I never gave you aught," Hamlet says to Ophelia, in an especially ungenerous moment, before she goes off and drowns) and Milton ("To do aught good never will be our task / But ever to do ill our sole delight," Satan declares near the beginning of *Paradise Lost*, before slinking up to tempt Eve). To call the decade "the aughts" is a compromise that pleases no one, and that has more than a whiff of resigned settling about it.

> This turned out to be the decade in which there were no good answers.

But perhaps that's appropriate, since 3 this turned out to be the decade in which there were no good answers. It began in overwrought hysteria: Recall that, this time ten years ago, the fear was abroad that civilization would come to a standstill, if not an end, when the world's computers failed to recognize a date that didn't begin with the digits 1 and 9. Having readied ourselves for that disaster, the one that actually did materialize, a year and a half later — the terrorist attacks of September, 2001 — came as a surprise, even, apparently, to those who had been privy to intelligence memos warning of impending harm from militant-Islamist quarters. It has been suggested that the appropriate designation for this decade might be "the post-9/11 era" — an unswingy if otherwise apposite sobriquet. Others argue that to name the decade thus would be letting the terrorists win — as if the cumulative casualties of war and the infringements of civil liberties that took place under President Bush were not already evidence of at least partial victory on that score.

The events of and reaction to September 11th seem to be the decade's defining catastrophe, although it could be argued that it was in the voting booths of Florida, with their flawed and faulty machines, that the crucial historical turn took place. (In the alternate decade of fantasy, President Gore, forever slim and with hairline intact, not only reads those intelligence memos in the summer of 2001 but acts upon them; he also ratifies the Kyoto Protocol and invents something even better than the Internet.) And if September 11th marked the beginning of this unnameable decade, its end was signalled by President Obama's Nobel acceptance speech, in which he spoke of what he called the "difficult questions about the relationship between war and peace, and our effort to replace one with the other," and painstakingly outlined the absence of any good answers to the questions in question.

4

In between those two poles, the decade saw the unimaginable unfolding: the depravities of Abu Ghraib, and, even more shocking, their apparent lack of impact on voters in the 2004 Presidential election; the horrors of Hurricane Katrina and the flight of twenty-five thousand of the country's poorest people to the only slightly less hostile environs of the Superdome; the grotesque inflation and catastrophic popping of a housing bubble, exposing an economy built not even on sand but on fairy dust; the astonishing near-collapse of the world financial system, and the discovery that the assumed ironclad laws of the marketplace were only about as reliable as superstition. And, after all this, the still more remarkable: the election of a certified intellectual as President, not to mention an African-American one.

5

There was the ascent of the digital realm — with the happy surrender, on the part of hundreds of millions, to the congenial omniscience and possibly less congenial omnipotence of Google, and the perplexingly popular appeal of making available online all manner of information of the sort formerly considered private. Who would have dreamed, at the decade's outset, not only that something like Facebook would exist but that, thanks to it, anyone would be able to view photographs of the company's C.E.O., Mark Zuckerberg, in pajama bottoms and with red-eye uncorrected, lounging in an armchair and clutching a Teddy bear to his chest? Or that anyone would want to? And what of those other unlikely innovations and unforeseen blights of the era — small plates, Bump for the iPhone, Sarah Palin, Chinese drywall, jeggings?

6

Given all that has emerged in the past ten years, the failure to invent a satisfactory name for the period seems overdetermined — a reflection of our sense that the so-called aughts were not all they ought to have

7

been, and were so much less than they promised to be. With its intractable conflicts and its irresolvable crises, its astonishing accomplishments
and its devastating failures, the decade just gone by remains unnamed
and unclaimed, an orphaned era that no one quite wants to own, or own
up to — or, truth be told, to have aught else to do with at all.

VOCABULARY/USING A DICTIONARY

1. What does it mean to be *overwrought* (para. 3)? How do the words
   imbedded within *overwrought* give clues to its meaning?
2. From what language does the word *sobriquet* (para. 3) come? What is its
   definition?
3. When is something *comprehensible* (para. 1)? What is the root of the word?

RESPONDING TO WORDS IN CONTEXT

1. Mead speaks of "infringements of civil liberties" (para. 3) that took place
   under President Bush. What does it mean to *infringe* upon something?
   How do you understand what is meant by *civil liberties*?
2. What do the words *intractable* and *irresolvable*, used in the same sentence in paragraph 7, mean? How are they similar in meaning?
3. What is the difference between *omniscience* and *omnipotence* (para. 6)?
   What does their shared prefix *omni* mean?

DISCUSSING MAIN POINT AND MEANING

1. Are the events of the last decade viewed in a positive or a negative light
   in this article? How can you tell?
2. What do the terms *naught* and *aught* (para. 2) suggest about the general
   perception of the last decade?
3. Is Mead surprised that no "satisfactory name for the period" (para. 7) has
   yet emerged? Why or why not?

EXAMINING SENTENCES, PARAGRAPHS, AND ORGANIZATION

1. An "alternate decade of fantasy" is included in paragraph 4 of the article.
   What is the effect of the inclusion of Mead's interpretation of what
   might have been? What is the effect of putting it in parentheses?
2. Potential names for the decade are listed in paragraph 1. What similarities
   are shared by these names? Why does Mead list them in this fashion?
3. How does Mead organize her evidence to underscore the difficulties of
   naming this particular decade?

THINKING CRITICALLY

1. The decade preceding the turn of the century is described as the "reassuringly comprehensible nineties" (para. 1). Why might the previous decade
   be viewed in that light?

2. Mead lists much of the history of the last decade in this article. What does she suggest is the defining event of the turn of the century? Given the other events named, do you agree with that assessment?

3. Why are names so powerful? How does a name or definition influence one's perception of events that are already in the past?

IN-CLASS WRITING ACTIVITIES

1. Consider Mead's conclusion that the inability to name the first decade of the twenty-first century suggests a belief that the "so-called aughts were not all they ought to have been" (para. 7). Briefly respond to this assertion in writing. Expand on one of her points or bring in aspects of this decade that she may not have touched upon.

2. The election of President Obama and his Nobel acceptance speech are mentioned as critical to our understanding of the decade. Research Obama's political beginnings and the path that led to his election. Alternately, research the speech in question and consider the events that led to Obama's receipt of the Nobel Peace Prize. Using that information, construct an essay that explores the impact of Obama's presidency on the early twenty-first century.

3. What events are unfolding as we now pass beyond the first decade of the twenty-first century? Does any one event stand out? How might that event define the time we are currently in?

Brittany Bergstrom (student essay)

The Fighting Sioux: The End of a Legacy?

[*The Spectrum*, University of North Dakota, September 29, 2009]

BEFORE YOU READ

Consider the names of sports teams and their logos. Might any of them be construed as offensive to a particular group? Why? When might the identification of a name with a particular group be a source of pride?

Brittany Bergstrom graduated in 2009 from the University of North Dakota, where she majored in psychology. She currently attends The William Mitchell College of Law and expects to graduate in 2013. As a contributing writer, she regularly wrote one to two articles a week for The Spectrum.

WORDS TO LEARN

lawsuit (para. 1): a case brought to court (noun).

connotation (para. 1): the associated meaning of a word or expression (noun).

alumnus (para. 3): a graduate of a school, college, or university (noun).

incidentally (para. 3): apart from the main subject; by the way (adverb).

unveiling (para. 4): the act of presenting or revealing (noun).

indefinitely (para. 5): without a fixed limit (adverb).

retire (para. 9): withdraw (verb).

legitimate (para. 9): lawful, reasonable (adjective).

unity (para. 9): the absence of diversity (noun).

powwows (para. 10): ceremonies performed among North American Indians (noun).

implemented (para. 11): carried out (verb).

Two years ago, the University of North Dakota and the NCAA found themselves in a lawsuit against the Standing Rock and Spirit Tribes, both of which represent the Sioux people, over the connotation of the school's mascot. According to the tribes, the term "Fighting Sioux" and the Indian head logo are disrespectful and, in fact, 1

© AP Photo/Dale Wetzel.

The University of North Dakota's "Fighting Sioux" mascot.

racist toward their heritage. In late October of 2007, they settled out of court with the agreement that the tribes had three years to decide about the use of the "Fighting Sioux" mascot before UND would have to transition into retiring the name and logo.

Originally, UND had until Jan. 1, 2010, before the president had to begin the process toward retiring the school's nickname. However, on May 14, 2009, the State Board of Higher Education moved the date to Oct. 1, 2009. Right now, we are just waiting to see what happens. "The State Board is meeting this week on campus, and if they decide to keep the Oct. 1, 2009, date, we will not be able to use the logo and nickname as of Aug. 1, 2010," Peter Johnson, UND Spokesman of University Relations, said. 2

UND's mascot was originally nicknamed the "Flickertails" and was officially changed to the "Sioux" in 1930 (the "Fighting" of today's "Fighting Sioux" was added later). The "Sioux" logo was created by Bennet Brien, who is a local artist, UND alumnus, and incidentally, of Ojibwa ethnicity. According to the *Dakota Student* (the UND student newspaper), the nickname was fitting for the school because the Sioux tribe was known for exterminating bison and the North Dakota State University "Bison" was UND's biggest rival at the time. 3

From its first unveiling, the Sioux nickname was greeted with protest from a small group of students on campus and has been a source of conflict within the University ever since. Supporters of the nickname maintain the notion that the "Fighting Sioux" is representative of a powerful nation and feel a sense of pride toward it. However, critics view the nickname as racially offensive. "When the 'Fighting Sioux' lawsuit came about, I had never really thought one way or the other about the nickname — it was a nickname just as any other. But once people started making such a big deal out of it, I became very defensive over the name. I am proud to be a 'Fighting Sioux,' and I think the majority of the campus would agree with me in that the name should stay," Gina Anderson, a UND senior, said. Megan Talley, a UND sophomore, agreed with Anderson: "We are proud of our name, and it is outside people who are bashing it. But we, as a student body, are proud of our name." 4

> From its first unveiling, the Sioux nickname was greeted with protest.

Perhaps most of the outrage is behind what will come of the infamous Ralph Engelstad Arena if the "Fighting Sioux" name is retired. Ralph Engelstad, former UND hockey player, donated $100 million for the construction of the arena that has been dubbed the "finest facility of its kind in the world" according to www.theralph.com. The arena is 5 adorned with granite floors, leather and cherry wood seats, and brass accents. In his agreement with the University, Engelstad made the condition that the arena was only to be used if the "Fighting Sioux" name was kept indefinitely. If at any time the name was deserted, the University was no longer permitted to use the facility.

In order to keep this condition in effect, Engelstad strategically   6
placed 2,200 "Fighting Sioux" heads throughout the building, one of which is in the entryway of the building and made out of marble, making the removal of all of the heads expensive, if not impossible. "I am outraged that the Sioux tribes do not feel honored to have one of the nation's best hockey teams, not to mention one of the best hockey facilities, named in its honor! To see the 'Fighting Sioux' name go would be the end of a legacy and would result in the waste of one of the greatest facilities around," Melissa Leathers, a UND law student, stated.

It is not just the UND student body that has an opinion on the   7
"Fighting Sioux" controversy. Many people on North Dakota State's campus are supportive of the nickname, even though the UND/NDSU rivalry lives on. "I feel that a name change is completely unnecessary. The 'Fighting Sioux' name should be looked upon as a compliment. The name reflects power and pride. I never understood why the name was considered offensive, and I don't think I ever will," said Amanda Booke, an NDSU senior majoring in nursing.

Richard Olson, an NDSU junior majoring in civil engineering,   8
agreed: "If I were a native Sioux, I would be proud to have my tribe being represented as the mascot of a college who gets national attention. It states they are a tribe that is powerful and fights for their beliefs — not that they are vicious and such." Many UND supporters argue that the success behind the UND women's basketball, men's hockey and football teams should make the tribes proud to have their heritage connected with the University. "I think they should look at it as more of an honor that a great school such as UND would choose to have their name to represent them as an institution. As long as it's used in a respectful manner, I think the name should be allowed to be kept," argued Stephanie Franzen, an NDSU environmental design senior. "There's too much history surrounding it to be lost," she added.

Although there may be no perfect solution, Dr. Dennis Cooley, an   9
NDSU professor of philosophy and religious studies, claimed that the best for all involved might be to retire the nickname. "There are a number of legitimate moral facts on both sides which need to be carefully considered and weighed before a decision can be made. Merely on practical grounds, it seems that the nickname should go. Although if we accept that it was intended to be a tribute to the Native Americans in the area,

the fact is that it is too divisive to be useful for what UND wanted it to do. UND wants to promote unity in their University community; however, the fact that the nickname hurts some of its members means that UND is not going to achieve its goal," Cooley said.

Furthermore, he added, "On the grounds of unity and avoidance of   10
unnecessary harm, the nickname should go. UND would do well to begin thinking about an image and name that would unite rather than divide its community." In an attempt to gain the respect of the Sioux tribes, UND has implemented a video tribute to the Sioux tribes that is played before every sporting event, built a Native American Center, and hosts two pow-wows a year. These efforts may be respectful gestures; however, the tribes still may not budge on their opposition of the nickname and logo.

"If it comes down to UND losing the 'Fighting Sioux' nickname and   11
logo, a new nickname may not be implemented for some time, if at all," stated UND Spokesman of University Relations Johnson. If, however, the tribes allow the use of nickname and logo, UND will remain the "Fighting Sioux" for the next thirty years.

VOCABULARY/USING A DICTIONARY

1. Define *logo* (para. 1). Is the word interchangeable with *nickname* (para. 4)? How is it different from or similar to a *mascot* (para. 1)?
2. The article discusses the *rivalry* (para. 7) between the UND and NDSU campuses. What is a *rival* (para. 3)? In what other situations (beyond sports events) might the term be used?
3. The argument in the essay revolves around the *connotation* (para. 1) associated with UND's mascot. What does it mean to *connote* something? How does a *connotation* differ from a *denotation*?

RESPONDING TO WORDS IN CONTEXT

1. In the article, a professor is quoted as saying the term "Fighting Sioux" is "too divisive" (para. 9) and that UND wants to promote "unity." What does it mean to "divide"? To "unify"?
2. What is an *alumnus* (para. 3)? How is an *alumnus* different from an *alumna* or *alumni*?
3. The concepts of race (para. 4) and *ethnicity* (para. 3) occur in this essay as pertaining to what's at stake in the acceptance or rejection of the Fighting Sioux nickname and logo. Is race the same as ethnicity?

DISCUSSING MAIN POINT AND MEANING

1. The history of the name "Fighting Sioux" dates back to a rivalry with the NDSU's team, the Bison (the Sioux were "known for exterminating bison"). Why doesn't this explanation satisfy the opponents of the name?

2. The article suggests the term "Fighting Sioux" could be harmful to some people (para. 9). Who might the nickname "Fighting Sioux" harm?
3. A student is quoted as being in favor of keeping the "Fighting Sioux" nickname. She states, "There's too much history surrounding it to be lost" (para. 8). What does she mean by that?

EXAMINING SENTENCES, PARAGRAPHS, AND ORGANIZATION
1. Does Bergstrom want to persuade or inform her readers? What about her presentation of material leads you to that conclusion?
2. Bergstrom doesn't interview anyone specifically involved in the lawsuit. Who does she interview? How might the article be different if she had discussed the matter with representatives from the Standing Rock and Spirit tribes?
3. Do the quotations sprinkled throughout strengthen the article? Why does Bergstrom include them?

THINKING CRITICALLY
1. The history of the "Fighting Sioux" name and "respectful gestures" (para. 10) made to the Sioux tribes by the school are mentioned here. In light of all of this, why might opposition to the name still exist?
2. The Sioux nickname has stirred controversy since it was first unveiled (para. 4). Why is the controversy so much more powerful (resulting in a lawsuit) today?
3. How important are sports to the UND faculty and student body? How is this information conveyed in the article?

IN-CLASS WRITING ACTIVITIES
1. Research the Ralph Engelstad Arena. Using your research and the details from this article, write an essay explaining the importance of the arena to the school. Why was the nickname "Fighting Sioux" so important to Ralph Engelstad?
2. What is a legacy? Does it only refer to sports teams? What other legacies have you encountered, and how do you understand their importance?
3. The Sioux tribes consist of people of particular ethnic groups within the Great Sioux Nation speaking particular dialects. They are distinct from the other many and varied Native American tribes scattered throughout the United States. What do you know about the perception and treatment of Native Americans in this country? How does that knowledge connect to what you do or do not know about the experience of the Sioux tribe specifically?

Integrating Quotations

Two types of quotations are routinely used in nonfiction. One type, more common in essays and criticism, is the use of a famous or previously published quote. For example, a writer might begin an essay: "As Franklin D. Roosevelt once said, 'We have nothing to fear but fear itself.'" A book like *Bartlett's Familiar Quotations* is a rich source of memorable quotes and has been used by several generations of writers, artists, celebrities, and political figures. (Many well-known quotations and their sources can now be found online.)

More commonly seen in journalism, however, are quotations gathered from live interviews. In writing news or feature stories, the journalist usually needs to collect interviews from a number of people — experts, eyewitnesses, accident victims, etc. — who will have something relevant to say about a topic. But gathering the interviews is only one part of the process. The writer then needs to integrate the quotations so that they work effectively within the body of the essay.

In "The Fighting Sioux: The End of a Legacy?" Brittany Bergstrom used direct and pertinent quotations from six students who display a variety of majors, from a professor, and from a university spokesperson. Note that her quotations compose practically the entire body of her essay and that they are drawn from students and staff at two different North Dakota schools. A major point of her essay was to show how many students appear to support the Sioux nickname.

1
The point quotations will support

2
First student quote offers a reason for keeping the nickname

3
Second student quote agrees with first to show added support

From its first unveiling, the Sioux nickname was greeted with protest from a small group of students on campus and has been a source of conflict within the University ever since. Supporters of the nickname maintain the notion that the "Fighting Sioux" is representative of a powerful nation and feel a sense of pride toward it. (1) However, critics view the nickname as racially offensive. "When the 'Fighting Sioux' lawsuit came about, I had never really thought one way or the other about the nickname — it was a nickname just as any other. But once people started making such a big deal out of it, I became very defensive over the name. I am proud to be a 'Fighting Sioux,' and I think the majority of the campus would agree with me in that the name should stay," Gina Anderson, a UND senior, said. (2) Megan Talley, a UND sophomore, agreed with Anderson: "We are proud of our name, and it is outside people who are bashing it. But we, as a student body, are proud of our name."(3)

1

STUDENT WRITER AT WORK
Brittany Bergstrom

On Writing "The Fighting Sioux: The End of a Legacy?"

RA. What inspired you to write this essay? And publish it in your campus paper?

BB. I graduated from the University of North Dakota, so the Fighting Sioux logo and nickname controversy is something I am interested in and know a lot about. When I began taking courses at North Dakota State University and writing for the campus paper, I wanted to bring the issue to students that do not have first-hand knowledge of it.

RA. How long did it take for you to write this piece? Did you revise your work? What were your goals as you revised?

BB. The piece took a total of two days to write. I knew which sources I needed, so that made the process much quicker. Plus, after working with *The Spectrum,* I learned how to work under a deadline! My revisions were done throughout the two-day span and my main focus was on how to make the article flow — where to put the quotes and information to best get the message across without boring the audience.

RA. What topics most interest you as a writer?

BB. I like to put my own spin on serious topics such as the new health plan, student loans from the government, and environmental issues.

RA. Are you pursuing a career in which writing will be a component?

BB. Yes, in the legal profession, writing is a large part of the career.

RA. What advice do you have for other student writers?

BB. Even if you are not a journalism, English, or communications major, if you enjoy writing, write! Most campus newspapers are looking for contributing writers to add depth and interest to their issues. Writing is a great way to express yourself and bring issues that are important to you to the forefront. Also, don't get discouraged by constructive criticism from others. The suggestions will only make you a stronger writer.

DEBATE

Liz Breslin

Does a Family Need to Share a Surname? Yes

[*Brain, Child*, Winter 2009]

BEFORE YOU READ

The tradition of sharing a surname has been called into question since women gained a voice and claimed more rights in the twentieth century, yet some women continue to take their husband's name and pass on the male surname to their children. Why do many women in the twenty-first century continue to follow this tradition? What influences their choice to do so?

WORDS TO LEARN

awkward (para. 4): clumsy, causing discomfort (adjective).
tradition (para. 6): something that is handed down (noun).
precedence (para. 7): priority (noun).
paternal (para. 7): derived from a father (adjective).
staunchly (para. 7): firmly; strongly (adverb).

simplicity (para. 8): the state or quality of being simple (noun).
poignant (para. 8): affecting or distressing (adjective).
schnitzel (para. 9): a veal cutlet (noun).
intrinsically (para. 12): belonging to a thing by its very nature (adjective).

My kids have their father's last name. And when I marry him next year, I'll take his name, too, and give mine away. 1

Let's get one thing straight. I am a feminist. And my kids, and their dad, know it. But this is not a feminist issue for me. It's a family one. 2

When I found out I was pregnant with twins, I was an unmarried mother in a stable relationship. We found out we were expecting a boy and a girl, and amicably settled on first names. 3

One day the question of a surname reared its awkward head. My significant other looked like his whole world had been shattered when 4

Liz Breslin has published essays, short stories, and poetry, and is the mother of twins.

I informed him that just because (he thinks) everyone else in the entire universe gives their kids their father's last name, it didn't necessarily follow that we would, too.

But then I thought about it. And in the end we did. Here's why.   5

It's good to question tradition, and good to question guys in your life   6
who uphold tradition without giving it some thought. But it's not good to change just for change's sake. We decided, after thinking it through, that tradition works for us — having the same name is part of the shared identity we treasure.

It's true that passing on the father's name gives precedence to   7
the paternal line, but is that really a bad thing? Children need fathers, research says. It also shows that masculinity is being shoved to the sidelines in the family. I'm grateful (albeit in a staunchly feminist way) that my significant other cares so much. Let's celebrate dads and families. I don't want to use my family to make a political point.

> I don't want to use my family to make a political point.

Why is having a public, shared name so important? Ask the clans   8
in Scotland or the small-towners with streets named after them. Living, working, warring together promotes a sense of unity. And this is what it's really about: a collective family identity. Christmas cards come to our house addressed to us, to the family. The simplicity of this is poignant. We are exclusively, inclusively us.

Of course, our shared name is only a symbol of our togetherness.   9
What make us a family are shared time, meals, songs, traditions, and customs. These come from our histories and the futures we're creating. We have schnitzel nights like my fiancé's family did; we celebrate name days the way my Polish grandmother does; we've started our very own tradition of going for an early morning Christmas Day swim no matter what the weather.

We could do all that with separate names, but what are the implica-   10
tions? How strange would it be if, for example, my daughter took my last name and my son took his father's? Or vice versa? What message would that give our children about our family unit? To me it would set up exclusions: My daughter's mine. Our son is yours. Names have the power to unite or divide. And I want my family united.

Perhaps double-barrelling or blending would be the way to go. But   11
think of the strife involved in that. I have friends who went down that route. Their separate surnames are Redbourne and Woodward. They've kept their own names and couldn't face the double-barrelled mouthful of Redbourne-Woodward. So they compromised and called their kids

Redwoods. It sounds fine, but it causes issues at kindergarten, in school, at the doctor's office and at immigration. Unknowing officials have questioned their family links in the absence of a name to tie them together. Whether it's right or not, our wider administrative world operates largely on an assumption that a family shares the same name.

Would keeping my birth surname in the family make me closer to my children? No. We had the growing, nurturing, breastfeeding times. I am the default setting for comfort in our home (especially between midnight and seven a.m.). We are intrinsically linked far beyond words. So why not let the kids have a tangible, visible bond with their father? They are now, at four and a big half, proud to share his name. He's proud, too. I'm proud that my politics didn't get in the way of letting them.   12

Ah, now there's that word. You let him. With the implication that he wouldn't let me. No: We chose. We knew our family meant more than words or titles, and that it was going to be one name or the other. We chose one. Now it's ours.   13

VOCABULARY/USING A DICTIONARY

1. When choosing a surname, the words *feminist* and *paternal* become important. Define the words *feminist* (para. 2) and *paternal* (para. 7) and explain why they are part of the discussion.
2. What is an *exclusion* (para. 10)? Can you think of other words that share that word's root?
3. What is an *assumption* (para. 11)? How does an assumption differ from a known fact?

RESPONDING TO WORDS IN CONTEXT

1. What is a *default setting* (para. 12)? How do you equate the idea of one with a mother?
2. In Breslin's opinion, the receipt of Christmas cards to a family sharing one name means "we are exclusively, inclusively us" (para. 8). What does she mean by that statement?
3. What happens when a woman considers "double-barrelling" a name for herself or her family?

DISCUSSING MAIN POINT AND MEANING

1. How do you understand Breslin's statement that the taking of her husband's name is not a feminist issue but a family one?
2. Breslin asks, "Would keeping my birth surname in the family make me closer to my children?" She then answers, "no." Why not?
3. What difficulties are faced by children (and their parents) who take their mother's name or a new name?

EXAMINING SENTENCES, PARAGRAPHS, AND ORGANIZATION

1. Breslin asks several questions in the essay and then offers answers to them (paras. 6, 7, 9, 12). What is the effect of the introduction of questions into the body of the essay?
2. What details are offered in this article to suggest the writer has given this question a good deal of thought? Has she considered the other side of the argument?
3. When does Breslin mention her husband-to-be's thoughts about his children's surnames? What role does his opinion play in her argument?

THINKING CRITICALLY

1. What traditions do you follow in your life? Why? Do you ever call those traditions into question?
2. Breslin calls herself a feminist. What evidence, if any, can you find in this article that supports that assertion? Do you question her claim at any points in the essay?
3. Have you ever questioned the assumption that children and wives should take on their fathers' and husbands' names? Do you agree or disagree with the argument Breslin is making? Can you think of other reasons for making the decision for or against a shared surname?

IN-CLASS WRITING ACTIVITIES

1. Not so long ago, there would have been very little question that a woman and her children would give up her name for her husband's name. Explain why this was so and what has changed in our understanding about family relationships in recent times to open debate.
2. Breslin insists a shared name is important, saying, "Ask the clans in Scotland or the small-towners with streets named after them" (para. 8). What does she mean? Write a brief essay explaining how those groups might answer if asked about the importance of names.
3. Breslin's family participates in a variety of traditions, from schnitzel nights and name days to sharing a surname and early morning Christmas swims. What traditions can you think of that many people share? What traditions are unique to your family?

DEBATE

Laura Williamson

Does a Family Need to Share a Surname? No

[Brain, Child, Winter 2009]

BEFORE YOU READ

Why do some women buck tradition and keep their names when married or give their children their birth name? What difficulties or opposition do these women and children encounter? How does the decision to give a child its mother's name influence the perception of that child's identity?

WORDS TO LEARN

vainly (para. 1): unsuccessfully; uselessly (adverb).

quibble (para. 5): minor objection or point of contention (noun).

wedlock (para. 5): the state of being married (noun).

surname (para. 6): the name used in common by members of a family (noun).

irk (para. 8): to bother (verb).

inflated (para. 8): swollen (adjective).

aioli (para. 8): a garlic-flavored mayonnaise (noun).

sever (para. 8): to divide or separate (verb).

genealogical (para. 8): having to do with family ancestries and histories (adjective).

ribbing (para. 9): an act of teasing (noun).

demur (para. 16): to make an objection (verb).

My mother-in-law had dropped the phone. Or so it seemed. All I could hear was my husband calling her name vainly into the mouthpiece.   1

"I think she fainted," he said.   2

The poor man. He'd just delivered the happiest news of his mother's life — that her first grandchild had been born — and followed it up with a sucker punch to the heart. The baby was going to have my last name.   3

Laura Williamson is a freelance author and part-time teacher.

How could a woman be so offended when I had done something so   4
patently pro-woman?

Her quibble, it seems, was this: A family without the same name is   5
not a family. It was bad enough that I still had my last name. But by giving
my name to our son, we'd effectively severed his connection to his father.
He might as well have been born out of wedlock!

Her attitude is more common than you might think. My son is over   6
three now, and I am confronted almost every day by someone who is
appalled that my child has my surname. Even those who admire my
choice still ask me why I did it. My answer is always the same: Why
wouldn't I?

For one thing, the assumption that a mother, a father, and their chil-   7
dren should have the same surname is almost always underwritten by a
second assumption: that the shared surname should be the father's. It's
the male's prerogative.

Late in my pregnancy this thought really started to irk me. There I   8
was, belly distended, ankles inflated, avoiding aioli and red wine while
my blood mingled with the blood of the
child inside me. I could not be more connected to another being, yet I was supposed
to sever our genealogical ties the minute
the umbilical cord was cut. It was unfair.

> Families create
> collective histories.

But what about your husband, you ask. *Didn't he get a say?* He did, and   9
he agreed with me. It was a brave decision; he must have known that he
was condemning himself to a lifetime of beer-induced ribbing from other
men. He also must have known that he was in for decades of confused
looks at the dentist's office, immigration checkpoints, and PTA meetings.

These pressures aside, he made a smart move. That my son had my   10
last name made me feel a lot better when my husband snored through the
five-breast-feeds-a-night phase. Had things been the other way around,
he would have been confronted by a beet-faced madwoman shrieking:
"There you go, buddy. He's got your name — let him gnaw on your nipples for a while!"

That my child's father was willing to let go of his name made me feel   11
closer to him then, and continues to make me proud. What could be better for our family?

It turns out a lot of women envy me. You wouldn't believe the num-   12
ber of mothers who have said to me: "I wish I'd been as strong as you," or,
"I wanted to do that, but I felt like we wouldn't be a family."

But family is more than a single surname. Families grow up and grow   13
old together. Families love their children even when they run the garden
hose into the fuel tank. Families create collective histories. All of these

things are possible with more than one surname in place; just ask all the people out there parenting successfully who are remarried, unmarried, in same-sex unions, or fostering.

Most important for my husband and me, though, is understanding that we are a family because we live by a shared set of values. We believe that automatically naming a child for his or her father because the majority says so isn't necessary. So we didn't. This doesn't mean we'll tell our son how to name his children, but we hope that he and his partner will make a decision that is true to their beliefs, not society's. Because that is what our family does. 14

As for my mother-in-law, she has come around. She points out to her friends that her son and I are a "modern couple," and then brags about her grandchild, just like any grandmother. 15

She does slip up, however. Every so often, she sends a card or a letter to her grandson addressed the way she really wants to: his first name and his father's last name. My husband threatens to telephone her to straighten things out, but I demur, She's had enough shocking phone calls for now. And I forgive her. 16

After all, she's family. 17

VOCABULARY/USING A DICTIONARY

1. Where does the term "sucker punch" (para. 3) come from? In what context is it usually used?
2. Define *prerogative* (para. 7). What does it mean when Williamson says the shared father's surname is the "male's prerogative"?
3. What does it mean that one assumption is *underwritten* (para. 7) by another assumption? Have you ever heard it used in other contexts?

RESPONDING TO WORDS IN CONTEXT

1. What is an *immigration checkpoint* (para. 9)? Why would that be a place where a difference in surname would cause confusion?
2. When Williamson speaks of the "pressures" (para. 10) faced by her husband if the child assumes her surname, what is she referring to?
3. Why does Williamson use the word "gnaw" in paragraph 10 to refer to her breastfeeding child? What does "gnaw" convey about her experience?

DISCUSSING MAIN POINT AND MEANING

1. What is Williamson's view of family? Why is a shared surname not so important to her definition?
2. How has Williamson's mother-in-law "come around" (para. 15) to the idea of her grandchild having his mother's name? What is there in Williamson's argument to suggest that this turnaround is inevitable?
3. Does Williamson's pregnancy influence her feelings about whose name her child will receive after birth? Explain.

EXAMINING SENTENCES, PARAGRAPHS, AND ORGANIZATION

1. At times, Williamson speaks of her child in gender-neutral terms; at other times, she refers to his gender. Identify where she makes the decision to withhold information about gender and where she refers to it. Do you think it's a conscious decision? Why might she have made those choices?
2. Williamson includes an italicized question: *But what about your husband?* (para. 9). What is the effect of that question in the essay? How would the essay have read without it?
3. How does the information she includes about her mother-in-law shape the essay and influence its tone? Does the decision to include her make sense? Why?

THINKING CRITICALLY

1. What problems do individuals face when they challenge societal norms? Where does Williamson find support for her decisions?
2. Williamson says she feels strongly that she should stand up for her beliefs even if the majority is against them. Do you believe her when she says, "This doesn't mean we'll tell our son how to name his children" (para. 14)? Why or why not?
3. Speaking of her mother-in-law, Williamson asks: "How could a woman be so offended when I had done something so patently pro-woman?" (para. 4). Do you see the question of surnames as a pro-woman or a pro-man question? Why or why not?

IN-CLASS WRITING ACTIVITIES

1. Both Williamson and Breslin invoke pregnancy and their children's infancies as influences on their decisions about surnames. Write a paper that compares their experiences of these two conditions and then explores where they differ.
2. Williamson reminds us that the configuration of the family has changed in recent years to include those who are "remarried, unmarried, in same-sex unions, or fostering" (para. 13). How do you understand what constitutes a family? Do these different configurations make you lean more toward the tradition of giving children a father's name or more toward the idea that sharing a surname is not so important?
3. The question on surnames has been broached largely because of the gains made by and the response to the feminist movement of the last several decades. Research the history of the feminist movement in this country. What status-quo decisions have changed over the years as a result of that movement? What sort of reactions against the movement have you discovered? Relate your findings in a short essay.

Who Named America?

When Christopher Columbus reached the shores of San Salvador on October 12, 1492, he incorrectly thought that he had achieved his commercial goal and successfully had proven to the Spanish royalty, who supported his mission, that a trade route to India could be found by sailing west across the Atlantic. He did not realize that he had instead reached a previously unknown part of the globe. Obviously, he was not the first to "discover" this region, since he encountered native populations everywhere he sailed. Many, many people had arrived at these lands long before he did. But, convinced that he had reached the outskirts of India, he knew what to call these people: Indians.

Most historians believe it was another Italian navigator, Amerigo Vespucci, who first realized that the world Columbus visited was actually a new world. Vespucci in 1501 reached what is now Brazil. In 1503 he wrote about his voyage and titled it, appropriately, *Mundus Novus* (*The New World*). When a German mapmaker named Martin Waldseemüller came across Vespucci's writings, he decided to place these newly discovered lands on the world map he was preparing in 1507. The mapmaker — acknowledging that Europe, Asia, and Africa had been widely explored but that this fourth new world remained both mysterious and unnamed — took the liberty of naming it. He wrote, "I do not see why anyone should rightly forbid naming it Amerigo, land of Americus as it were, after its discoverer Americus, a man of acute genius, or America, inasmuch as both Europa and Asia have received their names from women." So after turning the Italian name *Amerigo* into its Latin version *Americus* and then feminizing it to be consistent with the other continents, he inked the word *America* across the new lands, and the vast new world west of Europe received its permanent name.

In 2003, the only surviving copy of the Waldseemüller map was purchased by the Library of Congress, which claims in its information bulletin: "The map has been referred to in various circles as America's birth certificate and for good reason; it is the first document on which the name 'America' appears. It is also the first map to depict a separate and full Western Hemisphere and the first map to represent the Pacific

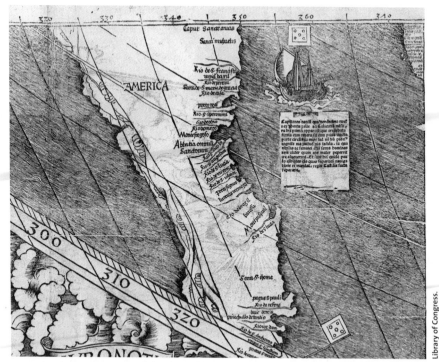

Detail from the first map of America.

Ocean as a separate body of water. The map, printed on twelve separate sheets, measures over 4 feet by 8 feet."

For a full and recent account of how America received its name and identity, interested readers should consult Toby Lester's informative study, *The Fourth Part of the World* (2009).

Discussing the Unit

SUGGESTED TOPIC FOR DISCUSSION

Each of these authors explores the importance of and often the difficulty of choosing a name. What difficulties does each author encounter when choosing a name? How is it more or less difficult to name a person rather than a school team, a country rather than a decade? After reading these essays, consider what choices are made when naming anyone or anything, and all that a name comes to stand for.

PREPARING FOR CLASS DISCUSSION

1. What kind of information sways you when you think about why a child should share his or her father's or mother's name? Whose interests get taken into account when the name of a school mascot or the name of a decade is controversial? How do you sort through all of the factors and feelings that go into a name?

2. We often think of names as solid, solitary, and unchangeable. When are you sure a name "fits" its subject? Can a time or a country or a person take on many names and still be "named"? Consider examples of this from the essays in this chapter.

FROM DISCUSSION TO WRITING

1. How do we decide who has the power to name something that belongs to more than one person (like a decade or a country, or two parents deciding on a surname for a child)? Which arguments in this chapter did you find particularly persuasive about who gets to choose a name and why? Write an essay that explains why one argument is more compelling than another.

2. Compare and contrast two of the more unlike essays (such as Olsen with Bergstrom, or Mead with Williamson) and examine the ways in which each author deals with the problems involved in deciding on a name. Where are their considerations in line with each other? Where do they differ?

TOPICS FOR CROSS-CULTURAL DISCUSSION

1. Does gender or race play a part in how these authors approach the question of naming? How so? Cite examples from at least three of the essays you read in this chapter and explain how gender or race come into play in the discussion of names.

2. "The Fighting Sioux: The End of a Legacy?" deals with the importance of respect for a particular ethnicity in the naming process. While "America Then ... 1507" doesn't deal directly with the influence of ethnicity on naming, it is clear that the names considered for America were the names of Europeans (or a European's misrepresentation of the peoples found there). Is it dangerous in a country like the United States for one ethnic group to be in charge of the naming of people or things? Do you see examples of a shift in the last one hundred years toward giving minorities a say in the naming process?

Happiness: Can It Be Defined?

Perhaps it's the result of America's long recession or perhaps a response to the widespread climate of fear (see Chapter 5), but in recent years we have seen an unprecedented number of articles, books, and scientific studies on the subject of happiness. Clearly, people, especially philosophers, have always been attentive to the issue of what makes human beings happy, but only recently has that topic become a focus of scientific attention. In "What You Don't Know Makes You Nervous," one of the leading figures in what might be called "Happiness Studies," the Harvard psychologist Daniel Gilbert, explores some reasons why "people feel worse when something bad *might* occur than when something bad *will* occur."

Gilbert bases his opinions on scientific experiments. Although what makes people happy or unhappy may seem resistant to scientific measurement, research studies are increasingly being conducted to investigate this subtle emotional topic. As another example, note the strange phenomenon that reporter Adriana Barton considers in "If You're Happy and You Know It, You're in Third": Why do Olympic athletes who finish third and win the bronze medal appear happier than those who finish second and win the silver? Wouldn't finishing second make someone happier than finishing third? Barton cites scientific research to demonstrate why this isn't necessarily so, and the implications of the study go far beyond athletic competitions.

As a people, Americans possess an unusual "right" that is famously mentioned at the start of the Declaration of Independence—the right not only to "Life" and Liberty," but to the "pursuit of Happiness." In "Get Happy" the noted mystery novelist Walter Mosley argues for "the institution of a government department that has as its only priority the happiness of all Americans." This may be the only way, he suggests, we can survive the complexities and turmoil of the twenty-first century.

On an everyday basis, happiness, although hard to define, often consists of seeing our situation in the context of others who may be far less fortunate, economically or physically, than we are. In "Learning from Tison," Tom Hewitt, a student at the University of Alaska Fairbanks, explains how his experiences with a ten-year-old Indonesian burn victim continue to teach him a valuable lesson about happiness: "I don't know where I stack up," he writes, "but the most important thing Tison taught me was that while things don't always turn out the way we want them to, all we can do is our best."

The chapter concludes with a "Spotlight on Research" that features an interview with Barbara Fredrickson, the noted psychologist and author of the recent bestselling book *Positivity,* who discusses her investigations into the elusive science of happiness.

Daniel Gilbert

What You Don't Know Makes You Nervous

[*The New York Times*, May 21, 2009]

BEFORE YOU READ

Would you rather know if and when something awful is going to happen, or do you prefer to live not knowing if something bad will happen or not? Why might knowing about something bad that will happen eventually lead to more happiness than sitting with the uncertainty of what will happen?

WORDS TO LEARN

quaint (para. 3): strange, peculiar, or unusual in an interesting, pleasing, or amusing way (adjective).

immaterial (para. 3): irrelevant (adjective).

funk (para. 5): a dejected mood (noun).

profusely (para. 7): freely and abundantly (adverb).

genetic (para. 10): pertaining to or influenced by genes (adjective).

consciousness (para. 11): awareness of one's own existence, sensations, thoughts, surroundings, etc. (noun).

circumstances (para. 11): conditions or details (noun).

insufficient (para. 12): not adequate for the purpose (adjective).

S eventy-six years ago, Franklin Delano Roosevelt took to the inaugural dais and reminded a nation that its recent troubles "concern, thank God, only material things." In the midst of the Depression, he urged Americans to remember that "happiness lies not in the mere possession of money" and to recognize "the falsity of material wealth as the standard of success." 1

"The only thing we have to fear," he claimed, "is fear itself." 2

As it turned out, Americans had a great deal more to fear than that, and their innocent belief that money buys happiness was entirely correct. 3

Daniel Gilbert is a professor of psychology at Harvard University and author of the 2006 best-selling book Stumbling on Happiness. *His research has received numerous professional awards and has been widely covered by the media.*

Psychologists and economists now know that although the very rich are no happier than the merely rich, for the other 99 percent of us, happiness is greatly enhanced by a few quaint assets, like shelter, sustenance and security. Those who think the material is immaterial have probably never stood in a breadline.

Money matters and today most of us have less of it, so no one will be   4 surprised by new survey results from the Gallup-Healthways Well-Being Index showing that Americans are smiling less and worrying more than they were a year ago, that happiness is down and sadness is up, that we are getting less sleep and smoking more cigarettes, that depression is on the rise.

But light wallets are not the cause of our heavy hearts. After all, most of   5 us still have more inflation-adjusted dollars than our grandparents had, and they didn't live in an unremitting funk. Middle-class Americans still enjoy more luxury than upper-class Americans enjoyed a century earlier, and the fin de siècle was not an especially gloomy time. Clearly, people can be perfectly happy with less than we had last year and less than we have now.

So if a dearth of dollars isn't making us miserable, then what is? No   6 one knows. I don't mean that no one knows the answer to this question. I mean that the answer to this question is that no one knows — and not knowing is making us sick.

Consider an experiment by researchers at Maastricht University in the   7 Netherlands who gave subjects a series of 20 electric shocks. Some subjects knew they would receive an intense shock on every trial. Others knew they would receive 17 mild shocks and 3 intense shocks, but they didn't know on which of the 20 trials the intense shocks would come. The results showed that subjects who thought there was a small chance of receiving an intense shock were more afraid — they sweated more profusely, their hearts beat faster — than subjects who knew for sure that they'd receive an intense shock.

That's because people feel worse when something bad *might* occur than   8 when something bad *will* occur. Most of us aren't losing sleep and sucking down Marlboros because the Dow is going to fall another thousand points, but because we don't know whether it will fall or not — and human beings find uncertainty more painful than the things they're uncertain about.

But why?   9

A colostomy reroutes the colon so that waste products leave the   10 body through a hole in the abdomen, and it isn't anyone's idea of a picnic. A University of Michigan–led research team studied patients whose colostomies were permanent and patients who had a chance of someday having their colostomies reversed. Six months after their operations, patients who knew they would be permanently disabled were happier than those who thought they might someday be returned to normal. Similarly, researchers at the University of British Columbia studied people who had undergone genetic testing to determine their risk for developing the neurodegenerative disorder known as Huntington's disease. Those who learned that they had a very high likelihood of developing the condition were happier a year after testing than those who did not learn what their risk was.

Why would we prefer to know the worst than to suspect it? Because when we get bad news we weep for a while, and then get busy making the best of it. We change our behavior, we change our attitudes. We raise our consciousness and lower our standards. We find our bootstraps and tug. But we can't come to terms with circumstances whose terms we don't yet know. An uncertain future leaves us stranded in an unhappy present with nothing to do but wait. 11

> We find our boot-straps and tug.

Our national gloom is real enough, but it isn't a matter of insufficient funds. It's a matter of insufficient certainty. Americans have been perfectly happy with far less wealth than most of us have now, and we could quickly become those Americans again — if only we knew we had to. 12

VOCABULARY/USING A DICTIONARY

1. What is a *breadline* (para. 3)?
2. Define the term *fin de siècle* (para. 5). From what language has the term been borrowed?
3. If someone experiences a *dearth of dollars* (para. 6), is she finding herself with a good deal of cash or is she broke?

RESPONDING TO WORDS IN CONTEXT

1. What is an *inaugural dais* (para. 1)? How might you guess what it is from the context of the sentence?
2. Why would *psychologists* and *economists* (para. 3) have something to say about whether people who are richer are happier than those who are poorer?
3. Define the word *unremitting* in paragraph 5. What part of speech is it?

DISCUSSING MAIN POINT AND MEANING

1. Why does Gilbert quote Franklin Delano Roosevelt in the beginning of the essay? How does the introduction of Roosevelt make sense with what follows?
2. What does the shock experiment quoted in paragraph 7 reveal about how people respond to certainty vs. uncertainty?
3. According to Gilbert, why do we feel better knowing what's going to happen instead of living in uncertainty?

EXAMINING SENTENCES, PARAGRAPHS, AND ORGANIZATION

1. In paragraph 3, Gilbert writes, "Those who think the material is immaterial have probably never stood in a breadline." What does that sentence mean? Do constructions like this one refer back to anything similar earlier in the piece?
2. Two sentences in paragraph 12 encapsulate the thesis of the essay: "Our national gloom is real enough, but it isn't a matter of insufficient funds. It's a matter of insufficient certainty." Why does Gilbert phrase the issue in this manner?
3. Explain Gilbert's tone when he refers to "quaint assets, like shelter, sustenance and security" in paragraph 3.

THINKING CRITICALLY

1. Do you believe that learning the greater certainty of developing a degenerative disorder like Huntington's disease (para. 10) leads one to become happier in the long run than assuming the possibility of risk but not learning for sure what that risk is? Why or why not?
2. What sort of things are Americans today anxious about? Why do you think these concerns affect their ability to be happy?
3. Do you agree that money influences happiness? Explain.

IN-CLASS WRITING ACTIVITIES

1. Consider the body's physical responses to anxiety. Consider the thoughts that go through one's head when anxious. Write a brief essay describing a situation, real or imagined, in which you don't know if there will be a favorable or unfavorable outcome. What do you experience? Explain why it is worse to be in a state of uncertainty, given the workings of the mind and body when it is anxious, than to know that an unfavorable outcome is inevitable.
2. Think about the statement, "Middle-class Americans still enjoy more luxury than upper-class Americans enjoyed a century earlier . . . " (para. 5). Since Gilbert establishes that Americans a century ago were not wealthier, do you think the Americans of a century ago were less anxious? Why might this have been or not been true? Research the turn of the twentieth century and argue whether or not anxiety might have come into play and what has changed in the early years of the twenty-first century.
3. Research the Great Depression. How did people get through it? Given the uncertainty of a having a job or enough food, how did people living through those times cope with their anxieties? Or did they? Try to look at the Great Depression from a variety of angles and examine any methods used to cope at that time.

Adriana Barton

If You're Happy and You Know It, You're in Third

[*The Globe and Mail*, February 18, 2010]

BEFORE YOU READ

Would it surprise you to learn that winning second place in a competition might bring less happiness than winning third place? Why is it surprising? Why might someone be happier in third place rather than second?

WORDS TO LEARN

crestfallen (para. 1): dejected (adjective).

ecstatic (para. 2): rapturous (adjective).

psychologist (para. 2): a specialist in psychology (the science of mental states and human behavior) (noun).

native (para. 4): pertaining to the place in which a person was born (adjective).

blunt (para. 5): abrupt (adjective).

shoo-in (para. 6): someone certain to win (noun).

multiple (para. 6): more than one (adjective).

When Shannon Bahrke won bronze in women's moguls Saturday [February 2010], she hugged first-place winner Hannah Kearney so tightly that she almost knocked her U.S. teammate over. Under the cloud cover of Cypress Mountain, Ms. Bahrke was seeing the bronze lining. By contrast, Canadian skier Jennifer Heil looked crestfallen after taking silver. 1

According to experts, Ms. Bahrke's ecstatic reaction wasn't simply due to her bubbly personality. "On average, bronze medalists are happier than silver medalists," said Victoria Medvec, a psychologist and professor at Northwestern University's Kellogg School of Management in Illinois. The phenomenon is a case of counterfactual thinking — thoughts about "what might have been," she explained. Third-place winners have upward 2

> "On average, bronze medalists are happier than silver medalists."

Adriana Barton is a journalist in Vancouver who covers visual arts, music, and sports.

thoughts ("at least I won") that increase satisfaction, researchers have found, whereas those who come in second tend to have downward "if only" thoughts that decrease happiness.

The most telling study involving athletes used footage from medal   3
ceremonies at the 1992 Summer Olympics in Barcelona. Researchers including Dr. Medvec asked subjects to rate the satisfaction of bronze and silver medal winners based on their facial expressions. The study revealed a disconnect between performance and satisfaction, said Dr. Medvec. "Those who perform objectively better can actually feel worse than those who they outperformed."

Expectations from sponsors, teammates and fans can contribute   4
to an athlete's sense of disappointment, according to Saul Miller, a Vancouver-based clinical psychologist and author of *Performing Under Pressure: Gaining the Mental Edge in Business and Sport*. For an athlete like Ms. Heil — lauded as Canada's first hope of a gold medal on native soil — "winning silver is a mixed thing," he said.

Olympic slogans emphasize participation over winning, Dr. Miller   5
pointed out, but "that's a bit of BS these days." According to Dr. Miller, the prevailing attitude is summed up in a controversial 1996 Nike ad, which said, "You don't win silver — you lose gold." Ms. Heil was blunt with reporters after taking second place: "There's no doubt about it, I was going for gold."

No one goes for bronze, Ms. Bahrke said. Unlike Ms. Heil, however,   6
she wasn't considered a shoo-in for the podium. "Just being recognized as one of the top three Olympic skiers is truly an honor," she said. Ms. Bahrke won a silver medal at the Winter Games in Salt Lake City, Utah. Then aged 21, Ms. Bahrke was "in shock" on the podium, she said, and didn't understand the scope of the Olympics. Eight years later, with a bronze medal in Vancouver, Ms. Bahrke became the first U.S. women's freestyle skier to win multiple Olympic medals.

Ms. Bahrke says she prizes the bronze even more than her silver   7
medal, which is locked in a safety deposit box in Salt Lake City. "This one means a lot more," she said. "I've been pretty much sleeping with it." The 29-year-old skier said she plans to retire from competition, and on 10/10/10, she will marry her long-time boyfriend, Matt Happe.

"It's great," she said. "I'm going to be 'Mrs. Happy.'"   8

VOCABULARY/USING A DICTIONARY

1. What are *moguls* (para. 1)?
2. What is the root of the word *objectively* (para. 3)? What part of speech is *objectively*?
3. What does it mean to *disconnect* something? What part of speech is the word *disconnect* in paragraph 3?

RESPONDING TO WORDS IN CONTEXT

1. Define the two words that make up the compound *counterfactual*. Based on what you say, what do you think Barton means by *counterfactual thinking* (para. 2)?
2. Barton includes a *controversial* 1996 ad (para. 5) in her argument. It said: "You don't win silver—you lose gold." What does *controversial* mean? What is a controversy?
3. If someone uses *footage* (para. 3) from a ceremony to get evidence of something, what are they using?

DISCUSSING MAIN POINT AND MEANING

1. What explanation does Barton give for why someone might be happier with a third-place medal than a second-place medal?
2. Why was winning so important to Jennifer Heil in the Vancouver Olympics, beyond an athlete's regular dream of winning gold?
3. What factors, according to Barton, can influence an athlete's feelings about performance in a competition?

EXAMINING SENTENCES, PARAGRAPHS, AND ORGANIZATION

1. Why does Adriana Barton say, in the first paragraph, "Under the cloud cover of Cypress Mountain, Ms. Bahrke was seeing the bronze lining"?
2. Do the quotations used throughout the article add to what's being said by the writer? Choose one quotation and explain your reasoning.
3. Why does the writer include information about Ms. Bahrke's personal life at the end of the article? Does it add or detract from the main point being made?

THINKING CRITICALLY

1. Does it surprise you that Shannon Bahrke was so happy to win the bronze after she'd won a silver medal in a previous Olympics?
2. What thoughts might an athlete have after winning a silver that might decrease the satisfaction of winning a medal?
3. What sort of portrait does the article paint of Ms. Bahrke and Ms. Heil that sheds more light on their reactions to their different medals?

IN-CLASS WRITING ACTIVITIES

1. Research the careers of Shannon Bahrke and Jennifer Heil. Write an essay that outlines the trajectories of their athletic careers up to the Vancouver Olympics. Discuss the findings of Barton's article as a way to conclude your essay.
2. Have you ever won a competition of any kind? If so, how did you feel about your placement in the event? Do you feel that any of Barton's findings hold true in your own experience? Explain. If you haven't been

judged in a competition before, try to imagine yourself in the various spots of first, second, and third place.

3. In a brief essay, describe the history of the Olympics. When did they begin? Have you ever watched an Olympic Games? What did you notice? How have the aims of the athletes changed over the years? Do you think there are appreciable differences between the early Games and the current ones? Between the Vancouver Games and the Olympics ten or twenty years ago?

Walter Mosley

Get Happy

[*The Nation*, October 5, 2009]

BEFORE YOU READ

If our inalienable rights as Americans are defined as "life, liberty, and the pursuit of happiness," how do we protect our right to pursue happiness? Are we, as Americans, a happy people? Why or why not?

WORDS TO LEARN

province (para. 2): territory; scope (noun).

downturn (para. 3): a decrease or decline (noun).

unequivocally (para. 3): unambiguously (adverb).

rampant (para. 3): unchecked (adjective).

consumerism (para. 3): an ever-expanding consumption of goods within an economy (noun).

aberrant (para. 4): abnormal (adjective).

glean (para. 4): to learn or discover slowly (verb).

bedrock (para. 5): bottom layer of rock; basis (noun).

bureaucracy (para. 9): government of many bureaus, administrators, and petty officials (noun).

frivolous (para. 11): characterized by a lack of seriousness or sense (adjective).

propagate (para. 11): to reproduce (verb).

durable (para. 14): lasting or enduring (adjective).

incursions (para. 14): invasions (noun).

flummox (para. 16): to confuse (verb).

slovenly (para. 16): untidy (adjective).

The prominent American novelist Walter Mosley is the author of more than thirty books. Although he writes in a variety of genres, he is best known for his popular Easy Rawlins *mystery series and for his first novel,* Devil in a Blue Dress *(1990), which was turned into a highly successful film starring Denzel Washington.*

We hold these truths to be self evident, that all men are cre-
ated equal, that they are endowed by their Creator with certain
unalienable rights, that among these are Life, Liberty, and the
pursuit of Happiness.

A mericans are an unhappy, unhealthy lot. From the moment we   1
declared our independence from the domination of British rule,
we have included the people's right to pursue happiness as one of
the primary privileges of our citizens and the responsibility of our government. Life and liberty are addressed to one degree or another by our
executive, legislative and judicial branches, but our potential for happiness has lagged far behind.

As the quote above says (and does not say), freedom was once the   2
province of white men; now the lack of that freedom and the subsequent
loss of the potential for happiness belongs to all of us. Our happiness is
kept from us by prisonlike schools and meaningless jobs, un(der)employ-
ment and untreated physical and psychological ailments, by political leaders who scare the votes out of us and corporate "persons" that buy up all
the resources that have been created and defined by our labor.

Citizens are not treated like members of society but more like   3
employees who can be cut loose for any reason large or small, whether
that reason be an individual action or some greater event like the downturn of the stock market. We are lied to by our leaders and the mass
media to such a great extent that it's almost impossible to lay a finger
on one thing that we can say, unequivocally, is true. We wage a "war on
drugs" while our psychiatrists prescribe mood-altering medicines at an
alarming rate. We eat and drink and smoke too much, and sleep too little.
We worry about health and taxes and the stock market until one of the
three finally drags us down. We fall for all sorts of get-rich-quick schemes,
from the stock market to the lottery. We practice rampant consumerism,
launch perpetual wars and seek out meaningless sex.

Through these studies we create aberrant citizens who glean their   4
empty and impossible hopes from television, the Internet and stadium
sports. These issues, and others, form the seat of our discontent, a throne
of nails under a crown of thorns.

Happiness is considered by most to be a subset of wealth, which   5
is not necessarily true. But even if it was true, most Americans are not
wealthy, and most of those who are will lose that wealth before they
die. Besides, money cannot buy happiness. It can buy bigger TVs and
comelier sex partners; it can pay for liposuction and enough fossil fuel to
speed away from smog-filled urban sprawls. Money can influence court

verdicts, but it cannot buy justice. And without the bedrock of justice, how can any American citizen be truly happy?

Happiness is a state of mind cultivated under a sophisticated understanding of a rapidly changing world. In times gone by the world didn't change so fast. As recently as the early twentieth century it would take a generation or more for knowledge to double; now the sum total of our knowledge doubles each year, perhaps even less than that. As technology and technique change, so does our world and our reactions to it. The Internet, gene-splicing, transportation, overpopulation and other vast areas of ever-growing knowledge and experience force significant changes in our lifestyles every few years. 6

> As technology and technique change, so does our world and our reactions to it.

The pursuit of happiness implies room to move, but the definition of that space has changed — from open fields to Internet providers, from talk with a friend or religious leader to psychotherapy and antidepression drugs. 7

If you are reading this essay and believe that you and the majority of your fellows are happy, content, satisfied and generally pleased with the potentials presented to you and others, then you don't have to continue reading. I certainly do not wish to bring unhappiness to anyone who feels they fit into this world like a pampered foot into a sheepskin slipper. 8

Some of us are naturally happy; others have had the good fortune to be born at the right moment, in the right place. But many of us suffer under a corporatized bureaucracy where homelessness, illiteracy, poverty, malnourishment (both physical and spiritual) and an unrelenting malaise are not only possible but likely. 9

One cure — for those who feel that their pursuit of happiness has been sent on a long detour through the labor camps of American and international capitalism — is the institution of a government department that has as its only priority the happiness of all Americans. 10

At first blush this might seem like a frivolous suggestion. Each and every American is responsible for her or his own happiness, whatever that is, you might say. Furthermore, even if a government department was designed to monitor, propagate and ensure the happiness of our citizens, that department should not have the power or even the desire to enforce its conclusions on anyone. 11

But the suggestion here is to expand the possibilities for happiness, not to codify or impose these possibilities. Our Declaration of Independence says that the pursuit of happiness is an "unalienable right." 12

This language seems to make the claim that it is a government responsibility to ensure that all Americans, or as many as possible, are given a clear path toward that pursuit.

This is not and cannot be some rocky roadway through a barren landscape. Our world is more like the tropics, crowded by a lush forest of fast-growing knowledge. The path must be cleared every day. How can a normal person be happy with herself in this world, when the definition of the world is changing almost hourly?

What we need is a durable and yet flexible definition (created by study and consensus) that will impact the other branches of government. If we can, through a central agency, begin to come to a general awareness of what we need to clear the path to the pursuit of happiness, I believe that the lives we are living stand a chance of being more satisfying. If we can have a dialogue based on our forefathers' declaration, I believe that we can tame the shadowy government and corporate incursions into our lives.

What do we need to be assured of our own path to a contented existence? Enough food to eat? Health? Help with childcare? A decent, fulfilling education? Should we feel that the land we stand on is ours? Or that our welfare is the most important job of a government that is made up by our shared citizenship?

These simple interrogations are complex in their nature. All paths are not the same; many conflict. But we need a government that assures us the promise of the Declaration of Independence. We need to realize that the ever more convoluted world of knowledge can flummox even the greatest minds. We need to concentrate on our own happiness if we expect to make a difference in the careening technological and slovenly evolving social world of the twenty-first century.

VOCABULARY/USING A DICTIONARY

1. What is *domination* (para. 1)? What other words do you know that share the root of that word?
2. Define *codify* (para. 12). What part of speech is it?
3. What is a *subset* (para. 5)? What does the prefix *sub* mean? How does a subset differ from a set?

RESPONDING TO WORDS IN CONTEXT

1. What is the difference between a *barren* landscape and one that is more like the *tropics* (para. 13)?
2. What is *urban sprawl* (para. 5)? To what does it refer in this context?
3. How is *consensus* (para. 14) achieved?

DISCUSSING MAIN POINT AND MEANING

1. What evidence does Mosley give that "Americans are an unhappy, unhealthy lot"?
2. Does Mosley think happiness is tied to wealth? Why or why not?
3. Mosley says of our happiness that "what we need is a durable and yet flexible definition." Based on what he says in the essay, does he define our unhappiness?

EXAMINING SENTENCES, PARAGRAPHS, AND ORGANIZATION

1. Why does Mosley begin with the excerpt from the Declaration of Independence? What effect does that quotation have on the piece overall?
2. Mosley asks a series of questions in paragraph 15. Do these questions shed light on what a government department charged with Americans' happiness would have to address? Explain.
3. Mosley nods in paragraphs 8 and 9 to those who might disagree with his opinion of Americans' unhappiness. What is the effect of doing so at this midpoint in the essay?

THINKING CRITICALLY

1. Why does Mosley suggest establishing a government department to help Americans in their "pursuit of happiness"?
2. Do you think that the happiness (or unhappiness) Mosley talks about is the same happiness referred to in the Declaration of Independence? Why?
3. Do you think the ever-increasing speed with which we live our lives has a direct impact on our happiness, as Mosley describes? Explain your answer.

IN-CLASS WRITING ACTIVITIES

1. Mosley suggests establishing a government agency that takes upon itself "the pursuit of happiness." He mentions that our executive, legislative, and judicial branches are in place to protect our rights to life and liberty. Explain what the executive, legislative, and judicial branches are and how they protect our rights. Do you think they also protect our pursuit of happiness? Does your argument refute Mosley's?
2. What do you think is the cure for our unhappiness? Would you suggest something as unusual as Mosley does (a government agency) or something else? How would you address the wide scope of unhappiness brought out in this essay?
3. Examine the way "we" as Americans are described in paragraph 3. Choose one of the statements Mosley makes and write an essay that explores why that action, or concern, or way of thinking affects our happiness. Look at how it affects our outlook on life and our standard of living.

Tom Hewitt (student essay)

Learning from Tison

[*The Sun Star*, University of Alaska Fairbanks, December 15, 2009]

BEFORE YOU READ

Have you ever considered how the life you have compares with the life of someone less fortunate? What sorts of things create happiness and unhappiness in your life? How do you determine what is really important to you and your happiness?

WORDS TO LEARN

victim (para. 3): someone who suffers from an injury (noun).

journalistic (para. 3): characteristic of journalism (adjective).

noticeable (para. 7): attracting attention (adjective).

fulfillment (para. 9): completion (noun).

detect (para. 10): to discover or catch (verb).

L ast week at this time, I was waking up in a Jakarta hotel in preparation for a 36-hour flight back to Alaska. 1

Let me back up. 2

I left Thanksgiving morning to travel to Indonesia, where I would begin filming a documentary about a 10-year-old burn victim named Tison who was coming to Fairbanks for reconstructive surgery. The whole opportunity had come together relatively at the last minute, but some journalistic opportunities are difficult to turn down. 3

It was a long haul traveling to the clinic where Tison lived — planes from Fairbanks to Seattle to Los Angeles to Hong Kong to Singapore to Manado to Ternate, then a speed boat from Ternate to the island of Halmahera, and a cab for the final three-hour drive to the clinic. I like traveling, but after four days en route, I was ready to stay in one place for a while. 4

The travel wasn't the only thing bothering me. I would be missing over a week of school — and an issue of the *Sun Star* — right before 5

Tom Hewitt is a senior at the University of Alaska Fairbanks, where he is a journalism major. He is the online editor and regular contributor for the student-run weekly paper, The Sun Star.

finals, and I had several papers and projects to complete before my return, in addition to filming Tison and life at the clinic full time. My stress level was high.

What finally brought my mind back to my work was a trip to a soc-   6
cer game at a nearby village, where the clinic's soccer team had a match against the locals. The twelve players, Tison, and I piled into a minivan and rumbled off.

The villagers were poor. They lived in aluminum-and-wood shacks with   7
tiny yards. The soccer field was mostly dirt, and a noticeable rise in the pitch near one goal provided a terrain obstacle. The bridge to the field couldn't support a car — the villagers had to ferry us across the river on rafts.

Despite all this, everyone at the game was happy. The whole village   8
turned out, and the visiting clinic team was treated like royalty, with cold water before the match and hot tea and baked bananas after. When the home team won, 3-1, the players' mothers and sisters stormed the field cheering.

Life isn't fair. Sometimes there's no good reason why some people   9
get to travel halfway around the world to see incredible things while others sleep on dirt floors and don't know where their next meal will come from. The Indonesians know that, but it doesn't stop them from finding fulfillment.

> No matter how long I pointed the camera his direction, I never got tired of telling his story.

Nor did having burns over 40 percent   10
of his body diminish Tison's spirit in any way I could detect. On his worst day, he was several times cheerier than I am in the best of times. No matter how long I pointed the camera in his direction, I never got tired of telling his story. And he pretended not to mind me tagging behind him everywhere he went.

We get thrown curves sometimes, and part of the way we may be   11
measured is how we respond not to situations we expect, but those we don't. I don't know where I stack up, but the most important thing Tison taught me was that while things don't always turn out the way we want them to, all we can do is our best. And if I can do half as well as Tison, I'll count myself a success.

VOCABULARY/USING A DICTIONARY

1. What is a *documentary* (para. 3)?
2. What does it mean to be *en route* (para. 4)?
3. What is meant by the word *terrain* in paragraph 7? From what language is the word derived?

RESPONDING TO WORDS IN CONTEXT

1. What is a *clinic* (para. 4)? How do you know what kind of clinic Hewitt is talking about?
2. How do you define *reconstructive surgery* (para. 3) based on your understanding of what it means to reconstruct something?
3. Explain what it means to *measure* something. How is the word "measured" used in paragraph 11?

DISCUSSING MAIN POINT AND MEANING

1. Who is Tison? Why was Hewitt sent to film a documentary about him?
2. What are some of the differences between Hewitt's life and the lives of the villagers?
3. Why does the soccer game create such happiness for the people of the village?

EXAMINING SENTENCES, PARAGRAPHS, AND ORGANIZATION

1. Why does the essay begin with Hewitt leaving Jakarta and then quickly switch gears? How does it "switch"?
2. Consider that this is a student essay on which you might provide feedback. If the essay were expanded to include more information, where would you want that information? What exactly would you like to hear more about?
3. Hewitt writes, "On his worst day, [Tison] was several times cheerier than I am in the best of times" (para. 10). Do you have a sense of Hewitt's personality and demeanor elsewhere in the essay? Where?

THINKING CRITICALLY

1. How does Hewitt view the lives of the villagers in Indonesia?
2. Do you wish you had more information about Tison in the essay? What do you wish you knew?
3. Would you expect a person like Tison to feel and behave the way Hewitt reports he does? Why or why not?

IN-CLASS WRITING ACTIVITIES

1. Choose a country that would be considered part of the "developing world" (like Indonesia), and do some research about conditions there. How do people live? Write an essay that compares your lifestyle with the lifestyles of people who come from much poorer countries. What are the similarities? What are the differences?
2. How does a group sport like soccer promote a sense of community and social connection? Consider soccer or another "easily translatable" activity (one that you would find in a very different part of the world) and

describe what aspects of it bring people together and allow for some sort of important interaction.

3. Consider the life of a journalist. Does a good journalist bring himself into the story or not? How might Hewitt influence his documentary, even though a documentary is supposed to be objective? How do you think journalists present objective truths, and how do you think they might fall into presenting subjective truths?

Using Repetition for Effect

Most of the time when writing essays you will want to avoid repetition. Wordiness — using more words than needed — is considered a compositional flaw, and instructors will often flag unnecessary repetition. But repetition also can be used for emphasis and rhetorical effect. A famous example of emphatic repetition is Lincoln's conclusion to the Gettysburg Address: "and that government of the people, by the people, for the people, shall not perish from the earth."

Observe how Tom Hewitt, a University of Alaska student, uses repetition effectively in his essay, "Learning from Tison." To emphasize the distance and tedium of his flight to Indonesia he uses the word "to" repeatedly in his account of the trip. In doing so, he makes his reader feel just how long the trip felt to him. To see how this effect works, try substituting the word "to" between all the airport stops with a comma and compare the two versions.

1
Repeating the word to *empha-sizes the length of the trip*

It was a long haul traveling to the clinic where Tison lived—planes from Fairbanks to Seattle to Los Angeles to Hong Kong to Singapore to Manado to Ternate, then a speed boat from Ternate to the island of Halmahera, and a cab for the final three-hour drive to the clinic. (1) I like traveling, but after four days en route, I was ready to stay in one place for a while.

STUDENT WRITER AT WORK
Tom Hewitt
On Writing "Learning from Tison"

RA. What inspired you to write this essay? And publish it in your campus paper?

TH. As the editor-in-chief, I was responsible for writing an editorial on a topic of my choice each week. Since we're a college paper, usually the topic relates to a specific issue affecting students (tuition, facilities, or the like) but because it was finals week, and it was my last editorial before handing off the editorship to the paper's incoming editor, I wanted the topic to be a little more universally meaningful. I had just had an amazing experience spending time with Tison in Indonesia and traveling with him to America, and I felt like there was something everyone who read the paper could take away from him.

RA. What response have you received to this piece? Has the feedback you have received affected your views on the topic you wrote about?

TH. I received a fair amount of feedback on this piece. It was overwhelmingly positive, and many of the people who talked to me about the piece were interested in Tison and how he was doing. As of June 2010, Tison has been in America for half a year receiving treatment for his burns and will likely stay for several more months before heading home to Indonesia. I see Tison once every couple of weeks; to my chagrin, he has learned enough about video games in his time here that he beats me at Mario Kart every time we play.

RA. Have you written on this topic since? Have you read or seen other work on the topic that has interested you? If so, please describe.

TH. I haven't written on this topic since writing this piece, but my experience with Tison has made me much more interested in Indonesian issues than I had been previously. I frequently think of the workers at the clinic where Tison lived on the island of Halmahera and have become friends with a few of them on Facebook.

RA. Are you pursuing a career in which writing will be a component?

TH. If my life goes the way I hope it will, writing will be fundamental to my career. I had the opportunity to embed with an army brigade in Iraq in August 2009, and that experience wiped out whatever previous doubts I might have had about whether I wanted to pursue a career in journalism. I hope to write for one of the major publications I read now, and I'm confident that I will.

RA. What advice do you have for other student writers?

TH. First and foremost, always keep writing. Writing more is the only surefire way to improve. What also helps is finding someone who can help you improve your writing. This can be a professor, friend, or colleague — anyone who can look at your work with a critical eye and tell you what you're doing right and where you're going astray. I've been lucky to have a couple such people in my life, and they make all the difference.

Another thing that can aid in developing your style is to read a lot, especially things that are similar to the way you want to write. Want to write for *Vanity Fair*? You'd better read it and find out the sort of thing they publish. Having your own voice is key, obviously, but there's no point in completely reinventing the wheel.

Beyond that, just make sure you're having fun.

Spotlight on Research

Barbara Fredrickson
The Science of Happiness

[*The Sun*, May 2009]

Barbara Fredrickson is the Kenan Distinguished Professor of Psychology at the University of North Carolina at Chapel Hill and the author most recently of Positivity *(2009). The following excerpt is from a long interview with Fredrickson conducted by Angela Winter that appeared in* The Sun *magazine in May 2009.*

Fredrickson: Scientists most often measure happiness by asking how strongly   1
a person agrees with statements like "I'm satisfied with my life" or "If I could
live my life over, I wouldn't change a thing." These kinds of questions are
much broader in scope than questions that are used to measure positive emotions, such as "Are you feeling amused, silly, or lighthearted?" Positive emotions are much more narrow-band feelings, not overall judgments about your
life. Sometimes we use happy to refer to a specific emotion, but, scientifically
speaking, it's not OK to use a single word, like *happy*, in multiple ways. I view
happiness as the overall outcome of many positive moments.

My goal as a scientist has always been to pull apart the process of how   2
one state leads to another and ultimately guides us to a useful outcome. Over
the last decade researchers have found some stunning correlations between
expressing more positive emotions and living longer. My role is to ask, How
does that happen? How do you go from experiencing these pleasant momentary states to living longer — perhaps even ten years longer?

Other researchers have found that the number of positive emotions   3
a person feels predicts his or her satisfaction with life. What we've done is
uncover how positive emotions actually cause us to be happier by helping
us build our resources for managing day-to-day life. When we have better
resources, we emerge from adverse situations feeling more satisfied with the
outcome.

My colleagues and I have a paper forthcoming in the journal *Emotion*   4
called "Happiness Unpacked." We're trying to take this word *happiness*,
which is a little bit of a garbage-can term — people put too many things
in it — and look under the hood at the dynamics of the process. And what
we've found is that we should be focusing on how we feel from day to day,
not on how we can become happy with life in general. If you focus on day-
to-day feelings, you end up building your resources and becoming your
best version of yourself. Down the road, you'll be happier with life. Rather
than staring down happiness as our goal and asking ourselves, "How do I
get there?" we should be thinking about how to create positive emotions in
the moment.

Discussing the Unit

SUGGESTED TOPIC FOR DISCUSSION

Each of the essays in this chapter illustrates that happiness is highly subjective— there is no one straight path to it. Who or what would these authors say is responsible for happiness? Were you surprised by the descriptions of happiness or unhappiness in any of the selections?

PREPARING FOR CLASS DISCUSSION

1. When are these writers drawing their information about happiness from personal experience and when are they following the trajectories of the happiness of others? Do you feel more convinced of the argument when it comes from the writer's experience or from research?

2. How do these writers define happiness? How do you define it? Do you believe happiness is a lack of anxiety (as in Gilbert's essay) or something so hard to find we need help imposing it on our modern lives (as in Mosley's essay), or is it accepting and enjoying ourselves in some way (as in Barton's and Hewitt's essays)?

FROM DISCUSSION TO WRITING

1. In "What You Don't Know Makes You Nervous," Gilbert quotes Franklin D. Roosevelt's famous phrase, "The only thing we have to fear is fear itself." How does fear affect our happiness? Write an essay that explores this statement in more detail, and pull in evidence from some of the other essays to support your point.

2. Choose two essays from this chapter that present a definition of happiness in a similar light. Try to encapsulate the "definition" of happiness being presented. Then write an essay that explores the similarities but also presents some of the differences you find.

TOPICS FOR CROSS-CULTURAL DISCUSSION

1. The happiness of Americans, or lack of it, is under scrutiny in many of these essays. How does the happiness of other people of other countries and cultural backgrounds compare to the happiness (or unhappiness) of Americans described here?

2. Mosley quotes the Declaration of Independence, which states that we have "certain unalienable rights, that among these are Life, Liberty, and the pursuit of Happiness." How, in the history of the United States, have non-whites or immigrants experienced the right to the pursuit of happiness? How does that experience match or not match Mosley's interpretation of that right?

3

Is There an Ethics of Eating?

Many of us, especially the health conscious, have grown accustomed to reading the labels on food products, studying the amount of fat, the number of calories, and the list of artificial ingredients. But such labels are no longer our only source of food information. More and more cities are looking into legislation that would require the menus of fast food chains to disclose the total calories a particular item or meal contains. There is also a growing movement for labels on supermarket products to reveal the energy costs (the carbon footprint) that went into the item, so that consumers will know how their purchase has affected the planet. Do you actually want to buy that carbon-intensive package of frozen hamburgers? Or all those environmentally hazardous plastic water bottles?

As Americans become increasingly aware of the impact their eating habits have on personal, public, and planetary health, we have seen a growing literature that addresses the ethics of eating, ranging from the risks of obesity to the slaughter of animals for human consumption. One aspect of ethical eating is the controversy over locally grown food. Though many assert the benefits of using local farms and markets, others, such as Warwick Sabin in "The Rich Get Thinner, the Poor Get Fatter," worry that local, wholesome food is fast becoming a luxury item that the poor cannot enjoy: "By an extraordinary twist of economics," he writes, "the fresh, local produce once available cheaply at the back-road farm stand has become the preserve of the elites, available in gourmet-food shops at inflated prices."

If local, organic food is beyond the means of many citizens, are the alternatives McDonald's and Burger King? Are these fast food chains and many others like them the perpetual enemy of the various ethical eating movements? In "Why Investing in Fast Food May Be a Good Thing," the socially conscious financial investor Amy Domini tries to take a realistic approach to the fast food problem. Herself a "Slow Food" advocate, who favors locally farmed organic foods, she realizes that the chains are here to stay and—citing a number of ways that fast food can become healthier and more environmentally responsible—she maintains that it will be best to improve them rather than fight them.

One controversy surrounding the topic of eating ethically is age-old: *meat*. Are we justified in slaughtering cows, pigs, chickens, and other creatures to satisfy our own appetites? Does a truly ethical response to food require that we all become vegetarians or vegans? Responses to this topic often follow conventional arguments on each side of the debate. But rarely does anyone respond in a complex personal essay that looks at the issue from a wide variety of perspectives. For Brian Jay Stanley in "Confessions of a Carnivore," eating, whatever the food, seems to compromise us morally. Eating is essentially consumption, he suggests, and is at the root of our consumer society: "Considering we are consumers by essence, no wonder we have built a consumer society, adding voluntary sins of acquisition to our necessary sin of eating."

An eighteenth-century French politician and one of the earliest culinary experts famously said: "Tell me what you eat, and I will tell you who you are." In the final selection, "Remembering Johnny Appleseed," Jacob Swede, a student at the University of Minnesota Twin Cities, takes this widely quoted remark far beyond the personal as he examines it in the context of today's numerous food abuses.

Warwick Sabin

The Rich Get Thinner, the Poor Get Fatter

[*Oxford American*, #68, March 2010]

BEFORE YOU READ

When you eat, do you reach for fresh, locally grown foods, or are you more likely to eat prepackaged, processed foods? What influences your choices about food? Are price and availability factors in your decision about how to eat?

WORDS TO LEARN

indicate (para. 3): show (verb).

intuitively (para. 6): being perceived or known by insight (adverb).

phenomenon (para. 6): an observed or observable occurrence (noun).

prevalence (para. 6): wide extent (noun).

disproportionally (para. 7): out of proportion (adverb).

attributable (para. 7): designated (adjective).

indulgences (para. 12): something gratifying to one's desires or feelings (noun).

dominant (para. 14): in an elevated position (adjective).

efficient (para. 15): performing in the best possible manner (adjective).

requisite (para. 17): required or necessary (adjective).

O ur appreciation of Southern cuisine has a dark side. We usu-   1
ally acknowledge it with a laugh, or a devil-may-care sense of
recklessness.

That fried chicken leg may kill you; that pork rib is going to take a year   2
off your life. But it's worth it, you say. You are willing to live on the edge.

This apparent choice between good health and good eating is   3
made even starker with every new report issued by the U.S. Centers
for Disease Control and Prevention. The latest, issued in November
2009, was titled "Highest Rates of Obesity, Diabetes in the South," and
it included some sobering statistics. Most Southern states have obesity

---

Warwick Sabin has been a journalist for the Arkansas Times *and is publisher of
the well-known Southern magazine* Oxford American, *which comes out of the
University of Central Arkansas.*

rates hovering near, or above, the thirty-percent mark, and projections indicate that the problem is going to get much worse in the years ahead.

Of course, it doesn't take long for the researchers to trace the expanding waistlines back to the biscuits and gravy.   4

"Southern culture plays a role in the rising obesity rates in the region,"   5
reports a 2008 article in the *Chattanooga Times Free Press*. "Traditional Southern foods — even vegetables such as fried green tomatoes and fried okra — can be land mines for the weight-conscious, health experts said."

Intuitively, that may seem true, but it does not explain why our nation's   6
skyrocketing obesity problem is a relatively recent phenomenon that is not confined to the South. The CDC data indicates that no state had an obesity rate higher than fifteen percent in 1990. By 1998, no state had a prevalence of obesity *less* than ten percent. As our lives become less physically demanding (with fewer jobs in agriculture and blue-collar trades), and our diets become less wholesome (with more sugar and artificial ingredients), all Americans are at risk of becoming ensnared in the obesity trap.

> By an extraordinary twist of economics, the fresh, local produce once available cheaply at the back-road farm stand has become the preserve of the elites, available in gourmet-food shops at inflated prices.

Still, there is a particularly sad irony in   7
the South disproportionally suffering from an obesity epidemic that could be attributable to its regional cuisine. Many of what are now considered traditional Southern dishes were to a large degree designed to fill empty stomachs and provide essential energy when work was hard and food was scarce.

Then, like now, the South had a higher rate of poverty than almost   8
anywhere else in the nation. So what has changed?

Take a walk through the aisles of your grocery store and compare the   9
prices of fresh fruits, vegetables, and meats to those of the mass-produced processed foods. It will quickly become clear that the poor people of the South are making the exact same decisions they made during the time of James Agee and Walker Evans — they are opting for the affordable calories.

The cruel fact is that fewer than one hundred years ago being poor   10
meant you were painfully thin. Now, it means you are dangerously fat.

But this time, it's probably not the biscuits and gravy that are to   11
blame so much as candy bars, soft drinks, and fast food.

In fact, our favorite Southern foods actually have become indulgences   12
because an increasing number of Southerners cannot afford them. By an

extraordinary twist of economics, the fresh, local produce once available cheaply at the back-road farm stand has become the preserve of the elites, available in gourmet-food shops at inflated prices.

It used to be that keeping a few free-range chickens, tending some 13 grain-fed hogs, and raising a small vegetable garden was how people simply survived. Now these are often vanity projects for young hipsters and retired hedge-fund executives who have discovered the forgotten pleasures of "heirloom" tomatoes and artisanal sausage. Incredibly, we've reached a point in our society where things that humans have done for thousands of years — grow a vegetable, smoke or cure a piece of meat — now provide the grounds for smug satisfaction. (Think of Marie Antoinette at Versailles, playing shepherdess and milking the cows.)

In a region where farming is still a dominant industry, how can food 14 that is fresh, local, and organic be beyond the reach of so many Southerners? Our states are among the nation's leaders in the cultivation of fruits, vegetables, rice, peanuts, poultry, and other agricultural products. Yet schoolchildren in poor, rural districts, surrounded by fields and chicken houses, eat processed lunches delivered by food-service tractor-trailers from facilities that are thousands of miles away.

In the end, this paradox can be traced back to those fields and 15 chicken houses, which are now incorporated elements of the devastatingly efficient agribusiness giants. Mechanization, genetic engineering, herbicides, pesticides, growth hormones, and massive economies of scale ensure that anything grown in the next town over is as likely to end up in a grocery store in Maine as in your neighborhood supermarket. In this environment, running a small farm according to organic principles and traditional methods requires greater commitment and investment, which explains why fresh produce is rarer and more expensive.

It is therefore easy to understand how the local food movement also 16 has become another form of social protest against the forces that are corporatizing and homogenizing our society. Fair enough, but it should not make wholesome food so precious and inaccessible that it becomes a luxury item.

Already there has been a noticeable elevation of familiar Southern 17 cuisine from the dairy bar to the martini bar; from the checkered tablecloth to the white tablecloth; from the blue plate to fine china. We're getting used to exclusive restaurants offering their interpretations of fried chicken, greens, pork rinds, and grits — with the requisite menu credit of the nearby organic farm where the meat and produce was raised.

In a bizarre reversal, now it is the wealthy who are rail-thin and eat- 18 ing beans and cornbread. And the poor? The message seems to be: Let them eat (Little Debbie) cake.

VOCABULARY/USING A DICTIONARY

1. What is the root of the word *ensnared* (para. 6)? What does its prefix mean?
2. What is a *processed* food (para. 9)? How does it differ from a fresh food?
3. What is an *epidemic* (para. 7)? How do you understand the phrase *obesity epidemic*?

RESPONDING TO WORDS IN CONTEXT

1. What is an *obesity rate* (para. 3)?
2. From what language is the word *cuisine* (para. 1) derived? What is a Southern cuisine (para. 1)? A regional cuisine (para. 7)?
3. Sabin says forces are "corporatizing and homogenizing our society" (para. 16). Given that pronouncement, how do you understand what these forces are doing to our food choices?

DISCUSSING MAIN POINT AND MEANING

1. Why are "traditional" Southern foods so high in calories?
2. Explain why the poor people of a hundred years ago were likely to be very thin while the poor people of today are more likely to be very fat.
3. Why are fruits and vegetables grown so close to some people in rural areas often very difficult to find in their local supermarkets?

EXAMINING SENTENCES, PARAGRAPHS, AND ORGANIZATION

1. What is the effect of the change in point of view (from first-person plural to second-person singular to third person) throughout the article? Which point of view is dominant?
2. Sabin writes, "By an extraordinary twist of economics, the fresh, local produce once available cheaply at the back-road farm stand has become the preserve of the elites. . . ." (para. 12). How do you understand the phrase "an extraordinary twist of economics," based on the statement that follows?
3. Why does the writer end the essay by stating that the message to the poor of this country seems to be "Let them eat (Little Debbie) cake" (para. 18)?

THINKING CRITICALLY

1. Sabin quotes some startling statistics about the change in obesity rates in this country from 1990 to 1998 (para. 6). Do you agree with the reasons given for this change? What other factors might be at play?
2. What sort of foods are available in your grocery store? Do you know where they are from? What affects your choices when buying food to eat?
3. Why might a "local food movement" (para. 16) be considered a "form of social protest"?

IN-CLASS WRITING ACTIVITIES

1. Research "Southern cuisine" and include the examples of foods given by Sabin in this essay. Consider the history of the South pre– and post–Civil War. What do you know about the region? Based on your research, explain how the cuisine of the area is a reflection of the region agriculturally and economically.
2. In a brief essay, agree or disagree with the argument Sabin lays out for why the poor of this country seem to be suffering from obesity disproportionately when compared with more affluent people. Are there points left out that Sabin didn't make?
3. What is the Centers for Disease Control and Prevention? Why is it concerned with the issues of obesity and food choices brought out in this article? Is it a good organization to monitor such issues? Why?

Amy Domini

Why Investing in Fast Food May Be a Good Thing

[*Ode Magazine*, March 2009]

BEFORE YOU READ

People invest in different companies for different reasons. If you consider yourself health-conscious or environmentally conscious, do you think you would ever invest your money in a fast food company? Why or why not?

WORDS TO LEARN

incalculable (para. 1): beyond calculation (adjective).

invest (para. 2): to put money into something that offers a potential return of interest or income (verb).

competitors (para 4): rivals (noun).

ban (para. 5): to prohibit (verb).

impact (para. 7): effect or influence (noun).

endangered (para. 7): threatened with danger or extinction (adjective).

industry (para. 9): trade or manufacturing activity (noun).

Amy Domini is the founder and CEO of Domini Social Investments. She is the author of The Challenges of Wealth: Mastering the Personal and Financial Conflicts *(1988) and* Socially Responsible Investing: Making a Difference and Making Money *(2001). She was named one of the top 100 most influential people in the world by* Time *magazine in 2005.*

My friends and colleagues know I've been an advocate of the   1
Slow Food movement for many years. Founded in Italy 20
years ago, Slow Food celebrates harvests from small-scale family farms, prepared slowly and lovingly with regard for the health and
environment of diners. Slow Food seeks to preserve crop diversity, so
the unique taste of "heirloom" apples, tomatoes and other foods don't
perish from the Earth. I wish everyone would choose to eat this way. The
positive effects on the health of our bodies, our local economies and our
planet would be incalculable. Why then do I find myself investing in fast-
food companies?

The reason is social investing isn't about investing in perfect compa-   2
nies. (Perfect companies, it turns out, don't exist.) We seek to invest in
companies that are moving in the right direction and listening to their
critics. We offer a road map to bring those companies to the next level,
step by step. No social standard causes us to reject restaurants, even fast-
food ones, out of hand. Although we favor local, organic food, we recognize it isn't available in every community, and is often priced above the
means of the average household. Many of us live more than 100 miles
from a working farm.

> **Fast food is a way of life.**

Fast food is a way of life. In America,   3
the average person eats it more than 150
times a year. In 2007, sales for the 400 largest U.S.-based fast-food chains totaled $277
billion, up 7 percent from 2006.

Fast food is a global phenomenon. Major chains and their local com-   4
petitors open restaurants in nearly every country. For instance, in Greece,
burgers and pizza are supplanting the traditional healthy Mediterranean
diet of fish, olive oil and vegetables. Doctors are treating Greek children
for diabetes, high cholesterol and high blood pressure — ailments rarely
seen in the past.

The fast-food industry won't go away anytime soon. But in the mean-   5
time, it can be changed. And because it's so enormous, even seemingly
modest changes can have a big impact. In 2006, New York City banned
the use of trans fats (a staple of fast food) in restaurants, and in 2008, California became the first state to do so. When McDonald's moved to non-
trans fats for making French fries, the health benefits were widespread.

Another area of concern is fast-food packaging, which causes forest   6
destruction and creates a lot of waste. In the U.S. alone, 1.8 million tons of
packaging is generated each year. Fast-food containers make up about 20 percent of litter, and packaging for drinks and snacks adds another 20 percent.

A North Carolina-based organization called the Dogwood Alliance   7
has launched an effort to make fast-food companies reduce waste and

source paper responsibly. Through a campaign called No Free Refills, the group is pressing fast-food companies to reduce their impact on the forests of the southern U.S., the world's largest paper-producing region. They're pushing companies to:

- Reduce the overuse of packaging.
- Maximize use of 100 percent post-consumer recycled boxboard.
- Eliminate paper packaging from the most biologically important endangered forests.
- Eliminate paper packaging from suppliers that convert natural forests into industrial pine plantations.
- Encourage packaging suppliers to source fiber from responsibly managed forests certified by the Forest Stewardship Council.
- Recycle waste in restaurants to divert paper and other material from landfills.

Will the fast-food companies adopt all these measures overnight? No. But along with similar efforts worldwide, this movement signals that consumers and investors are becoming more conscious of steps they can take toward a better world — beginning with the way they eat.   8

While my heart will always be with Slow Food, I recognize the fast-food industry can improve and that some companies are ahead of others on that path.   9

VOCABULARY/USING A DICTIONARY

1. *Advocate* (para. 1) is used in this essay as a noun. What does it mean? What other forms does *advocate* take, and how is it defined?
2. Is an *ailment* (para. 4) different from an illness?
3. What happens when you *eliminate* (para. 7) something?

RESPONDING TO WORDS IN CONTEXT

1. What does the word *phenomenon* mean? What is a *global phenomenon* (para. 4)?
2. What does the word *consumers* in paragraph 8 refer to? What other kinds of consumers are there?
3. If paper and other materials are *diverted* from landfills (para. 7), what happens to them?

DISCUSSING MAIN POINT AND MEANING

1. What's the difference between Slow Food and fast food?
2. What does Domini mean when she says, "Fast food is a way of life" (para. 3)?
3. Which two harmful aspects of the prevalence of fast food does Domini point to in her discussion of problems caused by the industry?

EXAMINING SENTENCES, PARAGRAPHS, AND ORGANIZATION

1. Why does Domini include information about the Dogwood Alliance? Does it surprise you that the essay is more about investing in fast food companies and less about supporting groups like the Dogwood Alliance? Why?
2. What is the effect of using bulleted points in the essay? Do you feel they are appropriately situated?
3. The essay begins and ends with a reference to Slow Food. What would the effect be on the essay if the information about Domini's relationship with Slow Food was left out?

THINKING CRITICALLY

1. Is investing in fast food a good thing? Why?
2. What sort of fast food companies (or other companies) would Domini consider investing in? Why?
3. How do you suppose individuals and groups begin to affect the choices made by large companies? How is change begun and achieved?

IN-CLASS WRITING ACTIVITIES

1. The Dogwood Alliance is only one of many watchdog groups that have an effect on our consumer society. Research the Dogwood Alliance or another such group and write about who formed the group, how it came into being, what its goals or mission statements are, and how it has begun to exert pressure on a corporation or industry.
2. Do you recycle? Consider how many things there are to reuse and what you recycle in everyday life. What don't you recycle that could be reused? Why? Describe the sort of effort that goes into recycling and the effect you think it has on the world.
3. Domini calls fast food a "global phenomenon." What do you know about fast food in other nations? Write an essay that explains why other countries might be more or less susceptible to the fast food lifestyle.

Brian Jay Stanley

Confessions of a Carnivore

[*The North American Review*, September/October 2009]

BEFORE YOU READ

Do you give much thought to the fact that the foods you eat, whether animal or vegetable, were once alive? Do such thoughts bother you? Do you continue to eat meat (or if you gave it up, do you run into other problems when you consider your role as a consumer of products of the earth)?

WORDS TO LEARN

deviants (para. 1): those who depart (usually markedly) from the norm (noun).

contemptuously (para. 3): disdainfully (adverb).

mulch (para. 3): a soil cover to prevent erosion or enrich the soil (noun).

deft (para. 4): skillful (adjective).

blithely (para. 4): merrily (adverb).

hypocrite (para. 6): a person who feigns virtues, morals, or religious beliefs he or she doesn't actually possess (noun).

thoracic (para. 6): pertaining to the central cavity in the body (adjective).

queasy (para. 6): nauseated (adjective).

carnivore (para. 6): animal that eats flesh (noun).

consummate (para. 7): complete or perfect (adjective).

prudery (para. 7): excessive modesty (noun).

martyrdoms (para. 8): extreme sufferings (noun).

plunderers (para. 9): robbers, pillagers (noun).

edifice (para. 10): a large, complex system (noun).

finitude (para. 10): a finite state or quality (noun).

paradigmatic (para. 11): of or pertaining to a paradigm (adjective).

defecate (para. 11): to void excrement (verb).

procreation (para. 13): generation of offspring (noun).

hydrate (para. 13): to supply water to something to maintain fluid balance (verb).

Brian Jay Stanley is a software developer who lives in Asheville, North Carolina. His essays, which combine personal experience with philosophical reflection, have been published in such literary journals as The Antioch Review, The North American Review, The Hudson Review, Connecticut Review, *and others. He holds a master's degree in library and information science from the University of Illinois and another master's degree in theology from Duke University.*

assuage (para. 14): to relieve (verb).

gametes (para. 14): sperm or eggs that unite with other sexual reproductive cells to form a new organism (noun).

animists (para. 15): those who believe that natural objects and the universe itself possess souls (noun).

expiation (para. 15): the means by which atonement or reparation is made (noun).

Into what rare air did the manna dissolve that we harry the free things, each other?

— Annie Dillard

One afternoon while sitting in my car, I saw two insects clasped together on my windshield. My first thought was that they were mating, but a closer look revealed a robber fly feeding on a small grasshopper. I leaned forward to watch what turned out to be a drama without much action. The victim neither struggled nor screamed as its life was sucked out, the aggressor displayed no rage, but each party killed or was killed without the least apparent emotion or surprise. For them, death was just an ordinary deed on an ordinary day in nature, whereas I shivered with interest, unaccustomed to witnessing crime scenes. The utter nonchalance of the miniature murderer chiefly struck me. In human society, we lock away killers as deviants, but every citizen of insect society that ever buzzed past your head probably had some other bug's blood on its proboscis. I felt an odd humility toward the fly. We think of animals as simple and innocent, but no, we are the innocents, for they calmly possess a knowledge of death that is strange and forbidden to us.

I recall having similar feelings growing up when my cat, Lucy, would deposit half-eaten moles, chipmunks, and rabbits at my family's doorstep. My siblings and I had chosen Lucy from the litter when she was a helpless, mewing fur ball of a kitten. We had brought her home, fed her, petted her, protected her from tumbling down the stairs, kept her safe in a world she might not have survived without us. Children enjoy having a pet for the same reason they enjoy having a younger sibling: it elevates them to a position of relative maturity. Yet only a few years later, the daily carnage at our door made me rethink who was whose senior. At twelve years old I was riding bikes and throwing baseballs, while here was my three-year-old cat dragging home enough corpses to fill a charnel house, no longer my helpless pupil but my teacher, initiating me into the secrets of the world.

Death was disturbing to see, especially since the victims were often 3
not actually dead but slowly dying on the garage floor, a wet red hole in
their fur and several slimy, unidentifiable organs lying a few feet away.
I thought of the vast expanse of woods behind our house where the
cat hunted. There were wildflowers there, rocks, broken twigs, mossy
stumps, tree bark, dirt, last year's leaves. Of so many choices, why must
the cat's claws crave the only things alive and moving? In my conception,
animals alone had worth amid the inanimate worthlessness of nature. I
tramped contemptuously through briars and brush but stopped in awe
for any woodchuck, vole, or deer — anything that could look back at me.
By what ill design were the worthy things eating each other instead of
eating unworthy things? Why not have stomachs get full on pebbles or
mulch or air?

With age my cat became too lazy to hunt, and, absent her grisly 4
reminders, I seldom thought of nature's war of all against all, until, years
later in college, a zoology course renewed my unease and tuned my eyes
to scenes of predation around campus and town. On the sidewalks after
rains, I would pause to observe a shriveled earthworm that, having fled
the underground flood just in time to be cooked by the reemerging sun,
was now being bitten to bits and carted off by a gang of ants. On the highway, driving past a crow slurping the gizzards of a squashed opossum, I
would cringe at nature's deft yet disgusting method of discarding trash:
giving living mouths a taste for the rotting dead. At a lakeside park on
a single afternoon, I watched a sharp-shinned hawk scoop up a chicka-
dee, and a great blue heron gulp down a wriggling trout, while children
blithely played on monkey bars and their parents read magazines. I also
glutted myself watching nature documentaries, which were fascinating
but became redundant, since all were invariably chronicles of hunting
behavior. Gray wolves chasing elk through the snows of Yellowstone,
orcas attacking harbor seal pups in Puget Sound, spotted hyenas licking
wildebeest bones in the Serengeti — earth has not one unbloody corner.
I always pulled for the prey to get away, yet I had to admit that in wishing escape for the hunted, I unwittingly wished starvation for the hunter.

One documentary recorded a monthly event in Costa Rica called 5
the arribada, meaning "arrival," in which thousands of Ridley sea tur-
tles converge on a stretch of sandy beach in Ostional to lay millions of
eggs. As the hordes of hatchlings climb simultaneously from the sand
and clamber toward the sea, most are picked off by vultures, crabs, rac-
coons, coyotes, and dogs who come to the beach for an easy feast. I felt
amazed at so many new lives meeting immediate deaths. Inside each egg,
nature fashions an intricate factory of tiny cooperating parts, assembling
carbons and hydrogens into working livers and lungs, wraps these inner

wonders in the durable package of skin and shell, gives each turtle senses and instinct and movement and breath — only so that, a minute after birth, nine of ten of these miniature masterpieces can go to their graves down a vulture's gullet. What five-star chef ever went to such trouble preparing a meal? Is this not a warped world in which babies are born to be snacks for adults, and death is stock in the soup of life?

Man is such a hypocrite: I often watched these documentaries in fascinated horror while casually chomping a chicken breast sandwich on my couch. But occasionally my food, notably when it had a face, would look back at me and say "Thou art the man!" I remember the first time I ate a lobster served whole, on a trip to Maine. I felt an unexpected shock when I lifted the lid from the pot, for though I had seen many lobsters, I had never seen one served in a pot for me, garnished and steaming, yet otherwise in the form nature gave it — looking like it ought to snap at me, and I ought to throw it back in the bay beside the restaurant. As its beady eyes watched me dismember it, I felt a slight nausea at the lobster's internal smorgasbord: the green liver that dripped from the gaping thoracic cavity, the juices squirting from the shell's seams, the black intestine running the length of the white flesh. These queasy sights gave me queasy thoughts of the guts of the lobster traveling through my own guts. I pictured my dinner getting gulped down my esophagus, swirled in my stomach acid, squeezed through burping sphincters, winding through pitch dark intestines in route to my colon. My realization of being a carnivore was as if I had looked in a mirror and seen a lion's face dripping with zebra gore. In my khaki pants and collared shirt, a civilized beast!

> Culture has removed us far from the time when all were hunters.

Another time I had a similar epiphany at the supermarket, as I walked past the meat bins containing every kind and cut of our four favorite fleshes — fish, fowl, beef, and pork — and I looked at the butcher whistling a tune with pink stains on his apron. Is not man the consummate predator? Do I not brush chewed flesh from my teeth every night before bed? Yet to free me from the awareness that I am an animal, society delegates callused cattlemen, industrialists, and butchers to do my killing for me. They clean, package, and garnish the corpse to remove all hint of my food's original identity. On a plastic plate wrapped in cellophane, a rib eye or pork chop no longer looks like a quadruped which was mooing or oinking yesterday. Since no one wants to eat a dead cow or dead pig, we change their names to beef and pork. Culture has removed us far from the time when all were hunters and must first spear the mammoth their bellies growled to eat. Modern man still has

6

7

the growling belly, but after two hundred thousand years of moral development, the mind's prudery recoils from the body's savagery.

Eating is such a solemn affair, no wonder prayers are said before   8
meals in most religions. Yet looking through prayer books, all I find are prayers of thanksgiving, whereas I feel more inclined to ask forgiveness. Every turkey on my plate is a savior slain for me, to give me life from lunch until dinner, at which time another savior must die to give me life until breakfast tomorrow. By the time I die, who can count the martyrdoms I'll have caused, each victim extending my existence a few more hours?

Perhaps I ought to be a vegetarian, but it is hard to fight with a body   9
evolved for meat-eating. Though my taste buds can tolerate steamed broccoli and a bowl of rice, my stomach growls *is that all?* I have to spend an hour shoveling forkfuls of greens into my inner abyss, getting bored before full. Besides, as I watch a hungry crowd piling items at a salad bar, I feel a vague misgiving about any eating, not only of meat. Even vegetarians seem greedy plunderers, like herds of goats that strip a hillside. More than any body part, there is something obscene about the mouth, a hole for stuffing the outside world inside us. We are constantly eating, and for contradictory reasons. We eat because we are lonely, and we eat because we have company. We eat to celebrate and we eat to mourn, toasting newlyweds with a feast and comforting the bereaved with casseroles. We do business over lunch, then unwind from doing business over dinner. Is there any mood or occasion we have not made an excuse for eating?

Our bodies, being products of eating, are immoral by essence. Food   10
is not merely the fuel we put in our body, food *is* our body. Every atom in this moving breathing edifice called Me was looted from other existences, through the food that I, or while I was in the womb my mother, ate. My living tissues are compacted bits of the dead, my muscles were once cows' muscles, my eyeballs were carrots. Why do we disparage tapeworms and flukes as parasites because they pilfer a living from others? Every life is parasitic. We should not all eat plants, as vegetarians say, but all *be* plants, making our own food and leaving others alone. We should stretch our arms like branches and feed on the sun, or we should have a sun inside us, an inner principle of life. But only gods have inner life, whereas we are manufactured incomplete. The stomach is the symbol of our finitude, an empty space at the body's core. Theologians speak of original sin, and to me the stomach is sin's seat. We creatures are necessary sinners by virtue of our very creatureliness, forced to feed our inborn lack or waste and die. The creator is complete and has no need to rob others for substance. God's only sin was creating us as sinners.

Considering we are consumers by essence, no wonder we have built   11
a consumer society, adding voluntary sins of acquisition to our necessary
sin of eating. Eating is our paradigmatic behavior, and all our consumer
habits are variations of eating — attempts to fatten our emptiness with
the meat of otherness. Go to the mall at holidays and watch people gorging
on the buffet of stores, pushing carts of gifts which cannot possibly fit in
their homes with all the prior years' gifts. We buy goods to furnish our
homes, then eventually must buy bigger homes to hold all our goods. Or
else, to avoid this consumer's obesity, we must defecate our used goods
to make room for new ones, leaving mounds of waste at the landfill.
Sometimes I look around my house and feel a horror of my possessions.
I recline in a leather chair which was a cow's skin whose flesh I probably
ate. I stack paper books and picture frames of mined metal on shelves
made of chopped-down trees. Not content with the matter appropri-
ated as my body, nor with the matter I put in my body to keep it going, I
must also surround myself with rooms and rooms of matter whose only
purpose is to supplement my existence. I feel like a fat emperor ruling a
kingdom of inanimate serfs.

Food is the fuel that powers our walking, but since walking is too   12
slow, we build cars with metal stomachs for drinking oil, which consists
of long-dead organisms, to add to the newly-dead ones we eat at dinner.
The automobile is representative of freedom, its four wheels taking
us wherever we want, yet I feel ashamed to see rows of exhausted cars
stopped every mile by the highway with gas hoses stuck in their tanks,
like patients on IVs. Man being finite, even our freedoms are built of
dependency. When I drive past a field of oil drills, they look like giant
mosquitoes sucking the earth's black blood, and I imagine that the
ground must be so hollow that it will collapse beneath me.

True, our siphoning causes no pain to the nerveless earth. But con-   13
sumption not only bites the world but lessens the leftovers for everyone
else. Just as plants, though they do not eat each other, eat the soil and sun
each other needs — consuming, not others' lives, but others' chance of
life — so too our mere existence is hazardous to others. In Genesis, God
tells the first humans to be fruitful and multiply, but now, through excess
of obedience, procreation has become an unintentional act of aggression
against the fellow multitudes already cramming the planet, each trying
to get a mouth on nature's nipples. Because I exist, there are fewer fertile
acres to feed the starving. To hydrate my cells, water tables have dropped.
Turning on my toaster speeds the hour when the last block of coal will
burn and New York City will go black. All I have added to earth are more
pollutants in the sky. Worse, if I have two children, and they have two
children each, in four generations I will have multiplied myself into

sixteen people, who will nibble the earth sixteen times as fast as I can alone. Will our great-great-grandchildren have to stand shoulder-to-shoulder to fit on the continents? Will air itself become a commodity and nations fight wars for the right to breathe, until everyone finally suffocates on everyone else's exhaled breath?

Conscientious people wonder what they should do about the ruts and gullies they carve by existing. Should they bike to work, plant a vegetable garden, wear three coats in winter instead of running heat? Should they (as some people now do) pay companies to plant trees to assuage their guilt for driving, like medieval Christians paying the pope for indulgences? These are half-measures. The logic of conscience would bid us whittle our lives far thinner. We should trade our tract homes for desert caves and sell our suits for sackcloth, to live like ancient monks. We should fast until our collarbones poke through our skin, like the anorexic models who are our modern ascetics, fleeing food as a wickedness punishable by saggy thighs. We should cut our cords so that none of our gametes will grow up like us to feast on their surroundings. Follow the logic's final step, and we should all cut our wrists and commence the diet of death. Only the unborn are sinless; only the dead are forgiven.

This morbid tendency of conscience is as horrid as the gobbling greediness of hunger. Who will we have died and dieted for, when all of us are dead? Such philosophizing is moot anyway, since most of us lack the will to starve ourselves. Every afternoon spent writing this essay on the evils of eating has ended embarrassingly. Though I have a saint's scruples, I have a Neanderthal's stomach, and promptly at 6 p.m. my stomach clubs my conscience on the head and directs me to dinner. I place a pork chop on the backyard grill and sip a bottled beer in the pleasant evening air. Tribal animists believe all life is sacred, but instead of therefore refraining from killing, their compromise is to kill their dinners with ceremonial solemnity, praying to the animal's spirit and offering rites of expiation. Perhaps the best we hungry immoral mortals can do is destroy with respect. I give conscious thought to the roasting pig, the barley mown to brew my beer, and the propane gas combusting in my grill — yet more kindling for the bonfire of my being. By way of repentance, I make a point to enjoy the evening and live appreciatively, knowing how costly I am.

VOCABULARY/USING A DICTIONARY

1. What does *nonchalance* (para. 1) mean? From what language is it derived?
2. What is a *smorgasbord* (para. 6)? From what language is it derived?
3. How may legs does a *quadruped* (para. 7) have?

RESPONDING TO WORDS IN CONTEXT

1. What is a *proboscis* (para. 1)?
2. What does *callused* (para. 7) mean? What part of speech is it? What is the root of the word?
3. How does one feel if one has a *misgiving* (para. 9) about eating meat?

DISCUSSING MAIN POINT AND MEANING

1. According to Stanley, how do insects and animals differ from humans in their experience of death?
2. Based on Stanley's argument, can humans ever avoid the problem of causing another animal's death, whether they eat meat or not?
3. Does Stanley offer any solutions to the dilemmas he presents in his essay? Or are his "confessions" simply that?

EXAMINING SENTENCES, PARAGRAPHS, AND ORGANIZATION

1. Stanley says, "Every turkey on my plate is a savior slain for me, to give me life from lunch until dinner, at which time another savior must die to give me life until breakfast tomorrow" (para. 8). Describe the writing in this sentence. Why does he talk about eating turkey (or other meats) in this way?
2. Does Stanley write long or short paragraphs? Does the choice influence his style of writing (or vice versa)?
3. Stanley begins the first paragraph with a description of an insect devouring another insect. He ends the paragraph with the statement, "We think of animals as simple and innocent, but no, we are the innocents, for they calmly possess a knowledge of death that is strange and forbidden to us." What difference would it make if this statement began the essay and the description followed? Do you think it is better the way it is?

THINKING CRITICALLY

1. Why does Stanley refer to death as the "stock in the soup of life" (para. 5)?
2. Explain what Stanley means when he says human beings are consumers (para. 11).
3. What does Stanley mean at the end of the essay when he says, "I make a point to enjoy the evening and live appreciatively, knowing how costly I am"?

IN-CLASS WRITING ACTIVITIES

1. Stanley begins the essay with an epigraph from Annie Dillard. What do you know about Dillard's writing? Is it similar to Stanley's? In what ways? Try to find points of comparison based on bits and pieces of her work that you find on the Web if you haven't read her books.
2. When discussing how much he owns and consumes, Stanley writes, "I feel like a fat emperor ruling a kingdom of inanimate serfs." Does this

simile sound right to you in terms of your own experience as a consumer? Did Stanley's argument change the way you view your own world of food and things? Explain in writing.

3. Issues of pollution and overpopulation, as well as other global problems, are alluded to in Stanley's essay. Write a brief essay on how you, as a human being, contribute to one such problem. Include anything you do to counteract your "carbon footprint," as well as any way in which you affect the world adversely simply by living in it.

Jacob Swede (student essay)

Remembering Johnny Appleseed

[*The Minnesota Daily*, University of Minnesota Twin Cities, March 10, 2010]

BEFORE YOU READ

There once was a time when people grew their own food and knew where it came from. Do you know where your food comes from? How did it get to your grocery store? Where was it grown? And how?

WORDS TO LEARN

sojourned (para. 1): lived temporarily (verb).

conceive (para. 2): to form an idea of (verb).

regulation (para. 4): a law or rule prescribed by an authority (noun).

obese (para. 5): very fat or overweight (adjective).

cognitive (para. 6): relating to the mental processes of perception and reasoning (adjective).

rift (para. 6): an opening or fissure (noun).

apathy (para. 6): lack of interest or concern (noun).

livelihood (para. 8): a means of supporting oneself (noun).

perilous (para. 8): dangerous (adjective).

impoverished (para. 9): reduced to poverty (adjective).

menial (para. 9): lowly or degrading (adjective).

unscrupulous (para. 10): unprincipled (adjective).

interstice (para. 10): a small or narrow space (noun).

tenuous (para. 10): weak (adjective).

paradigm (para. 11): an example serving as a model (noun).

Jacob Swede graduated from the University of Minnesota Twin Cities in the fall of 2010. He was a philosophy major and wrote weekly columns for The Minnesota Daily.

Today is Johnny Appleseed Day. While many of us haven't thought 1 of Johnny since fourth grade, his legacy belies a serious critique of modern life. Appleseed sojourned the Midwest cultivating apple orchards for frontiersmen at the turn of the nineteenth century. Unfortunately, forgetting the legacy Appleseed strived to circulate has obscured the agricultural process in American eyes.

We conceive of food as it arrives to us: the apple at breakfast, that 2 half-price turkey on Russian rye you had for lunch. Rarely in our nourishment do we reflect on the process of food production. The legacy of Appleseed makes it clear that food needs to become more than abstract in the American consciousness. French politician Jean Brillat-Savarin said, "Tell me what you eat, and I will tell you who you are." Willful ignorance of the food we consume says much about us.

Some agricultural corporations, such as those in Taiwan, still use 3 phosphate insecticides and herbicides, which have been linked to cancer and birth defects. But food producers today have taken on new risks, like genetically grafting plants and reducing seed diversity with Monsanto's Roundup Ready line. Rarely do we compare JIF, Skippy or Smucker's reputations or the nutrition labels of our foods.

But food ignorance has immediate consequences. Imports from 4 countries with ineffective or weak regulations often find their way onto our dinner table. Despite USDA regulation, the Centers for Disease Control estimates that 76 million cases of foodborne disease occur in the United States yearly, 325,000 leading to hospitalization and 5,000 leading to death. Recognizing the underlying causes that account for differences between an American-grown banana and one that comes from a dangerous area, such as Ecuador, allows consumers to make healthier choices.

Food ignorance, such as uncertainty about nutrition or food prepa- 5 ration, has substantial physical effects. The prevalence of obesity among Americans can be largely attributed to Americans' penchant for dining out, says a 2007 Temple University study. The research found that Americans eat out five times a week on average, and those who consume fast food three to six times per week have measurably higher body mass indexes than those who eat fast food two or less times a week. This high obesity trend is borne out in 2009 data by the Trust for America's Health, which found 25.3 percent of adults in Minnesota to be obese. The same Temple study indicates that if people were more conscious of their eating habits, they would willingly choose differently.

This is true not merely because people make bad decisions (we all 6 crave that Big Mac every once in a while) but because people don't take the time to understand what they eat. Living life away from the fields creates a cognitive rift between the consumer and the consumed. Certainly the intimate relationship Appleseed maintained with his food is an unachievable standard for the busy modern American, but one's apathy toward food suggests one's health will suffer.

Appleseed's legacy is not an example merely for consumers. Pro-   7
ducers neglect the burden of providing beneficial food while maintaining the land for future use with tilling techniques which erode topsoil for greater harvest. Indeed, Appleseed's lifestyle of environmental altruism is the antithesis of the modern agricultural industry. The cultivation techniques that agricultural corporations employ to maximize yield make soil maintenance of secondary importance. In the past 30 years this problem has been drastically reduced in the U.S., but not in many poorer nations where corporations outsource their production.

A 2008 Food and Agriculture Organization of the United Nations   8
study, taken over 20 years, found that land degradation is increasing rapidly due to farming practices. Some areas previously used for agriculture are now so nutrient-depleted or salinated that they have been completely abandoned. This may seem a concern for conservationists, but the same study found that the survival of nearly 1.5 billion people depends on the maintenance of this land's agricultural capacity. Irresponsible farmland management is perilous both for those ecosystems and for those whose livelihood falls within those ecosystems.

> Some areas previously used for agriculture are now so nutrient-depleted or salinated that they have been completely abandoned.

Concerns aren't purely environmental; many are economic. Imported   9
foods require cheap labor in order to turn a substantial profit. Those exploited for cheap labor are impoverished people in poor countries. To compound the problem of erosion, the people doing the menial tasks are rarely paid living wages. These circumstances are rampant in poor countries that agribusiness corporations import from, but they're not unheard of in the United States, either.

Despite its "Food with Integrity" motto, even the enlightened   10
Chipotle chain had been buying from unscrupulous Florida tomato growers since 2009. The Florida farm managers had hired immigrants at slave wages and forced them to live in a ventilated box truck while Chipotle remained willfully ignorant. Filling the interstice between consumers and oppressive systems of agribusiness with knowledge is the first step toward changing the tenuous reality of modern farming.

Johnny Appleseed Day is a neglected holiday in the United States, but 11 Appleseed's legacy can be a model for changing the paradigm of both producers and consumers, as well as a model to bridge the gap between the two.

VOCABULARY/USING A DICTIONARY
1. What is a *legacy* (para. 1)?
2. What is an *ecosystem* (para. 8)? How is the definition built into the word itself?
3. What does it mean if something is *rampant* (para. 9)?

RESPONDING TO WORDS IN CONTEXT
1. What does Swede mean by a *critique* of modern life (para. 1)?
2. How do you understand what Swede means by the *substantial physical effects* (para. 5) that are the outcome of food ignorance?
3. What is *land degradation* (para. 8)?

DISCUSSING MAIN POINT AND MEANING
1. How does today's American public view food? Why might that perspective be dangerous?
2. What are some of the environmental concerns Swede voices about our lack of interest in food production? What are some of the economic concerns?
3. If you experience food as "the apple at breakfast, the half-price turkey on Russian rye you had for lunch," what do you know about your food? What are you missing?

EXAMINING SENTENCES, PARAGRAPHS, AND ORGANIZATION
1. Why is Jacob Swede's essay titled "Remembering Johnny Appleseed"?
2. Does the Appleseed reference run throughout the essay? Is the connection to Appleseed made paragraph by paragraph or is it made less often?
3. Swede's diction in this essay is sometimes complex. For example, "Unfortunately, forgetting the legacy Appleseed strived to circulate has obscured the agricultural process in American eyes" is a sentence using high diction. Rewrite it using simpler language to show that you understand the writer's meaning.

THINKING CRITICALLY
1. How have American consumers lost sight of Johnny Appleseed's legacy? How have American producers lost sight of it?
2. Do you believe Swede when he says bad food choices are not just because of bad decisions, "but because people don't take the time to understand what they eat"? Explain.
3. What do you think Johnny Appleseed Day is about, based on your reading of this essay?

IN-CLASS WRITING ACTIVITIES

1. Why did Johnny Appleseed Day become a holiday? Is it one you are familiar with? Research the holiday and write a brief essay on Appleseed and his legacy. Explain why Johnny Appleseed Day "is a neglected holiday in the United States" and argue why that should or should not be so.

2. Consider the food you buy at the grocery store. What have you bought recently? How much do you know about it? Write as much as you think you know and consider the various things you may not know.

3. Swede quotes Jean Brillat-Savarin, who said, "Tell me what you eat, and I will tell you who you are." Consider issues of food ignorance, environmental destruction, and economic hardship brought up in this essay. Focus on one in a brief essay and argue how our current practices regarding food divorce us from ourselves, our land, and our fellow humans.

LOOKING CLOSELY

Using Statistical Evidence to Support an Argument

One convincing way to support an argument is by citing statistical data. Throughout this book you will see many selections that use statistical information to bolster an opinion or assertion. When citing such data it is important to remember that you should (a) use reliable sources, (b) mention the source of the information, and (c) employ data that is relevant to your claim. In informal essays you may — unless otherwise stipulated by your instructor — simply mention what research study or institution released the data, but in a formal research paper you will need to cite more fully the source of your information. You should always be suspicious of data that may be politically or commercially biased; for example, a poll indicating the popularity of a candidate for Senate issued by that candidate's own party may not be reliable data, nor may safety statistics released by an automobile manufacturer that will help sell its cars.

In "Remembering Johnny Appleseed," Jacob Swede, a student at the University of Minnesota Twin Cities, uses several statistical studies to support his point about the importance of learning more about the food we eat. In the following paragraph, Swede introduces statistics from a highly reliable source, the Centers for Disease Control, to establish his contention that what we don't know about food could be deadly.

But food ignorance has immediate consequences.   1
Imports from countries with ineffective or weak regulations often find their way onto our dinner table. <u>Despite
USDA regulation, the Centers for Disease Control estimates that 76 million cases of foodborne disease occur
in the United States yearly, 325,000 leading to hospitalization and 5,000 leading to death.</u> (1) Recognizing the
underlying causes that account for differences between an
American-grown banana and one that comes from a dangerous area, such as Ecuador, allows consumers to make
healthier choices.

1
*Statistical data
from a reliable
source supports
the writer's claim*

STUDENT WRITER AT WORK
Jacob Swede

RA. What inspired you to write this essay? And publish it in your campus paper?

JS. My editor informed me that my publication date was set for March 10 — which I knew was Johnny Appleseed Day. I honestly hadn't thought of Johnny Appleseed in years before writing the column, but while brainstorming I began to think back to traditions we had at our school of planting trees and visiting the local farms. At the time I had also been researching genetic engineering, agri-globalization, and factory farming, so the narrative of Johnny Appleseed worked well for my purposes.

RA. Who was your prime audience?

JS. I write for anyone who will read. Ideally anyone who will understand and question the arguments I set forward in the piece is the audience I'm looking for. To challenge beliefs of others, or reinforce ideas with stronger arguments and information, lays the groundwork for meaningful discussion. If, as is often the case, the audience comes to disagree with the opinion advanced in my column, then I've considered my job well done by provoking informed and critical discussion.

RA. How long did it take for you to write this piece? Did you revise your work? What were your goals as you revised?

JS. It took me approximately five hours to write this piece. The first draft started out very broad and with a much more general scope than the final piece, but as I worked and reworked the column it evolved into a much more narrowly aimed argument. As I revised it as well as continued researching the subject, my goals became attuned to citing specific agricultural problems as opposed to the general claim made in the introduction and conclusion.

RA. What topics most interest you as a writer?

JS. Topics that are broadly applicable and yet intimately personal interest me most. Trying to navigate complex questions such as rights to abortion, understanding death, how to deal with the environment, etc., are incredibly general matters and yet all of us have an intense personal stake in resolving them.

RA. What advice do you have for other student writers?

JS. Be intrepid; whatever you think you can write, you can. No issue is too vast or complicated that you can't make a successful go at it if you try.

Discussing the Unit

SUGGESTED TOPIC FOR DISCUSSION

Our society must educate itself about the food we eat. Gone are the days of having a direct connection to the farms where our food comes from and the people who grow produce and tend to livestock. Given our lack of connection to food, how do the writers in this chapter educate us about what we put in our bodies and how we should behave as consumers? At the very least, does "Confessions of a Carnivore" raise our awareness so we can consider, if not change, how and what we consume?

PREPARING FOR CLASS DISCUSSION

1. How did good food become harder to come by and more expensive than high-calorie, low-nutrient foods? Why do we choose to pack our diets with the less healthy foods? Discuss these questions with an eye on two or more of the essays in the chapter.

2. How do the authors in these essays portray our relationship with our fellow man, or even with ourselves? How is this relationship made manifest in our choices about what we eat?

FROM DISCUSSION TO WRITING

1. Do the authors of the essays in this chapter have a common philosophy about food and eating? Explain. Where are their philosophies similar and where do they diverge?

2. Each of these writers looks at the history of food production, preparation, and consumption in some way. How do the histories provided add depth and strength to the arguments being presented? How would the essays be different without them?

TOPICS FOR CROSS-CULTURAL DISCUSSION

1. "The Rich Get Thinner, the Poor Get Fatter" considers the influence of region, culture, and economics on diet and health. How and why are the people of the South affected by trends in eating? How do those factors translate to people of other regions, cultures, and economic backgrounds in the United States?

2. Consider how the cultures that Domini mentions have changed due to the proliferation of fast food across the globe. How has fast food affected cultures unlike our own? Should we try to pull out or isolate our seemingly bad habits from the rest of the world? Will the "Old World" idea of "Slow Food" ever take off in this country? Why are we able to influence the eating habits of other cultures when it is so difficult for them to influence ours?

4

Photography: Can We Believe What We See?

It's often said that "one picture is worth a thousand words," meaning that a picture can convey a message more effectively and more economically than words could ever do. That expression has become such a driving force in journalism that no news story can be considered complete without photographs or videos. Such images, it is argued, can show us at a glance something that might take several pages to describe. And such images, the argument continues, offer us reliable, eyewitness testimony to what has occurred, for unlike a writer's words, as we are often told, the photographer's camera doesn't lie.

But is that expression correct? One photography expert thinks not. In "This Photo Is Lying to You," Rob Haggart claims that the old saying "'the camera never lies' is, in fact, backwards — the camera *always* lies. Since the birth of the medium, photographers have been crafting their images with lens selection, film type, and all manner of darkroom tricks." His argument is being increasingly supported by today's new digital media and a technology that makes "with a few mouse clicks" the alteration of photos a simple task for anyone who can use a computer.

Few questioned the accuracy and authenticity of the infamous photographs that showed American prison guards torturing Iraqis at the Abu Ghraib prison. But in "Picture Imperfect," the noted art critic Jed Perl wonders what the pictures both tell us and don't tell us. "Photographic truth," he maintains, "is a particular kind of truth, and that is the case even when the photograph has not been doctored or edited."

Having lost many precious photos after a hard drive crash, Elizabeth Svokos, a student at Bryn Mawr College, discovers the joy of taking pictures the old-fashioned way, with film. She discovers also the pleasure of "imperfection" that her old camera offers. With digital, she observes in her essay, "Head to Head — Print Photographs," "There's no room for imperfection when you can remove red eyes and blot out pimples with a click of your mouse."

Rob Haggart

This Photo Is Lying to You

[*Outside*, September 2009]

BEFORE YOU READ

Do you think that "the camera never lies"? What is the relationship between photographic images and truth? How does photography shape our sense of reality?

WORDS TO LEARN

inherent (para. 1): existing as an essential element, quality, or attribute of something (adjective).

myopic (para. 3): relating to near-sightedness (adjective).

intrinsically (para. 5): belonging to a thing by its very nature (adverb).

insidious (para. 15): secretly treacherous or deceitful (adjective).

Photographer Ed Freeman is working on a book about surfing, though he's never surfed a day in his life. A couple of years ago, while shooting stock in Hawaii, he stumbled upon some surfers on the North Shore of Oahu. He was blown away by the "athleticism, the intimate relationship with nature, and the inherent danger of it all," he says. "I knew I wanted to do something that was art, not sports photography. I wanted the pictures to be about how surfing feels to me. Not how it is."

Freeman readily admits the images he created were "Photoshopped halfway to death." He spent hours on his computer, crafting the skies, combining different pictures of waves, and in one instance stitching together a Frankensurfer out of multiple riders. Two of the finished products won awards in an annual contest judged by *Photo District News*, a leading professional-photography publication.

When I was the photo editor at *Outside*, earlier this decade, I used to look through *PDN* winners for photos to publish. I'm a freelancer now, but I'm still excited to see the selections. When I first viewed Freeman's

1

2

3

Currently a freelance editor, Rob Haggart was the photo editor for Outside *magazine from 2000 until 2006.*

© Ed Freeman.

Freeman's image of a surfer on Oahu's North Shore has been "Photoshopped halfway to death," says the photographer.

photos this past June, I was blown away. I should have caught on that they were composites — there are some obvious clues, like overly brooding skies and myopic lighting — but I didn't. I saw surfers riding 20-foot-tall freight trains of water and thought, *These are amazing.* Then I went to Freeman's Web site and saw his disclaimer about making art images. So I did what people do these days: I posted one of his photos on my blog, aphotoeditor.com.

Commenters immediately blasted Freeman, claiming he'd betrayed   4 the sport by ginning up a photo that supposedly captures an authentic athletic achievement. Freeman replied with his own comments, shrugging off the criticism, and when I called him recently he remained unapologetic. "I'm an artist," he told me. "I'm interested in creating great pictures, not documentary images. I couldn't care less if they're 'real' or not."

That's a common defense in cases like this, and a reasonable point   5 of view. But it fails to take into account that the value of manufactured pictures is intrinsically tied to the authentic shots that came first. No matter how forthright one is about alterations, fake photos cause collateral damage. They devalue the work of photographers with the skills and patience to capture awing images in real time. Even worse, modern photo manipulation is seriously screwing up our concept of reality and our willingness to believe what we see in magazines like *Outside*.

Of course, truth in photography has always been fuzzy. The old trope "The camera never lies" is, in fact, backwards — the camera *always* lies. Since the birth of the medium, photographers have been crafting their images with lens selection, film type, and all manner of darkroom tricks.

6

> Of course, truth in photography has always been fuzzy.

"Photographs have always been tampered with," says Hany Farid, a computer-science professor at Dartmouth College who works with federal law-enforcement agencies on digital forensics. "It's just that the digital revolution has made it much easier to create sophisticated and compelling fakes." Farid keeps a greatest-hits list of forgeries online, which includes a photograph of Abraham Lincoln from around 1860 that's actually a composite: Lincoln's head propped on southern politician John Calhoun's body.

7

In the late 19th century, photographers were intent on proving that their images deserved a place in galleries alongside paintings. Like Ed Freeman, these "pictorialists" espoused the practice of manipulating photographs to achieve artistic intent. In 1932, in response to this movement, a group that included Ansel Adams[1] formed f/64 to champion "straight" photography. Ironically, Adams was known to be a master of dodging and burning (i.e., lightening and darkening), darkroom techniques that allowed him to produce a print reflecting his vision for what the photograph *should* be.

8

Over the years, even the most hallowed curators of documentary photos have been seduced by the temptation to doctor images for creative and commercial reasons. The infamous Pulitzer Prize–winning photo from the 1970 Kent State massacre,[2] which showed a 14-year-old girl leaning over a dead body, was retouched to remove an awkward-looking

9

---

[1] Ansel Adams (1902–1984) (para. 8): American environmentalist and photographer known for his photographs of the American West.

---

[2] Kent State massacre (para. 9): In 1970, four students were killed and nine others were wounded when the Ohio National Guard opened fire during an antiwar protest at Kent State University.

pole behind her head before being published in *Life, Time,* and other magazines. In 1982, *National Geographic* moved the Pyramids of Giza in order to run a horizontal shot on its vertical-format cover.

One of the earliest milestones in our current digital age of manipulation occurred in 1994, four years after the introduction of Adobe Photoshop,[3] when a rising wildlife photographer named Art Wolfe published *Migrations,* in which a third of the images were photo illustrations. An early adopter of digital tools, Wolfe added elephants and zebras to photos and turned the heads of birds to fit his perfectionist notion of natural patterns. In the introduction, he stated that it was an art book and that he had enhanced images "as a painter would on a canvas," but *Migrations* still started a stampede of accusations. Celebrated outdoor photographers Frans Lanting and the late Galen Rowell criticized the book, with Rowell warning of the changes set into motion once the trust is broken between nature photographers and viewers.   10

Which brings us to our current crisis. Wolfe told me that if *Migrations* were published in 2009, nobody would bat an eye. "In today's natural-history world, the idea of removing a telephone pole or lightening a shadow or removing a distracting out-of-focus branch is acceptable," he says. Only "purists" would complain, and he "can't even have a dialogue with them."   11

That's too bad, because some of those purists have smart ideas. Natural-history photographer Kevin Schafer argues that manipulation "waters down the power of real documentary photography." Our reactions to a photo — amazement, delight, excitement — are, Schafer says, "intimately tied with its impact as a record of a real event." This is nearly identical to the lesson that memoirist James Frey learned in 2006, when fabrications discovered in *A Million Little Pieces* made him a national disgrace.   12

When I called surf photographer and *Outside* contributor Yassine Ouhilal for his opinion on altering photos, he cited a photo he'd taken in Norway, a guy riding a wave in front of snowcapped peaks. Viewers always assume Ouhilal Photoshopped in the mountains. But he didn't. "The biggest satisfaction I get," he says, "is when people ask me if a picture is real, and I say, 'Yes, it is.'"   13

And yet the amount of manipulated photography in circulation only grows along with the number of publications willing to push boundaries. The July cover of *Outdoor Photographer* is an Art Wolfe picture of Utah's Delicate Arch — with a full moon plopped in the middle. Wolfe had captured the moon with a nifty double exposure that required him to switch   14

---

[3] Adobe Photoshop (para. 10): A well-known graphic and photograph editing application.

to a telephoto lens, but the magazine's extended photo caption cites only the 17-35-millimeter lens Wolfe used for the shot of the arch. That would make a full moon the size of a pinprick; this one is more like a dime. (*Outdoor Photographer* claims the omission was an oversight.)

Equally worrisome are the insidious digital alterations — used to "improve" photos — which have become commonly accepted practice: darkening skies, oversaturating colors, and sharpening everything. These subtle but significant tweaks are now so easy that many photographers (and photo editors) do them out of habit.   15

David Griffin, director of photography at *National Geographic*, says that imperceptible digital fixes are a serious threat to integrity. He feels the sly use of manipulation in photojournalism threatens "to erode the veracity of the honest photographic covers that may come in the future." *National Geographic* does permit some enhancements, like slight darkening of highlights, opening of shadows, color correction, and the removal of defects (dust and scratches) — all part of what used to be industry-accepted "old darkroom techniques." But the magazine also requires all assignment photographers to submit their images in raw format — essentially a digital negative — so it can oversee all the changes in-house.   16

That kind of policy would have prevented an embarrassing incident last year for *Outside*, which published Rod McLean's stunning photo of sailboats on San Francisco Bay in its Exposure section. Several readers pointed out impossible contradictions in wind, light, and color, and *Outside* printed a correction. McLean, who created the image by stitching together nine shots, had told the magazine he'd retouched the image — removing a buoy, adding waves and clouds — but the editors didn't realize the extent of the alterations. When I called him, he sounded a lot like Ed Freeman. "I'm looking at photography from my ability to create an image," he said. "Other people look at photography as capturing a moment. Both approaches have always existed."   17

McLean explained that he knows some photographers feel threatened by his techniques, but insisted that he doesn't retouch images because it's "the easy way out." He noted in an e-mail that he spends hours taking photos — then spends many more crafting "seamless images that are very real."   18

I don't buy that argument, but McLean did bring up one really good point: Many of the same photographers pointing fingers at his work are quite happy to stage action for the camera. Rock-climbing photography has a particularly bad reputation in this regard. It's common for climbers to complete an ascent on their own, then replicate the most dangerous moments with a photographer in tow — along with better lighting, more protection, and shampooed hair. Magazines typically run these images without noting   19 that they're re-creations. (When I was at *Outside,* we published a shot of Dean Potter on Yosemite's El Capitan in 2002, with a caption citing his historic free climb, but omitted the fact that photographer Jimmy Chin had taken the picture a couple of weeks after the ascent.)

Christian Beckwith, founder and former editor of *Alpinist,* a climbing magazine defined by its pursuit of authenticity, believes that this dishonest practice "undermines the power and drama" of images capturing actual accomplishments. "Climbing photography is best when it's spontaneous," he says. "Those photos have much more value than an image that was created using the same climbers but with perfect everything."   20

The result of the race among photographers and magazines to create a better, brighter (or darker) version of reality is that "our relationship with photography is changing," says Hany Farid. "A more savvy public is becoming skeptical of the images they see — perhaps overly so. Many are quick to tag photos as Photoshopped."   21

Skepticism does have an upside. One of the more positive trends taking hold is the policing of photos. Earlier this year, judges in the Picture of the Year contest in Denmark created a stir when they disqualified Klavs Bo Christensen for excessive Photoshopping in his series of photos of Haitian slums. In July, *The New York Times Magazine* ran a portfolio of abandoned construction projects across the U.S. taken by Portuguese photographer Edgar Martins. When the *Times* posted them online, commenters on the community weblog MetaFilter jumped on apparent cloning and mirroring techniques, causing *Times* editors to quickly pull the images.   22

What I think is happening — what I hope is happening — is that we're finally fed up with all the tampering. Too many published photographs are unhinged from reality, morphed by a few mouse clicks into slick advertisements for perfect moments in time. Our relationship to photography is clearly changing, as Farid notes, but so is our taste: There's a growing hunger for truth. We'll never get all the way there — no camera will ever see as honestly as our eyes — but the idea that photographers set out to pursue truth is about to have its moment. And it's about time.   23

VOCABULARY/USING A DICTIONARY

1. In the second paragraph, Haggart describes a photographer "stitching together a Frankensurfer out of multiple riders." What do you think the word *Frankensurfer* means? What does it reference?

2. According to the writer, the "old trope" that "the camera never lies" is backwards (para. 6). What is a *trope*?

3. Haggart cites a photography editor who worries that artificial images may "erode the veracity" of honest photojournalism. Where does the word *veracity* come from? What does it mean?

RESPONDING TO WORDS IN CONTEXT

1. Haggart writes that "fake photos cause collateral damage" (para. 5). What is *collateral damage*? What is the usual context for this phrase?
2. In paragraph 9, the writer refers to the "most hallowed curators of documentary photos." How is Haggart using the word *hallowed* here? What connotations does it have?
3. Why does Haggart place quotation marks around *improve* in paragraph 15? How does this choice affect the meaning of the word?

DISCUSSING MAIN POINT AND MEANING

1. Haggart discusses *Migrations* by the photographer Art Wolfe. Why was the book a "milestone" (para. 10)?
2. The practice of manipulating images may break the trust between photographer and viewer. However, the resulting skepticism may have an "upside" according to Haggart (para. 22). What is the "upside"?

EXAMINING SENTENCES, PARAGRAPHS, AND ORGANIZATION

1. The opening sentence of the essay reads: "Photographer Ed Freeman is working on a book about surfing, though he's never surfed a day in his life" (para. 1). Why does Haggart highlight the fact that Freeman is not a surfer? How do the opening sentence—and Freeman's example—introduce the themes of the essay?
2. What purpose do paragraphs 6 to 11 serve in the essay? How are they all related?
3. While Haggart refers to the broken trust between photographers and viewers as a "crisis," he remains optimistic about the prospects for honest photojournalism. How is the overall structure of the essay designed to support this view?

THINKING CRITICALLY

1. Ed Freeman considers himself an "artist" (para. 4). He defends his work by arguing, "I'm interested in creating great pictures, not documentary images. I couldn't care less if they're 'real' or not" (para. 4). What is your reaction to this defense? Do you find his point convincing?
2. Haggart provides examples of altered photography; he also quotes specific photographers like Ed Freeman and Rod McLean, who offer their counterarguments. Why does he do this? How does including these opposing points of view help Haggart's overall argument?
3. According to the writer, "There's a growing hunger for truth" (para. 23). What does he mean? Do you agree with the statement? Do you think it has any application outside the context of photography?

IN-CLASS WRITING ASSIGNMENTS

1. Do you have a favorite photographic image or a picture that stays in your memory? What is it? Write a brief description of the photograph, as well as an explanation of its appeal or its hold on your imagination.

2. According to Haggart—and contrary to conventional wisdom—"the camera *always* lies" (para. 6). How do you understand this statement? How can photographic images (even unaltered ones) change our "concept of reality" (para. 5)? Write an essay examining the assertion that photographs "always" lie in some way.

3. Photographer Art Wolfe refers to "purists," whom he "can't even have a dialogue with" (para. 11). What does it mean to be a "purist"? Are you a "purist" about anything? Do you know anyone whom you would describe as a "purist"? What are the upsides and downsides of such an attitude?

Jed Perl

Picture Imperfect

[*The New Republic*, June 17, 2009]

BEFORE YOU READ

What is the significance of the 2005 prisoner abuse scandal at Abu Ghraib? Do photographs ever lie or conceal the truth? Does having more information always make us more knowledgeable?

WORDS TO LEARN

inured (para. 4): toughened, habituated, made hard or insensitive (verb).

perpetrators (para. 5): those who commit crimes (noun).

succumbing (para. 6): giving in, surrendering, submitting (verb).

autonomous (para. 6): independent (adjective).

abhorrent (para. 7): shocking, disgusting, repellent (adjective).

amelioration (para. 8): the act of improving something, or making it more satisfying (noun).

Jed Perl has been the art critic for The New Republic *since 1994. His most recent books are* New Art City: Manhattan at Mid-Century *(2005) and* Antoine's Alphabet: Watteau and His World *(2008).*

What is there to say about photographs we have not seen? There is a good deal to say, when those photographs document the abuse of prisoners in Iraq and Afghanistan. The U.S. government has in its possession as many as 2,000 images that have not been made public, a cache that will add to, but probably not significantly alter, the story we know from the photographs and videos first seen five years ago, taken as U.S. military personnel brutalized prisoners at Abu Ghraib. The lawsuits demanding the release of these photographs under the Freedom of Information Act date back to the middle years of the Bush administration, and now, the Obama administration, after initially agreeing to a court-ordered release, has reversed course, citing the security of our troops and the danger of giving further material for propaganda to terrorists in the Arab world.

The arguments of the American Civil Liberties Union and other organizations that support release cannot be taken lightly. The courts have already concluded, in a number of decisions, that even the possibility that these photographs might endanger American troops does not justify their being withheld. Some have said Obama realizes that the release of the photographs will occur sooner rather than later and has been mostly trying to avoid their being published on the eve of his trip to Egypt. So is the Obama administration standing in the way of the truth? If we do not see these photographs, are we being denied some information that we need to have now? I am not convinced.

Photographic truth is a particular kind of truth, and that is the case even when the photograph has not been doctored or edited. In going back to the courts to urge that these pictures not be released, the Obama administration is acknowledging this very fact. The argument against releasing them is not that they are not truthful, but, rather, that they represent an aspect of the truth about U.S. behavior in Iraq that Islamic militants will be able to use to create lies about the United States. The repetition of images on television and the Internet — and this is as much the case with our 24/7 news cycle as with the propaganda campaigns of Islamic militants — is a form of editorializing that, by its very nature, reshapes the photographic image, which in the first place represents a singular act of brutalization or the results of a particular sequence of acts.

The argument has been made that the wide distribution of torture photographs helps to concentrate the public's imagination, rendering ideas of brutality and suffering concrete. This is surely true, but it is also true that the public can become inured to even the most violent pictures, can claim image overload, can simply turn away. Photographic images should never become a substitute for the development of the moral imagination, for the ability to comprehend horrors we have not ourselves experienced or for which there is little or no documentation. Sometimes we need to believe things we cannot see, not as a matter of religious faith but of moral conviction.

Everybody can call to mind some of the photographs from Abu 5 Ghraib. There is the shot of Lynndie England, the boyish military prison guard, holding a leash at the other end of which is a naked prisoner flat on the floor, pulled half out of his cell. And there is another photograph of a prisoner, his head covered by a conical hood, his outstretched arms attached to wires, standing on a box. These pictures derive from a three-month period, October to December 2003, that has been the subject of a number of military trials and convictions. That these pictures were taken by the perpetrators, as trophies of a kind, has been, for some viewers, nearly as unsettling as the abuse itself. Here is a glimpse of a mentality that Americans did not want to see, certainly not in their countrymen. From a legal point of view, the self-satisfied looks on the faces of the torturers as they pose for the camera certainly reveals a good deal about their mental state. But the ugliness of the self-documentation — the guys-and-gals-having-a-wild-time-together side of the photographic record — can also confuse the issue. The stupidity of the photographs should not be allowed to detract from their monstrousness, which is exactly what Rush Limbaugh[1] and callers on his show were trying to do when they argued that this was just frat-house stuff, people letting off steam, horsing around.

Photographs, in and of themselves, do 6 not necessarily tell us very much. A certain kind of photographic literalism has made it easier for some to argue that these were isolated acts. All there is, so this argument goes, is in the photograph. What you see is what you get. But the grotesque particularity of certain shots can be said, if not to exactly distort the truth, then certainly to skew the truth. There are several close-up photographs of a male prisoner's nipple with a smiley face inscribed in what looks like magic marker. The pop culture sadism is sick-making, no question about it, but if you linger too long here you are succumbing to a diversion. The picture cannot tell us who encouraged or ignored such behavior, or who was responsible for creating an atmosphere in which such things took place. While much of what we know about the lawless conduct of some American soldiers in Iraq comes from these photographs, more probably derives from non-photographic sources: from military documents, congressional

> Photographs, in and of themselves, do not necessarily tell us very much.

---

[1] Rush Limbaugh (para. 5): Conservative radio talk show host.

testimony, evidence of many kinds. Certainly, the photographs should not be considered without captions. To study them without being aware of the circumstances under which they were produced is to accept them as autonomous images with their own integrity, and that is obscene.

In the five years since these pictures were first seen on *60 Minutes*,[2] there have been a number of efforts to decode them, and some of the interpretation strikes me as not so much mistaken as beside the point. It is easy to see that TV news, which is always looking for the next flashpoint, can collapse a complex story into an image that, however horrific, is only one piece of evidence in a story that is even more terrible, if understood in its entirety. But there is also a danger in lingering for too long over the individual photographs, in submitting them to psychological or sociological or art-historical analysis. Soon after the first pictures from Abu Ghraib were released, they were compared to online S&M pornography, and the suggestion was made that soldiers who had not seen Internet porn would have never thought of the leashes, the stress positions, the mortifying nudity, the simulated sex. I worry that this recourse to theories about the psychology of the perpetrators, this effort to give their pathological behavior a sociological setting, can blunt the plain horror of what was done, can make it all seem somehow interesting, the material for a novel or a movie. There have also been comparisons made between the Abu Ghraib photographs and Robert Mapplethorpe's[3] photographs of consensual S&M sex, and this is another line of thinking I find inherently troubling, a form of aggrandizement. The very mention of Mapplethorpe's name adds interest, even cachet to these abhorrent acts. Why dress up the ugly truth? My feeling is that violent power relationships are inherently appealing to certain individuals, and that there could have been military police on duty at Abu Ghraib who felt the urge to act as they did even without a little nudge from Internet porn.

I also resist the connections that have been made between photographs from Abu Ghraib and various works of art, whether Goya's *Disasters of War*[4] or Picasso's *Guernica*.[5] The impulse to see connections

7

8

---

[2] *60 Minutes* (para. 7): CBS television newsmagazine.

---

[3] Robert Mapplethorpe (para. 7): American photographer (1946–1989).

---

[4] Goya's *Disasters of War* (para. 8): A series of prints illustrating the violence of war by Spanish painter Francisco Goya (1746–1828).

---

[5] Picasso's *Guernica* (para. 8): Painting by Spanish artist Pablo Picasso (1881–1973) depicting the bombing of Guernica, a town in the Basque region of Spain, by German and Italian warplanes in 1937.

between the art of the past and photographic images taken without any conscious thought of creating art can be very strong, especially among those who are familiar with the art in the museums. Sometimes the associations are almost impossible to avoid. Who can forget the news photograph taken at Kent State in 1970, with a young woman kneeling over the body of a student who has just been shot to death, her arms outstretched and mouth open in horror, in a pose that might have come straight out of the iconography of ecstasy and grief in Hellenistic art? But what precisely does this comparison tell us except that the artists of the past were acute observers of human behavior? A recent book by the art historian Stephen F. Eisenman, *The Abu Ghraib Effect*, traces certain gestures and situations that we encounter in the Abu Ghraib images all the way back to the Greeks, and, although Eisenman is very judicious about the connections that he makes, I cannot help wishing that he would have left the pictures from Abu Ghraib as what they are, namely evidence of particular, terrible things done by particular men and women at a particular moment. When heinous acts are associated with artistic acts, there is a danger of amelioration, or, at least, the appearance of amelioration.

Whatever the courts decide, however, we would do well to remember that we can expect too much from photography, that we need to respect the limits of photographic truth. Living in a society that is as widely and vibrantly uncensored as ours, we have an obligation to consider the value of self-censorship, of a reticence or discretion that can shape the onslaught of information. While we cannot achieve knowledge without information — this is a fundamental fact in any democratic society — information does not always advance knowledge, and photographic information in its raw form can mean many different things. We did not need the Abu Ghraib photographs to tell us that men and women do terrible things. The significance of these pictures is particular, specific. And their specificity should be approached with a certain reticence. We must not aggrandize the torturer's photographic acts of self-aggrandizement. And then there is the matter of the privacy of the victims, some of whom may well recognize themselves in these photographs and, I would presume, would not want such images disseminated around the world. No wonder some of the photographs have been published with the faces or genitals blurred, a distortion of photographic truth that brings home to us in the most immediate way the reality of these awful images.

Photographs turn current events into historical events. Precisely because photographers operate in the moment, their work has the effect of emphasizing the speed with which the present becomes the past. If this is a paradox, it is one that everybody embraces when they rush to see

9

10

the photographs of the vacation or the party — to see what they've just experienced reframed as a story. It is surely true that, in order for the full historical record of American terror and abuse in Iraq and Afghanistan to finally be revealed, all the photographs in the possession of the U.S. government will need to be seen. But, even if some of the photographs show us significantly different aspects of what went on, it is unlikely that our understanding will be significantly altered, and, in any event, the fragmentary reports of what these photographs contain do not suggest that major revelations are in store. What we have already seen in the photographs from Abu Ghraib will not be better understood by seeing more photographs, that is for sure. Photography can provide evidence. But people have to make the judgments.

USING A DICTIONARY

1. Perl writes that releasing more photographs of abused prisoners in Iraq and Afghanistan might give terrorists "material for propaganda" (para. 1). What is *propaganda*? What are the origins of the word?

2. According to Perl, some of the photographs have a "grotesque particularity" (para. 6). What does *grotesque* mean? What purpose does the word serve in this phrase?

3. The writer refers to the "pop culture sadism" (para. 6) of the photographs. What does the word *sadism* mean? Where does it come from?

RESPONDING TO WORDS IN CONTEXT

1. Perl writes, "Photographic images should never become a substitute for the development of the moral imagination . . ." (para. 4). What does he mean by "moral imagination"?

2. What is the difference between the words *cache* (para. 1) and *cachet* (para. 7)?

3. Perl disagrees with attempts to "give their [the perpetrators'] pathological behavior a sociological setting" (para. 7). What do *pathological* and *sociological* mean in this section?

DISCUSSING MAIN POINT AND MEANING

1. In the third paragraph, Perl discusses "photographic truth" as a "particular kind of truth." How is this point related to his overall argument?

2. How have the images of prisoner abuse been decoded and interpreted over the last five years? What connections, parallels, and contexts have observers proposed for the photographs? What is Perl's attitude toward these interpretations?

3. According to Perl, how does TV news incorporate photographic images into its coverage of events? Why is this a problem?

EXAMINING SENTENCES, PARAGRAPHS, AND ORGANIZATION

1. Where in the article does Perl use rhetorical questions? How do they help structure his argument?
2. Throughout the essay, Perl writes in relatively long paragraphs. Why does he do this? Do you think they are necessary? What do you think this says about his readers and *The New Republic*?
3. How does Perl address counterarguments? Does he do so effectively?

THINKING CRITICALLY

1. Perl wants to "resist the connections that have been made between photographs from Abu Ghraib and various works of art" (para. 8). He also believes there is "danger" in submitting the images to "psychological or sociological" analysis (para. 7). Do you agree with his point of view?
2. According to the writer, photographic truth "is a particular kind of truth" (para. 3). Do you agree? How do unaltered photographs "skew" or even conceal truth?
3. Perl writes: "While we cannot achieve knowledge without information — this is a fundamental fact in any democratic society — information does not always advance knowledge, and photographic information in its raw form can mean many different things" (para. 9). Do you agree? What is the connection between knowledge, information, and democracy?

IN-CLASS WRITING ACTIVITIES

1. Perl writes that images of prisoner abuse may be used for "propaganda" purposes. How do you define *propaganda*? What are its characteristics? Choose an example of propaganda and then write an essay that analyzes its techniques, strategies, and other defining characteristics. What makes your example effective — or ineffective — as propaganda?
2. "Picture Imperfect" is an argument against the release of photographs by the U.S. government. Do you agree with Perl? In an essay, make your own case for or against making the images public.
3. Perl argues that unaltered photographs and images can be be misleading. Think of an example — either from your personal experience or from history or popular culture — and write about it in a brief essay.

Elizabeth Svokos (student essay)

Head to Head — Print Photographs

[*The Bi-College News*, Bryn Mawr College/Haverford College, November 18, 2009]

BEFORE YOU READ

Do you prefer digital photography or printed photographs from film cameras? What is your favorite photograph? Do new technologies bring a sense of loss, as well as a sense of progress?

WORDS TO LEARN

embossed (para. 2): raised in a decorative or ornamental way (adjective).

gratification (para. 4): great satisfaction (noun).

anticipation (para. 4): hopeful expectation (noun).

Two weeks ago my computer crashed. I lost all my photographs. My trip to China last summer, my mom's 50th birthday party, a really embarrassing picture of Juliana Reyes from freshman year: gone, gone, gone. Digital photographs, you are the worst. 1

Didn't you grow up looking at old pictures of your family and friends? We've replaced passing those weathered photos around the table with crowding around a laptop to click our ways through a Facebook album of "enhanced" photos with embossed edges. 2

Digital cameras? Don't get me started. The ability to see a picture you just took has made it nearly impossible to find a bad picture of someone these days. But isn't the best picture in your family album the one of your uncle looking constipated? Well, that photo wouldn't exist if he could have seen the monstrosity and deleted it off the camera right then and there. There's no room for imperfection when you can remove red eyes and blot out pimples with a click of your mouse. 3

We live in a world of instant gratification. Wanting to see a photograph an instant after it was taken is basically second nature. So much for building anticipation. So much for trips to the drug store to pick up the film and tear it open before you even reach your car, wondering what 4

Elizabeth Svokos currently attends Bryn Mawr College with a double major in anthropology and Italian. She has worked both as the photography editor and a staff writer for The Bi-College News.

kind of crazy stuff you captured on this film. Oh, that night! Where did we find a kiddie pool?

> There is also something incredibly exciting about the one-shot chance you get with a film camera.

There is also something incredibly exciting about the one-shot chance you get with a film camera. Everyone knows you only get one moment to make the shot count, and the excitement builds. There's no pre-flash red light to warn you when to smile your best; you just go for it, giggling, and hope no one's finger is blocking the lens. And if it is, well now they're just in the picture too. The more the merrier.

These reasons and the Great Computer Crash of 2009 prompted me to buy a $10 film camera from the thrift store down the street. My first prints came out perfectly. Now at least I can show my kids photos of my life by handing them the actual pictures instead of e-mailing them a link to an online album.

If I had printed with film earlier, I would still be able to look at my sisters and myself posing on the Great Wall of China. And I'd still have the option of using that picture of Juliana as blackmail someday. But now that we can't physically hold photographs, they are entirely in the hands of technology. They can be altered, enhanced, touched up, and even lost forever.

I, for one, would rather look back on my memories the way my mom does: opening the tin box of photographs in her side table drawer and flipping through them, smiling at her life captured in those imperfect and beautiful photographs with their smudge marks and rips on the edges from passing them around so much. One has a crack down the middle from carrying it in her wallet for twenty years.

VOCABULARY/USING A DICTIONARY

1. Svokos discusses her dissatisfaction with digital photography. What does *digital* mean in this context, and what are its roots?
2. The writer refers to a bad photographic image as a "monstrosity" (para. 3). What are the origins of this word? Are there synonyms Svokos could have used to achieve the same effect?
3. According to Svokos, our photographs are "entirely in the hands of technology" (para. 7). Where does the word *technology* come from? What does it mean?

RESPONDING TO WORDS IN CONTEXT

1. Svokos writes that we now crowd around laptops to look at pictures rather than "passing those weathered photos around the table" (para. 2).

What is a more typical context for the word *weathered*? What connotations does it have?

2. Why does the writer place quotation marks around "enhanced" in the second paragraph? How does the punctuation affect the meaning of the word?

3. According to Svokos, our assumption that we can see a photograph "an instant after it was taken is basically second nature" (para. 4). What does *second nature* mean? Does it have a positive or negative connotation?

DISCUSSING MAIN POINT AND MEANING

1. Svokos experiences advances in digital photography with a sense of loss. What has been lost, according to the writer?

2. We usually value "good" pictures as opposed to "bad" ones. What point does Svokos make about "embarrassing" or imperfect photographs?

3. What contrasts does Svokos establish between digital photography and print photography? How does each represent different values?

EXAMINING SENTENCES, PARAGRAPHS, AND ORGANIZATION

1. Describing nondigital photography, Svokos writes: "There's no pre-flash red light to warn you when to smile your best; you just go for it, giggling, and hope no one's finger is blocking the lens" (para. 5). How does the writer use a semicolon in this sentence? Is it correct? Effective?

2. Svokos refers to Juliana Reyes in her first paragraph; then, she mentions her again in the second-to-last paragraph. What point is Svokos making? Does it matter if we know who Juliana Reyes is? Why or why not?

3. In what ways is this a personal essay? How does Svokos move beyond the personal essay?

THINKING CRITICALLY

1. What relationship does Svokos attempt to have with her reader? How would you describe it? What strategies does she use?

2. According to the writer, "We live in a world of instant gratification" (para. 4). What do you think she means? Do you agree? Is it a problem?

3. How would you describe Svokos's attitude toward technology and technological progress? Do you agree with it?

IN-CLASS WRITING ACTIVITIES

1. Svokos clearly prefers printed film photography over digital photography. How would you refute her argument?

2. Do you have a favorite photograph — of yourself, a family member, or a friend? Describe the picture and try to explain its appeal. Is it print or digital? Is it a "good" picture or a "bad" one?

3. According to the writer, advances in digital photography may have more drawbacks than advantages. Describe another technological advance or example of high technology that has caused us to "lose" or devalue something important.

Using Concrete Language

A sure way to make your writing vivid and memorable is to select words that convey specific and concrete meanings. Very often in the process of writing we are confronted with the choice of using either a general noun, such as *tree* or *bird* or *fence*, or a more exact noun, such as *maple*, or *cardinal*, or *chain-link fence*. So it's always a good idea, especially in revising, to look closely at your word choice to avoid language that is so generalized that readers cannot visualize your images or get an exact sense of what you are attempting to convey. The terms *maple* and *cardinal* can be distinctly pictured, unlike *tree* or *bird*, and a *chain-link fence* conveys a specific type of fence we can readily picture, not just the abstract idea of one.

Observe how Elizabeth Svokos, a student at Bryn Mawr College, makes a deliberate decision throughout her essay to use concrete words. In her final paragraph, especially, she paints a specific word picture that helps us understand her main point about the difference between digital and print photography. She wants us to understand why someone could be fond of the imperfections of old photographs, and her concrete details of a tin box in a side table drawer where her mother's smudged and wrinkled photos are kept help us see clearly the physical condition of the pictures.

1
We see exactly where the old photos are kept

2
We see exactly the condition of the photos

I, for one, would rather look back on my memories the way my mom does: opening the tin box of photographs in her side table drawer (1) and flipping through them, smiling at her life captured in those imperfect and beautiful photographs with their smudge marks and rips on the edges from passing them around so much. One has a crack down the middle from carrying it in her wallet for twenty years. (2)

STUDENT WRITER AT WORK
Elizabeth Svokos

RA. What was your main purpose in writing this piece?

ES. The purpose I had in mind was to show that technology isn't always better than the way things used to be. It helps us in many ways, but we lose a little of that imperfection that is so endearing.

RA. What response have you received? Has the feedback affected your views on the topic you wrote about?

ES. The responses I received were positive. I think it was an accessible piece that many people can easily relate to, since I had people come up to me in the cafeteria to tell me they miss disposable cameras, too. This feedback helped me to recognize that writing about something that inspires me can also hit home for readers. It made me more open to giving my opinion.

RA. How long did it take for you to write this piece? Did you revise your work? What were your goals as you revised?

ES. This article didn't take me too long to write since it's a subject very close to my heart. It's an opinion piece, so I didn't need any sources or interviews, which usually take a lot of time. I revised my work a couple (hundred) times, moving paragraphs and changing the wording to give it the feel I wanted. My goal as I revised was to create a piece that had a comfortable writing style that makes the reader feel like they are listening to a friend, while also getting my point across without forcing it.

RA. Do you generally show your writing to friends before submitting it? Do you collaborate or bounce your ideas off others?

ES. Yes. This is the most important aspect of my writing process. My best friend is also a writer and we regularly exchange articles, not just for copy editing, but to truly dig into the details of our writing and help to make our articles clean, clear, and meaningful. We devote a significant amount of time to sitting down with each other and delving into our writing. This not only helps the writer, but also the editor, who becomes more aware of things to look out for in her own articles.

RA. What topics most interest you as a writer?

ES. The topics I like most are personal stories about people. There are so many interesting people in the world and when a good writer covers their stories, I feel really connected. Which is what journalism is all about, right?

Elián González

On Saturday, April 22, 2000, the fate of a six-year-old Cuban boy, Elián González, was decided. The boy's mother had drowned while fleeing Fidel Castro's Cuba, but Elián was rescued and allowed to stay with relatives in Miami for several months, where the predominately anti-Castro Cuban community felt that it was in the boy's best interests to remain. The U.S. government, however, believed it was the nation's obligation to return Elián to his native land into the custody of his father. In the early hours of April 22 — under orders from President Bill Clinton's attorney general, Janet Reno, Immigration and Naturalization Service agents broke into the house of the Miami relatives, seized the six-year-old, and whisked him off to Washington. Two photographs quickly captured the public's attention: in one, an armed and helmeted agent seizes the boy at gunpoint; in the other, a boy smiles in his father's arms. Those who supported the anti-Castro cause of Cuban Americans focused on the shot of Elián being forcibly removed, while those who supported the government's position pointed to the shot of a happy boy reunited with his father.

© AP Photo/Alan Díaz.

The photo of Elián at gunpoint, which ran in many papers and on TV news programs, raised suspicion. Writing for *Slate* immediately after the photos, the award-winning journalist William Saletan brilliantly analyzed the González photos and called the gunpoint photo into question to counter claims that federal agents were ready and willing to shoot a six-year-old boy. According to Saletan, "The reason you can see the agent's trigger finger clearly is that it's extended *alongside* the gun, *not* curled around the trigger. And the impression that the gun is pointed at Elián is an optical illusion caused by compressing a three-dimensional scene into a two-dimensional photograph." Saletan points out that the gun was aimed instead at Donata Dalrymple, one of the fishermen who had pulled Elián out of the ocean and wanted to hide him from the agents. They had been warned of possible violence and therefore prepared for a struggle. But, as Saletan continues, if you saw the photo on TV stations that Saturday morning, "You had no idea the gun was pointed at anyone other than Elián because Dalrymple had been squeezed out of the picture."

"Pictures, like words," Saletan reminded his readers, "can project illusions and take events out of context."

Discussing the Unit

SUGGESTED TOPIC FOR DISCUSSION

Most of our conventional wisdom—and our clichés—about photography refer to its singular ability to convey truth: "The camera never lies." "A picture is worth a thousand words." Perhaps even "Seeing is believing." But all the writers in this unit challenge this point of view. As Jed Perl notes, "Photographic truth is a particular kind of truth, and that is the case even when the photograph has not been doctored or edited." What is your own view of "photographic truth"? Do you usually trust images, whether you see them on the news, on the Internet, in a family album, or on a friend's Facebook page? Why or why not? Does context matter? If photographs often lie or mislead, why are platitudes about their truthfulness so common and persistent?

PREPARING FOR CLASS DISCUSSION

1. According to Rob Haggart, there is a "growing hunger for truth": We are fed up with the unreality of the images that surround us. Do you agree? Would Jed Perl and Elizabeth Svokos agree? Do their essays reflect a "hunger for truth"?

2. Jed Perl argues that the media, "which is always looking for the next flashpoint, can collapse a complex story into an image that, however horrific, is only one piece of evidence...." How does his point relate to the photograph of Elián González? Can you think of other examples of a "complex story" being "collapsed into an image"? How might written words be better at conveying truth than photographs?

FROM DISCUSSION TO WRITING

1. Our sense of history and the world is shaped by photographs. But as the essays in this unit suggest, such images often represent "photographic truth": They simplify reality, leave out facts and details, and shape our perceptions. Choose an iconic or famous photograph. Then, research the facts behind the picture, as well as the ways in which the photograph has been used, understood, and interpreted. Are there discrepancies between "photographic truth" and truth, or between the meaning of the photograph and the reality it supposedly captured?

2. Both Haggart and Svokos express skepticism about and dissatisfaction with high-tech digital photography. Svokos goes so far as to reject it altogether, in favor of a ten-dollar film camera from a thrift store. Would you ever consider replacing a newer technology with an older one? Which one would you replace, and why?

QUESTIONS FOR CROSS-CULTURAL DISCUSSION

1. Jed Perl writes that the release of more prisoner abuse photographs could give "further material for propaganda to terrorists in the Arab world." Setting aside specific questions about extremist propaganda, what happens to photographic and video images when they cross national, ethnic, racial, and cultural borders through more mainstream channels? How might such differences affect "photographic truth"? How do they shape interpretation—not only a specific event (like the prisoner abuse), but also views of an entire culture or country?

2. There are some cultures and religions that forbid photography—either completely, or at certain times and places. For example, some Amish do not allow themselves to be photographed because of the biblical injunction against graven images. Why do you think there are taboos around the practice? Are there things, people, places, and occasions that should not be photographed? Why or why not?

5

What Do We Fear?

Many more people on the planet are killed each year by falling coconuts than by sharks — so why are sharks considered terrifying creatures and coconuts an enjoyable fruit? Why do people fear the unlikely event of dying in an airline crash but not the more likely event of dying in a car accident? According to the best-selling authors of *Freakonomics*, humans are "quite bad at assessing risk." In "What Should You Worry About?" Steven D. Levitt and Stephen J. Dubner list some of the topics, such as sharks and strangers, "about which our fears run far out of proportion to reality."

Fear, as Irwin Savodnik reminds us in "All Crisis, All the Time," can lead to overreaction and can transform what is merely a problem into a crisis. "Overreaction," he claims, "points to mythical thinking, a way of embodying our emotions and impulses in tales of our fears, vulnerabilities, and guilt in strange, often colorful, stories." Overreaction is also the subject of Erica Zucco's essay, "Quit Living in Swine Fear." A student at the University of Missouri Columbia, she uses her own excessive responses to the recent swine flu epidemic to call attention to the way our fears of exaggerated dangers can interfere with our lives: "We should live in such a way," she advises, "that the only stress we have is real stress, and the things we fear are actually real."

Although the terrorist attacks of 9/11 and subsequent incidents worldwide have contributed to a climate of fear, the phenomenon is not entirely new to America. In "America Then . . . The 1950s," we look back on a nation terrified of nuclear attack.

Steven D. Levitt and Stephen J. Dubner

What Should You Worry About?

[*Parade*, October 18, 2009]

BEFORE YOU READ
What do you worry about? How does the media influence our concerns and fears? Can science and technology solve our biggest problems?

WORDS TO LEARN
jargon (para. 2): the language or vocabulary peculiar to a particular trade, profession, or group (noun).

dubbed (para. 3): named (verb).
conjure (para. 15): to bring to mind or call into existence (verb).

Humans are good at many things — typing, inventing stuff — but   1
we're quite bad at assessing risk. Day after day, we get bent out of shape over things we shouldn't worry about so much, like airplane crashes and lightning strikes, instead of things we should, like heart disease and the flu.

So how can we find out what's truly dangerous? Economics. Upon   2
hearing the word, most people think of incomprehensible charts and jargon and promptly change the subject. However, we can use the field's powerful ideas and tools, along with huge piles of data, to understand topics that aren't typically associated with economics. Topics like shark attacks.

Think back to the summer of 2001, or what the U.S. media dubbed   3
the "Summer of the Shark." The prime example was the story of Jessie Arbogast, an 8-year-old who was playing in the warm, shallow Pensacola,

---

Steven D. Levitt and Stephen J. Dubner are the authors of the influential best seller Freakonomics: A Rogue Economist Explores the Hidden Side of Everything *(2005) and* Superfreakonomics: Global Cooling, Patriotic Prostitutes, and Why Suicide Bombers Should Buy Life Insurance *(2009). A graduate of Harvard University with a PhD from the Massachusetts Institute of Technology, Levitt has been an economics professor at the University of Chicago since 1997. A nonfiction author and journalist, Dubner holds an MFA from Columbia University, and his books include the memoir* Confessions of a Hero-Worshiper *(2003).*

Florida, waves when a bull shark ripped off his right arm and a big chunk of his thigh.

The media was full of such chilling tales. Here's the lead paragraph from one article published that summer: 4

"Sharks come silently, without warning. There are three ways they strike: the hit-and-run, the bump-and-bite, and the sneak attack. The hit-and-run is the most common. The shark may see the sole of a swimmer's foot, think it's a fish, and take a bite before realizing this isn't its usual prey." 5

A reasonable person might never go near the ocean again. But how many shark attacks do you think actually happened that year? 6

Take a guess — and then cut that figure in half, and now cut it in half a few more times. During all of 2001, there were 68 shark attacks worldwide, of which just four were fatal. 7

Not only were the numbers lower than the media hysteria implied, but they were not much higher than those of previous years or of the years that followed. Between 1995 and 2005, there were on average 60.3 shark attacks worldwide each year, with a high of 79 and a low of 46. There were on average 5.9 fatalities per year, with a high of 11 and a low of three. In other words, the headlines during the summer of 2001 might just as easily have read "Shark Attacks About Average This Year." 8

Elephants, meanwhile, kill at least 200 people a year. Why aren't we petrified of them? Probably because their victims tend to live far from the world's media centers. It may also have to do with our perceptions gleaned from the movies. Friendly elephants are a staple of children's films like *Babar* and *Dumbo*; sharks are typecast as villains. 9

> There are any number of topics about which our fears run far out of proportion to reality.

There are any number of topics about which our fears run far out of proportion to reality. For instance, whom are you more afraid of: strangers or people you know? 10

While "strangers" is the obvious answer, it's probably wrong. Three out of four murder victims knew their assailants; about seven of 10 rape victims knew theirs. While the public is justifiably horrified when a stranger snatches a child off the street, the data show that such kidnappings are extremely rare. 11

As for the crime of identity theft, most of us fear nameless, faceless perpetrators — say, a far-off ring of teenage hackers. We try to thwart them by endlessly changing our PINs (and forgetting them). 12

But it turns out that nearly half of identity-theft victims are ripped off by someone they know. And fully 90% of thefts happen offline, not on the Internet.

Fear sometimes distorts our thinking to the point where we become 13 convinced that certain threats are so enormous as to be unstoppable. Every generation has at least one such problem — the plague, polio. Today, it's global warming.

The average global ground temperature over the past 100 years has 14 risen 1.3 degrees Fahrenheit, or .74 degrees Celsius. But even the most brilliant climate scientists are unable to predict exactly what will happen to the Earth as a result of those atmospheric changes and when anything will happen.

We humans tend to respond to uncertainty with more emotion — fear, 15 blame, paralysis — than advisable. Uncertainty also has a nasty way of making us conjure the very worst possibilities. With global warming, these are downright biblical: hellish temperatures, rising oceans, a planet in chaos.

But instead of panicking and collectively wringing our hands, it 16 might help us to look at other "unsolvable" problems humanity has had to deal with.

Like, well, horse manure. As urban populations exploded in the 17 nineteenth century, horses were put to work in countless ways, from pulling streetcars and coaches to powering manufacturing equipment. Our cities became filled with horses — for example, in 1900, New York City was home to some 200,000 of them, or one for every 17 people.

Unfortunately, they produced a slew of what economists refer to as 18 "negative externalities." These included noise, gridlock, high insurance costs, and far too many human traffic fatalities.

The worst problem was the manure. The average horse produces 19 about 24 pounds of it a day. In New York, that added up to nearly 5 million pounds. A day. It lined the streets like banks of snow and was piled as high as 60 feet in vacant lots. It stank to the heavens. And it was a fertile breeding ground for flies that spread deadly disease.

City planners everywhere were confounded. It seemed as if cities 20 could not survive without the horse — but they couldn't survive with it, either.

And then the problem vanished. The horse was kicked to the curb by 21 the electric streetcar and the automobile.

Virtually every unsolvable problem we've faced in the past has turned 22 out to be quite solvable, and the script has nearly always been the same: A band of clever, motivated people — scientists usually — find an answer. With polio, it was the creation of a vaccine. If the best minds in the world focus their attention on global warming, hopefully we can handle that, too.

Yes, it is an incredibly large and challenging problem. But, as history   23
has shown us again and again, human ingenuity is bound to be even
larger.

VOCABULARY/USING A DICTIONARY

1. What are the origins of the word *flu* (para. 1)? What terms is it related to?
2. What does the word *hysteria* (para. 8) mean and where does it come from?
3. What are the roots of the word *paralysis* (para. 15)?

RESPONDING TO WORDS IN CONTEXT

1. In paragraph 15, the writers note that problems like global warming seem "downright biblical." What does the adjective *biblical* mean in this context?
2. Levitt and Dubner argue that when we face our current crises and challenges, we might "look at other 'unsolvable' problems humanity has had to deal with" (para. 16). Why do the writers put the word *unsolvable* in quotation marks?
3. According to the writers, news headlines in 2001 could have read "Shark Attacks About Average This Year" (para. 8). What point are Levitt and Dubner making here? How is it related to their overall argument?

DISCUSSING MAIN POINT AND MEANING

1. The authors argue that economics can help us "find out what's truly dangerous" (para. 2). What does economics offer that other ways of assessing risk may not?
2. According to Levitt and Dubner, our fears and our perceptions of risk are shaped in a number of ways. What are they?
3. Besides taking an economist's view of "unsolvable" problems, the writers provide historical context, as well. What is the historical "script" that has "nearly always been the same," according to Levitt and Dubner?

EXAMINING SENTENCES, PARAGRAPHS, AND ORGANIZATION

1. Several times in their essay, Levitt and Dubner use sentence fragments or even one-word sentences. Why do you think they do this? Point out specific examples.
2. What purpose does paragraph 5 serve? How does it support the writers' overall argument?
3. Levitt and Dubner are primarily interested in global warming and our responses to the threat of climate change, but they do not mention the topic until paragraph 13. Why do the writers organize the essay in this way?

THINKING CRITICALLY

1. Levitt and Dubner write that the field of economics can help us "find out what's truly dangerous" and offers "powerful ideas and tools, along with huge piles of data" (para. 2). Does this essay seem to be about "economics," as you understand the term?

2. The authors propose an analogy between global warming and the "negative externalities" once created by horses in New York City. Does this seem like a legitimate, persuasive, and effective comparison? Why or why not?

3. How would you characterize Levitt and Dubner's view of people, generally? Do you agree with it? Are there any problems with their attitude?

IN-CLASS WRITING ASSIGNMENTS

1. Levitt and Dubner write, "Every generation has at least one [enormous, seemingly unstoppable problem]. . . . Today, it's global warming" (para. 13). Do you agree with them? Is global warming perceived as the biggest threat to the current generation? Should it be? Write an essay either agreeing or disagreeing with Levitt and Dubner's premise.

2. According to Levitt and Dubner, "there are any number of topics about which our fears run far out of proportion to reality" (para. 10). The writers partially blame the media for this, as in the 2001 coverage of shark attacks. Can you think of other examples of the media distorting or sensationalizing coverage "out of proportion to reality"? Are you influenced by such stories or images?

3. The writers claim that "upon hearing the word [economics], most people think of incomprehensible charts and jargon and promptly change the subject" (para. 2). How do you react to economics — as a word, an idea, and a field of study? Write down your associations with and attitudes toward the subject.

Irwin Savodnik

All Crisis, All the Time

[*The Weekly Standard*, November 2, 2009]

BEFORE YOU READ

What is a "crisis"? Does our society overreact to perceived "crises"? How do
we balance logic and emotion in our response to a serious problem?

WORDS TO LEARN

surfeit (para. 2): overabundance,
 excess (noun).
dint (para. 5): force, power (noun).
unequivocally (para. 7): clearly, with
 no other possible meanings
 (adverb).
dichotomy (para. 10): division of two
 opposing ideas or kinds (noun).
alienation (para. 11): the state of
 being isolated from the objective
 world or reality (noun).

panoply (para. 11): a wide-ranging
 and impressive display (noun).
usurped (para. 11): seized or held
 without right or authority, often
 by force (verb).
serial (para. 13): sequential, coming
 as a series rather than all at once
 (adjective).

Americans are overreacting to events: to the "Great Depression" of 1
2009, to the increasing numbers of young people with Attention
Deficit Disorder, to the histrionic fantasy that climate change
will become global boiling. None of these issues is without substance,
and none of them should be ignored; but in one way or another, we are
overreacting by turning each of them into a crisis.

We seem to have fallen in love with crises, and the more crises we 2
find the more animated we seem to be. We are immersed in a Crisis of
Crises, replete with illogic, a surfeit of emotion, and strings of events
vying for crisis status.

"Crisis," literally, means separation, and involves a break with the 3
past by supplanting the existing order with a new one. Tectonic departures from precedent such as the transition from BC to AD, from the

---

*Irwin Savodnik is a psychiatrist and clinical faculty member at the UCLA School
of Medicine. His writing appears in both the popular press and professional
journals.*

ancien régime[1] to the French Republic, from the Romanovs[2] to the Bolsheviks,[3] were set off by crises. Both the Russian and French revolutions included a change in their calendars. Illegal immigration, farm "crises," daily energy "crises," credit card "crises," E. coli contamination "crises," and education "crises" express substantive concerns, but they are not and never were crises in the strict sense of the term.

So what is overreaction? Simply put, overreaction is characterized by its reliance on emotion, its episodic time frame and, ultimately, its retreat from reality. Take the worldwide swine flu pandemic. No doubt, researchers have locked onto a serious health threat that will require a forceful response — immunization, rapid diagnosis, public health precautions, and ongoing research. An important moderating factor is the high probability that anyone who was infected with the virus between 1946 and 1953 is likely to be immune to the disease.   4

But the public has responded with less moderate emotions, donning surgical masks, avoiding crowds, and gulping down "immune-boosting" pills. No doubt, swine flu infection is a real phenomenon, and a scary one which, by dint of a single mutation, could cast a giant shadow across the American continent. But when we look at the facts we find both our feet on the ground. H1N1, as infectious disease specialists call it, is closely related to influenza virus A, which brings the flu each winter. The most recent attack, one that was carefully studied, took place in Mexico in late April, and the death rate was calculated at 0.6 percent.   5

Admittedly, H1N1 has hogged the airways because it is the same virus that caused the Spanish Influenza of 1918 and killed 50–100 million people worldwide. But the reaction to the news about H1N1 has been nearly hysterical, not by researchers who calmly poke their noses into high-risk settings but by ordinary people who imagine large-scale scenarios of death and dying. Given the changes in our ability to launch an antiviral "war" we should regard this disease as a serious problem — and one for which we have a coordinated repertoire of responses. A serious problem, Yes; a crisis, No.   6

---

[1] *ancien régime* (para. 3): The social, political, and aristocratic system in France from the Middle Ages to the eighteenth century, which was replaced by the French Republic after the French Revolution in 1789.

---

[2] Romanovs (para. 3): Russia's last imperial family dynasty, which ruled the country from 1613 to the Russian Revolution of 1917.

---

[3] Bolsheviks (para. 3): Revolutionary Communist political party that came to power in Russia in 1917.

A captivating example of overreaction involves the volatile responses   7
to a 1998 article in *Lancet*,[4] which described an alleged new disorder
called autistic enterocolitis. The authors stated unequivocally that they
had *not* established a connection between the measles, mumps, and
rubella (MMR) vaccine and this new condition. But at a post-publication
press conference, one of the authors surprised his coauthors and recom-
mended that children should have the opportunity to receive the vaccines
separately, with a year between doses. Though the article itself had not
made a splash, this single remark ignited a furious reaction that caught
the imagination of the media. The result was a decrease in the number of
children whose parents approved of the vaccine, a decrease that produced
a *real* threat of an outbreak of measles — and all because of the overreaction of the press and public to one stray remark from one coauthor that
was disavowed by his colleagues.

In the firefight that followed that single comment, the debate on   8
the subject turned into a "crisis," and collective emotions crowded out
potential candidates for the cause of autism.
Researchers seek to provide premises that
are true, and the combination of logic and
fact is at the heart of science. Denying
the value of either is what overreaction is
about. But by avoiding reality, some parents
ignored the ordinary standards of evidence,
and crazy ideas flourished.

> We have a choice
> between thinking
> in Dr. Seuss terms,
> and in reflective
> adult ways.

Overreaction points to mythical thinking, a way of embodying our   9
emotions and impulses in tales of our fears, vulnerabilities, and guilt in
strange, often colorful, stories. We dread our powerlessness and concoct
magical cures for our weakness. Such thinking is regressive. That myths
are the outcome of the flight from reality, that we hop from one myth
to the other and supplant reason with emotion, tells us that we have
regressed. We've chosen ways of thinking found in children, tribal cultures, and dreams.

There is a moral dimension to all this. We are not children anymore.   10
We are not mere mythmakers. We know fairy tales don't solve the problems that plague us. We have a choice between thinking in Dr. Seuss
terms, and in reflective adult ways. When we don't acknowledge this
internal dichotomy, we are acting in bad faith.

A troubling side to this collective self-deception — the detach-   11
ment of people from themselves — is what we call alienation. In order

---

[4] *The Lancet* (para. 7): A well-respected, peer-reviewed, weekly medical journal,
which has been published since 1823.

to construct myths that replace reality, we deny not merely the world beyond ourselves, but the world within. To varying extents, we have to distance ourselves from our own identity, from the knowledge of who we are, what we want, and how we want to live. That many Americans have fled from themselves seems self-evident, given their total immersion in diversionary activities, in multiple iterations of ESPN or the Internet, in their surrender to the panoply of forces that have usurped their privacy and in their vague displeasure that things are not going their way.

What is the difference between reaction and overreaction? At the 12 simplest level, a reaction to a *real* event means responding in a realistic way — taking facts into account, avoiding fairy tales, and being logical. People who act in their own best interest assess things realistically. They don't use mythical ideas; they don't reason with their emotions; they don't hop from one crisis to another.

In the case of overreaction, just the opposite applies. The hyper- 13 emotionality attached to the mythical imagination eclipses logical reflection, while the serial, episodic nature of excess emotion moves on to new pastures with strange regularity. Overreaction, by definition, ignores reality — even though reality is the provenance of the challenging event. Instead of realism, it withdraws into a private, subjective realm of dreamy thought, lacking logical structure and ignoring the facts of the case.

In increasing numbers, we are choosing our own interiors over the 14 real world in which we live.

VOCABULARY/USING A DICTIONARY
1. What are the meaning and origin of the word *animated* (para. 2)? What terms are related to it?
2. What is a *mutation* (para. 5)? What other words share its origins?
3. What is the origin of the word *volatile* (para. 7)? What does it mean?

RESPONDING TO WORDS IN CONTEXT
1. In paragraph 3, Savodnik refers to "tectonic" historical departures and changes. What does the word *tectonic* suggest in this context?
2. The writer discusses "mythical thinking" in paragraph 9, a practice he associates with "children, tribal cultures, and dreams." What connotations do *tribal cultures* have? Why do you think he uses the phrase?
3. According to Savodnik, when we do not acknowledge the "internal dichotomy" between childish, mythical thinking and "reflective adult" thinking, we act "in bad faith" (para. 10). What does it mean to act in *bad faith*?

DISCUSSING MAIN POINT AND MEANING

1. What is Savodnik's thesis? Where does he state it?

2. According to the writer, Americans are "overreacting to events" (para. 1). How does he define *overreaction*? What are its characteristics?

3. Savodnik makes general claims that Americans are overreacting to perceived crises. What specific examples does he provide to support his argument?

EXAMINING SENTENCES, PARAGRAPHS, AND ORGANIZATION

1. In paragraph 8, Savodnik writes: "Researchers seek to provide premises that are true, and the combination of logic and fact is at the heart of science. Denying the value of either is what overreaction is about." Could that second sentence be worded in a better way? How would you rewrite it?

2. What is the purpose of paragraph 3? How does it further Savodnik's overall argument?

3. In paragraph 10, Savodnik writes: "We have a choice between thinking in Dr. Seuss terms, and in reflective adult ways." Throughout the essay, he relies on a series of interrelated oppositions to structure his argument. What are these oppositions? How are they related to one another?

THINKING CRITICALLY

1. According to Savodnik, how does the media encourage overreaction? Why do you think this occurs?

2. Savodnik writes, "Overreaction points to mythical thinking..." (para. 9). What is "mythical thinking," according to the writer? Does it provide an accurate explanation for overreactions to contemporary "crises"? Are there any problems with his account of "mythical thinking"?

3. In paragraph 10, Savodnik writes: "There is a moral dimension to all this." What does that mean, exactly? Do you agree? Explain.

IN-CLASS WRITING ASSIGNMENTS

1. According to Savodnik, "We have a choice between thinking in Dr. Seuss terms, and in reflective adult ways" (para. 10). Write a compare-and-contrast essay explaining, in your own terms, the difference between these two kinds of thinking.

2. Savodnik writes, "Americans are overreacting to events" (para. 1). Have you ever "overreacted" to an issue, problem, or crisis? Give a specific example and explain your response.

3. Near the end of his article, Savodnik generalizes about the "alienation" of Americans. He claims that many "have fled from themselves" and

chosen "total immersion in diversionary activities, in multiple iterations
of ESPN or the Internet, in their surrender to the panoply of forces that
have usurped their privacy and in their vague displeasure that things are
not going their way" (para. 11). Do you agree with this assessment? How
do you respond to Savodnik's claims?

Erica Zucco (student essay)

Quit Living in Swine Fear

[*The Maneater*, University of Missouri Columbia,
September 4, 2009]

BEFORE YOU READ
How did you respond to the recent swine flu outbreak? What kinds of threats
and dangers worry you the most? Do you think our culture and media over-
hype crises?

WORDS TO LEARN
Chancellor (para. 1): Chief executive
of a university (noun).
anthrax (para. 5): An often fatal bac-
terial infection that afflicts cattle,

sheep, and other mammals and
can be transmitted to humans by
contaminated animal products
(noun).

A s a (self-diagnosed) hypochondriac, this is not a good week for   1
me. Since the college's Chancellor sent out the swine flu e-mail
to students Monday, I've made three "emergency" trips to Wal-
greens for essentials. Three kinds of hand sanitizer? Got 'em. An economy
pack of surface wipes? Check. Bottled water, canned food and processed
snacks? On it.

Starting yesterday, I've turned all public doorknobs with a tissue. I   2
wash my hands so often they're probably going to chap soon and I ingest
Vitamin C like it's my job. I am 100 percent convinced that tomorrow

---

*Erica Zucco, a journalism major, graduated from the University of Missouri in
2010. She worked for* The Maneater, *where this article first appeared, for three
years as staff writer, section editor, and columnist.*

I will be quarantined to my room with only *Dawson's Creek*[1] and oatmeal to keep me company.

> It's essentially a normal flu — so why are people in such hysterics about it? Call it the Culture of Fear.

The thing is, there's really nothing I can   3
do. The flu spreads fast and easily and if you (a) go to class, (b) go to the Student Recreation Complex or (c) step on campus regularly, chances are you've at least brushed shoulders with someone who has it, so we've probably all at least been exposed. It's essentially a normal flu — so why are people in such hysterics about it? Call it the Culture of Fear.

We live in a time and place where the interaction of the media, public policymakers and corporations, sometimes by accident and at other times on purpose, constantly issue widespread reports of danger. Right now the hot topic is H1N1. I've reported at a TV station, a newspaper and a radio station, and in many cases in all of these media outlets we chose to include (or to lead with) a hot-issue story even if it wasn't really that newsworthy or a huge danger. And when we call for the government to do something and they do, it can confirm there actually is a threat. When bottled water companies warned us to stock up before the new millennium, people bought it because they had already been assured by the government this will "protect" them.   4

In *False Alarm: The Truth about the Epidemic of Fear*, Marc Siegel asserts we fear things we shouldn't and we don't fear the things we should. We prepare for instances of mass bio-terrorism and forget to turn hair straighteners off in the bathroom. Chances are, it's much more likely the straightener will set off a cosmetic fire than an entire city will be affected by anthrax. We ignore the threat of more probable dangers and instead take precautions against irrational fears. And while we may take comfort in the fact that we're doing something, we are actually creating for ourselves a culture of fear. There are probably a few positive results from this, but for the most part, it means we live in a constant state of concern.   5

So what can we do to fix this? The easiest way is to think about all of the realistic things we could be doing instead of preparing for the worst. Considering that the probability of a disastrous event is minimal, you can respond to an overblown threat by changing the channel or turning the page. There are certainly some dangers that are very real, but we need   6

---

[1] *Dawson's Creek*: American television drama series that initially aired from 1998 to 2003.

to use both our own judgment and that of people we trust to discern between the actual and the exaggerated.

With all of this in mind, I'm still swigging the orange juice and carrying a mini Bath and Body Works hand gel in my purse . . . but I'm done freaking out about touching doorknobs or going to class. We should live in such a way that the only stress we have is real stress, and the things we fear are actually real. Become a part of that change.   7

VOCABULARY/USING A DICTIONARY

1. Zucco uses "three kinds of hand sanitizer" (para. 1). Where does the word *sanitizer* come from? What other terms are related to it?
2. What does the word *quarantined* mean (para. 2)? What are its origins?
3. According to Zucco, we should "live in such a way that the only stress we have is real stress" (para. 7). Where did the word *stress* originate? What other words share its roots?

RESPONDING TO WORDS IN CONTEXT

1. Zucco is a self-described (and "self-diagnosed") "hypochondriac" (para. 1). What is a *hypochondriac,* and why is this detail important in the context of her essay?
2. What does it mean to be in "hysterics" (para. 3) about the swine flu? What other words might Zucco have used?
3. At the end of the essay, Zucco writes that she is "done freaking out about touching doorknobs or going to class" (para. 7). What word or phrase could be used as a synonym for *freaking out*? Would it be as effective? Why or why not?

DISCUSSING MAIN POINT AND MEANING

1. According to Zucco, *why* are people in "hysterics" over the swine flu?
2. Zucco argues that the media contributes to the "Culture of Fear" (para. 3). What role does it play? How is it complicit with both the government and corporations?
3. The writer claims that we live in a "constant state of concern" (para. 5). What does she propose as a solution?

EXAMINING SENTENCES, PARAGRAPHS, AND ORGANIZATION

1. In her first paragraph, Zucco deliberately uses sentence fragments and bad grammar ("Got 'em"). Why do you think she does this? What does such usage contribute to her essay?
2. Where in the essay does Zucco incorporate outside research? Does she do so effectively?

3. In paragraph 4, the writer refers to her time as a reporter at a TV station, a newspaper, and a radio station. Why does she bring up this personal experience at this point in the essay?

THINKING CRITICALLY

1. According to Zucco, "bottled water companies warned us to stock up before the new millennium" (para. 4). What is she referring to? Is it a good example? How might she make this point about the "new millennium" stronger?

2. The writer implies that the media, public policy makers, and corporations deliberately cultivate the "Culture of Fear" (para. 3). Do you agree? Why would they do this?

3. Zucco indirectly raises questions about trust in government. Does the government play a helpful role in determining real "threats" and effective responses? Do you trust the government to protect you from danger?

IN-CLASS WRITING ACTIVITIES

1. Zucco writes that, too often, people "ignore the threat of more probable dangers and instead take precautions against irrational fears" (para. 5). Do you agree? Have you observed this phenomenon in your own life or in your observations of others and of society in general?

2. "Quit Living in Swine Fear" argues that we live in an agitated, anxious, and fearful culture. Could the opposite case be made, as well? Is there any evidence that people are complacent or even oblivious about major problems and dangers?

3. According to Zucco, we live in a "Culture of Fear" (para. 3). What other qualities or characteristics define our culture? Choose one, and then write an essay in which you explain and illustrate how we live in a Culture of _____.

Summarizing Professional Research and Opinion

In writing a short opinion paper, you will frequently find it necessary to summarize briefly an article, a book, or a professional research study that supports your position. Why is this necessary? You need to do this because it demonstrates to readers that your position is not simply based on your own impressions or experiences but has been confirmed by those who are presumably experts. Observe how Erica Zucco, a student at the University of Missouri Columbia, does this in her essay, "Quit Living in Swine Fear." In informal opinion essays, writers — unless the assignment requires it — do not need to cite a full bibliography. Zucco simply and clearly mentions the author and title of a book that supports her point that our fears are often exaggerated. Given the scope of her paper, she can't quote extensively from the book, but she does offer an effective summary that's relevant to her main point.

1
Brief citation of the book and author

2
Book's summary supports writer's main argument

In *False Alarm: The Truth about the Epidemic of Fear,* Marc Siegel (1) asserts we fear things we shouldn't and we don't fear the things we should. We prepare for instances of mass bio-terrorism and forget to turn hair straighteners off in the bathroom. Chances are, it's much more likely the straightener will set off a cosmetic fire than an entire city will be affected by anthrax. We ignore the threat of more probable dangers and instead take precautions against irrational fears. (2) And while we may take comfort in the fact that we're doing something, we are actually creating for ourselves a culture of fear. . . .

STUDENT WRITER AT WORK
Erica Zucco

RA. What inspired you to write this essay? And publish it in your campus paper?

EZ. I read Marc Siegel's *False Alarm: The Truth about the Epidemic of Fear* right when the H1N1 scare was gaining traction, and it all clicked. Because I am a journalist, the role of the media in creating a "culture of fear" especially interests me, and I wanted to decode the common response to H1N1 and find a way that we could avoid unnecessary panic.

RA. Have you written on this topic since? Have you read or seen other work on the topic that has interested you? If so, please describe.

EZ. Not this specific topic, no. I think Siegel's book is a great starting point, though, for anyone interested in the topic!

RA. Do you generally show your writing to friends before submitting it? Do you collaborate or bounce your ideas off others? To what extent did discussion with others help you develop your point of view on the topic you wrote about?

EZ. My college roommates were the best sounding board! Most of my friends and I have very different experiences, backgrounds, and points of view, so throwing out ideas always brings in ideas from everywhere on the ideological spectrum.

RA. What do you like to read? What magazines and newspapers do you read most frequently?

EZ. I love reading — books, newspapers, magazines, Web content, all of it. It's hard for me to narrow magazines down, especially, because I read through stacks every month. When it comes to writing, though, my favorites are *The Economist, The Atlantic, Vanity Fair, Mother Jones,* and *Rolling Stone.* Each day, I also skim through the *Chicago Tribune,* the *New York Times,* the *LA Times,* and the *Washington Post.*

RA. Are you pursuing a career in which writing will be a component?

EZ. I plan to pursue a career in journalism, working across mediums, and writing forms the foundation of any good broadcast, Web, or print story — so yes, absolutely!

RA. What advice do you have for other student writers?

EZ. Write! Write about anything and everything for anyone that will let you. Find people who are willing to work with you, to read what you write, and to help you make your voice stand out. Anyone can learn how to write well: how to use appropriate grammar, spelling and style — but only you have your own unique voice. Use it!

The Cold War and the Fallout Shelter

A half century ago, Americans were terrified that their country would be attacked by the Soviet Union. The struggle between the two nations, usually referred to metaphorically as the Cold War (since we never formally declared war against each other), began shortly after World War II and lasted for decades, though it had subsided by the 1970s and was generally considered over by the time the Soviet Union fell in 1991. The Cold War was at its height in the 1950s, when Americans daily felt the threat of nuclear missiles and Soviet bombers. Every town had its fallout shelters (the old black and yellow signs can still be seen in many cities), and millions of citizens volunteered for Civil Defense posts where they would search the skies for enemy aircraft that could be identified from government-distributed booklets. Schoolchildren experienced frequent emergency drills and at the sound of an alarm would crawl under their desks as they prepared themselves for a devastating explosion. Hoping to be more secure, countless Americans built or purchased their own fallout shelters. Some, like the one pictured on the next page, could be quite elaborate.

© Bettmann/Corbis.

© Bettmann/Corbis.

Discussing the Unit

SUGGESTED TOPIC FOR DISCUSSION

No one disputes the existence of real threats, from environmental concerns to terrorism. Yet, how should we respond to them? How can we differentiate sensational or media-hyped crises from real crises? Does society pay political, social, and economic costs for being in a constant state of anxiety? If so, what are those costs?

PREPARING FOR CLASS DISCUSSION

1. All the essays in this unit discuss the role that the media plays in encouraging a sense of crisis and fear. Zucco even writes that "you can respond to an overblown threat by changing the channel or turning the page." Yet to be informed, we must rely on the media and other sources. Where do you go for your information? How do you evaluate sources? How do they help you distinguish between problems, crises, and hysteria?

2. Both "What Should You Worry About?" and "All Crisis, All the Time" discuss the tendency of Americans to overreact. Do you think Savodnik would

agree with Levitt and Dubner? How would you compare and contrast their essays? How do the tones and styles of the authors differ?

FROM DISCUSSION TO WRITING

1. Savodnik seems pessimistic about our ability to handle crises in the future, as people are increasingly choosing "their own interiors over the real world in which we live." In contrast, Levitt and Dubner believe human ingenuity will be stronger than any problems we face. Which position do you agree with, and why?

2. Savodnik argues that contemporary forms of entertainment lead to alienation, self-deception, disconnection, and detachment from reality. He writes, "That many Americans have fled from themselves seems self-evident, given their total immersion in diversionary activities. . . ." Do you agree with his assessment?

QUESTIONS FOR CROSS-CULTURAL DISCUSSION

1. These writers focus on fear and crisis in the United States as a whole. But to what degree do our backgrounds and identities—national, ethnic, racial, religious, class, gender—inform and shape our fears and our reactions to crises? Do you see differences, in your own life and in the lives of others?

2. The essays in this unit cover crises such as global warming and swine flu. But in the United States, racial, ethnic, and cultural differences have often led to conflict, fear, and crisis. For example, immigration remains a controversial topic that drives the anxiety of many Americans. Black Americans and white Americans have a long history of conflict, tension, and mutual fear. More recently, fears about terrorism have led to heightened tensions with Muslim communities, both in America and abroad. How do such cultural differences create anxiety and fear? Do you think these fears are overblown, or valid? How might they be alleviated?

6

How Is Today's Media Altering Our Language?

Can educators blame the new media technology for encouraging sloppy writing and careless reading—or are the new styles of writing and reading a blessing in disguise? How will blogs, Web sites, and social media affect the way we understand meaning and evaluate information? In "The New Literacy," Clive Thompson, a media columnist for *Wired* magazine, examines new educational research which shows that one result of all the new ways we can now instantly communicate is that "young people today write far more than any generation before them." In a "Spotlight on Research" feature called "This Is Your Brain on the Web," *The Wilson Quarterly* magazine offers a brief survey of additional research on how the new media is affecting today's reading and writing. All these new forms of communication—Facebook, Twitter, Web sites, etc.—will also supply us with a new, vital source for understanding language, as Erin McKean forecasts in "Redefining Definition." A prominent dictionary expert, McKean sees the Web as dramatically altering what traditional dictionaries do.

With more and more people, especially college students, dependent on the Internet as a source of information, how will the growing popularity of blogs and instant opinion change the way we respond to news? A University of Central Arkansas student, Aprille Hanson, worries that the public is growing increasingly negligent about journalistic standards. In "Stop Relying on Bloggers for News," she cites a recent opinion poll that deeply troubles her: "I believe this poll brings about a horrifying realization: Non-reporters are more trusted than actual journalists." Bloggers are often ridiculed by serious journalists, and in "How to Write an Incendiary Blog Post" Chris Clarke, a popular blogger himself, satirically suggests why blogging may be more artifice than art.

How did people "instant message" before the days of the Internet? "America Then . . . 1844–2006" features the cutting-edge communication technology of its time — the telegram, an item that most young people have only seen, if at all, in old movies.

Clive Thompson

The New Literacy

[*Wired*, September 2009]

BEFORE YOU READ

How do you perceive your intended audience when you write on a social-networking site? What about when you write a school paper? What, if anything, changes when you put your thoughts into words for a class assignment vs. in "everyday" writing?

WORDS TO LEARN

pundits (para. 1): learned people or authorities (noun).

dehydrated (para. 1): deprived of water (verb).

illiteracy (para. 1): a lack of ability to read and write (noun).

rhetoric (para. 2): the ability to use language effectively (noun).

mammoth (para. 2): huge (adjective).

scrutinize (para. 2): to examine in detail (verb).

paradigm (para. 5): model or pattern (noun).

adept (para. 6): very skilled (adjective).

asynchronous (para. 6): not occurring at the same time (adjective).

quotidian (para. 7): something that occurs daily (noun).

brevity (para. 8): briefness (noun).

deploy (para. 8): to arrange or move strategically (verb).

proliferation (para. 8): a rapid increase (noun).

exegesis (para. 8): critical explanation or interpretation of a text (noun).

As the school year begins, be ready to hear pundits fretting once again about how kids today can't write — and technology is to blame. Facebook encourages narcissistic blabbering, video and PowerPoint have replaced carefully crafted essays, and texting has dehydrated language into "bleak, bald, sad shorthand" (as University College of London English professor John Sutherland has moaned). An age of illiteracy is at hand, right? 1

Andrea Lunsford isn't so sure. Lunsford is a professor of writing and rhetoric at Stanford University, where she has organized a mammoth 2

Clive Thompson, who covers science, technology, and culture, is a contributing writer for the New York Times Magazine *and a columnist for both* Wired *and* Slate *magazines. He appears regularly on NPR, CNN, and other media outlets.*

project called the Stanford Study of Writing to scrutinize college students' prose. From 2001 to 2006, she collected 14,672 student writing samples — everything from in-class assignments, formal essays, and journal entries to emails, blog posts, and chat sessions. Her conclusions are stirring.

"I think we're in the midst of a literacy revolution the likes of which we haven't seen since Greek civilization," she says. For Lunsford, technology isn't killing our ability to write. It's reviving it — and pushing our literacy in bold new directions.   3

The first thing she found is that young people today write far more than any generation before them. That's because so much socializing takes place online, and it almost always involves text. Of all the writing that the Stanford students did, a stunning 38 percent of it took place out of the classroom — life writing, as Lunsford calls it. Those Twitter updates and lists of 25 things about yourself add up.   4

It's almost hard to remember how big a paradigm shift this is. Before the Internet came along, most Americans never wrote anything, ever, that wasn't a school assignment. Unless they got a job that required producing text (like in law, advertising, or media), they'd leave school and virtually never construct a paragraph again.   5

> But is this explosion of prose good, on a technical level? Yes.

But is this explosion of prose good, on a technical level? Yes. Lunsford's team found that the students were remarkably adept at what rhetoricians call *kairos* — assessing their audience and adapting their tone and technique to best get their point across. The modern world of online writing, particularly in chat and on discussion threads, is conversational and public, which makes it closer to the Greek tradition of argument than the asynchronous letter and essay writing of 50 years ago.   6

The fact that students today almost always write for an audience (something virtually no one in my generation did) gives them a different sense of what constitutes good writing. In interviews, they defined good prose as something that had an effect on the world. For them, writing is about persuading and organizing and debating, even if it's over something as quotidian as what movie to go see. The Stanford students were almost always less enthusiastic about their in-class writing because it had no audience but the professor: It didn't serve any purpose other than to get them a grade. As for those texting shortforms and smileys defiling *serious* academic writing? Another myth. When Lunsford examined the work of first-year students, she didn't find a single example of texting speak in an academic paper.   7

Of course, good teaching is always going to be crucial, as is the mastering of formal academic prose. But it's also becoming clear that online media are pushing literacy into cool directions. The brevity of texting and status updating teaches young people to deploy haiku-like concision. At the same time, the proliferation of new forms of online pop-cultural exegesis — from sprawling TV-show recaps to 15,000-word videogame walkthroughs — has given them a chance to write enormously long and complex pieces of prose, often while working collaboratively with others.   8

We think of writing as either good or bad. What today's young people know is that knowing who you're writing for and why you're writing might be the most crucial factor of all.   9

VOCABULARY/USING A DICTIONARY

1. What does it mean if something is *asynchronous* (para. 6)? How does it differ from something *synchronous*?
2. From what language is the word *rhetoric* (para. 2) derived? What is a *rhetorician*?
3. What does the word *collaboratively* (para. 8) mean? What part of speech is it? What does it mean to *collaborate* on something?

RESPONDING TO WORDS IN CONTEXT

1. Thompson quotes a professor who says texting is an example of "bleak, bald, sad shorthand" (para. 1). What is the definition of *bald* in this context?
2. Thompson writes that "Facebook encourages narcissistic blabbering" (para. 1). What is a *narcissist*?
3. How do you understand what is meant by the phrase "online pop-cultural exegesis" (para. 8)? To what does this refer?

DISCUSSING MAIN POINT AND MEANING

1. Do we write more or less than we used to? How does Thompson explain the similarities and differences between past and current approaches to writing?
2. What role does technology play in the lives of people writing today? How do you understand writers and good writing based on Thompson's version of the "new literacy"?
3. In this essay, what alternative is presented to viewing writing as "good" or "bad"?

EXAMINING SENTENCES, PARAGRAPHS, AND ORGANIZATION

1. What is the benefit of including the data from Lunsford in the early sections of this essay? What would be the effect of using it later or not at all?

2. What is the effect of including the information about *kairos* (para. 6) in the essay? Does it connect to other ideas in the essay?

3. What sections of the essay validate the conclusion that "today's young people know … that knowing who you're writing for and why you're writing might be the most crucial factor of all" (para. 9)?

THINKING CRITICALLY

1. Do you believe that texting or writing on social-networking sites counts as a form of literacy? Why or why not?

2. How do you understand the idea of an audience for one's writing? How does the audience change depending on what's being written?

3. Do you believe that the "brevity of texting and status updating" (para. 8) equals concise writing? Why or why not?

IN-CLASS WRITING ACTIVITIES

1. Explore Facebook or another social-networking site. What can you gather about the individuals who are writing on it from what you see there? Do you think they have a sense of their audience, as Thompson suggests? Why or why not?

2. In a brief essay, examine your writing process. Consider a school paper you've written recently or something you've blogged about — or both. What sort of preparation took place before you wrote it? What sort of revisions took place? Describe how you feel about the work that went into the writing and the end result, and consider elements of good writing as you do so: structure, word choice, style, and anything else that comes to mind.

3. Write an essay that explores the effect of technology on writing today. What sort of innovations have taken place? How has it changed the way we write and the way we read? Do you believe Andrea Lunsford's comment: "I think we're in the midst of a literacy revolution the likes of which we haven't seen since Greek civilization"? Give evidence in your essay that supports your position.

Spotlight on Research

Rebecca J. Rosen

This Is Your Brain on the Web

[*The Wilson Quarterly*, Autumn 2009]

Rebecca J. Rosen is associate editor at The Wilson Quarterly.

As scientists begin to bear down on the cognitive differences between reading 1
online and off, they are discovering that the two activities are not the same at all.

Numerous studies have shown that we don't so much *read* online as *scan*. 2
In a series of studies from the early 1990s until 2006, Jakob Nielsen, a former
Sun Microsystems engineer, and Don Norman, a cognitive scientist, tracked
the eye movements of Web surfers as they skipped from one page to the next.
They found that only 16 percent of subjects read the text on a page in the
order in which it appeared. The rest jumped around, picking out individual
words and processing them out of sequence. "That's how users read your precious content," Nielsen cautions Web designers in his online column. "In a
few seconds, their eyes move at amazing speeds across your Web site's words
in a pattern that's very different from what you learned in school."

Nielsen recommends that designers create Web sites that are easy to 3
comprehend by scanning: one idea per paragraph, highlighted keywords, and
objective-sounding language so readers don't need to perform the mental
heavy-lifting of determining what's fact and what's bias or distortion.

It is particularly hard to hold readers' attention online because of all the 4
temptations dangled before them. Psychologists argue that our brains are
naturally inclined to constantly seek new stimuli. Clicking on link after link,
always looking for a new bit of information, we are actually revving up our
brains with dopamine, the overlord of what psychologist Jaak Panksepp has
called the "seeking system."

This system is what drives you to get out of bed each day, and what 5
causes you to check your e-mail every few minutes; it's what keys you up
in anticipation of a reward. Most of your e-mail may be junk, but the prospect of receiving a meaningful message — or following a link to a stimulat-
ing site — is enough to keep your brain constantly a bit distracted from what
you're reading online.

What are the effects on the brain of all this distraction? Scientists are only 6
beginning to answer this question. A recent study by three Stanford researchers found that consummate multitaskers are, in fact, terrible at multitasking.
In three experiments, they were worse at paying attention, controlling their
memories, and switching between tasks than those who prefer to complete
one task at a time. Clifford Nass, one of the researchers, says, "They're suckers
for irrelevancy. Everything distracts them." Unable to discriminate between
relevant material and junk, multitaskers can get lost in a sea of information.

The things we read on the Web aren't likely to demand intense focus 7
anyway. A survey of 1,300 students at the University of Illinois, Chicago,
found that only five percent regularly read a blog or forum on politics,
economics, law, or policy. Nearly 80 percent checked Facebook, the social
networking site.

Maryanne Wolf, director of the Center for Reading and Language 8
Research at Tufts University, says it's not just what we read that shapes us,
but the fact that we read at all. She writes, "With [the invention of reading],
we rearranged the very organization of our brain, which in turn expanded the
ways we were able to think, which altered the intellectual evolution of our
species." When children are just learning to read, their brains show activation in both hemispheres. As word recognition becomes more automatic, this
activity is concentrated in the left hemisphere, allowing more of the brain to
work on the task of distilling the meaning of the text and less on decoding it.
This efficiency is what allows our brains the time to think creatively and ana-
lytically. According to Wolf, the question is, "What would be lost to us if we
replaced the skills honed by the reading brain with those now being formed
in our new generation of 'digital natives'?"

In the end, the most salient difference isn't between a screen and a page 9
but between focused reading and disjointed scanning. Of course, the former
doesn't necessarily follow from opening a book and the latter is not inherent to opening a Web browser, but that is the pattern. However, that pattern
may not always hold true. Google, for example, recently unveiled Fast Flip, a
feature designed to recreate the experience of reading newspapers and magazines offline. Other programs, such as *The New Yorker*'s digital edition or *The
New York Times*' Times Reader 2.0, have a similar purpose, allowing readers
to see on the screen something much like what they would normally hold
between their two hands. And with the Kindle and other e-readers quickly
catching on, we may soon find that reading in the future is quite like reading
in the past.

Until such innovations move into wider use, the surest bet for undis- 10
tracted reading continues to be an old-fashioned book. As historian Marshall
Poe observes, "A book is a machine for focusing attention; the Internet is [a]
machine for diffusing it."

Erin McKean

Redefining Definition: How the Web Could Help Change What Dictionaries Do

[*New York Times Magazine*, December 20, 2009]

BEFORE YOU READ

Have you ever considered where dictionary definitions come from? Who writes them? How might consensus be reached on what a word "means"?

WORDS TO LEARN

blithely (para. 1): merrily (adverb).

incontrovertible (para. 1): indisputable (adjective).

arbiter (para. 1): a judge (noun).

tentative (para. 2): unsure or uncertain (adjective).

consensus (para. 2): general agreement (noun).

derive (para. 2): to reach by reasoning (verb).

ostensible (para. 3): apparent (adjective).

abstract (para. 3): apart from concrete realities (adjective).

arbitrarily (para. 5): randomly (adverb).

preface (para. 5): the introductory part (noun).

dissimilitude (para. 5): dissimilarity (noun).

optimal (para. 6): most favorable (adjective).

organic (para. 9): derived from living organisms (adjective).

If anything is guaranteed to annoy a lexicographer, it is the journalistic habit of starting a story with a dictionary definition. "According to *Webster's*," begins a piece, blithely, and the lexicographer shudders, because she knows that a dictionary is about to be invoked as an incontrovertible authority. Although we may profess to believe, as the linguist Dwight Bolinger once put it, that dictionaries "do not exist to define but to help people grasp meanings," we don't often act on that belief. Typically we treat a definition as the final arbiter of meaning, a scientific pronouncement of a word's essence.

Erin McKean was formerly the editor-in-chief of American dictionaries for Oxford University Press and currently is chief executive and founder of Wordnik.com.

But the traditional dictionary definition, although it bears all the   2
trappings of authority, is in fact a highly stylized, overly compressed and
often tentative stab at capturing the consensus on what a particular word
"means." A good dictionary derives its reputation from careful analysis of
examples of words in use, in the form of sentences, also called citations.
The lexicographer looks at as many citations for each word as she can find
(or, more likely, can review in the time allotted) and then creates what is,
in effect, a dense abstract, collapsing into a few general statements all the
ways in which the word behaves. A definition is as convention-bound as
a sonnet and usually more compact. Writing one is considered, at least by
anyone who has ever tried it, something of an art.

Despite all the thought and hard work that go into them, defini-   3
tions, surprisingly, turn out to be ill suited for many of the tasks they
have been set to — including their ostensible purpose of telling you the
meaning of a word. Overly abstract definitions are often helpful only
if you come to them already primed by context. It's difficult to read a
definition like "(esp. of a change or distinction) so delicate or precise
as to be difficult to analyze or describe," and have *subtle* immediately
spring to mind; or to come across "reduce the force, effect or value of"
and think of *attenuate*.

Definitions are especially unhelpful to children. There's an oft-cited   4
1987 study in which fifth graders were given dictionary definitions and
asked to write their own sentences using the words defined. The results
were discouraging. One child, given the word *erode*, wrote, "Our family
erodes a lot," because the definition given was "eat out, eat away."

Neither are definitions complete pictures of all the possible mean-   5
ings of a word. One study found that in a set of arbitrarily chosen passages from modern fiction, an average of 13 percent of the nouns, verbs
and adjectives were used in senses not found in a large desk dictionary.
And of course there are some words that simply elude definition, a problem even Samuel Johnson faced. In the preface to his groundbreaking
Dictionary of the English Language, he wrote, "Ideas of the same race,
though not exactly alike, are sometimes so little different that no words
can express the dissimilitude, though the mind easily perceives it when
they are exhibited together." We all have had Johnson's experience of
"easily perceiving" differences between words that we cannot as easily
describe — quick: what's the difference between *louche* and *raffish*? Most
people, when asked what a word means, resort to using it in a sentence,
because that's the way we learn words best: by encountering them in
their natural context.

Given these shortcomings of definitions, and the advantages of   6
examples, why do we still cling to definitions? The short answer, for

hundreds of years, has been a practical one: space — specifically the lack thereof. Print dictionaries have never had sufficient page-room to show enough real, live, useful examples to create an optimal and natural word-learning experience. Even the expert lexicographers at the *Oxford English Dictionary,* which famously includes "illustrative quotations" alongside its definitions, still put the definition and its needs first, making new words wait their turn to make it through the definition bottleneck.

The near-infinite space of the Web gives us a chance to change all 7
this. Imagine if lexicographers were to create online resources that give, in addition to definitions, many living examples of word use, drawn not just from literature and newspapers but from real-time sources of language like Web sites, blogs and social networks. We could build people's confidence in their ability to understand and use words naturally, from the variety of contexts in which words occur. Indeed, this is what my colleagues and I are trying to accomplish at the online dictionary Wordnik. com: we're using text-mining techniques and the unlimited space of the Internet to show as many real examples of word use as we can, as fast as we can.

This approach is especially useful for grasping new words and uses: 8
if you look up *tweet* on a site like mine, for example, you understand that the word is used to refer to messages sent via Twitter; there's no waiting for an editor to write you a definition; plus there are examples of tweets right on the page. Online, you can also look up just the form of a word you're interested in — say, *sniped* instead of *snipe* — and find precise examples. A word is so much more than its meaning: it's also who uses it, when it was used, what words appear alongside it and what kinds of texts it appears in.

> A word is so much more than its meaning.

Without privileging definitions, dictionary-making would involve 9
more curation and less abridgment, less false precision and more organic understanding. If we stop pretending definitions are science, we can enjoy them as a kind of literature — think of them as extremely nerdy poems — without burdening them with tasks for which they are unsuited.

VOCABULARY/USING A DICTIONARY

1. McKean writes that "overly abstract definitions are often helpful only if you come to them already *primed* by context" (para. 3) What does it mean to *prime* something?
2. What is a *lexicographer* (para. 1)? What is a *lexicon*?
3. What is the root of the word *dissimilitude* (para. 5)?

RESPONDING TO WORDS IN CONTEXT

1. What does it mean for a dictionary to have a *reputation* (para. 2)?
2. If a book is *abridged* (para. 9—*abridgment*), what has happened to it?
3. Who do you think McKean is referring to when she mentions her "colleagues" (para. 7)?

DISCUSSING MAIN POINT AND MEANING

1. A child learns the meaning of *erode* is to "eat out, eat away" and misuses *erode* in a sentence: "My family erodes a lot." Why does that sort of thing happen even when the definition is clear?
2. Why is the suggestion made to think of definitions as poems and not as science?
3. According to McKean, what will change our need to "cling to definitions" (para. 6)?

EXAMINING SENTENCES, PARAGRAPHS, AND ORGANIZATION

1. How does the inclusion of so many words and definitions within the essay influence the reader's view of what a dictionary can do?
2. McKean states: "Typically we treat a definition as the final arbiter of meaning, a scientific pronouncement of a word's essence" (para. 1). What does she mean?
3. What problem does McKean have with the pronouncement "According to *Webster's*" that often begins an essay?

THINKING CRITICALLY

1. Do you feel convinced that the Web will create new possibilities for the dictionary and how words are understood? Why or why not?
2. Why is writing a definition to a word considered "something of an art" (para. 2)? How do you imagine the people who write definitions begin their process?
3. How can an Internet dictionary make use of the Internet's "near-infinite space"?

IN-CLASS WRITING ACTIVITIES

1. Go to Wordnik.com. After exploring the site, write an informative essay that gives the reader an overview of the site and its usefulness or difficulties as you see them. How does it compare to a regular dictionary? Include examples of words you might search for and various approaches to defining them.
2. What is your experience with print dictionaries? How often do you use them to find the meaning of a word? If you don't ever use a dictionary, how do you approach learning the meaning of words you don't know?

3. Research the creation of important dictionaries, such as *Webster's*, and write an essay that provides an outline of how the dictionary came into being and how its reputation was established. Who worked on it? How has it been revised? Why is it still revered today?

Aprille Hanson (student essay)

Stop Relying on Bloggers for News

[*The Echo*, The University of Central Arkansas, April 7, 2010]

BEFORE YOU READ
Where do you go to get information about current events? Do you rely on older, trusted news sources, or do you go to a blog or other source? Why is one source more appealing than the other? Do you believe you are getting accurate information you can trust?

WORDS TO LEARN
controversial (para. 1): debatable; polemical (adjective).
assassination (para. 1): a sudden, secret, premeditated murder of someone (noun).
satirical (para. 3): pertaining to or characterized by satire (the use of sarcasm or ridicule to expose a truth) (adjective).
analyze (para. 4): to examine critically (verb).

crusaders (para. 5): people who engage in a crusade (a vigorous movement that defends or advances a cause) (noun).
blog (para. 6): a Weblog of personal thoughts (noun).
burden (para. 9): a load; something borne with difficulty (noun).
deter (para. 10): to discourage or prevent (verb).
bulk (para. 12): the greater part (noun).

On July 17, 2009, Walter Cronkite, one of the world's most   1
respected journalists, died at the age of 92. Not only was
Cronkite respected, but he proudly wore the title of the "most
trusted man in America." The title came from a 1972 magazine poll for

Aprille Hanson graduated magna cum laude from the University of Central Arkansas in the spring of 2010. She worked for The Echo *in various capacities for all four years of her college career, including as editor-in-chief for three semesters.*

his constant coverage on controversial issues such as the Vietnam War and President John F. Kennedy's assassination.

Time magazine conducted an online poll on July 24, 2009, to try to figure   2
out who is the most trusted newscaster in America now that Cronkite is no longer in our midst. The choices given were: Katie Couric, Charlie Gibson, Brian Williams, and shockingly, the comedic newscaster Jon Stewart of *The Daily Show with Jon Stewart*. The results were as follows: Couric, 7 percent; Gibson, 19 percent; Brian Williams, 29 percent; Stewart, 44 percent.

Yes, ladies and gents, the most trusted man in America is in fact a   3
satirical newscaster, whose main priority is not to report the news, but to make people laugh. Cronkite shaped journalism for generations and had such a following that he even caused President Lyndon B. Johnson to make the remark: "If I've lost Cronkite, I've lost Middle America."

Let's analyze Jon Stewart's achievements in journalism. He is a show-   4
man, a comedian, a television writer and an actor. He's won a Grammy, but has he ever won a Pulitzer? Though this may be comical to some, I believe this poll brings about a horrifying realization: Non-reporters are more trusted than actual journalists. *USA Today* journalist DeWayne Wickham stated a valid point in a past column that really brings this point home: "What should worry us is that as the ranks of newspaper journalists shrink, no amount of satirists will be able to fill this void."

After the Watergate scandal, government wasn't trusted and hasn't   5
been able to regain the trust it had before that fateful event. At the time, journalists were revered as the crusaders of truth. Sometime between then and now, journalists have been placed on that same platform of mistrust. Though it's not clear when this divide happened, one thing is certain: it doesn't look like it's changing anytime soon.

Politics play a big role in where people find their news. For conserva-   6
tives, it's Fox News. Liberals hate Fox News for claiming it's a "No Spin Zone," when it is clear it caters to a conserva-tive outlook. For liberals, it's MSNBC. Conservatives hate MSNBC for trying to push the "Liberal Agenda." For the Americans who don't fit into the categories of highly conservative or highly liberal, finding a news source is difficult. To simply avoid the whole political circus, most of today's youth are getting their information from anyone with a computer who wants to add their commentary on a subject — in short, a blog.

> For the Americans who don't fit into the categories of highly conservative or highly liberal, finding a news source is difficult.

Getting information from anywhere but a trained reporter makes as   7
much sense as getting surgery from someone who plays the board game

"Operation" every day as opposed to a real surgeon. This is not to say that all bloggers or satirical journalists cannot do a decent job of reporting the news or are always wrong. However, they do not have the necessary skills it takes to hold themselves to a higher standard of reporting.

Like it or not, journalists are trained in Associated Press style, how   8
to interview, how to research the facts, how to be objective and above all, report the truth. Bloggers or satirical journalists do not have these boundaries to follow. Though these differences may seem minor, it's these lines that dictate who is more credible. To be clear, it is not the job of a journalist to be objective in every type of article he or she writes. Reviews and columns are not meant to be objective, but offer a means for us to share the author's opinion on a subject. Other articles, however, should be held to the highest standard of objectivity.

Every reader should realize the difference in professionalism between   9
a blogger or a comedian and a reporter and stop selling themselves short when it comes to knowledge. However, the burden does not only fall upon the reader — it's also up to the journalists.

As in every job there are those that don't do their best. Some jour-   10
nalists, news stations and newspapers don't take the concept of objectiv-
ity as seriously as they should. But those few rotten apples should not ruin journalism's professional respectability. The challenge is for publish-
ers and owners to hold its staff to a higher standard, but regardless of whether this will ever fully be achieved, it is our challenge as readers not to let it deter us from getting our news.

There are many credible news sources out there and committing   11
yourself to finding them will be more beneficial in the long run than trying to find a credible blog. Though there's no clear way of finding a completely credible source, there are some things to watch out for. If a newspaper or news station has been around for decades, it will usually be a more valuable source than one that hasn't been around long. Also, if a news source has won several prestigious awards, such as Pulitzer's, it's safe to say it is being praised for its credibility. For example, the *New York Times* has been around since 1851 and every year for the past ten years and on, it has won at least one Pulitzer.

If you're still not sure about the credibility of news sources, picture   12
this scenario: When we're old, how comforting will it be to know that we've gained the bulk of our knowledge from a jobless, middle-aged man sitting in his underwear, eating a burrito, typing his latest thought on a subject to his blog? Or would we rather take a chance and trust a trained, professional journalist? The answer is obvious, but the choice is yours. Do your job as readers and we'll do our job as journalists and strive to become the most trusted people in America once again.

VOCABULARY/USING A DICTIONARY

1. What does the word *priority* (para. 3) mean?
2. What is the difference between *liberals* and *conservatives* (para. 6)?
3. Explain what Hanson means by *professionalism* (para. 9).

RESPONDING TO WORDS IN CONTEXT

1. What is *spin* (para. 6) in the news?
2. What does Hanson mean in paragraph 5 when she refers to a "platform of mistrust"?
3. Define the word *credible* (para. 11). How is it related to the word *incredible*?

DISCUSSING MAIN POINT AND MEANING

1. What are the differences that Hanson points out between a journalist and a blogger?
2. Why is it surprising that Jon Stewart is more trusted as a newscaster than Katie Couric, Charlie Gibson, or Brian Williams? Why is it not surprising?
3. What sort of skills are needed to be a reliable journalist? What skills are needed to be a blogger?

EXAMINING SENTENCES, PARAGRAPHS, AND ORGANIZATION

1. Do you think Hanson's use of questions is effective in the final paragraph? How do they affect her conclusion?
2. What is the effect of including the percentage results of the poll about "most trusted newscasters"?
3. Hanson offers a metaphor in paragraph 7, saying, "Getting information from anywhere but a trained reporter makes as much sense as getting surgery from someone who plays the board game 'Operation' every day as opposed to a real surgeon." Does she back that metaphor up elsewhere in her essay? Where?

THINKING CRITICALLY

1. Do you think that bloggers are credible as journalists? Why or why not?
2. How might a comedian report the "truth" about current events?
3. If a publisher or newspaper owner wants to hold its journalists to a standard of objective truth, how might they do that?

IN-CLASS WRITING ACTIVITIES

1. Why do you think people have come to trust bloggers as much as or more than trained journalists? Do you go to multiple news sources to learn about different events? Do you trust one "reporter" in particular? Why? Write an essay that explains your point of view on these questions. Include details about what sources you trust for news.

2. Hanson provides some information on Walter Cronkite. Research Cronkite's career online and the events taking place at the time he was reporting. Choose one particular news event and write about Cronkite's coverage. Discuss why his reporting might have been valuable, and why it was valued by the public at the time.

3. In this essay, Hanson states, "The *New York Times* has been around since 1851 and every year for the past ten years and on, it has won at least one Pulitzer." Take a look at the front page of the *New York Times* (online or in print). Describe the stories you see there. What topics are covered on the front page? Do you have a sense of the scope of the news beyond the front page? Do you think the reporting you see there is Pulitzer-worthy? Explain why or why not.

Developing Ideas through Comparison and Contrast

One of the most common ways to develop the central idea of a paragraph or even an entire essay is by setting up two contrasting positions. A historian, for example, examines the Battle of Gettysburg by contrasting the different military strategies of Union versus Confederate generals. Or a sportswriter contrasts the tennis tactics of Venus Williams with those of her sister, Serena. Depending on the writer's goal, such contrasts can be briefly stated or compose nearly the entire body of the essay. Observe how University of Central Arkansas student Aprille Hanson effectively develops several paragraphs by contrasting the differences between trained journalists and bloggers or satirical journalists.

Hanson's point is that there is a difference of professionalism between a trained journalist who has strict guidelines to follow and someone who doesn't but writes news stories just the same. Note how she maintains the contrast in the following two paragraphs.

1
Hanson contrasts two common sources of news information

Getting information from anywhere but a <u>trained reporter</u> makes as much sense as getting surgery from someone who plays the board game "Operation" every day as opposed to a real surgeon. This is not to say that all <u>bloggers or satirical journalists</u> (1) cannot do a decent job of reporting the news or are always wrong. However, they do not have the necessary skills it takes to hold themselves to a higher standard of reporting.

1

2
Hanson offers reasons for her contrast

Like it or not, journalists are trained in Associated Press Style, how to interview, how to research the facts, how to be objective and above all, report the truth. Bloggers or satirical journalists do not have these boundaries to follow. Though these differences may seem minor, it's these lines that dictate who is more credible. (2) To be clear, it is not the job of a journalist to be objective in every type of article he or she writes. Reviews and columns are not meant to be objective, but offer a means for us to share the author's opinion on a subject. Other articles, however, should be held to the highest standard of objectivity.

STUDENT WRITER AT WORK
Aprille Hanson

RA. What inspired you to write this essay? And publish it in your campus paper?

AH. I was inspired to write this essay after sitting in my persuasion class and listening to a discussion my fellow students were having. Many students in the class were discussing the unreliability of the media and how they frequently go to blogs or Twitter to get their news. Since I am a print journalism major, I understand how much training goes into becoming a reporter, and to actually trust someone with no training over a reporter does not seem like a thought-out decision. I wanted to write an article that emphasizes protecting the intelligence of the future generation by pushing them to once again trust the media.

RA. Are your opinions unusual or fairly mainstream given the general climate of discourse on campus?

AH. My opinions in this article tend to be unusual compared to the thoughts of most students on campus. However, the reason for writing the article was to help show students that relying on Twitter, Facebook, and satirical comedians for news is not logical. You wouldn't go to a journalist to get a laugh, so why go to a comedian for news?

RA. How long did it take for you to write this piece? Did you revise your work? What were your goals as you revised?

AH. With research included, it probably took me about two hours to write the article. I have been writing columns for *The Echo* for years and have taken an editorials and review writing class so it usually doesn't take me very long to sort out my thoughts for a column. My main goal as I revised was clarity. Since this was somewhat a persuasion column, I wanted to make sure my point was clear and easy for the reader to understand or else my point wouldn't have gotten across.

RA. What do you like to read? Please let us know what specific magazines and newspapers (print and online) you read most frequently.

AH. I like to read a variety of publications because I believe that if you're going to be a well-rounded individual, it's best to branch out. I enjoy reading articles on MSNBC.com, the *New York Times*, the *Arkansas Democrat-Gazette*, *Time* magazine, and *Reader's Digest*.

RA. What advice do you have for other student writers?

AH. Write for your college's publication. Whether it is a student newspaper or a literary magazine, having the freedom to try new styles of writing, make mistakes, and learn from them is the best thing student writers can do. The main question at every newspaper where I applied for a job was, "Have you ever worked on your college newspaper?" It's the same for most writing jobs. Flexing those writing muscles outside of the classroom in a college setting will help you use the tools you've learned in class. Being pushed out of your writing comfort zone is the only way to improve and learn.

Chris Clarke

How to Write an Incendiary Blog Post

[*Boston.com*, February 14, 2010]

BEFORE YOU READ

How do you understand and absorb what you read on the Internet? Is the material you read expected or unexpected? Does it ever provoke a response from you?

WORDS TO LEARN

tenuous (para. 1): weak (adjective).

inference (para. 1): conclusion (noun).

trite (para. 2): hackneyed; stale (adjective).

egregiously (para. 3): glaringly; flagrantly (adverb).

intemperate (para. 3): unrestrained (adjective).

refutation (para. 3): the act of showing a statement to be false (noun).

acronyms (para. 3): abbreviations formed by initial letters (noun).

intent (para. 5): purpose (noun).

incendiary (para. 7): pertaining to the setting on fire of something; to inflame or excite (adjective).

corollary (para. 7): something; that naturally follows (noun).

ingratiate (para. 8): to gain favor with effort (verb).

T his sentence contains a provocative statement that attracts the readers' attention, but really has very little to do with the topic of the blog post. This sentence claims to follow logically from the

1

Environmental and natural history author Chris Clarke has published in a wide variety of print and online journals, including Camas, Orion, Bay Nature, California Wild, *the* New Internationalist, Berkeley Insider, *and* The East Bay Monthly. *He is the author of the popular blog* Coyote Crossing, *and the memoir* Walking with Zeke: A Familiar Story *(2008).*

first sentence, though the connection is actually rather tenuous. This sentence claims that very few people are willing to admit the obvious inference of the last two sentences, with an implication that the reader is not one of those very few people. This sentence expresses the unwillingness of the writer to be silenced despite going against the popular wisdom. This sentence is a sort of drum roll, preparing the reader for the shocking truth to be contained in the next sentence.

This sentence contains the thesis of the blog post, a trite and obvious statement cast as a dazzling and controversial insight.   2

This sentence claims that there are many people who do not agree with the thesis of the blog post as expressed in the previous sentence. This sentence speculates as to the mental and ethical character of the people mentioned in the previous sentence. This sentence contains a link to the most egregiously ill-argued, intemperate, hateful, and ridiculous example of such people the author could find. This sentence is a three-word refutation of the post linked in the previous sentence, the first of which three words is "Um." This sentence implies that the linked post is in fact typical of those who disagree with the thesis of the blog post. This sentence contains expressions of outrage and disbelief largely expressed in Internet acronyms. This sentence contains a link to an Internet video featuring a cat playing a piano.   3

This sentence implies that everyone reading has certainly seen the folly of those who disagree with the thesis of the blog post. This sentence reminds the reader that there are a few others who agree. This sentence contains one-word links to other blogs with whom the author seeks to curry favor, offered as examples of those others.   4

This sentence returns to the people who disagree with the thesis of the blog post. This sentence makes an improbably tenuous connection between those people and a current or former major political figure. This sentence links those people and that political figure to a broad, ill-defined sociodemographic class sharing allegedly similar belief systems. This sentence contains a reference to the teachings of Jesus; its intent may be either ironic or sincere.   5

This sentence refers to a different historic period, and implies that conditions relevant to the thesis of the blog post were either different or the same. This sentence states that the implications of the previous sentence are a damned shame. This sentence says that the next sentence will explain the previous sentence. This sentence contains a slight rewording of the thesis of the blog post, a trite and obvious statement cast as a dazzling and controversial insight.   6

This sentence contains an apparent non sequitur phrased as if it follows logically from the reworded thesis of the blog post. This sentence is a wildly overgeneralized condemnation of one or more entire classes of   7 people phrased in as incendiary a fashion as possible which claims to be an obvious corollary to the thesis and non sequitur.

This sentence proposes that anyone who might disagree with the wildly overgeneralized condemnation is, by so disagreeing, actually proving the author's point. This sentence explains that such people disagree primarily because of the author's courageous, iconoclastic approach. This sentence mentions the additional possibilities that readers who express disagreement with the wildly overgeneralized condemnation are merely following political fashion or trying to ingratiate themselves with interest groups. This sentence is a somewhat related assertion based in thoughtless privilege and stated as dispassionate objective truth. This sentence explains that if the scales would merely fall from those dissenting readers' eyes, they would see the wisdom and necessity of the author's statements. 8

> This sentence invites readers to respond freely and without constraint as long as those responses fall within certain parameters.

This sentence invites readers to respond freely and without constraint as long as those responses fall within certain parameters. This sentence consists of an Internet in-joke that doesn't quite fit the topic. 9

VOCABULARY/USING A DICTIONARY
1. Define the word *blog* (para. 1).
2. What is meant by the word *folly* in paragraph 4?
3. What is an *iconoclast*? What is an *iconoclastic approach* (para. 8)?

RESPONDING TO WORDS IN CONTEXT
1. What is a *non sequitur* (para. 7)?
2. What does it mean "to curry favor" (para. 4)?
3. Clarke writes: "This sentence contains a reference to the teachings of Jesus; its intent may be either ironic or sincere" (para. 5). What does it mean to "be either ironic or sincere"?

DISCUSSING MAIN POINT AND MEANING
1. Do you feel that the writer has instructed you on how to write an incendiary blog post?
2. The writer describes those who disagree with the "thesis of the blog post" and writes, "This sentence contains expressions of outrage and disbelief largely expressed in Internet acronyms." How does the sentence shed light on how you are to read this essay?
3. Why might this essay be considered "incendiary"?

EXAMINING SENTENCES, PARAGRAPHS, AND ORGANIZATION

1. What is the effect of organizing the sentences in this essay to repeat or be very similar in structure?
2. Is there anything confusing about the way this author puts sentences together within each paragraph? Where or why do you feel lost?
3. What is the effect of starting a sentence with the phrase "this sentence"?

THINKING CRITICALLY

1. Would you describe the information presented here as abstract or concrete? Explain.
2. Why might the writer include "a link to an Internet video featuring a cat playing a piano," "a reference to the teachings of Jesus," and a reference to people "merely following political fashion or trying to ingratiate themselves with interest groups" in this essay?
3. Why do you think this essay includes a sentence that "invites readers to respond freely and without constraint as long as those responses fall within certain parameters"?

IN-CLASS WRITING ACTIVITIES

1. This essay was first written as a blog post and then reprinted in a newspaper. How does knowing where it appeared change your impression of the essay, if at all? Explain in a short essay.
2. Explain the uses of a blog. Based on what you have come in contact with, what information is usually covered in a blog? How is a blog similar to or different from other kinds of writing?
3. Who is the audience for this essay? How can you tell? Write a brief essay explaining your answer.

The Telegram

Radio relay towers, about 50 miles apart, will gradually replace thousands of miles of telegraph poles and wires.

Now, telegrams "leapfrog" storms

through RCA Radio Relay

With the radio relay system, developed by RCA, Western Union will be able to send telegraph messages without poles and wires between principal cities.

"Wires down due to storm" will no longer disrupt communications. For this new system can transmit telegrams and radiophotos by invisible electric microwaves. These beams span distances up to fifty miles between towers and are completely unaffected by even the angriest storms. Moreover, the radio relay system is less costly to build and maintain.

This revolutionary stride in communications was made possible by research in RCA Laboratories— the same "make it better" research that goes into *all* RCA products.

And when you buy an RCA Victor radio or television set or Victrola* radio-phonograph, or even a radio tube replacement, you enjoy a unique pride of ownership. For you know, if it's an RCA it is one of the finest instruments of its kind that science has achieved.

Radio Corporation of America, RCA Building, Radio City, New York 20, N.Y. . . . Listen to The RCA Victor Show, Sundays, 4:30 P.M., Eastern Time, over NBC Network.

Research in microwaves and electron tubes at RCA Laboratories led to the development by the RCA Victor Division of this automatic radio relay system. Here you see a close-up view of a microwave reflector. This system also holds great promise of linking television stations into networks.

 RADIO CORPORATION of AMERICA

*Victrola, T. M. Reg. U. S. Pat. Off.

An ad (c. 1940) promoting the technology of the telegram.

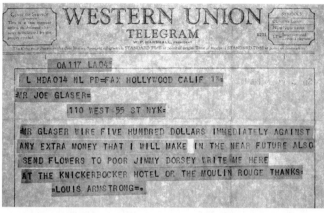

© Mario Tama/Getty Images.

An undated telegram, probably sent in the early 1940s, from the legendary jazz musician Louis Armstrong (1901–1971) to his manager.

Long before text-messaging and e-mail, and earlier than fax machines and long-distance telephone calls, there was the telegram. Through much of the nineteenth and the first half of the twentieth centuries, sending a telegram was the easiest and fastest way of communicating with someone at a distance. European inventors and scientists experimented with various machines to send written messages as early as the 1790s. In the United States, working independently, a Yale graduate and well-known portrait painter Samuel F. B. Morse (1791–1872) received a patent for an electrical telegraph in 1837. Because so many others had worked up telegraphic systems with codes, it is difficult to credit Morse as *the* inventor of the telegraph. What he did essentially was, with the assistance of other scientists and instrument designers, to develop the first "user-friendly" machine with a convenient code of dots and dashes representing the alphabet and numeric system. Though there were other codes, the Morse code quickly became the worldwide standard.

Despite some successful early demonstrations, Morse encountered difficulties for years in persuading Congress to grant him the money to lay a telegraph line between Washington, D.C., and Baltimore so he could prove once and for all the value of his idea. The central idea, of course, was that messages could be sent by means of electrical current. He and his small group of associates kept fine-tuning the system, extending the power of batteries and transmission capacity, and simplifying the machine's "finger-key" and the code so that more words could be tapped out per minute. In 1844, Congress finally approved funds. After a few errors — Morse first tried laying the wires underground and then found it worked better to string them on poles — Washington, D.C., was electrically connected with Baltimore. On May 24, 1844, Morse sent from the U.S. Supreme Court a one-sentence message, the first electrical telegram. The message, apparently chosen by the daughter of a patent official, was "What hath God wrought!" She borrowed the exclamation from the King James Bible: "Surely there is no enchantment against Jacob, neither is there any divination against Israel: according to this time it shall be said of Jacob and of Israel, What hath God wrought!" (Num. 23:23).

Over the next decade, Morse's telegram system grew tremendously, as America became "wired" for the first time. In 1857, the Western Union Company, which became synonymous with *telegram*, was born. In January 2006, Western Union, unable to compete with the ease of e-mail, sent its last telegram. An entire verbal culture, one that often prided itself on brief, economical messages (since senders paid for telegraphs by the word) came to an end, as one technology inevitably replaced another.

Discussing the Unit

SUGGESTED TOPIC FOR DISCUSSION

All of the essays in this unit explore the ways in which language is being used and broadcast, written and interpreted. Are we becoming more literate in new and bold ways? Is the Internet furthering our understanding of language or is it adding to our confusion? Where do you go for information and "truth," and how do you help shape that truth?

PREPARING FOR CLASS DISCUSSION

1. Who are bloggers? What are they trying to achieve? Draw information from at least two of the essays in this chapter to support your answer.
2. What is the role of the Internet today? Does it determine most of our interests and activities? How do the writers in this chapter support or contradict your idea of the place the Internet holds in your life?

FROM DISCUSSION TO WRITING

1. If you were to go to a blog frequently for news or to gather other information, what would you hope to find there? Using the essays that

explore the use of the Internet as a tool for knowledge, write a brief essay that shows how we use this technological tool to deepen our understanding of the world.

2. How do the writers of these essays convince you that one type of writing is "good" and another "bad"? Using their criteria, what is good or bad writing? Are their standards similar to yours? Write a brief essay that compares the viewpoint of the authors in this chapter to your own.

TOPICS FOR CROSS-CULTURAL DISCUSSION

1. Today's students grew up with computers as a way of life; students of previous generations did not. What cultural differences between generations are pointed out in these essays? How does the new literacy compare with the old literacy? Are the values held by the followers of Cronkite the same values held by the followers of Stewart? How might you "define" the generation who uses the print dictionary as opposed to the generation who uses the Internet?

2. Thompson states, "Students today almost always write for an audience (something virtually no one in my generation did)" (para. 7) and that "gives them a different sense of what constitutes good writing." Does that hold true for Americans of various cultural and ethnic backgrounds? How do audiences vary depending on these backgrounds? How do their differences shape what is thought of as good writing?

7

Gender Roles: Should Women Act More Like Men?

Whether there are real, biologically caused differences between the ways men and women think, act, speak, and behave has remained an important sidebar in the debates over feminism and sexism. If, aside from trifling physical differences, men and women are more or less exactly alike psychologically, doesn't that indicate conclusively that they should be treated alike? But what if they aren't? Take the character traits of aggression and arrogance. In his well-publicized controversial blog "A Rant about Women," Clay Shirky, a New York University communications teacher, worries that even the most talented women fall behind men because they are less willing to be self-assertive and self-promoting: "I sometimes wonder what would happen," he writes, "...if my college spent as much effort teaching women self-advancement as self-defense." Responding to Shirky's advice in an *American Prospect* column, "Swagger Like Us," Ann Friedman argues that just acting like men will not alone advance women's professional lives: "It will take a long time—and a lot of conscious effort—to dispel deeply ingrained stereotypes about work and gender."

Workplace gender stereotypes can occur in many industries, even the most glamorous, as Kim Elsesser provocatively maintains in "And the Gender-Neutral Oscar Goes To...." Americans would be outraged, Elsesser claims, if there were separate awards for white and black actors, so why "is it considered acceptable to segregate nominations by sex, offering different Oscars for best actor and best actress?"

For centuries women were considered the "weaker sex," and men were expected to protect, respect, and honor them according to a medieval code known as "chivalry." But with the expansion of feminist ideals and the rise of independent women, the practice of chivalry began to seem quaint and condescending. Writing on the occasion of Valentine's Day, Boise State University student Shannon Morgan decides to take a new look at medieval gender roles. In "Defending Camelot: Chivalry Is Not Dead," she imagines a new chivalry for the twenty-first century: "I propose that modern chivalry should be gender-neutral; it can apply to any sexual orientation, and can cross cultures." Modern chivalry, she suggests, would encourage women to behave more like men and men more like women.

Finally, in our "Spotlight on Research" feature, journalist Tom Jacobs cites a recent study that examines how the titles of popular romance novels help answer the age-old question: "What do women want?"

Clay Shirky

A Rant about Women

[Clay Shirky Blog, *Shirky.com*, January 2010]

BEFORE YOU READ

Do you ever engage in self-promotion? Are men better at promoting themselves than women are? How much do you care about what people think of you? Is it ever okay to lie to get ahead in your career?

WORDS TO LEARN

superlative (para. 1): surpassing or superior to all others (adjective).

incarceration (para. 7): imprisonment, time in jail (noun).

fickle (para. 12): likely to change, unstable, unsteady (adjective).

correlates (para. 20): establishes an orderly connection between; places in a mutual relationship (verb).

So I get email from a good former student, applying for a job and asking for a recommendation. "Sure," I say, "Tell me what you think I should say." I then get a draft letter back in which the student has described their work and fitness for the job in terms so superlative it would make an Assistant Brand Manager blush.

So I write my letter, looking over the student's self-assessment and toning it down so that it sounds like it's coming from a person and not a PR department, and send it off. And then, as I get over my annoyance, I realize that, by overstating their abilities, the student has probably gotten the best letter out of me they could have gotten.

Now, can you guess the gender of the student involved?

Of course you can. My home, the Interactive Telecommunications Program at NYU, is fairly gender-balanced, and I've taught about as

1

2

3

4

Clay Shirky is a specialist in the field of Internet technologies and teaches new media at New York University's Interactive Telecommunications Program. His writing has appeared in the New York Times, *the* Wall Street Journal, Wired, *the* Harvard Business Review, *and other periodicals. His books include* Voices from the Net *(1995) and* Here Comes Everybody: The Power of Organizing without Organizations *(2008).*

many women as men over the last decade. In theory, the gender of my former student should be a coin-toss. In practice, I might as well have given him the pseudonym Moustache McMasculine for all the mystery there was. And I've grown increasingly worried that most of the women in the department, past or present, simply couldn't write a letter like that.

This worry isn't about psychology; I'm not concerned that women   5
don't engage in enough building of self-confidence or self-esteem. I'm worried about something much simpler: Not enough women have what it takes to behave like arrogant self-aggrandizing jerks.

Remember David Hampton, the con artist immortalized in *Six*   6
Degrees of Separation,[1] who pretended he was Sidney Poitier's son? He lied his way into restaurants and clubs, managed to borrow money, and crashed in celebrity guest rooms. He didn't miss the fact that he was taking a risk, or that he might suffer. He just didn't care.

It's not that women will be better off being con artists; a lot of con   7
artists aren't better off being con artists either. It's just that until women have role models who are willing to risk incarceration to get ahead, they'll miss out on channelling smaller amounts of self-promoting con artistry to get what they want, and if they can't do that, they'll get less of what they want than they want.

There is no upper limit to the risks men are willing to take in order   8
to succeed, and if there is an upper limit for women, they will succeed less. They will also end up in jail less, but I don't think we get the rewards without the risks.

* * *

When I was 19 and three days into my freshman year, I went to see Bill   9
Warfel, the head of grad theater design (my chosen profession, back in the day), to ask if I could enroll in a design course. He asked me two questions. The first was "How's your drawing?" Not so good, I replied. (I could barely draw in those days.) "OK, how's your drafting?" I realized this was it. I could either go for a set design or lighting design course, and since I couldn't draw or draft well, I couldn't take either.

"My drafting's fine," I said.   10
That's the kind of behavior I mean. I sat in the office of someone   11
I admired and feared, someone who was the gatekeeper for something I wanted, and I lied to his face. We talked some more and then he said, "OK, you can take my class." And I ran to the local art supply place and bought a drafting board, since I had to start practicing.

---

[1] *Six Degrees of Separation*: A 1990 play by John Guare, made into a film in 1993.

That got me in the door. I learned to draft, Bill became my teacher   12
and mentor, and four years later I moved to New York and started doing
my own design work. I can't say my ability to earn a living in that fickle
profession was because of my behavior in Bill's office, but I can say it was
because I was willing to do that kind of thing. The difference between me
and David Hampton isn't that he's a con artist and I'm not; the difference
is that I only told lies I could live up to, and I knew when to stop. That's
not a different type of behavior, it's just a different amount.

And it looks to me like women in general, and the women whose edu-   13
cations I am responsible for in particular, are often lousy at those kinds of
behaviors, even when the situation calls for it. They aren't just bad at behaving like arrogant self-aggrandizing jerks. They are bad at behaving like self-
promoting narcissists, anti-social obsessives, or pompous blowhards, even
a little bit, even temporarily, even when it would be in their best interests
to do so. Whatever bad things you can say about those behaviors, you can't
say they are underrepresented among people who have changed the world.

Now this is asking women to behave   14
more like men, but so what? We ask people
to cross gender lines all the time. We're in
the middle of a generations-long project
to encourage men to be better listeners
and more sensitive partners, to take more
account of others' feelings and to let out our

> We ask people to
> cross gender lines
> all the time.

own feelings more. Similarly, I see colleges spending time and effort teaching women strategies for self-defense, including direct physical aggression.
I sometimes wonder what would happen, though, if my college spent as
much effort teaching women self-advancement as self-defense.

* * *

Some of the reason these strategies succeed is because we live in a world   15
where women are discriminated against. However, even in an ideal future,
self-promotion will be a skill that produces disproportionate rewards, and
if skill at self-promotion remains disproportionately male, those rewards
will as well. This isn't because of oppression, it's because of freedom.

Citizens of the developed world have an unprecedented amount of free-   16
dom to choose how we live, which means we experience life as a giant distributed discovery problem: What should I do? Where should I work? Who
should I spend my time with? In most cases, there is no right answer, just
tradeoffs. Many of these tradeoffs happen in the market; for everything from
what you should eat to where you should live, there is a menu of options, and
between your preferences and your budget, you'll make a choice.

Some markets, though, are two-sided — while you are weighing your 17
options, those options are also weighing you. People fortunate enough
to have those options quickly discover that it's not enough to decide you
want to go to Swarthmore, or get money out of Kleiner Perkins.[2] Those
institutions must also decide if they will have you.

Some of the most important opportunities we have are in two-sided 18
markets: education and employment, contracts and loans, grants and
prizes. And the institutions that offer these opportunities operate in an
environment where accurate information is hard to come by. One of
their main sources of judgment is asking the candidate directly: Tell us
why we should admit you. Tell us why we should hire you. Tell us why we
should give you a grant. Tell us why we should promote you.

In these circumstances, people who don't raise their hands don't get 19
called on, and people who raise their hands timidly get called on less.
Some of this is because assertive people get noticed more easily, but
some of it is because raising your hand is itself a high-cost signal that you
are willing to risk public failure in order to try something.

That in turn correlates with many of the skills the candidate will 20
need to actually do the work — to recruit colleagues and raise money,
to motivate participants and convince skeptics, to persevere in the face
of both obstacles and ridicule. Institutions assessing the fitness of candidates, in other words, often select self-promoters because self-promotion
is tied to other characteristics needed for success.

It's tempting to imagine that women could be forceful and self-confident 21
without being arrogant or jerky, but that's a false hope, because it's other people who get to decide when they think you're a jerk, and trying to stay under
that threshold means giving those people veto power over your actions. To
put yourself forward as someone good enough to do interesting things is,
by definition, to expose yourself to all kinds of negative judgments, and as
far as I can tell, the fact that other people get to decide what they think of
your behavior leaves only two strategies for not suffering from those judgments: not doing anything, or not caring about the reaction.

* * *

Not caring works surprisingly well. Another of my great former students, 22
now a peer and a friend, saw a request from a magazine reporter doing a
tech story and looking for examples. My friend, who'd previously been
too quiet about her work, decided to write the reporter and say "My
work is awesome. You should write about it."

---

[2] *Kleiner Perkins* (para. 17): Well-known venture capital firm that has invested in
companies such as Amazon.com and Google.

The reporter looked at her work and wrote back saying, "Your work   23
is indeed awesome, and I will write about it. I also have to tell you you
are the only woman who suggested her own work. Men do that all the
time, but women wait for someone else to recommend them." My friend
stopped waiting, and now her work is getting the attention it deserves.

If you walked into my department at NYU, you wouldn't say, "Oh   24
my, look how much more talented the men are than the women." The
level and variety of creative energy in the place is still breathtaking to me,
and it's not divided by gender. However, you would be justified in saying,
"I bet that the students who get famous five years from now will include
more men than women," because that's what happens, year after year. My
friend talking to the reporter remains the sad exception.

Part of this sorting out of careers is sexism, but part of it is that men   25
are just better at being arrogant, and less concerned about people thinking we're stupid (often correctly, it should be noted) for trying things
we're not qualified for.

Now I don't know what to do about this problem. (The essence   26
of a rant, in fact, is that the ranter has no idea how to fix the thing
being ranted about.) What I do know is this: It would be good if more
women see interesting opportunities that they might not be qualified for, opportunities which they might in fact fuck up if they try to
take them on, and then try to take them on. It would be good if more
women got in the habit of raising their hands and saying, "I can do that.
Sign me up. My work is awesome," no matter how many people that
behavior upsets.

VOCABULARY/USING A DICTIONARY

1. In paragraph 4, Shirky says that he might as well have given his former
   student the "pseudonym Moustache McMasculine." What is a *pseudonym*? What are the word's origins?

2. The writer claims that women "are bad at behaving like self-promoting
   narcissists . . ." (para. 13). What is a *narcissist*? Where did the term
   originate?

3. Several times in his essay, Shirky refers to "con artists." What is a *con artist*,
   and where does the term come from?

RESPONDING TO WORDS IN CONTEXT

1. Shirky recounts a time that he lied to Bill Warfel, a professor who "was
   the gatekeeper for something I wanted . . ."(para. 11). How is Shirky using
   the word *gatekeeper* here? What connotation does it have? What is its
   significance in this context?

2. According to the writer, we live in a market of choices (professional,
   personal, geographical, etc.). Some markets are one-sided, while others

are "two-sided" (para. 17). What does Shirky mean by a two-sided market? Why is this idea important for his argument?

3. In paragraph 13, Shirky writes, "And it looks to me like women in general, and the women whose educations I am responsible for in particular, are often lousy at those kinds of behaviors, even when the situation calls for it." What sort of word is "lousy"? What does it mean to you? Do you think it's an appropriate word for Shirky to use in this context?

DISCUSSING MAIN POINT AND MEANING

1. In what way is Shirky concerned about women? What distinction does he make in paragraph 5?
2. Shirky discusses the character David Hampton, a con artist in John Guare's 1990 play *Six Degrees of Separation*. How does Shirky distinguish between Hampton's cons and his own?
3. The writer acknowledges that his argument asks "women to behave more like men" (para. 14). Is this a problem? How does he respond to those who might take issue with requiring women to meet a standard set by men?

EXAMINING SENTENCES, PARAGRAPHS, AND ORGANIZATION

1. What is the purpose of paragraphs 9 through 12? How does this story support Shirky's overall argument?
2. Shirky's third paragraph is one sentence long: "Now, can you guess the gender of the student involved?" Is this choice effective? Did you guess the gender of the student? Does it matter if you did or not?
3. The writer's concluding paragraph begins: "Now I don't know what to do about this problem. (The essence of a rant, in fact, is that the ranter has no idea how to fix the thing being ranted about.)" (para. 26). What is a "rant"? Do you accept this disclaimer? Why do you think Shirky placed it here, rather than at the beginning of his essay?

THINKING CRITICALLY

1. Shirky describes a time that he lied to advance his education and career. How do you react to his dishonesty? Do you think he was justified?
2. Shirky refers to qualities like arrogance, narcissism, self-aggrandizement, and pomposity. He writes, "Whatever bad things you can say about those behaviors, you can't say they are underrepresented among people who have changed the world" (para. 13). Do you agree?
3. In evaluating the prospects of women students, Shirky acknowledges that sexism plays a part in the "sorting out of careers" (para. 25). Where do you see sexism? Are you hurt by it? Does it benefit you in any way?

IN-CLASS WRITING ACTIVITIES

1. Shirky wrote his former student a recommendation that sounded like it came "from a person and not a PR department" (para. 2). He notes that applicants for jobs, grants, and other opportunities are often asked directly: "Tell us why we should admit you" (para. 18). How do you respond to situations like this? Is it possible to promote yourself—either in person or in writing—without sounding like a "PR department"? Write a brief "how-to" guide for achieving this balance. What kind of language should you use? What should you avoid?

2. The writer discusses con artists and con artistry in "A Rant about Women." Have you ever been conned? Have you ever conned anyone? Write an essay about the experience.

3. Shirky makes a strong case for the necessity of self-promotion, even if it occasionally requires dishonesty or other kinds of "bad" behavior. Will this essay change the way you "promote" yourself or the way you think about the process? Does your gender play a part in your "self-promotion" skills? Why or why not?

Ann Friedman

Swagger Like Us

[The American Prospect, March 2010]

BEFORE YOU READ

Should women act more like men to compete in the business world? Do women have special talents for leadership and management just because they are women? Are men and women's career prospects shaped by cultural attitudes toward gender?

WORDS TO LEARN

refrain (para. 2): a phrase or verse recurring at intervals in a song or poem (noun).

extolling (para. 4): praising highly (verb).
testosterone (para. 5): male sex hormone (noun).

Ann Friedman is the deputy editor of The American Prospect *and a frequent contributor of political commentary to that periodical and others. She holds degrees in journalism and Spanish literature from the University of Missouri, Columbia and currently lives in Washington, D.C.*

E ver since women began making serious workplace gains in the 1970s, there has been a debate about the best way for them to climb the professional ladder. More often than not, the answer has been to "act like a man" — if you can't beat the boys' club, join it. Oversell yourself in job interviews. Ask for more raises. Demand a better title. Be assertive in expressing your opinion. You're gonna make it after all.

Women have made only marginal professional and political progress over the last decade, yet this simple refrain — be aggressive! B-E aggressive! — still makes for a convenient, can-do solution. In January, new-media guru Clay Shirky published "A Rant about Women" on his blog, summing up this view: "I sometimes wonder what would happen, though, if my college spent as much effort teaching women self-advancement as self-defense. . . . Now this is asking women to behave more like men, but so what? We ask people to cross gender lines all the time."

> Even after decades of women suiting up in shoulder pads and trying to cross that line, we continue to simultaneously embrace the idea that powerful women promise to be different, somehow, from powerful men.

Even after decades of women suiting up in shoulder pads and trying to cross that line, we continue to simultaneously embrace the idea that powerful women promise to be different, somehow, from powerful men. Supposedly, women are natural mediators. Women know how to multitask. Women are more levelheaded. If women ruled the world, it would be more stable, less violent, and color-coordinated.

The idea that what's between your legs determines your management style is also nothing new. LouAnn Brizendine generated a flurry of style-section articles in 2006 when she released her book, *The Female Brain*, about how every woman is "a lean, mean communicating machine." Antifeminist crusader Christina Hoff Sommers has written that "a practical, responsible femininity could be a force for good in the world beyond the family, through charitable works and more enlightened politics and government." And in December, *The Economist* reported on a new breed of "feminist management theorists" who are extolling the virtues of women's kinder, gentler leadership style.

So which is it? Should women be amplifying their aggression to mimic successful men? Or should they try to get ahead by playing up what supposedly makes them different from the testosterone-fueled CEOs who fed one financial bubble after another? The more time you spend thinking about women's stalled progress in the working world — they were only 6.3 percent of corporate top earners last year — the clearer it becomes that neither of these two options is working.

Shirky does not acknowledge that his answer (which says women just need to man up) sets women up for backlash. Women who are loud and proud about their abilities and experience will be declared uppity bitches — or at least privately thought of that way. Studies have shown that employees, both male and female, are wary of working for high-achieving women. And what about women who follow Hoff Sommers' advice (which says women just need to, well, woman up)? They won't even get their applications read, let alone taken seriously. When was the last time you saw "responsible femininity" among desired qualities in a job listing?   6

This is a broad, cultural problem. If, like me, you believe that your biology is not the primary factor in determining your strengths and weaknesses in the workplace, you believe that we are shaped by the society in which we live. Which is to say, there are cultural, structural reasons why men are typically more assertive, more self-promotional, and more successful everywhere from the boardroom to the op-ed pages to the halls of Congress. This is much bigger than women's individual behavior.   7

To use Shirky's own example: Just as self-defense classes are not a solution to the problem of campus rape, self-advancement classes will not, on their own, improve things for women in the professional world. It will take a long time — and a lot of conscious effort — to dispel deeply ingrained stereotypes about work and gender. Women can't do that alone. The burden also falls on people in positions of power — those who are doing the hiring, promoting, recommending, and mentoring — to understand the gender dynamics at play and to push back against them. In my line of work, that means I not only write publicly about the "byline gap" between men and women in political journalism — I actively seek out women writers and encourage them to pitch their ideas. And I'm fairly certain I see more results than an editor who simply professes to care about this issue in the abstract.   8

For decades, we've told women how to get ahead in an unjust system. It's high time we all work to change the system itself.   9

VOCABULARY/USING A DICTIONARY

1. Friedman refers to the common assumption that women are "natural mediators" (para. 3). What is a *mediator*? Where does the word come from? What other words is it related to?

2. According to the writer, "feminist management theorists" extol the "virtues" of women's leadership (para. 4). What is the origin of the word *virtue*? Why might its roots be important in the context of Friedman's essay?

3. The writer claims that assertive women are perceived as "uppity bitches" (para. 6). What does *uppity* mean? What connotations does it have?

RESPONDING TO WORDS IN CONTEXT

1. Friedman concludes her opening paragraph with the sentence, "You're gonna make it after all." What allusion is the writer making here? How does it fit with her overall argument?

2. The writer claims that women have spent decades "suiting up in shoulder pads and trying to cross that line" (para. 3). What is the double meaning in this phrase? How is it related to her main point?

3. According to Friedman, the "idea that what's between your legs determines your management style is also nothing new" (para. 4). Why do you think she chose this specific wording? Is she being euphemistic?

4. The phrase "responsible femininity" appears twice in this essay. How does its meaning change depending on context?

DISCUSSING MAIN POINT AND MEANING

1. What characteristics supposedly distinguish powerful women from powerful men? What "special" skills or talents do women possess?

2. According to Friedman, career-minded women have two choices if they want to compete in the professional world. What are they? What does she think of the two paths?

3. What is Friedman's solution to the problem? What is she doing about it, personally?

EXAMINING SENTENCES, PARAGRAPHS, AND ORGANIZATION

1. How does Friedman use repetition near the end of the third paragraph? What is her tone in these sentences? How is that attitude related to her main point?

2. What is the purpose of paragraph 4? Would the essay be as effective without it? Could she have summarized the paragraph's content more briefly?

3. In paragraph 2, Friedman includes a long quotation from "new media guru" Clay Shirky's blog. Why does she do this? What is the relationship between Shirky's "rant" and "Swagger Like Us"?

THINKING CRITICALLY

1. Friedman writes, "The more time you spend thinking about women's stalled progress in the working world—they were only 6.3 percent of corporate top earners last year—the clearer it becomes that neither of these two options is working" (para. 5). How well does she support her view that women's progress in the working world is "stalled"? What would make her argument more effective?

2. What accounts for the differences between men and women, professionally, according to Friedman? Do you agree? Why or why not?

3. The writer refers to the hypothetical premise "If women ruled the world . . ." (para. 3). She uses the hypothesis to note several common positive stereotypes of women. How would you elaborate on the premise? Do you think the world would be fundamentally different if women "ruled" it?

IN-CLASS WRITING ACTIVITIES

1. Friedman considers debates about the best ways for women to "climb the professional ladder" (para. 1). What does that metaphor mean, exactly? Do you view your current or future career as a ladder? What other figures of speech could you use?

2. According to the writer, "Studies have shown that employees, both male and female, are wary of working for high-achieving women" (para. 6). Does this appear true from your own observations? Explain why you agree or disagree.

3. Do you think your gender will affect your career choices and prospects? How big a role, if any, will it play in shaping your professional life? Will your gender give you any advantages? Any disadvantages?

Kim Elsesser

And the Gender-Neutral Oscar Goes To . . .

[*The New York Times*, March 4, 2010]

BEFORE YOU READ

Why is there an Oscar given for the best "actress," but not for the best "directress"? Are men and women usually evaluated as equals when they work in the same profession? Is gender-neutral language important?

WORDS TO LEARN

segregate (para. 2): to separate (verb).

perpetuate (para. 5): to maintain or preserve (verb).

stereotype (para. 5): a conventional, formulaic, and oversimplified idea, opinion, characterization, or image (noun).

Kim Elsesser is a research scholar at the Center for Study of Women at the University of California, Los Angeles. She specializes in workplace issues.

M any hours into the 82nd Academy Awards ceremony this Sun-   1
day, the Oscar for best actor will go to Morgan Freeman, Jeff
Bridges, George Clooney, Colin Firth or Jeremy Renner. Suppose, however, that the Academy of Motion Picture Arts and Sciences
presented separate honors for best white actor and best non-white actor,
and that Mr. Freeman was prohibited from competing against the likes
of Mr. Clooney and Mr. Bridges. Surely, the academy would be derided
as intolerant and out of touch; public outcry would swiftly ensure that
Oscar nominations never again fell along racial lines.

Why, then, is it considered acceptable to segregate nominations by   2
sex, offering different Oscars for best actor and best actress?

Since the first Academy Awards ceremony in 1929, separate acting   3
Oscars have been presented to men and women. Women at that time had
only recently won the right to vote and were still several decades away from
equal rights outside the voting booth, so perhaps it was reasonable to offer
them their own acting awards. But in the twenty-first century women contend with men for titles ranging from the American president to the American
Idol. Clearly, there is no reason to still segregate acting Oscars by sex.

Perhaps the academy would argue that the separate awards guarantee   4
equity, since men and women have received exactly the same number of
best acting Oscars. And the academy is not
alone in this regard: the Golden Globes, the
Screen Actors Guild, the British Academy
of Film and the Independent Spirit Awards
all split acting nominees by sex as well.

> Just as stewardess-
> es are now called
> flight attendants,
> many actresses
> now prefer to be
> called actors.

But separate is not equal. While it is   5
certainly acceptable for sports competitions like the Olympics to have separate
events for male and female athletes, the biological differences do not affect acting per-
formances. The divided Oscar categories merely insult women, because
they suggest that women would not be victorious if the categories were
combined. In addition, this segregation helps perpetuate the stereotype
that the differences between men and women are so great that the two
sexes cannot be evaluated as equals in their professions.

Today, the number of female-run production companies, female direc-   6
tors and great roles for women continues to increase. Four of the five films represented in this year's best actress category center on strong female characters.

As women gain more influence in Hollywood, even the term   7
"actress" is disappearing. Just as stewardesses are now called flight attendants, many actresses now prefer to be called actors. The Screen Actors
Guild has eliminated the term "actress" in the presentation of its awards,

instead using "female actor." Perhaps, as the term "actress" falls further out of favor, the award-granting organizations will be forced to acknowledge that male and female actors do indeed have the same occupation.

Collapsing two major categories into one would have the added value of reducing the length of the awards show, a move that many viewers would laud. But if the academy wanted to preserve the number of acting awards, it could easily follow the lead of the Hollywood Foreign Press Association, which has, since 1951, offered genre-based Golden Globe honors, for best performances in dramatic, and comedic and musical roles. 8

For next year's Oscars, the academy should modify its ballots so that men and women are finally treated as full equals, able to compete together in every category, for every nomination. And if the academy insists on continuing to segregate awards, then it should at least remain consistent and create an Oscar for best directress. 9

VOCABULARY/USING A DICTIONARY
1. Where does the word *ceremony* (para. 1) come from?
2. According to Elsesser, many viewers would "laud" (para. 8) the shortening of the Oscar awards show. What does *laud* mean? What are its origins? What words are related to it?
3. The writer notes that "even the term 'actress' is disappearing," much as the word "stewardess" has (para. 7). Where does the practice of adding an "-ess" to the end of a word to denote femininity come from?

RESPONDING TO WORDS IN CONTEXT
1. In paragraph 5, the author says, "but separate is not equal" and later in the paragraph uses the term "segregation." What is the origin of these expressions; in other words, in what context do these terms usually appear? Do you think these terms are being applied here appropriately? Why or why not?
2. Elsesser refers to the high number of Oscar-nominated films with "strong female characters" (para. 6). What is a "strong female character"? Why does she note the prevalence of these characters?
3. The writer proposes that the Oscars follow the format of the Hollywood Foreign Press Association, which gives "genre-based Golden Globe honors" (para. 8). What does "genre-based" mean?

DISCUSSING MAIN POINT AND MEANING
1. Elsesser makes her argument primarily by using an extended analogy. What is the comparison?
2. What are the benefits of eliminating gender-based Oscar awards, according to Elsesser?

3. How would you characterize Elsesser's overall tone? For example, does she sound optimistic in this article? Skeptical? Is there any attitude conveyed in her writing style?

EXAMINING SENTENCES, PARAGRAPHS, AND ORGANIZATION

1. How does Elsesser set up her argument in the first two paragraphs? Is it an effective strategy? Why or why not?
2. Does the writer acknowledge counterarguments? Does she address them effectively?
3. Where is the thesis of this essay? How would you restate it in your own words?

THINKING CRITICALLY

1. Elsesser writes that at the first Oscar ceremony, women "were still several decades away from equal rights outside the voting booth" (para. 3). Do men and women have equal rights now? Where do you see inequality between the sexes? Are some disparities justified?
2. When is gender separation acceptable, according to Elsesser? What is her standard for making this judgment? Do you agree?
3. The writer argues that the Academy of Motion Picture Arts and Sciences should change their ballots so that men and women are treated equally. Does this seem like an important issue? Does Elsesser justify its significance effectively?

IN-CLASS WRITING ACTIVITIES

1. Elsesser notes that the word actress is "disappearing," just as "stewardesses are now called flight attendants" (para. 7). Are you aware of gender in your writing? Do you try to write in "gender-neutral" ways? Do you think it matters? Why or why not?
2. The writer refers to "strong female characters" in films (para. 6). Choose such a character from film or fiction; then, explain how she fits this description. What qualities do you associate with "strong female characters"?
3. According to Elsesser, "the divided Oscar categories merely insult women, because they suggest that women would not be victorious if the categories were combined" (para. 5). Do you agree with her inference? Are there other ways of looking at the separate Oscars? Write a persuasive essay that argues either for or against the divided categories.

Shannon Morgan (student essay)

Defending Camelot: Chivalry Is Not Dead

[*Arbiter Online*, Boise State University, February 24, 2010]

BEFORE YOU READ

How would you define *chivalry*? Should men have a special code of manners and behavior in their relationships with women? What rules guide your behavior in romantic relationships?

WORDS TO LEARN

harking back (para. 3): going back to an origin or source (verb).

medieval (para. 3): referring to the "Middle Ages" in Europe, often dated between 476 and 1453 (adjective).

spontaneous (para. 4): arising from a momentary impulse or circumstance (adjective).

I've heard some women say they don't appreciate being patronized by antiquated gestures of chivalry. Women are not the "weaker sex" and we do not need protecting. I've heard some men say they are afraid to be chivalrous because they don't want to disrespect their partner. These men struggle with wanting to employ a time-honored tradition of chivalry without being sexist.

I propose that modern chivalry should be gender-neutral; it can apply to any sexual orientation, and can cross cultures. In honor of Cupid, I'll focus my arguments on the romantic aspects of chivalry, the code of how to treat our intimate partners. If both women and men should strive to be chivalrous, we must first discuss what this means. Chivalry is far more than having good manners. Opening someone's door, helping someone put on a jacket, or picking up the check at dinner are polite gestures, employed by women and men alike, in situations that extend beyond the pursuit of romance.

1

2

Shannon Morgan is the editor-in-chief of The Arbiter. *She will graduate in 2011 from Boise State University, where she is majoring in communications, with minors in political science and history.*

According to chivalrynow.net, "Chivalry spells out certain ethical standards that foster the development of manhood. Men are called to be: truthful, loyal, courteous to others, helpmates to women, supporters of justice, and defenders of the weak. They are also expected to avoid scandal." Harking back to Camelot,[1] chivalry is rooted in a medieval code of honor for knightly men. Let us bring chivalry into the twenty-first century, and have it serve as a moral and ethical code both sexes can follow to help guide relationships. I appreciate traditional gender roles in relationships (to a degree), but I also believe people should be free to find a partner to balance them in the effort to create a meaningful and supportive bond. Whether we are more comfortable in the role of protector, nurturer, or a combination of the two, we can subscribe to the code of chivalry. 3

> Let us bring chivalry into the twenty-first century, and have it serve as a moral and ethical code both sexes can follow to help guide relationships.

Chivalry should be a check on our urges, a compass to ensure we are behaving in ways that cultivate rewarding and supportive relationships. In committed relationships it means we will "avoid scandal" by being faithful, and that we will seek to be just, fair, and discreet with our criticism of our partners. Being chivalrous, in a romantic sense, is intimate. It's affectionate; it's a commitment to being supportive and encouraging of your partner. It is not a spontaneous act, but a concentrated and time-tested effort. It's expressed in small, everyday actions like brewing coffee in the morning, picking your wet towels up off the floor, or taking time to write a love letter or plan a romantic evening. It's also expressed in larger ways, such as being supportive when your partner is in a weakened state. Maybe someone lost a job, or lost a loved one, or experienced a crisis of faith, or suffered a medical catastrophe. Being chivalrous is a commitment to love your partner, not only when it's easy, but when it's hard. It is a commitment to work through problems, to seek to understand before being understood. It's being compassionate, dependable, strong, and kind. Chivalry is about respect. Respect for yourself and for your lover — and the commitment to serve and honor each other. 4

---

[1] *Camelot:* The site of the legendary King Arthur's palace and court, possibly near Exeter, England. Traditionally, it is associated with goodness, beauty, and knightly ideals.

VOCABULARY/USING A DICTIONARY

1. Morgan's article focuses on *chivalry* (para. 1). What are the origins of that word?

2. According to the writer, some women "don't appreciate being patronized by antiquated gestures of chivalry" (para. 1). What does *patronized* mean? What are its roots? What other words are related to it?

3. What does *antiquated* (para. 1) mean? What synonym could Morgan have used in its place?

RESPONDING TO WORDS IN CONTEXT

1. Morgan writes, "Women are not the 'weaker sex' and we do not need protecting" (para. 1). What does she mean, exactly? How do you interpret the phrase "weaker sex"?

2. According to the writer, chivalrous behavior includes being "just, fair, and discreet with our criticism of our partners" (para. 4). What does *discreet* mean in this context? How does it fit in with her definition of chivalry?

3. "Being chivalrous, in a romantic sense, is intimate" (para. 4). What "sense" of the word *romantic* is Morgan using here? What other meanings does that term have? Are any of them applicable here?

DISCUSSING MAIN POINT AND MEANING

1. Morgan wants to bring chivalry "into the twenty-first century" (para. 3). Why do older notions of chivalry need to be revised, according to the writer?

2. According to Morgan, "Chivalry should be a check on our urges" (para. 4). What does that mean? How might chivalric rules restrain "urges"?

3. How might chivalry be expressed, according to the writer?

EXAMINING SENTENCES, PARAGRAPHS, AND ORGANIZATION

1. Morgan begins her essay, "I've heard some women say they don't appreciate being patronized by antiquated gestures of chivalry" (para. 1). Would you describe this sentence as general or specific? How might you improve it as an introduction?

2. According to the writer, "Chivalry is far more than having good manners" (para. 2). Does she clarify this distinction effectively in the second paragraph, or elsewhere in the essay?

3. How would you describe the tone of Morgan's essay? What choices in style and diction contribute to that tone? Does it suit her argument? Why or why not?

THINKING CRITICALLY

1. The writer wants a "gender-neutral" chivalry, as opposed to patronizing, "antiquated," or even chauvinistic chivalry. How do you distinguish between chivalrous behavior and sexist behavior? Where do you draw the line between the two?

2. Morgan writes, "I appreciate traditional gender roles in relationships (to a degree), but I also believe people should be free to find a partner to balance them in the effort to create a meaningful and supportive bond" (para. 3). What part do "traditional gender roles" play in your own romantic relationships? Do you look for "balance"?

3. Do you think good manners are important? How would you define them? What specific practices do they include? What purpose do they serve?

IN-CLASS WRITING ASSIGNMENTS

1. Do you have a "moral and ethical code" that helps you guide your romantic relationships? What is it? Do you have "rules"? Where do they come from? Morgan emphasizes the goal of a "meaningful and supportive bond" (para. 3). Do you share that goal? Does your code reflect that purpose? Do you think your code will change?

2. Morgan cites a definition of *chivalry* from the Web. Research the term on your own. Are there aspects to chivalry that her explanation does not include? Do you think chivalric ideals still persist in our society? If so, where do you see them? What social forces work against them?

3. This essay proposes that we modernize chivalry (para. 3). Do you agree with Morgan? Are her arguments persuasive? Why or why not?

LOOKING CLOSELY

Clearly Expressing the Purpose of Your Essay

In composition, your purpose is your overall goal or aim in writing. It is basically what you hope to accomplish by writing — whether it is to promote or endorse a certain point of view, rally support for a cause, criticize a book or film, or examine the effects of a social trend. Your purpose may or may not be expressed explicitly (in creative writing it rarely is), but in essays and nonfiction it is usually important that the reader understand the purpose behind your writing. An explicitly stated purpose not only helps the reader follow your argument or perspective, but also helps ensure that everything you write reflects that purpose. A carefully expressed purpose will help anchor your essay and keep it from floating aimlessly.

Note how Boise State student Shannon Morgan expresses her purpose in "Defending Camelot: Chivalry Is Not Dead." She begins her Valentine's Day essay by pointing out how men and women feel about chivalric behavior and the difficulties they have with it. Then in paragraph 2 she immediately makes her purpose clear. She is writing the essay to propose a new form of chivalry for our age that benefits both sexes. Note, too, how the remainder of her essay is closely linked to her explicit purpose.

1
Clear statement of purpose

 <u>I propose that modern chivalry should be gender-neutral; it can apply to any sexual orientation, and can cross cultures. (1) In honor of Cupid, I'll focus my arguments on the romantic aspects of chivalry, the code of how to treat our intimate partners. If both women and men should strive to be chivalrous, we must first discuss what this means.</u> (2) Chivalry is far more than having good manners. Opening someone's door, helping someone put on a jacket, or picking up the check at dinner are polite gestures employed by women and men alike, in situations that extend beyond the pursuit of romance.

2
Clearly states how the remainder of the essay is linked to her purpose

STUDENT WRITER AT WORK

Shannon Morgan

On Writing "Defending Camelot: Chivalry Is Not Dead"

RA. What inspired you to write this essay? And publish it in your campus paper?

SM. Honestly, I got tired of arguing with my girlfriends about chivalry. It occurred to me that they hadn't thought through what the spirit of chivalry is. My goal was to start a dialogue. History is not static, and our ideas of intimacy, gender roles, and sex have evolved over time. I don't see why attitudes about chivalry can't also.

RA. How long did it take for you to write this piece? Did you revise your work? What were your goals as you revised?

SM. I wrote it over the course of two days and four different drafts. When I finish an article, I send it to editors and friends, and I almost always ask my Facebook and Twitter community if anyone has time to read a draft for me and give me feedback. I like to get at least five different perspectives, mostly just to make sure that the thesis of my article is accurately conveyed to my audience. It's important for me to get it right. There's nothing worse than sending an opinion article to print and getting torn apart in the comments because you have weak arguments. Showing my work to people before it gets published gives me an opportunity to identify weaknesses and fix them.

RA. Are you pursuing a career in which writing will be a component?

SM. I'm not quite sure what I will do for a career yet, but I am certain writing will be a component.

RA. What advice do you have for other student writers?

SM. Be bold. Be curious. Be tenacious. Develop a thick skin early on. Welcome feedback in all forms. Teach yourself as much as you can. Find a mentor. Learn to understand a variety of perspectives and worldviews, especially if they differ from your own. Learn how to listen and communicate effectively. Care about the world and the richness of life all around you. Great writing is a rare thing. It's more than just copying down what people say, or what you see and think. It's about research, accuracy, context, culture . . . so many things. My advice is to get as broad an education as possible because the more you know about the world, the better you are able to write about it.

Spotlight on Research

Tom Jacobs
Romance Novel Titles Reveal Readers' Desires
[*Miller-McCune*, March 2, 2010]

Great thinkers from Sigmund Freud to Mel Gibson have profitably pon- 1
dered the timeless question "What do women want?" Now, two Canadian
researchers — one of each gender — have taken a novel approach to solving
this purported puzzle.

In a paper titled "The Texas Billionaire's Pregnant Bride," recently pub- 2
lished in the *Journal of Social, Evolutionary and Cultural Psychology*, they analyze the titles of Harlequin romance novels. Anthony Cox of the Center of
Psychology and Computing and psychologist Maryanne Fisher of St. Mary's
University contend these best-selling volumes — and in particular their market-
tested titles — provide a unique insight into their buyers' desires.

Coming from an evolutionary psychology perspective, they hypoth- 3
esized these titles would reflect mating preferences that have evolved over the
millennia — specifically, a desire for a long-term relationship with a physically fit, financially secure man who will provide the resources needed to successfully raise a family.

They found considerable support for this theory, although some of their 4
speculative specifications were spelled out more directly than others.

The scholars created a database of just over 15,000 romance novels pub- 5
lished between 1949 and 2009. Not surprisingly, they found the most frequently used word in the title was "love," which appeared 840 times. "Bride"
was close behind at 835. "Baby" was slightly back at 696, followed by "man"
at 672 and "marriage" at 612.

These words "clearly suggest long-term commitment and reproduction 6
are important to readers," Cox and Fisher write. Indeed, commitment was
the most common theme they discovered, with words like *marriage, wedding,
bride, groom* and *honeymoon*. The second-most common was procreation,
with words like *baby, child, mommy, daddy* and *pregnant*.

The list of frequently used words does not specifically point to a desire 7
for wealth or good looks in a man. Surprisingly, "handsome" turns up only
six times, and the word "athletic" does not appear at all. Figuring such desires
were coded within the characters, the scholars decided to compile a list of the
20 most frequently occurring professions in these fictional works.

Doctor came in at No. 1, with 388 characters practicing medicine. No 8
surprise there: The authors note physicians "take care of others and earn a
generous salary," making them something of a two-fer as potential mates go.

But who would expect *cowboy* to come in second, at 314? Apparently the 9
archetype of the rugged frontiersman retains its appeal.

"We propose that the Western theme might relate to women's preference 10 for attractive mates," the researchers write — "attractive" not in the male-model sense, but rather in the muscular mold. "Cowboys are athletic and have high physical fitness, as their duties primarily involve physical labor," they note. That would presumably make them effective protectors against a variety of physical threats.

Nurse was the third most frequent occupation mentioned in the book 11 titles, at 224 (a lot of these stories feature doctors falling in love with nurses). Otherwise unspecified "boss" was fourth at 142 (many feature bosses falling in love with their secretaries). *Prince* was next, at 122 (the Sleeping Beauty myth lives!), followed by *rancher* at 79 (the Western motif returns), *knight* at 77 (there's something about a man who needs his armor polished) and *surgeon*, also at 77 (see *doctor*, above).

There is, of course, some danger in assuming women who purchase 12 romance novels are representative of their entire gender. While sales are admittedly huge (almost $1.4 billion in 2007, making it the largest fiction category in the U.S. by far), a significant number of women have no interest in them, and this study does not measure their desires.

Nevertheless, this smart, seductive study has inspired us to wonder if 13 we can reposition *Miller-McCune.com* headlines to appeal to what is clearly a huge demographic. Keep an eye out for our coming exposé *The Doctoral Candidate and the Ravishing Researcher.*

Discussing the Unit

SUGGESTED TOPIC FOR DISCUSSION

Women now make up the majority of the U.S. workforce, including management and professional positions (they still lag at the highest levels of executive leadership). Additionally, more women than men are earning college degrees. How would you account for these shifts? What do you think the consequences might be — socially, economically, and culturally? Which articles in this unit offer insight into this trend?

PREPARING FOR CLASS DISCUSSION

1. The essays in this unit cover a broad range of topics, from the Academy Awards to the nature of chivalry. What common themes unite the articles? If you had to characterize them in terms of one overriding preoccupation, what would it be?

2. Several of these essays touch upon gender stereotypes, whether directly or indirectly. Which stereotypes can you identify? Do you think they are

valid or "true" in any way? Are any of them pejorative or harmful, or just plain inaccurate? Do you identify with any of the gender stereotypes?

FROM DISCUSSION TO WRITING

1. While women have made enormous gains economically and socially, Friedman notes the "stalled" progress of women at the highest echelons of the business world, where they composed just 6.3 percent of the top earners in 2009. What do you think accounts for this disparity? Do you think that, ultimately, women will achieve parity with men—or even dominance over them? Why or why not?

2. All of these essays suggest that gender remains a significant factor in our society. How has gender shaped your choices in your education and your career ambitions? Has it been a limiting factor in any way? Has it been an advantage? How aware are you of your gender when choosing a particular path, professionally or personally?

TOPICS FOR CROSS-CULTURAL DISCUSSION

1. Unquestionably, our ideas about gender and gender roles are shaped by our culture. What cultural factors—familial, ethnic, religious, racial, or otherwise—have influenced your perceptions of men and women, as well as male and female "roles"? Do your beliefs ever conflict with dominant views of gender and gender roles? Have your views changed in any way? What caused them to change?

2. Do you see the differences between men and women (their behavior, their "roles," their relative places in society, their strengths and weaknesses, etc.) primarily as a matter of unchangeable biology, or do you understand them as culturally constructed? Should people work to eliminate the distinctions between men and women in society, or are such differences fundamental and essential, and therefore in need of preservation?

8

Does Our Need for Security Threaten Our Right to Privacy?

Ever since the attacks of 9/11, Americans have been concerned about balancing two needs—the need for security and the need for privacy. But these needs are not always easily balanced, as many travelers discover routinely at airports every day. As an increase in terror threats is met by new surveillance technologies, many Americans worry that our rights to privacy will become less and less respected. Is it possible to step up security measures while protecting privacy rights, as President Obama claimed when he said that he wants to "aggressively pursue enhanced screening technology . . . consistent with privacy rights and civil liberties"? And when security is at stake and lives are endangered, how much privacy are we willing to sacrifice?

In "Nude Awakening," one of the nation's prominent legal reporters, Jeffrey Rosen, worries that the new full-body scanning machines being rapidly installed at airports across the nation may seriously jeopardize our rights to privacy unless strict efforts are made to blur all personal characteristics. "Let's not mince words about these machines," Rosen argues: "They are a virtual strip search—and an outrage." Yet, not everyone feels so offended by the new airport scanning equipment: "If you think I'm making light of the full-body scanners on order for airports across the country, you're right," says columnist Connie Schultz in

"New Airport Policy: Grin and Bare It," who feels assured that authorities have implemented "numerous precautions to protect your privacy." Since terrorist techniques are constantly evolving, and racial profiling doesn't work, we need "high-tech devices" at airports, maintains Washington State University student Mohammed Khan, himself a victim of such profiling. Although Khan thinks it's understandable that people feel "uncomfortable with these invasive practices," he nevertheless believes, as the title states, that "Safety Is Paramount."

In the final selection, "The Tips of Your Fingers," nature writer Jay Griffiths takes a broader, transcendent look at the meaning of privacy in a surveillance society. She wonders why nations seem so intent on protecting their own borders while showing no respect for those of the individual citizen. "Through the twin prongs of ID cards and surveillance," she writes, "the borders of the private self are invaded."

Jeffrey Rosen

Nude Awakening

[*The New Republic*, February 4, 2010]

BEFORE YOU READ

Are airport security measures too intrusive? Are they effective? Would you submit to new airport scanning machines that create a graphic image of your naked body? How do you balance the need to be secure with the protection of your privacy?

WORDS TO LEARN

blurted (para. 1): uttered suddenly or accidentally (verb).

indignation (para. 2): anger at something considered unjust, offensive, or insulting (noun).

effusive (para. 2): overflowing, lacking hesitation or restraint (adjective).

estranged (para. 8): separated; unfriendly, hostile, or alienated (adjective).

L ast summer, I watched a fellow passenger at Washington's Reagan National Airport as he was selected to go through a newly installed full-body scanner. These machines — there are now 40 of them spread across 19 U.S. airports — permit officials from the Transportation Security Administration (TSA) to peer through a passenger's clothing in search of explosives and weapons. On the instructions of a security officer, the passenger stepped into the machine and held his arms out in a position of surrender, as invisible millimeter waves surrounded his body. Although he probably didn't know it, TSA officials in a separate room were staring at a graphic, anatomically correct image of his naked body. When I asked the TSA screener whether the passenger's face was blurred, he replied that he couldn't say. But, as I turned to catch my flight, the official blurted,

1

A professor at George Washington University Law School, Jeffrey Rosen is a graduate of Harvard University, Oxford University, and Yale Law School. He comments regularly on legal affairs for The New Republic. *His books include* The Unwanted Gaze: The Destruction of Privacy in America *(2000),* The Most Democratic Branch: How the Courts Serve America *(2006), and* The Supreme Court: The Personalities and Rivalries That Defined America *(2007).*

"Someone ought to do something about those machines—it's like we don't have any privacy in this country anymore!"

The officer's indignation was as rare as it was unexpected. In the wake of the failed Christmas bombing of Northwest Flight 253, the public has been overwhelmingly enthusiastic about these scanners. A recent *USA Today* poll found that 78 percent of respondents approved of their use at airports. Western democracies have been no less effusive. President Obama has ordered the Department of Homeland Security (DHS) to install $1 billion in airport screening equipment, and the TSA hopes to include an additional 300 millimeter-wave scanners. Britain, France, Italy, and the Netherlands have all made similar pledges to expand their use.

Let's not mince words about these machines. They are a virtual strip search—and an outrage. Body scanners are a form of what security expert Bruce Schneier has called "security theater." That is, they give people the illusion of safety without actually making us safer. A British MP who evaluated the body scanners in a former capacity, as a director at a leading defense technology company, said that they wouldn't have stopped the trouser bomber aboard the Northwest flight. Despite over-hyped claims to the contrary, they simply can't detect low-density materials hidden under clothing, such as liquid, powder, or thin plastics. In other words, the sacrifice these machines require of our privacy is utterly pointless. And, as it happens, it's possible to design and use the body scanners in a way that protects privacy without diminishing security—but the U.S. government has failed to do so.

> They give people the illusion of safety without actually making us safer.

Millimeter-wave scanners came on the market after September 11 as a way of detecting high-density contraband, such as ceramics or wax, that would be missed by metal detectors when concealed under clothing—while avoiding radiation that could harm humans. The machines also reveal the naked human body far more graphically than a conventional x-ray. But, from the beginning, researchers who developed the millimeter machines at the Pacific Northwest National Laboratory offered an alternative design more sensitive to privacy. They proposed to project any concealed contraband onto a neutral, sexless mannequin while scrambling images of the passenger's naked body into a nondescript blob. But the Bush administration chose the naked machine rather than the blob machine: Some blob skeptics argue that blotting out private parts would make it harder to detect explosives concealed, for example, in prosthetic genitalia. Of course, neither the blob nor the naked machine would have detected the suicide bombers who have proved perfectly willing to conceal explosives in real body cavities, as a Saudi suicide bomber proved in a failed attempt to assassinate a Saudi prince using explosives planted in a place where the sun doesn't shine.

Former DHS director Michael Chertoff, whose consulting firm now   5 represents the leading vendor of the millimeter machines, Rapiscan, has been a vocal cheerleader for body scanning: He called the Christmas bombing a "very vivid lesson in the value of that machinery." In 2005, under Chertoff's leadership, TSA ordered five scanners from Rapiscan, claiming that its naked images were less graphic than those of competitors. TSA also introduced one additional privacy protection: Agents who review the images of the naked bodies are in a separate room and, therefore, can't see the passengers as they're being scanned. According to the TSA website, the technology blurs all facial features, and, based on some news accounts, private parts have been blurred as well. But because the TSA remains free of independent oversight, it's impossible to tell precisely how they're being used.

Most troubling of all, the TSA website claims that "the machines   6 have zero storage capability" and that "the system has no way to save, transmit or print the image." But documents recently obtained by the Electronic Privacy Information Center reveal that, in 2008, the TSA told vendors that the machines it purchases must have the ability to send or store images when in "test" mode. (The TSA told CNN that the test mode can't be enabled at airports.) Because no regulations prohibit the TSA from storing images, the House (but not the Senate) voted last year to ban the use of body scanning machines for primary screening and to prohibit images from being stored.

As long as the TSA fails to blur images of both faces and private   7 parts, the machines will represent a serious threat to the dignity of some travelers from the 14 countries whose citizens will now be required to go through them (or face intrusive pat-downs) before entering the United States. Some interpretations of Islamic law, for example, forbid men from gazing at Muslim women unless they are veiled. It's also unfortunate that, a year after the Supreme Court declared, 8-1, that strip searches in schools are unreasonable without some suspicion of danger or wrongdoing, virtual strip searches will soon be routine for many randomly selected travelers at airports, rather than reserved for secondary screening of suspicious individuals.

But the greatest privacy concern is that the images may later leak. 8
As soon as a celebrity walks through a naked machine, some creep will
want to save the picture and send it to the tabloids. And the danger that
rogue officials may troll the database is hardly hypothetical. President
Obama's embattled nominee to head the TSA, Erroll Southers, conducted two searches of the confidential criminal records of his estranged
wife's boyfriend, downloaded the records, and passed them on to law
enforcement, possibly in violation of the Privacy Act, and then gave a
misleading account of the incident to Congress. That's why the images
should be anonymous and ephemeral, so agents can't save the pictures
or connect them to names.

Even if the body scanners protected privacy, Schneier insists, they 9
still would be a waste of money: The next plot rarely looks like the last
one. But, if we need to waste money on feel-good technologies that don't
make us safer, let's at least make sure that they don't unnecessarily reveal
us naked. President Obama says that he wants to "aggressively pursue
enhanced screening technology . . . consistent with privacy rights and
civil liberties." With a few simple technological and legal fixes, he can do
precisely that. Blob machine or naked machine — the choice is his.

VOCABULARY/USING A DICTIONARY

1. What does the word *enthusiastic* (para. 2) mean, and what are its origins?
2. What are the roots of the word *contraband* (para. 4), and what does it mean?
3. What are the origins of the word *hypothetical* (para. 8)? What other words is it related to?
4. What is the meaning of the word *ephemeral* (para. 8), and what are its origins?

RESPONDING TO WORDS IN CONTEXT

1. In paragraph 3, Rosen writes, "Let's not mince words." What does the phrase "mince words" mean? Why does he use it here?
2. The writer warns of "rogue officials" (para. 8), who might invade people's privacy. What connotations does the word *rogue* have?
3. Rosen describes the body scanners as "feel-good technologies" (para. 9). What does *feel-good* mean in this context?

DISCUSSING MAIN POINT AND MEANING

1. According to Rosen, what are the problems with the full-body scanners now being used in U.S. airports?
2. The writer claims that the scanners constitute a real privacy threat to airline passengers. How, specifically, do the machines threaten privacy and dignity?

3. Rosen argues that it is possible to "use the body scanners in a way that protects privacy without diminishing security" (para. 3). What solution does he propose in his essay?

EXAMINING SENTENCES, PARAGRAPHS, AND ORGANIZATION

1. In the final paragraph of the essay, Rosen quotes specific language from President Barack Obama. How does it support his point?
2. Rosen acknowledges the widespread public and political support for the body scanners in paragraph 2. Why does he include this paragraph, which highlights popular enthusiasm for these machines? In what way does it further his argument?
3. The writer begins his essay with a personal anecdote and observation. Following the first paragraph, how does he transition from his personal experience to the wider focus of his argument?

THINKING CRITICALLY

1. What are Rosen's main sources for his argument? How would you evaluate them?
2. In paragraph 8, Rosen writes that "the greatest privacy concern is that the images may later leak." How does he substantiate this claim? Does he do so effectively? Why or why not?
3. Rosen is writing about the Transportation Security Administration, as well as the body scanners. What view of the TSA comes across in the essay? How does the writer characterize the agency, specifically?

IN-CLASS WRITING ACTIVITIES

1. Rosen describes the TSA's use of body scanners as a "virtual strip search—and an outrage" (para. 3). Do you agree with him? How much privacy are you willing to give up to remain safe? In a response to this essay, explain how you view these issues, particularly with regard to balancing the need for security with the need to protect privacy.
2. The writer is critical of the TSA's "security theater" (para. 3) and the agency's ostensible commitment to "feel-good technologies" (para. 9). Rosen refers to the danger that "rogue officials" pose, citing the example of Erroll Southers (para. 8). Do you agree with Rosen's implicit view of government authority, generally?
3. In presenting his argument, Rosen suggests that, while others may soften their words or deploy euphemisms, he is being honest and candid about the subject. Why might people "mince words" on this issue? What arguments and issues seem to lead to this practice?

Connie Schultz

New Airport Policy: Grin and Bare It

[*Cleveland Plain Dealer*, January 10, 2010]

BEFORE YOU READ

Could airport security measures ever violate your privacy rights? Do you worry about terrorism? How much do you trust the government to keep you safe when you travel—and in other areas of your life?

WORDS TO LEARN

ambled (para. 5): walked at a slow, easy pace (verb).

confounding (para. 7): confusing (adjective).

emit (para. 9): to send forth (verb).

waist-highs (para. 12): panty hose or unfashionable, dated women's underwear (noun).

1   If you're one of the millions of Americans who resolved to get in shape this year but lack motivation, booking a flight at an airport near you might be just the ticket to push you to feel the burn.

2   Whenever you fly, you're used to tossing your bags on a conveyor belt and then removing shoes and enough clothing to leave you just this side of bare-naked. Soon you'll get to stand with your arms out and legs spread so that a stranger huddled over a computer can peer at an image of virtually nude, lumpy you.

> If you think I'm making light of the full-body scanners on order for airports across the country, you're right.

3   The stranger doesn't see your face, and you never see the stranger's face. But both of you will know that lurking under what's left of your clothing are more bumps and bulges than the Appalachian foothills have.

4   If you think I'm making light of the full-body scanners on order for airports across the country, you're right. For one

---

The winner of the 2005 Pulitzer Prize for commentary, Connie Schultz is a nationally syndicated columnist for The Plain Dealer *in Cleveland, Ohio. She is the author of a collection of columns,* Life Happens: And Other Unavoidable Truths *(2006), and . . . And His Lovely Wife: A Campaign Memoir from the Woman Beside the Man (2007).*

thing, I saw these computer-generated images up close and personal last summer, after two of the machines were installed at Cleveland's airport. These images are not pornographic unless your sexual fantasies steer toward cartoon characters and robots, in which case "ew" doesn't begin to diagnose your issues.

More importantly, on Christmas Day we allegedly came this close   5
to a would-be terrorist named Umar Farouk Abdulmutallab using plastic explosives sewn in his underwear to blow up a commercial flight headed for America. As I wrote just last summer, anyone wearing this travel accessory probably would not make it through a full-body scanner. But Abdulmutallab — a 23-year-old Nigerian with no coat, no luggage and cash for his ticket — ambled right through the metal detector in Amsterdam and onto Northwest Airlines Flight 253.

Not exactly Secret Agent Man.   6

Abdulmutallab's father had tried to warn American officials about his   7
son. Reportedly, an initial search misspelled his name, so no one discovered he had a multiple-entry visa. This error is confounding to some of us. Enter a misspelled name in a Google search and you immediately are greeted with "Did you mean" in bright red letters, followed by the correct spelling.

It's a little unsettling to think that security systems haven't figured   8
that one out.

The Transportation Security Administration has ordered 130 full-   9
body scanners, which emit low-level X-rays and produce computer images that look like chalk drawings. An additional 300 scanners are on order for next year.

There are numerous precautions to protect your privacy. The TSA   10
screener who waves you through is not the one who sees your computer image, which is deleted as soon as you're cleared. The images can't be stored, printed, or transmitted, and the person scanning the pictures is not allowed to bring a cell phone or camera into the room.

Nevertheless, some insist that these full-body scanners are a vio-   11
lation of privacy. It doesn't help when TV news anchors keep warning viewers about "graphic images" and praising grim-faced male volunteers as "brave" and "courageous" before walking in front of the scanners that pick up every piece of fake contraband they're wearing.

Last year, the American Civil Liberties Union championed the   12
privacy of celebrities who live and work in Los Angeles and fear their computer images could be posted on the Internet. People who regularly expose themselves for money and attention probably don't make the best victims, and so lately we aren't hearing that argument much. Now we're talking about how Grandma should be able to keep her waist-highs to herself.

There are also protests from the usual cast of angry Americans who   13
insist you can't trust the government to make travel any safer. A curious argument coming from an entire population of people who turn the
key in the ignition and pull out onto roads paved, painted and policed
by — how's this for coincidence? — the government.

Think about it. We carry licenses issued by the government, strap   14
on seat belts required by the government and then follow any number of
traffic laws passed by the government. We also assume that all the strangers sharing the road with us passed the same driver's test given by the
government.

So, c'mon, you're going to stand there and tell me you don't trust the   15
government?

Now, that's a funny image.   16

VOCABULARY/USING A DICTIONARY

1. What are the roots of the word *privacy* (para. 11)? What terms are related to it?
2. What does the word *visa* (para. 7) mean, and what are its origins?
3. What are the connotations of the word *violation* (para. 11)? What are its roots and related words?

RESPONDING TO WORDS IN CONTEXT

1. Why does the writer use the words "travel accessory" in paragraph 5? How would you characterize the tone of this phrase?
2. In paragraph 11, Schultz places quotation marks around the words "graphic images," "brave," and "courageous." How do the quotation marks affect the way we read the words? What point is she making?
3. How do the meaning and connotation of the word *image* change throughout the essay, especially in the context of the last paragraph?

DISCUSSING MAIN POINT AND MEANING

1. Schultz advocates for the new body-scanning machines. What are her main arguments for their use?
2. According to the writer, the TSA has numerous precautions to protect passenger privacy. What are they?
3. Schultz spends much of her essay describing and addressing opponents of the body-scanning machines. How does she characterize them?

EXAMINING SENTENCES, PARAGRAPHS, AND ORGANIZATION

1. The writer acknowledges that she is "making light" (para. 4) of the con-troversy around full-body scanners. What specific aspects of her style, tone, and diction demonstrate this attitude? Do they make her argument more persuasive?

2. In her essay, Schultz writes in the first person (both singular and plural), the second person, and the third person. What effects do these different grammatical choices produce? How do they support her main point?
3. What is the purpose of the last sentence in paragraph 4? What do you think she means, specifically? How does this statement fit in with her larger point?

THINKING CRITICALLY

1. Schultz makes an argument in favor of using the full-body scanners in airports. What specific evidence does she use to support her point of view?
2. In paragraph 11, Schultz writes, "some insist that these full-body scanners are a violation of privacy." She also refers to the "usual cast of angry Americans who insist you can't trust the government to make travel any safer" (para. 13). How effectively does she address counterarguments? What would make her position stronger?
3. Where in the essay does Schultz argue by using analogies? How persuasive and effective are these comparisons?

IN-CLASS WRITING ACTIVITIES

1. Schultz consciously makes light of airport security issues and even presents "would-be terrorist" (para. 5) Umar Farouk Abdulmutallab as a comic figure ("Not exactly Secret Agent Man"). How much do you worry about terrorism, in the context of traveling or other aspects of your life? Are people generally too concerned with the possibility of terrorist attacks? Not concerned enough?
2. While Schultz is writing specifically about airport security issues and travel safety, she also considers the role of government more generally. How much do you trust the government?
3. According to the writer, the TSA is taking "numerous precautions" (para. 10) to protect people's privacy. Do you see the scanners as too intrusive? Do the precautions seem thorough enough? Would they change your view of airport security or even your travel habits?

Mohammed Khan (student essay)

The Need for Safety Is Paramount

[*The Daily Evergreen*, Washington State University,
January 13, 2010]

BEFORE YOU READ

Should airport security officials and law-enforcement authorities use religious and ethnic profiling to thwart terrorist attacks? Is such profiling effective? What is more important in a time of global terrorism, safety or privacy?

WORDS TO LEARN

ascertaining (para. 3): finding out or learning with certainty (verb).

qualms (para. 7): feelings of uneasiness (noun).

naive (para. 8): lacking worldly experience and unsuspecting; unsophisticated (adjective).

Profiling is an element of airport screening intended to increase security, but it is not the ultimate solution to the problem. In light of what we learned from the attempted airliner bombing over Detroit on Christmas Day [2009], profiling is nowhere near effective in this age of global terrorism.

An enormous amount of evidence indicates racial profiling is not sufficient to protect us from terrorists. For instance, Richard Colvin Reid was stopped from igniting a device in his shoe on an American Airlines flight from Paris to Miami on Dec. 22, 2001. Reid, who is currently serving a life sentence in a supermax prison, was born in England and is half English, half Jamaican.

Umar Farouk Abdulmutallab, who failed with his Christmas Day bombing attempt over Detroit, is a Nigerian from a relatively rich family in London. Ethnic profiling of Arabs, Iranians, or Pakistanis would not have singled out either Reid or Abdulmutallab for specific attention. Officials could profile all Muslims, but given the difficulty of ascertaining individual religious beliefs and coupled with the fact that Muslims compose more than one-fifth of the world's population, such profiling is not feasible, at least on many international flights.

Mohammed Khan is a senior at Washington State University, where he is an opinion columnist for The Daily Evergreen *and majors in electrical engineering.*

Upon examining the facts, it is obvious there was a serious security 4
failure in the Detroit case. Abdulmutallab's father warned the United
States that his son was a threat. Nonetheless, Abdulmutallab's American
visa was not revoked, and he was allowed to board the plane without any
extra security measure. The bomb that he carried was undetected.

It is becoming increasingly apparent that our system needs to look 5
beyond the facades of profiling and employ tactics that are intelligence
based. High-tech devices like full-body scanners have recently come into
light. However, privacy advocates are concerned about the machines'
capability of virtually stripping people, leaving an image of their nude
body on the screen.

Many people are uncomfortable with these invasive practices, which is 6
understandable. The issues range from child pornography to obvious privacy infringements, all of them raising important questions. But the need for
safety is paramount. Considering al-Qaida's
evolving techniques, employing these high-
tech devices is the need of the hour.

> Considering
> al-Qaida's evolv- 7
> ing techniques,
> employing these
> high-tech devices
> is the need of the
> hour.

New protocols could be adopted to
address people's qualms about the devices.
Those who are uncomfortable with the
machines could arrive at the airport earlier
than others. This would give officials time to
thoroughly search uneasy passengers. Such a
rule would streamline the entire process and
improve security while giving people options.

It is naive to assume that racial profiling will eliminate any airport 8
security threats. Regardless, profiling inherently exists in our contemporary times. When I first came to the United States in 2005, I was held at
the Chicago O'Hare International Airport for two hours, sitting next to
a man whose leg was cuffed to the bench. When I asked an official why
I was being held, I was told, "With a name like Mohammed Farooq Ali
Khan, you are going to be held everywhere."

Since my arrival, there have been regular breaches in airport secu- 9
rity. Although racial profiling exists to prevent such breaches, it does not
work. There is no one solution to this predicament. But one thing is for
certain: As al-Qaida is evolving, so must security protocols.

VOCABULARY/USING A DICTIONARY

1. What does the word *feasible* (para. 3) mean? What are the word's origins?
2. According to the writer, the "need for safety is paramount" (para. 6). What
   does *paramount* mean, and what are its origins? How is its meaning different from that of the term *tantamount*?

3. Khan writes that new security devices could require "new protocols" (para. 7). What does he mean by *protocol*? Where does the word come from?

RESPONDING TO WORDS IN CONTEXT

1. Khan refers to "this age of global terrorism" (para. 1). How would you define the terms *terrorism* and *terrorist*? What characteristics make "terrorism" different from other kinds of crime, military action, or political violence?
2. What is "racial profiling" (para. 2)? What connotations does the term have?
3. According to Khan, security officials must "employ tactics that are intelligence based" (para. 5). What does the word *tactics* mean in this context, and how does it differ from the word *strategy*?

DISCUSSING MAIN POINT AND MEANING

1. How would you phrase Khan's thesis or main point in your own words?
2. Khan refers to Richard Reid and Umar Farouk Abdulmutallab in his essay. What do these two examples demonstrate, according to the writer?
3. How does Khan address privacy concerns in this essay?

EXAMINING SENTENCES, PARAGRAPHS, AND ORGANIZATION

1. According to the writer, "our [airport security] system needs to look beyond the facades of profiling and employ tactics that are intelligence based" (para. 5). What contrast is Khan making here? How is it related to his overall argument?
2. Khan writes, "Many people are uncomfortable with these invasive practices, which is understandable" (para. 6). How could this generalization be supported and made more convincing?
3. Why does Khan include his personal experience in paragraph 8? Would it be as effective if he included it earlier in the essay?

THINKING CRITICALLY

1. Khan suggests that "Officials could profile all Muslims," but then concludes that such a procedure would not be "feasible" (para. 3). Why does he come to this conclusion? What other reasons might make this approach infeasible?
2. Do you have any "qualms" about heightened security measures, such as full-body scanners? How do you respond to Khan's claim that "the need for safety is paramount" (para. 6)?
3. According to Khan, "An enormous amount of evidence indicates racial profiling is not sufficient to protect us from terrorists" (para. 2). Does he substantiate this claim adequately?

IN-CLASS WRITING ACTIVITIES

1. The practice of "racial profiling" (para. 2) implies that terrorists fit a certain profile. What image or stereotype comes to mind for you? Where do these images come from? How accurate is your stereotype? What do you see as the primary factor in creating terrorists?

2. Do you agree with Khan or disagree? Write an argumentative essay that either supports "The Need for Safety Is Paramount" or refutes it.

3. How much do you worry about terrorism in your own life? Where does it rank on your lists of concerns and fears? Do you think people overstate the threat of terrorist attacks? Or have we gotten too complacent about such threats?

LOOKING CLOSELY

Supporting Your Point with Examples

In any discussion or debate, nothing is more persuasive than well-chosen examples. We often use examples to back up a generalization with concrete instances or to support a claim. The examples *show* what we mean. We can see the effective use of appropriate examples in "The Need for Security Is Paramount," an essay by Washington State University student Mohammed Khan. Khan believes that airports should use screening devices because racial profiling does not work. He then offers two examples of would-be terrorists who would not have been stopped by racial profiling because their identities did not fit the ethnic groups being targeted.

1
Khan provides an instance that supports his point about profiling

An enormous amount of evidence indicates racial profiling is not sufficient to protect us from terrorists. For instance, Richard Colvin Reid was stopped from igniting a device in his shoe on an American Airlines flight from Paris to Miami on Dec. 22, 2001. Reid, who is currently serving a life sentence in a supermax prison, was born in England and is half English, half Jamaican. (1)

2
He strengthens his point by adding a second example

Umar Farouk Abdulmutallab, who failed with his Christmas Day bombing attempt over Detroit, is a Nigerian from a relatively rich family in London. Ethnic profiling of Arabs, Iranians, or Pakistanis would not have singled out either Reid or Abdulmutallab for specific attention. (2)

STUDENT WRITER AT WORK
Mohammed Khan

On Writing "The Need for Safety Is Paramount"

RA. What inspired you to write this essay? And publish it in your campus paper?

MK. As a Muslim student of Indian descent, I have far too many times experienced firsthand the extra scrutiny a person receives for belonging to a certain race. During the time I wrote the article, the Christmas bomber was being analyzed and the idea of racial profiling was being debated all over the twenty-four-hour news cycles. I had to make my voice heard as well and so I wrote the article with my perspective.

RA. What do you like to read?

MK. I am an avid fan of the *Huffington Post,* and my favorite magazines range from *National Geographic* to astronomy prints.

RA. What topics most interest you as a writer?

MK. Topics that are hot debates under the sociopolitical umbrella. I like to analyze the story with my perspective and write my opinions on it.

RA. What advice do you have for other student writers?

MK. I believe that writing is a direct result of passion towards a subject. If you really want to be heard, you will develop the skills to not only improve your language, but also the strength of your writing. Nothing can be imposed; it should come from within.

Jay Griffiths

The Tips of Your Fingers

[*Orion*, January/February 2010]

BEFORE YOU READ

What does *individuality* mean? Do you think that the government invades your privacy and your individualism? Does the average citizen have a real political voice? How does our society pressure people to conform?

WORDS TO LEARN

articulate (para. 2): to reveal, make distinct, or give clarity to (verb).

multifold (para. 4): numerous and varied (adjective).

alterity (para. 4): the quality or state of being other or profoundly different (noun).

homogeneity (para. 5): composition of similar parts, elements, or characteristics (noun).

bolsters (para. 5): supports or upholds (verb).

sequestered (para. 6): withdrawn, separated, or isolated (adjective).

biometrics (para. 9): the measurement of physical characteristics, such as fingerprints or DNA, to verify the identity of individuals (noun).

perennial (para. 11): enduring, lasting a long time (adjective).

In the woods near the border checkpoint from France to Britain, several people sit around a fire, pushing iron bars deeper into the flames until the metal is red hot. Taking out the iron, with searing pain they burn their own fingertips, trying to erase their identification. 1

The fingertips are a border checkpoint of the human body, and through them the self reaches out to touch the world. Fingertips are diviners, lovers, poets of the perhaps, emissaries of empathy. They are feelingful, exquisitely sensitive to metal, dough, moss, or splinter. They are also one of the body's places of greatest idiosyncrasy: a fingerprint 2

Jay Griffiths is the award-winning author of two nonfiction books, Pip Pip: A Sideways Look at Time *(2000), and* Wild: An Elemental Journey *(2006), and a short novel about Frida Kahlo,* A Love Letter from a Stray Moon *(2011).*

is the body's signature. Fingertips are at once highly selved and highly sensitive: They articulate difference and they distinguish difference.

Forced to erase the sign of themselves, people scar, burn, stitch, and 3
staple their fingertips at U.S. borders too, and indeed wherever people fear that their identification will be used against them, not because they are criminals but because they are refugees and victims of war, poverty, and neo-imperialism.

Border checkpoints bristle with state control, and this control now 4
encroaches within nations. In Britain, already the world leader in surveillance, the state is now pushing for nationwide ID cards. Identification, tagging, and surveillance are used to intimidate those at the margins, the borders of society: Refugees, whose individual stories of blood and horror give the lie to the glossy brochures of foreign policy; the insane with their flashes of specific mind-lightning; those who stand out, eccentrically, for their beliefs, who poke and provoke with the demeanor of a pitchfork in the cutlery drawer; young people at the borders of adulthood; protesters, with their multifold cries of "see it otherwise," demanding political alterity. All are harassed with surveillance.

Truly individualistic societies would cherish all such border cross- 5
ers, not punish them. But the dominant culture is a society of intolerant homogeneity that bolsters racism, ageism, and conformism. It supports monoism, destroying variety from biodiversity to linguistic diversity. Like the monoculture of Hollywood and the monocrops of agribusiness, the monopolitics of world powers erase the particular, searing away the idiomatic dialect of the self, symbolized so specifically by each person's fingertips. Burning away the signature of individuality, at the borders of those very countries that most profess individualism, is a metaphor of terrible reproach. And it tells a deep truth, for ours is not an individualistic society. Rather, it is a hyper-privatized one.

The word *private* originally meant to be "deprived of public life," 6
and most people today are so deprived. A vote every few years does not constitute a political voice. Terms for public political life, like *solidarity, trade unions, co-operatives,* or *collectives,* are unwelcome in a world of hyper-privatization. Employees engaged in public protest find their jobs threatened. Citizens are also deprived of public life in nature, fobbed off with parks and that hyper-privatized patch of green, the fenced-in private garden. Entertainment, traditionally a very communal affair, is now hyper-privatized, the individual watching TV in a room alone, where the sequestered self is more vulnerable to advertising.

Similarly, the etymology of the word *idiot,* from ancient Greek, 7
refers to a "purely private person" — one who takes no part in public life. In this hyper-privatized world, it is as if governments would prefer their

subjects to remain idiots, disengaged from the state's process but suffering its intrusions.

Humans need community and public life: we also need the secluded intimacy of privacy, and the latter is threatened by surveillance. Those in favor of surveillance argue that "if you have nothing to hide, you have nothing to fear," but this denies the very significance of privacy — a cache to shelter our tenderness and our name. Telling one's name is a gift. Withholding it is a right.

> Telling one's name is a gift. Withholding it is a right.

8

Through the twin prongs of ID cards and surveillance, the borders of the private self are invaded. I am declaring, here, that I am a sovereign state. I do not want alien states to use biometrics to crawl into my eyes like flies. I do not want my identity captured by strangers. But I, who am deprived of the human right to freely roam in my own free land, find that the state can roam freely through the territories of my self, violating the integrity of my borders.

9

When the state crosses the borders into my private self, it is an ugly act. But border crossing the other way — the self reaching outward — is an act of beauty and transcendence. Art, spirituality, environmentalism, and movements for political justice agree, seeking transcendence from the confines of the single self, and it is no surprise that people from backgrounds of faith, activism, and art are those who most vehemently oppose ID cards.

10

The perennial philosophy of a universal oneness suggests a reaching out beyond the ego. So does the traditional posture of fingertips touched together in prayer to set free the spirit, winged for infinity. Movements for political reform take wide, unprivate ideals, the wisest art goes beyond the individual, and at the heart of environmentalism is the extension of the borders of responsibility to encompass lands, times, selves, and species beyond the individual.

11

The human psyche, then, seems to find benevolence in the self transcending its boundaries. By contrast, the psyche finds malevolence in those who invade those boundaries: in the myths and mores of many cultures, people are wary about giving names to strangers. Belief in the Evil Eye is virtually a human universal, embodying the malignity of surveillance. Staring is inherently predatory, and we, as other animals, hate being watched because it is a prelude to attack. Mass surveillance — modernity's Evil Eye — is peculiarly nasty because of its cowardice; the watcher is hidden, unknowable and faceless.

12

Anyone can recognize a sense of guilt merely walking (innocently) through airport customs. Being trailed by a police car provokes a similar

13

guilt, even when unfounded. Surveillance provokes a pervasive sense of guilt and entrapment and this fusion has a practical history in the invention in 1785 of the Panopticon, the surveillance device designed to watch prisoners without their knowledge. If plans for compulsory ID cards succeed in the UK, we will be carrying our own Panopticons with us, and the protest against these plans is muted. In the U.S., thankfully, there is tougher resistance to ID cards, but a modern Panopticon, the microchip tag within the body, is in use already by an Ohio company (CityWatcher.com) whose business is in providing governments with surveillance tools, and which has inserted microchips under the skin of some of its employees.

Surveillance creates conformity. Anyone queuing at border control 14 attempts to look as "normal" as possible: like any animal under a predatory stare, humans try to fit in with the herd, not to stand out. The glare of surveillance is the opposite of the gaze of love, for under that gaze a person wants to be known, seen especially for themselves, flirting the peacock feathers of otherness, the distinguishing features of the soul. The law of evolution encourages individuation, and diversity is a signature of the vitality of nature. These laws of life agree with the law of love in nurturing true individuality, for the human heart cherishes "this-ness," the essential specificity of the beloved person.

"If you ask me why I loved him," said the Renaissance French human- 15 ist Michel de Montaigne of his friend Étienne de La Boétie, "I can only say: because he was he, and I was I." Delineating an exquisite uniqueness, it is as if their fingertips still touch, after all these centuries, and the fingertips of Montaigne's mind, like all great artists, transcend the borders of self and time to touch minds today with the inalienable signature of love.

VOCABULARY/USING A DICTIONARY
1. What does *idiosyncrasy* (para. 2) mean? What other words is it related to?
2. How does Griffiths use the word *psyche* (para. 12)? What are its origins?
3. In paragraph 13, the writer refers to the development of the Panopticon as a surveillance device to watch prisoners without their knowledge. What are the roots of that word?

RESPONDING TO WORDS IN CONTEXT
1. In paragraph 2, Griffiths writes that "Fingertips are diviners ..." (para. 2). What does the word *diviners* mean? What connotations does it have in the context of the essay?
2. Griffiths writes that privacy is "a cache to shelter our tenderness and our name" (para. 8). Why did she choose the word *cache* rather than a more common term like *hiding place*?

3. According to the writer, "the law of evolution encourages individuation" (para. 14). What is the difference between *individuation* and *individuality*?

DISCUSSING MAIN POINT AND MEANING

1. The writer argues against the use of "biometrics" (para. 9) and national ID cards. What problems does she see with them?
2. Griffiths criticizes the forces of conformity beyond surveillance and national identification requirements. Where else does she see them at work?
3. According to the writer, "it is no surprise that people from backgrounds of faith, activism, and art are those who most vehemently oppose ID cards" (para. 10). Why would that be the case, in the context of Griffiths's argument?

EXAMINING SENTENCES, PARAGRAPHS, AND ORGANIZATION

1. Griffiths shows a keen awareness of sound and figurative language, from the cadences of her writing and her surprising word choices and metaphors, to her use of rhyme and alliteration: "The fingertips are ... poets of the perhaps, emissaries of empathy" (para. 2). Point to some specific examples of lyrical or poetical prose within the essay. What are the benefits and drawbacks of writing this way?
2. What purposes do paragraphs 6 and 7 have in the essay? How do they further Griffiths's argument?
3. This article is titled "The Tips of Your Fingers." It begins with a description of people burning their fingertips near a border checkpoint to erase their identities. How does Griffiths use fingertips as an organizing device or theme in her essay?

THINKING CRITICALLY

1. Griffiths writes that genuinely "individualistic societies would cherish all such border crossers ... [but] the dominant culture is a society of intolerant homogeneity that bolsters racism, ageism, and conformism" (para. 5). How do you interpret these assertions? Do you agree with them?
2. According to the writer, most people today are "deprived of public life" (para. 6). What view does she take of contemporary political participation? Do you agree?
3. Griffiths refers to the "malignity of surveillance" and claims that its widespread presence is "modernity's Evil Eye" (para. 12). Where do you see such surveillance in your own life? Do you share her view of it as a malevolent force?

IN-CLASS WRITING ACTIVITIES

1. According to the writer, most people have no real political voice (para. 6). She then lists several terms for "public political life," which she claims are "unwelcome in a world of hyper-privatization" (para. 6). Choose one or all

of the words, and briefly discuss their meaning and connotations. Do you agree that they are "unwelcome" in our current political and economic climate? Are there other words that designate "public political life" that are just as important?

2. Griffiths writes about the value of—and need for—"true individualism," even as she argues that societies and countries are hostile to individualism. What does "individualism" mean to you? Do you share Griffiths's views?

3. The writer argues that even contemporary amusements are isolating: "Entertainment, traditionally a very communal affair, is now hyper-privatized, the individual watching TV in a room alone, where the sequestered self is more vulnerable to advertising" (para. 6). Consider your own experiences and habits of "entertainment." Do you agree with Griffiths that they generally tend to isolate people rather than connect them? Explain.

Discussing the Unit

SUGGESTED TOPIC FOR DISCUSSION

All the authors in this unit discuss the balance between security and privacy: the need for safety versus the need to guard the boundaries of our personal identities. None of the writers dismiss the real threat of terrorism. But who bears most of the responsibility for protecting us? Rosen is skeptical of "security theater." In contrast, Connie Schultz writes, "So, c'mon, you're going to stand there and tell me you don't trust the government?" To what degree do we need the government to keep us safe? How effective is it at that task? Do you think it should play more of a role in our safety? Less?

PREPARING FOR CLASS DISCUSSION

1. Griffiths writes, "I do not want alien states to use biometrics to crawl into my eyes like flies." Biometrics are the measurement of physical characteristics, such as fingerprints, DNA, or retinal patterns for the use of verifying the identity of individuals. What is your opinion of biometrics? Would you mind being part of a national or international database? Would you object to national ID cards, if they were made mandatory? Why or why not?

2. For Khan and Schultz, security takes precedence over privacy concerns—although Khan has reservations about the use of profiling. Rosen and Griffiths are more concerned with privacy. Which of these four essays do you find the most persuasive and effective? Why?

FROM DISCUSSION TO WRITING

1. Griffiths, Rosen, and Schultz all address privacy rights. How do you define *privacy*? Do you have a "right" to it? What are your own "privacy rights"? How do you balance them against matters of public safety or the interests of the state (e.g., regulating immigration)?

2. Khan writes that during his detention at Chicago's O'Hare airport, an official told him, "With a name like Mohammed Farooq Ali Khan, you are going to be held everywhere." Khan does not include or discuss his response to the official's remark. What is your response? What was the official's tone or goal in making the remark? How would you have responded if you were Khan?

QUESTIONS FOR CROSS-CULTURAL DISCUSSION

1. Griffiths takes a grim view of national and international border controls and checkpoints, which "bristle with state control." What are your own views on border security, immigration, and national identity? Why are these issues often so controversial in the United States?

2. How do cultural and ethnic backgrounds shape attitudes toward privacy rights? Should these considerations be taken into account when, say, formulating policies about airport security? Why or why not?

Barack Obama: What Does His Election Mean to America?

The election of America's first African American president filled the country, from left to right, with a momentary euphoria—even those who disagreed with his campaign felt a sense that the boundaries of American life had been suddenly and irreversibly expanded. Barack Obama's opponent, Senator John McCain, even called the election "historic" in his concession speech, telling his Republican supporters that the Democratic president-elect had "achieved a great thing for himself and for his country." The same emotion was felt all over the world: The prime minister of Ukraine declared to Obama, "Your victory is an inspiration for us. That which appeared impossible has become possible."

But as the elation subsided to the anxiety of a country facing two wars and a crippling economic recession, many began to question exactly what Obama's presidency meant—and means. Many observers bristled that despite the inspiring rhetorical power of Obama the candidate, Obama the president would represent more of the same: that he would perpetuate the same Washington policies they felt had failed the country. Moreover, commentators characterized him as a member of the Washington elite, out of touch with ordinary Americans, and particularly with his African American base—poor, uneducated, and powerless—that he had so inspired.

The debate was wide and important enough to spawn an entire issue of *Essence*, the country's premier African American magazine, shortly after Obama's election. In that issue, novelist Diane McKinney-Whetstone summarized the ebullient feeling so many black people had watching the election night ceremony in Chicago's Grant Park — a feeling that the long-promised piece of the American dream was finally really theirs, and that the Obama family members were the best ambassadors they could have asked for. "Barack's story is so familiar to us," she writes. "The child whose father goes away, the single mom struggling on welfare, the grandparents who step in and supplant." Obama represents the shared experience of all African Americans who have struggled through privation and prejudice to reach a purpose in life. "And for the Obamas," she says, "the moment came."

John Edgar Wideman, writing in the same issue of *Essence*, focuses on the realities of life for black children, a reality he sets off against the same pomp and circumstance McKinney-Whetstone celebrates in the election. Wideman describes the ongoing poverty and marginalization of New York's black poor, and wonders, "Is a President Obama too late to help the missing ones?" The problem of urban poverty will not be solved, Wideman argues, simply by having a president with a different skin tone; we have to be willing to actually "listen to our young people on the street corners."

This chapter's student essay, by Santa Clara University's Pearl Wong, agrees that a black president won't be able to fix America's many problems simply by virtue of his ethnicity. "While Obama embodies a milestone in America's history as the first African American president," she writes, "he is not the president of only African Americans." While Wong is skeptical of the specific identity politics she sees in the Obama campaign, Christopher Hedges, writing for *Tikkun*, takes a more generally critical view of Obama. What's interesting about Hedges's essay is that he attacks Obama not from the right but from the left, arguing that he represents a continuation of the conventional policies of the Bush administration, policies he believes are determined and orchestrated by a corporate oligarchy. All Obama's race means, for Hedges, is that the insiders are "rebranding" their message, just as a corporation might rebrand its products. "But like all branded products spun out from the manipulative world of corporate advertising," Hedges writes, "this product is duping us into doing and supporting a lot of things that are not in our interest."

Diane McKinney-Whetstone

The First Family

[*Essence*, January 2009]

BEFORE YOU READ

How do you see the African American family in America today? Is it even possible to think of a "typical" black family, or are all family units marked by too much diversity to entertain such stereotypes? Did the election of Barack Obama change your picture of black families at all? Why or why not?

WORDS TO LEARN

charismatic (para. 1): having a charm that wins people over (adjective).

exude (para. 1): to ooze out (verb).

ebullience (para. 1): energetic cheerfulness (noun).

dysfunction (para. 3): a failure or impairment, especially of a family (noun).

maladjusted (para. 3): unable to fit into a normal social environment (adjective).

intact (para. 3): together (adjective).

fractured (para. 4): broken (adjective).

culminate (para. 4): to reach a certain point in the end (verb).

supplant (para. 4): to replace (verb).

dearth (para. 4): lack (noun).

garner (para. 4): to get (verb).

buoyant (para. 5): staying afloat; optimistic and confident (adjective).

The Obamas made for a stunning visual as they took center stage in Grant Park on election night. When the crowd surged forward, hearts bursting with love and pride, the lens shifted and altered the world's view of the Black family. Here, in President-elect Barack Obama, was a handsome and charismatic father exuding adoration for his daughters; a husband whose affection for his wife was so evident that, as we watched them on the campaign trail, we got the sense that after 16 years of marriage, he still got weak in the knees at the sight of her walking toward him. Here, in Michelle Obama, was a brilliant wife and an attentive mother, eyes trained on her children, protective and strong. And here were the beautiful daughters, Malia and Sasha, in their ebullience and velvet-and-taffeta dresses and their Sunday school hair.

Diane McKinney-Whetstone has written five acclaimed novels, the most recent of which is Trading Dreams at Midnight *(2008). The recipient of many awards, she teaches at the University of Pennsylvania.*

President-elect Barack Obama with his family at Grant Park in Chicago, Illinois, November 4, 2008.

As the tears washed down our faces, we flashed on all the moments   2
over the past months that had filled us up, filled us with a recognition of
family that has for too long been missing from the public stage: There
was Barack, eyes closed for a moment, leaning against his wife in a Normal Rockwell-esque[1] diner, or scooping his daughters into his arms on
yet another airport tarmac. And Michelle, exchanging that playful fist
dap[2] with her husband, or wiping Malia's brow on a hot summer day,
or absently, tenderly, smoothing Sasha's flyaway hair. And there, in family snapshots were the girls, sprawled across their parents, owning them,
with perfect assurance that the man who would be president and his first
lady were theirs, first and forever; the campaign, the world, everything
else, came after.

And there, on election night, for all to witness, was the picture-perfect   3
image that the world has not seen enough of because the camera has too
often been trained on our dysfunction — the absent father, the hysterical
mother and the maladjusted kids. But in Grant Park on that night, we saw
an image that could have been lifted from those cardboard fans we used

---

[1] Norman Rockwell (para. 2): (1894–1978) A painter and illustrator famous for
   scenes of typical family life in the United States.

[2] fist dap (para. 2): A reference to a "fist bump" gesture Barack and Michelle
   Obama became famous for making on stage in July of 2008.

to sway in church, fans adorned with pictures of the smiling Black parents and their well-appointed children. We saw a family not unlike any number of Black families we know, who live quietly in towns and cities and suburbs throughout the nation. That night, watching the Obamas, even if we didn't leave our seats, inside we were jumping up and down just like the Kenyan relatives.[3] Finally, the world could see what we've always known: Black families can be loving, intact, nurturing worlds that produce confident, talented children.

> Finally, the world could see what we've always known.

We were moved by the image of the Obamas on that stage for other reasons too. 4
We knew intimately about the fractured pasts and defiant dreams that had culminated in a present that was so wonderfully whole. Barack's story is so familiar to us: the child whose father goes away, the single mom struggling on welfare, the grandparents who step in and supplant. We've lived Michelle's past as well, in the dearth of material privilege, and the sacrifice and the encouragement that never quit. Like Barack and Michelle, many of us were raised by those who would not allow excuses for underachievement. We studied our books and garnered scholarships, and began the quest for a purposeful life. Then there was the miracle of falling in love and partnering with one who had the capacity for compromise. The children came. And for the Obamas, the moment came.

It was our moment, too. On the stage at Grant Park the light passed 5 at just the right angle to capture the splendid realness of the Black family. We saw ourselves in the small gestures: Michelle touching Malia's shoulder; Barack sweeping Sasha into the air, the president-elect, buoyant in the presence of his family. And we felt the wonder of the moment, wrought by God's grace, through which even the fractured parts of our history could unfold into such miraculous wholeness. Deep down, we've always known what our families could be. Now with the Obamas' victory, the world knows, too.

VOCABULARY/USING A DICTIONARY

1. What does it mean to know something or someone *intimately* (para. 4)? What would one possible opposite of *intimately* be?
2. What does the word *culminate* (para. 4) mean? What part of speech is it? What does it mean for more than one thing to culminate?
3. What is *ebullience* (para. 1)? What language does it come from, and what did it mean in that language?

---

[3] Kenyan relatives (para. 3): Barack Obama has an extended family in Kenya, in eastern Africa, whose members were shown on election night celebrating.

RESPONDING TO WORDS IN CONTEXT

1. What exactly does McKinney-Whetstone mean when she refers to a "Norman Rockwell-esque diner" (para. 2)? What does the association the author makes to Rockwell imply about the scene?

2. McKinney-Whetstone refers to "the child whose father goes away, the single mom struggling on welfare, the grandparents who step in and supplant" (para. 4). What does *supplant* mean here?

3. The essay describes President-elect Obama as "buoyant" on the stage in Grant Park (para 5). What does it mean to be *buoyant*? What specific gestures or expressions do you imagine when you hear somebody described as *buoyant*?

DISCUSSING MAIN POINT AND MEANING

1. What is McKinney-Whetstone saying she felt watching the ceremony in Grant Park? How is the feeling related to her childhood?

2. What is the essay implying many people think about black families? How did the image of the Obamas on stage challenge that picture?

3. Who does McKinney-Whetstone mean when she repeatedly says "we" in the essay? (For instance, "We studied our books and garnered scholarships," para. 4.) What does this group have in common with the Obamas?

EXAMINING SENTENCES, PARAGRAPHS, AND ORGANIZATION

1. What is the effect of mentioning Malia and Sasha's "velvet-and-taffeta dresses and their Sunday school hair" in paragraph 1? Why does she include this detail?

2. Paragraph 4 of this essay contains several long sentences and then ends with one short sentence. Study these sentences in context. What is the effect of this organization on the reader?

3. How does the essay switch between its two major scenes — that of the Obamas themselves in Grant Park, and that of the audience? Which one does it start with, when does it transition, and when does it transition back? What is the effect of this back-and-forth motion?

THINKING CRITICALLY

1. What, if anything, do you believe the election of Barack Obama represents for American society? What, if anything, do you think it represents for the image of the black family in America?

2. Do you believe there's such a thing as a "typical" black family? If so, what is it? If not, why not?

3. McKinney-Whetstone focuses entirely on the visual impact of the Obama family, ignoring President Obama's policies and positions. What is the effect of this focus? What does an image of a politician tell us that a political speech or a debate cannot?

IN-CLASS WRITING ACTIVITIES

1. Watch a video of the Grant Park acceptance speech from November of 2008 (available on YouTube.) What is your reaction to President Obama as a public figure, to the Obama family, and to the speech itself? What elements of McKinney-Whetstone's essay resonate with you as you watch the video? Do you think she missed anything or got anything wrong?

2. What do you believe the status, the condition, and the future of the African American family is today? Do you think blacks have overcome the bigotry that has dogged them in the past, or is racism still a problem in America? Do you think the Obama administration will make an impact on race relations, positive or negative? If so, do you think this impact will come from policy decisions or simply from the presence of a black president? Give specific reasons and examples to back up your answer.

3. Describe a moment, like the one McKinney-Whetstone describes, where you saw yourself in a public figure or connected deeply to a person, people, or an idea you encountered in the public sphere, either in person or on TV. What was it about the moment that made such an impact on you? Was it the overall feeling of what was said or done, or was it, as in "The First Family," the details? Give a thorough account of your reaction.

John Edgar Wideman

Street Corner Dreamers

[*Essence*, January 2009]

BEFORE YOU READ

What, if anything, can be done about the crushing problem of poverty in America's cities? What, if anything, will the Obama administration be able to achieve that previous governments have not?

WORDS TO LEARN

scour (para. 1): to clean something by rubbing or wiping it hard (verb).

dour (para. 1): sad and gloomy (adjective).

harbor (para. 1): to have inside (verb).

dire (para. 1): extremely serious (adjective).

droning (para. 1): making a low humming sound (adjective).

predatory (para. 1): planning to attack (adjective).

alienated (para. 2): made to feel apart from (adjective).

phantoms (para. 2): ghosts (noun).

palpable (para. 2): able to be felt (adjective).

jeopardizing (para. 2): putting in danger (verb).

expendable (para. 2): not necessary (adjective).

roiling (para. 3): swirling around (adjective).

exuberance (para. 3): joy and excitement for life (noun).

daunted (para. 3): intimidated or nervous (adjective).

simulate (para. 3): imitate (verb).

motley (para. 3): made of many different colors or fabrics (adjective).

infatuated (para. 4): having a sudden, intense passion for something (adjective).

incarcerated (para. 4): in prison (adjective).

chasm (para. 4): a wide gap, like a cliff (noun).

perilous (para. 5): dangerous (adjective).

intractable (para. 5): unable to be changed or dealt with (adjective).

irrepressible (para. 6): unable to be restrained (adjective).

throng (para. 7): crowd (verb).

One of America's most respected novelists, John Edgar Wideman is the Asa Messer Professor of Africana Studies and Creative Writing at Brown University. He has twice won the prestigious PEN/Faulkner Award and has been a nominee for the National Book Critics Circle Award. His most recent books include a collection of stories, God's Gym *(2005), and a novel,* Fanon *(2008).*

It is the morning after Barack Obama has been elected the forty-   1
fourth president of the United States. In six hours or so, the corner
of Grand and Essex, a block from my apartment building on New
York's Lower East Side, will fill up with young people exiting Seward
Park High School. For more than two years, the city has been sandblast-
ing Seward Park's seven-story exterior walls. As the presidential candidates debated taxes, someone was paid a large chunk of scarce public
funds, originally designated for improving education, to clean the building. Unfortunately, the scouring barely altered the dour, dirty gray scowl
of the brick and stone. I don't know what was transpiring inside Seward
while its outside was being scrubbed, but given the dismal record of
public schools educating the poor, I harbor plenty of dire concerns:
Has anybody asked the students if they think they're learning more
and better after their school's facelift? Are the students being instructed
how to survive the droning, predatory streets waiting to eat them up? I
want to walk up to one of them and ask, "Do you think your life might
be different now that Barack Obama is president? What steps do you
believe President Obama will take to improve your life? What steps do
you think he should take?"

Of course there are many, many young people missing from the   2
corner — in jail, addicted or dead already from violence or neglect, many
alienated absolutely from school, citizenship, prospects of jobs and families. Not a lost generation exactly — their bodies survive, though as mere
phantoms of what they could have become, could have offered society.
They are ghosts whose absence is a palpable presence among the kids on
the corner, a shadow haunting and jeopardizing them. How long? Too
long. They are the predictable casualties, victims comprising a heart-
breakingly high percentage of youth of color, destroyed by marginalization. Why? Because America decided we could get along just fine without
them, thank you. Is a President Obama too late to help the missing ones?
What higher priority for a nation, for a new president, than to stop the
bleeding, to stop the blighting of youth and potential suffered by generation after generation of the colored and poor? Will they continue to be
treated as expendable? How will President Barack Obama attempt to seal
the cracks they slip through? Not cracks in the pavement of Grand and
Essex, but the cracks of broken promises, the cracks that have divided
and conquered the will of a nation to treat all citizens equally.

Walking the gauntlets of students on the sidewalks surrounding   3
that school, I admit to myself that I've been too busy, too consumed
by whatever's on my mind, to ask any of them anything. Though they'd
never guess it from my silence as I pass through their ranks, I'm hope-
lessly in love with them, worry about them, see my nieces, nephews,

granddaughter, myself in this unruly, roiling mass of teenagers — young people of amalgamated African, Asian, European descent, every shade of light and dark skin, bushy hair, straight hair, dreads, braids, shaved heads, raw exuberance and noise and eyes hungry only for each other. I am a bit intimidated by them, certainly daunted by the ruthless truth of the vast difference in age and circumstance separating us, overwhelmed finally by the spectacle of their absolute fragility and vulnerability as they pour out onto the streets, exposed by the clothing they wear, clothes manufactured from the cheapest synthetics to simulate expensive flash and flair, colorful clothing brimming with attitude, with confidence and humor and shame and shyness about physically coming of age, bodies sprouting, busting-out young bodies in motley costumes to disguise poverty, clothing calculated to reveal and conceal.

Is there such a thing, really, as a future in young minds infatuated,   4 incarcerated by the present moment? Why would these young people speculate about crossing the gulf between themselves and the future, any future, whether a President Obama's in it or not? How equipped are they to imagine bridging the chasm between a White House in Washington, D.C., and a local, recently scoured public school that serves the Lower East Side's children of color and poverty?

In a classroom inside the building, as a sponsored guest, maybe I   5 could undertake a conversation about who they are, who I am, and the uncertain, unsettling place where we find ourselves at this perilous juncture in our nation's evolution. Perhaps we would explore together the explosive, still almost unbelievable fact that our country finally seized the opportunity to turn away from one deeply rooted, intractable, self-destructive, dead-end understanding of itself as White and Black, finally began to create a new vision of itself, whatever that vision might shake out to be. Will we become a nation converted to a new faith, a new dream, a new political consciousness and commitment, embracing Obama's complex heritage, his courage, his determination, his call for us to be more, collectively, than the sum of our parts?

My vision of what's coming next goes no further. No crystal-ball   6 gazing. I see a swarm of young people congregating down the block, free at last, free at last, of closed rooms, regimented hours, hostility, chaos, good intentions. Young women and men energized by the immediate, compelling hunger and sweetness of being alive. I want to believe that these young people on the corner are not only capable of hearing change, but that they can also be bearers of that change. Do I glimpse that change in the way they walk and talk, the way they occupy space and flash looks at one another, urgent exchanges of joy, anger, longing, understanding, impatience, solidarity, challenge, like the undeniable, irrepressible reality embodied in singer Sam Cooke's[1] voice when he promises change that must come — music that might be in the general air now or playing just around the corner in the voice of Barack Obama?

Not Barack singing, but President Obama in charge, calling the meeting to order. Putting a finger to his lips: *Quiet, everybody, please.* Let's listen to our young people on the street corners. Let's begin making room for the voices they may not exactly understand they own yet, carve out space for them in this country they may not exactly comprehend belongs to them, too. The president of the United States of America, listening to the words of the young people who throng Grand and Essex, Obama listening to discover what he may do for them, do for us all.

> Quiet, everybody, please. Let's listen to our young people on the street corners.

7

VOCABULARY/USING A DICTIONARY

1. What exactly is *marginalization* (para. 2)? What does Wideman mean by this term, where does it come from, and how does it apply to the "youth of color" to whom he refers?

2. What kind of garments is Wideman describing when he calls them *motley* (para. 3)? To what specific thing did this word once refer, and in what sense is Wideman using it in the essay?

3. What does *amalgamated* (para. 3) mean? What noun is this word related to, and what is its origin?

RESPONDING TO WORDS IN CONTEXT

1. Wideman says that the cleaning of the school building was unable to remove its "scowl" (para. 1). What is a *scowl*, and what do you think he means by the *scowl* of a building?

2. Wideman refers to the "facelift" of the school building in the same paragraph. What is a *facelift*, and what is he implying by using the word in this context?

3. What does Wideman mean when he refers to the "blighting of youth and potential suffered by generation after generation of the colored and poor" (para. 2)? Look up *blighting* in a dictionary. Where does the word come from, and what is its meaning here?

---

[1] Sam Cooke (para. 6): An African American singer killed in 1964. Wideman is referring to his song "A Change Is Gonna Come," released just after his death, which became an anthem for the civil rights movement.

260 Barack Obama: What Does His Election Mean to America?

DISCUSSING MAIN POINT AND MEANING

1. What do the students at Seward Park High School stand for? Why is Wideman using them as examples, and how do they represent a larger group?
2. What forces does Wideman blame for the problem he is describing? What exactly is that problem?
3. What does Wideman mean when he says he will do no "crystal-ball gazing" (para. 6)? Do you get the sense that Wideman is optimistic or pessimistic that President Obama will bring real change to the lives of the students at Seward Park?

EXAMINING SENTENCES, PARAGRAPHS, AND ORGANIZATION

1. Wideman writes that "as the presidential candidates debated taxes, someone was paid a large chunk of scarce public funds" (para. 1) to clean the New York school. Why does Wideman point out that these things happened at the same time?
2. What do all the sentences in paragraph 4 have in common? How does this paragraph add to the tone of the essay as a whole?
3. What is the effect of beginning the essay with a descriptive scene? What sort of scene does it set, and how does the image the essay establishes evolve into its argument?

THINKING CRITICALLY

1. Wideman repeatedly invokes the "missing" young people (para. 2), and refers to the black students on the corner of Grand and Essex as "phantoms" and "ghosts." Do you agree that black people, especially young black people, have been ignored in America? If so, why? What forces account for society's lack of attention, and what can be done about it? If not, why do you think Wideman and others believe young black people are "missing"? What can be done to address the problems they raise?
2. Wideman asks why black youths would "speculate about crossing the gulf between themselves and the future, any future, whether a President Obama's in it or not" (para. 4), but stops short of predicting whether in fact they will—or what that future will look like for them. Look into your own crystal ball. Do you think Obama will have an impact on urban poverty? Why or why not?
3. Wideman writes that the best hope for America is to "turn away from one deeply rooted, intractable, self-destructive, dead-end understanding of itself as White and Black" (para. 5). What does he mean by this comment? Is he suggesting that Americans need to ignore racial differences, embrace them, or something in between? How much do you feel race should be a part of our individual identities or of the national conversation? Does it receive too much attention at the moment—or too little?

IN-CLASS WRITING ACTIVITIES

1. Research some statistics on the poverty gap between blacks and whites. What accounts for this disparity? Do you believe there is a solution to the overwhelming imbalance between black and white poverty? If so, detail how you believe this solution could be enacted. If not, why not? What makes the problem, to borrow Wideman's word, so "intractable"?

2. Write a brief description of a public school in your neighborhood or home town following Wideman's example, in which the outward look of the school serves as a metaphor for what kind of education goes on inside it. Is it (and are the students, in turn) suffering from neglect? Or is it a symbol of the class of people who attend it? Show, don't tell.

3. What do you expect President Obama can do for you and your community? Do you feel that politicians have any real impact on the way things stand on the street level anymore, or is it impossible for a disconnected Washington establishment to make any real changes? List three positive changes the federal government could make in your town or city in the next two years, and whether or not you think they will happen. If not, why not?

Pearl Wong (student essay)
Obama—President for All

[*The Santa Clara*, Santa Clara University, February 25, 2010]

BEFORE YOU READ
Have we transcended race in America? If not, will we ever transcend it? How conscious should we be of race in our everyday lives?

WORDS TO LEARN
assailed (para. 2): viciously and repeatedly attacked (adjective).
foundation (para. 3): structure on which something rests (noun).

maintain (para. 3): hold on to (verb).
vulnerable (para. 4): easy to hurt (adjective).

Pearl Wong is an economics major at Santa Clara University. She contributes to the school paper, The Santa Clara, *a few times a year and hopes to make a career out of writing. She expects to graduate in 2012.*

How can one expect others to look past our skin color and eth- 1
nic backgrounds if we can't? Now, I'm not talking about being
ashamed of one's heritage or about prancing in public with conspicuous banners demanding acceptance. A fine line exists between overtly
embracing who we are and quietly concealing our identity. However, by
conspicuously identifying themselves with a specific racial group, people
essentially allow others to classify them based only on their heritage.

Recently, President Barack Obama has been assailed with discon- 2
tentment from the African American community for not doing enough
for black Americans. Of course, black scholars are careful in their criticisms, but the message is clear: They think Obama needs to directly
address the issue of race.

Although our nation was built on a foundation to protect minority 3
groups, no one ever said one can only help one group of minorities; so, red
pill or blue?[1] Rather than focusing on one race, even if it's one particularly
close to Obama's heart, the President of the United States must maintain
his executive position as a representative of all people residing in America.

Addressing the rising grumbling from black scholars, Obama was 4
quoted in the *New York Times*, saying, "I can't pass laws that say I'm just
helping black folks. I'm the President of the United States. What I can do
is make sure that I am passing laws that help all people, particularly those
who are most vulnerable and most in need. That in turn is going to help
lift up the African American community."

Hence, while Obama embodies a 5
milestone in America's history as the first
African American president, he is not the
president of only African Americans. In
order for true equality to develop, we must
begin with ourselves and with each other.
Instead of calling for attention, take the
opportunity to make positive changes in
your local community.

> In order for true
> equality to develop,
> we must begin
> with ourselves and
> with each other.

Rather than shaking your heads at the news, ask yourself what you 6
can do to make the world a bit better for minorities. As Mother Teresa
said, "If you judge people, you will have no time to love them."

VOCABULARY/USING A DICTIONARY

1. What does the prefix *dis-* mean in "discontentment" (para. 2)? What does
   Wong mean by *discontentment*?

---

[1] red pill or blue (para. 3): A reference to the 1999 film *The Matrix*, in which the
choice of pills represents a particularly difficult decision between learning the
truth or being happy.

2. What is a *milestone* (para. 5)? What is the literal meaning of the word, and what figurative meaning does the dictionary offer? In which sense is Wong using it here?

RESPONDING TO WORDS IN CONTEXT

1. Wong repeats the word *conspicuous* in paragraph 1, in two different forms. What does this word mean, to what sort of behavior is she referring, and why does she emphasize it?
2. Wong writes that Obama "embodies a milestone in America's history." What does it mean to *embody* something (para. 5)? What is the origin of the word, and how is it used in Wong's essay?

DISCUSSING MAIN POINT AND MEANING

1. Summarize what Wong means by the "fine line" she introduces in paragraph 1. What are the two extremes she is arguing we must avoid?
2. Wong writes that "in order for true equality to develop, we must begin with ourselves and with each other" (para. 5). What do you think she means? What is she suggesting we have to do in order to achieve equality?

EXAMINING SENTENCES, PARAGRAPHS, AND ORGANIZATION

1. What does Wong mean by asking "red pill or blue" in paragraph 3? What two options do the pills represent? Why does she phrase the choice this way, and how does this phrasing enhance her point?
2. Describe how Wong uses quotations in her essay. What two sources does she quote, and what is the effect of each quotation? What is their combined effect?

THINKING CRITICALLY

1. Wong's argument rests in large part on her assertion in paragraph 1 that "by conspicuously identifying themselves with a specific racial group, people essentially allow others to classify them based only on their heritage." Do you agree? Do you think it's possible to make your ethnicity or heritage a major part of your identity without allowing others to judge you based on it?
2. What do you think of Wong's claim that change must come from individual action? What will be more important to solving problems like race relations in America—local efforts by individuals or government intervention? Why? Give specific examples.

IN-CLASS WRITING ACTIVITIES

1. Limited by space, Wong does not offer examples of how black scholars expect President Obama to do more for black Americans, or to "directly address the issue of race (para. 2)." Give three specific examples of actions

black leaders might hope the president would take on behalf of minorities, whether or not you agree he should follow them.

2. Wong challenges us to ask ourselves what we can do "to make the world a bit better for minorities" (para. 6). Do you think this is a reasonable challenge? Should we be considering minorities when we act on a local level, or, following Obama's example, should we simply worry about helping those who need it most, regardless of ethnic group? What do you think is the most useful thing people can do to help the needy in their communities?

Establishing Your Main Point

As you learn to express opinions clearly and effectively, you need to ask yourself a relatively simple question: Will my readers understand my main point? In composition, a main point is sometimes called a thesis or a thesis statement. It is often a sentence that summarizes your central idea or a position. It need not include any factual proof or supporting evidence — that can be supplied in the body of your essay — but it should represent a general statement that clearly shows where you stand on an issue or what exactly your essay is about. Although main points are often found in opening paragraphs, they can also appear later on in an essay, especially when the writer wants to set the stage for his or her opinion by opening with a relevant quotation, a topical reference, an emotional appeal, or a general point.

This is the way Pearl Wong, a student at Santa Clara University, proceeds in "Obama — President for All." She begins with a general point about ethnic identification that prepares the reader for her main point, which is not expressed until the third paragraph, as seen below.

1

In one sentence, Wong states the main point of her essay

Although our nation was built on a foundation to protect minority groups, no one ever said one can only help one group of minorities; so, red pill or blue? <u>Rather than focusing on one race, even if it's one particularly close to Obama's heart, the President of the United States must maintain his executive position as a representative of all people residing in America.</u> (1)

STUDENT WRITER AT WORK
Pearl Wong
On Writing "Obama—President for All"

RA. What was your main purpose in writing this essay?

PW. Writing is my main outlet for my emotions and thoughts. Mainly, that outlet comes from when I feel there is an injustice or a breach in my definition of ethics or when I feel very strongly about a situation in my life.

RA. How long did it take for you to write this piece? Did you revise your work? What were your goals as you revised?

PW. It took me about thirty minutes to write the very first draft. In the end, the final draft was sent after a couple more hours of revision and editing. Whenever I write a first draft, it is a very raw reflection of my viewpoints. I think my revisions usually incorporate more fairness and openness to whatever topic I am working on. I don't like to be biased or narrow-minded. My goals are always to be fair to the other side and understand where they are coming from, even if I don't agree.

RA. What topics most interest you as a writer?

PW. I'm most interested in topics relating to social justice, ethics, business, and international relations.

RA. Are you pursuing a career in which writing will be a component?

PW. Yes, I want to be a writer, but I'm not sure if I want to pursue journalism or be a novelist.

RA. What advice do you have for other student writers?

PW. Write. Write all the time. Keep a journal and let the words flow. Make that journal private — in other words, not a blog — so that you can completely let go of keeping up appearances or trying to be politically or grammatically correct. We all need a place where we do not feel judged, and sometimes that place is actually a physical object like a journal. And that's okay!

Christopher Hedges

Celebrity Culture and the Obama Brand

[*Tikkun*, January/February 2010]

BEFORE YOU READ
Can politicians offer real change, or are their promises more often than not empty? Does President Obama represent a real break from the policies of the past, or is he just part of an elaborate illusion?

WORDS TO LEARN

overlords (para. 1): powerful rulers (noun).

lobbyists (para. 1): people who try to influence government on behalf of an industry or a group (noun).

insolvent (para. 2): unable to pay debts (adjective).

forestalls (para. 2): delays for a little while (verb).

dismantle (para. 2): take down (verb).

inoculates (para. 3): gives someone a vaccine to prevent a disease (verb).

immune (para. 3): unable to be affected by something (adjective).

folksiness (para. 3): the appearance of being ordinary and unpretentious (noun).

artifice (para. 3): fakeness (noun).

precursors (para. 3): something similar that came before (noun).

risqué (para. 3): slightly shocking (adjective).

confound (para. 3): confuse (verb).

predatory (para. 4): attacking like a predator (adjective).

venue (para. 4): a place where something happens (noun).

redress (para. 4): a way of fixing a wrong (noun).

leached (para. 6): dripped (verb).

bequeath (para. 6): leave behind (verb).

reparation (para. 6): making right (noun).

interlocking (para. 6): connecting together (adjective).

braggadocio (para. 6): exaggerated arrogant behavior (noun).

mawkishness (para. 6): being overly sentimental (noun).

The Pulitzer Prize–winning reporter Christopher Hedges spent nearly twenty years as a foreign correspondent. His books include the best-selling War Is a Force That Gives Us Meaning *(2002) and* Empire of Illusion: The End of Literacy and the Triumph of Spectacle *(2009).*

bloating (para. 6): filling to capacity or overflowing (verb).

obliterate (para. 6): completely destroy (verb).

perpetual (para. 8): unending (adjective).

wanton (para. 8): intentional and unprovoked (adjective).

bereft (para. 8): lacking something, especially money (adjective).

potent (para. 8): powerful (adjective).

snuff out (para. 8): kill brutally (verb).

Barack Obama is a brand. And the Obama brand is designed to make us feel good about our government while corporate overlords loot the Treasury, armies of corporate lobbyists grease the palms of our elected officials, our corporate media diverts us with gossip and trivia, and our imperial wars expand in the Middle East. Brand Obama is about being happy consumers. We are entertained. We feel hopeful. We like our president. We believe he is like us. But like all branded products spun out from the manipulative world of corporate advertising, this product is duping us into doing and supporting a lot of things that are not in our interest.

What, for all our faith and hope, has the Obama brand given us? His administration has spent, lent, or guaranteed $12.8 trillion in taxpayer dollars to Wall Street[1] and insolvent banks in a doomed effort to re-inflate the bubble economy, a tactic that at best forestalls catastrophe and will leave us broke in a time of profound crisis. Brand Obama has allocated nearly $1 trillion in defense-related spending and the continuation of our doomed imperial projects in Iraq, where military planners now estimate that 70,000 troops will remain for the next fifteen to twenty years. Brand Obama has expanded the war in Afghanistan, increasing the use of drones sent on cross-border bombing runs into Pakistan, which have doubled the number of civilians killed over the past three months. Brand Obama has refused to ease restrictions so workers can organize and will not consider single-payer, not-for-profit health care for all Americans. And Brand Obama will not prosecute the Bush administration for war crimes, including the use of torture, and has refused to dismantle Bush's secrecy laws and restore habeas corpus.[2]

---

[1] Wall Street (para. 2): The location of the financial industry in New York, often used to represent large, wealthy banking interests and the stock market.

---

[2] habeas corpus (para. 2): The principle that an accused person should be allowed to know the charges against him or her exactly; the Bush administration suspended it during the War on Terror.

Brand Obama offers us an image that appears radically individualis-   3
tic and new. It inoculates us from seeing that the old engines of corporate power and the vast military-industrial complex continue to plunder
the country. Corporations, which control our politics, no longer produce products that are essentially different, but brands that are different.
Brand Obama does not threaten the core of the corporate state any more
than did Brand George W. Bush. The Bush brand collapsed. We became
immune to its studied folksiness. We saw through its artifice. This is a
common deflation in the world of advertising. So we have been given a
new Obama brand with an exciting and faintly erotic appeal. Benetton
and Calvin Klein[3] were the precursors to the Obama brand, using ads to
associate themselves with risqué art and progressive politics. This strategy gave their products an edge. But the goal, as with all brands, was to
make passive consumers confound a brand with an experience.

Obama, who has become a global celebrity, was molded easily   4
into a brand. He had almost no experience, other than two years in the
Senate, lacked any moral core, and could be painted as all things to all
people. His brief Senate voting record was a miserable surrender to
corporate interests. He was happy to promote nuclear power as "green"
energy. He voted to continue the wars in Iraq and Afghanistan. He
reauthorized the Patriot Act.[4] He would not back a bill designed to cap
predatory credit card interest rates. He opposed a bill that would have
reformed the notorious Mining Law of 1872.[5] He refused to support
the single-payer[6] health care bill HR 676, sponsored by Reps. Dennis
Kucinich and John Conyers. He supported the death penalty. And he
backed a class-action "reform" bill that was part of a large lobbying
effort by financial firms. The law, known as the Class Action Fairness
Act, would effectively shut down state courts as a venue to hear most
class-action lawsuits and deny redress in many of the courts where
these cases have a chance of defying powerful corporate challenges.

---

[3] Benneton and Calvin Klein (para. 3): Fashion designers famous for their racy
ads, which often feature minority models.

---

[4] Patriot Act (para. 4): A law passed shortly after 9/11 that expanded the government and, according to some liberals, violated civil liberties, as part of the War
on Terror.

---

[5] Mining Law of 1872 (para. 4): A United States law that oversees prospecting
and mining on federal public lands.

---

[6] single-payer (para. 4): A type of government-provided healthcare coverage in
which each taxpayer is automatically enrolled in government health insurance.

Obama's campaign won the vote of hundreds of marketers, agency   5
heads, and marketing-services vendors gathered at the Association of
National Advertisers' annual conference in October. The Obama campaign was named *Advertising Age's*[7] marketer of the year for 2008 and
edged out runners-up Apple and Zappos.
com. Take it from the professionals. Brand
Obama is a marketer's dream. President
Obama does one thing and Brand Obama
gets you to believe another. This is the
essence of successful advertising. You buy
or do what the advertisers want because of
how they can make you feel.

> President Obama
> does one thing
> and Brand Obama
> gets you to believe
> another.

Celebrity culture has leached into every aspect of our culture, includ-   6
ing politics, to bequeath to us what Benjamin DeMott[8] called "junk politics." Junk politics does not demand justice or the reparation of rights.
Junk politics personalizes and moralizes issues rather than clarifying
them. "It's impatient with articulated conflict, enthusiastic about America's optimism and moral character, and heavily dependent on feel-your-
pain language and gesture," DeMott noted. The result of junk politics
is that nothing changes — "meaning zero interruption in the processes
and practices that strengthen existing, interlocking systems of socioeconomic advantage." Junk politics redefines traditional values, tilting
"courage toward braggadocio, sympathy toward mawkishness, humility
toward self-disrespect, identification with ordinary citizens toward dis-
trust of brains." Junk politics "miniaturizes large, complex problems at
home while maximizing threats from abroad. It's also given to abrupt
unexplained reversals of its own public stances, often spectacularly bloating problems previously miniaturized." And finally, it "seeks at every turn
to obliterate voters' consciousness of socioeconomic and other differences in their midst."

The old production-oriented culture demanded what the historian   7
Warren Susman termed "character." The new consumption-oriented culture demands what he called "personality." The shift in values is a shift
from a fixed morality to the artifice of presentation. The old cultural values of thrift and moderation honored hard work, integrity, and courage.
The consumption-oriented culture honors charm, fascination, and like-
ability. "The social role demanded of all in the new culture of personality

---

[7] *Advertising Age* (para. 5): An industry magazine for advertisers.

---

[8] Benjamin DeMott (para. 6): American academic, writer, scholar, and cultural
critic (1924–2005).

was that of a performer," Susman wrote. "Every American was to become a performing self."

The junk politics practiced by Obama is a consumer fraud. It is about performance. It is about lies. It is about keeping us in a perpetual state of childishness. But the longer we live in illusion, the worse reality will be when it finally shatters our fantasies. Those who do not understand what is happening around them and who are overwhelmed by a brutal reality they did not expect or foresee search desperately for saviors. They beg demagogues to come to their rescue. This is the ultimate danger of the Obama Brand. It effectively masks the wanton internal destruction and theft being carried out by our corporate state. These corporations, once they have stolen trillions in taxpayer wealth, will leave tens of millions of Americans bereft, bewildered, and yearning for even more potent and deadly illusions, ones that could swiftly snuff out what is left of our diminished open society.

8

VOCABULARY/USING A DICTIONARY

1. Hedges twice describes American policy as "imperial" (paras. 1 and 2). What does he mean by *imperial*? What word does *imperial* derive from?
2. What does it mean if junk politics is *tilting* (para. 6) certain virtues toward extreme redefinitions, as Hedges quotes Benjamin DeMott as arguing?
3. Define *demagogue* (para. 8). What language does the word come from, and what does it mean in the original language? Does it have a positive or negative connotation?

RESPONDING TO WORDS IN CONTEXT

1. Based on the passage in which it occurs, what do you think the phrase "grease the palms of" (para. 1) means? Look it up online if necessary. How does Hedges suggest palms are being greased here?
2. Look up the word *trivia* (para. 1). What usages of the word are you familiar with? In what sense does Hedges mean it here?
3. What does Hedges mean by *deflation* (para. 3), judging from the context? What is the literal, dictionary definition of the word?

DISCUSSING MAIN POINT AND MEANING

1. Explain in your own words what Hedges means by a "brand" throughout this essay. What industry does the idea of a brand come from? What does it mean for Barack Obama to be a brand?
2. What does Hedges think of the presidency of George W. Bush? Why? What does he imply Barack Obama promised to do on assuming the presidency, and how does he assess Obama's keeping of those promises?

3. According to Hedges, who really controls American politics and government? How do they do so? How does his argument about "Brand Obama"
fit into this assertion?

EXAMINING SENTENCES, PARAGRAPHS, AND ORGANIZATION

1. Why does Hedges put the words *green* and *reform* in quotation marks in
paragraph 4? What is he implying, and what does this add to the tone of
the essay as a whole?
2. What is the effect of the short, choppy sentences in paragraph 1 ("We
are entertained. We feel hopeful," etc.)? What tone is Hedges using to
describe our reaction to the Obama presidency?
3. Does Hedges seem to be writing for an audience that agrees or disagrees
with his politics? How does he make his political leanings clear throughout the essay? Point out a few places where the author states a premise
that some might find controversial but with which he assumes his audience will agree.

THINKING CRITICALLY

1. Should the fact that advertisers admire the Obama campaign—as
evinced in *Advertising Age* naming it marketer of the year in
2008—automatically condemn President Obama or his administration?
Why or why not? Do you think politicians have an obligation to avoid the
sort of tactics and strategies that marketers use, or is some degree of
salesmanship unavoidable in electoral politics?
2. Do you agree that we have "junk politics" (para. 6) in America? Describe
in your own words what junk politics is, and judge our political system as
you know it against this definition. Do politicians stress the right issues
in America, or do they, as the essay alleges, aim only to distract voters?
3. Some critics would disagree with Hedges's thesis on the grounds that
Barack Obama has been the object of so much severe criticism since
taking office—much of it from George W. Bush's Republican Party. Do
you think the division between Democrats and Republicans proves that
corporations are not in fact pulling the strings behind the scenes of
American government, but that the two parties do actually represent
real ideological differences? How do you think Hedges would answer this
argument?

IN-CLASS WRITING ACTIVITIES

1. What do you think Hedges means by "gossip and trivia" when he
describes "corporate" media coverage in paragraph 1 of the essay? Give
a few specific examples of gossip and trivia in the media. Do you agree
that this kind of media coverage is a bad thing? Do you agree that it

is part of a plot to keep Americans uninformed and unquestioning? Whether or not you feel corporate interests control it, do you think the American media could do a better job of covering politics and government? If so, how?

2. Write a brief assessment of how things have changed, in your experience and research, since Obama entered the White House and Bush left it. Has America changed at all? Or have any changes been, as Hedges claims, superficial and minor?

3. Hedges describes the Obama brand as having an "exciting and faintly erotic appeal" (para. 3). Whether or not you agree with the author's belief that a deliberate effort is behind the Obama brand, offer your own assessment of what this brand is. Start by writing down your immediate associations with President Obama—what do you think of when you hear his name and how do you see him and his administration? What parts of this portrait, if any, may have been planted in your mind by Barack Obama himself or by his supporters? By his opponents?

Discussing the Unit

SUGGESTED TOPIC FOR DISCUSSION

If nothing else, the debate over the significance of the Obama presidency shows us that race is still a prominent and controversial topic in America today. What do you think of the issue of race? Is it overblown—a media invention contrived to keep us arguing about something when we actually live in an increasingly color-blind society? Or do we still live with the vestiges of slavery and discrimination, a civilization fundamentally hampered by our own racial tensions?

PREPARING FOR CLASS DISCUSSION

1. Both Diane McKinney-Whetstone and John Edgar Wideman discuss the nagging problem of black poverty from the vantage point of African Americans with a position of solidarity and conviction that the problem is solvable. What do you think is keeping so many African Americans in poverty in the United States?

2. Compare Christopher Hedges's view of Barack Obama to those of McKinney-Whetstone and Wideman. What would Hedges say about the way these two authors imagine Obama, and why? What do you think?

FROM DISCUSSION TO WRITING

1. Evaluate the Obama administration in terms of what it has done for African Americans. Has President Obama lived up to the promise McKinney-

Whetstone saw in him and his family on election night? Has he done anything about what Wideman calls the "marginalization" (para. 2) of African American youth? How do you perceive his impact on race relations as president?

2. Imagine you're a historian one hundred years from now writing the annals of the Obama administration. How does the presidency begin? How will history see Obama's election—as a significant historic moment, or something else? What are Obama's immediate successes and failures? What does he strive to do for America, and how does he fare?

TOPICS FOR CROSS-CULTURAL DISCUSSION

1. The selections in this chapter focus on racial relations between blacks and whites in America, but this is hardly the end of race as a topic of discussion. What other groups have a significant voice, or pose a significant problem, to our national discussion on race? Should these groups be encouraged by President Obama, or concerned about his administration? Why?

2. Hedges writes that "Brand Obama is a marketer's dream" (para. 5), but mentions only the domestic market—that is, how Obama appeals to Americans. As McKinney-Whetstone points out, Obama's extended family was seen cheering on election night in Kenya, and the Obama brand has certainly sold, for better or worse, overseas. How is the Obama presidency changing the *American* brand in the rest of the world's eyes? Is it a good or a bad change?

10

Social Networking—How Is It Transforming Behavior?

In what ways are social media like Facebook, MySpace, and Twitter transforming our social lives? Are these new forms of instant social connection causing us needless distraction? Do they have a serious impact on how we live today? Even though social media is quickly catching on across generations, many older people view them satirically, believing they are no substitute for traditional methods of communication. In "Hi, Dad," a segment from the popular comic strip *Doonesbury*, Garry Trudeau pokes fun at a college student's total absorption in her online relationships while she ignores her visiting father's presence.

Yet some adults don't mind "oversharing" online, as thirty-year-old journalist and blogger Mary Katharine Ham acknowledges in "We Shall Overshare." Admitting that she is "an enthusiastic user" of Twitter and Facebook, Ham concedes that it is easy to embarrass oneself online: "It's a daily game of public Frogger, hopping frantically to avoid being crushed under the weight of your own narcissism, banality, and plain old stupidity."

Ego is also an issue for Emerson College student Brent Baughman. In "Growing Older in the Digital Age: An Exercise in Egotism," he comically considers how all the new technology comes together when we have a birthday: "Birthdays are the one day of the year when compulsive e-mail checking finally pays off — every five minutes the latest note, e-card, or jotting of affection is waiting there in Gmail bold."

If birthdays provide opportunities to use new social media, what about the deaths of friends? How do we commemorate the loss of loved ones on Facebook? After one of her best students was fatally struck by a van in the summer of 2009, Elizabeth Stone, a Fordham University communications professor, monitored the responses of her many friends on Facebook. In "Grief in the Age of Facebook," she poignantly raises the issue of how social media deals with grief and mourning. She writes: "I've seen how markedly technology has influenced the conventions of grieving among my students, offering them solace but also uncertainty."

Garry Trudeau

Hi, Dad

[*Doonesbury, Boston Globe,* November 8, 2009]

BEFORE YOU READ

Are social media and social networking positive or negative forces in your life? Are they bringing you closer to or further from your friends and family?

WORDS TO LEARN

oversharing (panel 2): giving too much personal information (verb).

migrates (panel 8): moves (verb).

curating (panel 8): managing and controlling (verb).

Born in New York City in 1948, Garry Trudeau began publishing comic strips as an undergraduate at Yale University, where he also received an MFA in graphic design. He is best known for Doonesbury, *which was first syndicated in 1970, received a Pulitzer Prize in 1975, and now appears in well over a thousand newspapers across the globe.*

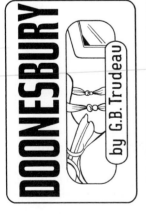

VOCABULARY/USING A DICTIONARY

1. What does *secs* stand for in panel 4 of the strip? Why is the use of the abbreviation here ironic?
2. What does it mean to *blog* (panel 7)? What part of speech is it in this case? What is the origin of this word?

RESPONDING TO WORDS IN CONTEXT

1. You're probably familiar with much of the social-networking vocabulary used in the strip. Look the terms up if you aren't. What does it mean to *tag* (panel 7)? To *strip* (panel 7)?
2. What does the daughter in the strip mean when she says in panel 8 she's *curating* her *brand*? What about *repositioning* her *presence*?

DISCUSSING MAIN POINT AND MEANING

1. What is the main point of the strip? What argument or idea is it advancing? Do you think Trudeau sympathizes more with the daughter or with the father? Defend your answer.
2. What do we assume the father is waiting to do? What clues suggest this to us? Why is this important to the main idea of the strip?

EXAMINING SENTENCES, PARAGRAPHS, AND ORGANIZATION

1. Where is the strip set? How can you tell? How does Trudeau give you hints to the setting without making it obvious, and why is this important?
2. Which character does virtually all of the speaking in the strip? What is the only thing the other character says? What is the effect of this imbalance?

THINKING CRITICALLY

1. Does the daughter's use of social networking resonate with you based on your own experiences? What aspects of it do you think are accurate, and what, if anything, did Trudeau get wrong? Is it an exaggeration, or do you and your friends spend the same amount of time and energy online as the young woman in the strip seems to?
2. Do you agree with the strip that social media could potentially be ruining our lives? Do you think sites like Facebook, MySpace, and Twitter have had an overall positive or negative influence on your life and on the way you work and socialize? Why? Give specific examples.

IN-CLASS WRITING ACTIVITIES

1. Describe in detail the way you use the Internet and social media in particular. How many hours a day do you spend on networking and media sites? What, if anything, do you accomplish by being on them? Do you feel addicted to these sites, or is there a real usefulness to them? If you disagree with Trudeau's premise, defend your use of social media to him. If you agree, explain why it is so worrisome.

2. Regardless of your feelings about social media, do you sympathize more with the daughter or the father in this strip? Why? Describe a time when you experienced the kind of generational gap the strip explores. Were you ever frustrated by someone older than you or befuddled by someone younger? How did it feel? Do you ever worry the situation will be reversed?

Mary Katharine Ham

We Shall Overshare

[*The Weekly Standard*, June 8, 2009]

BEFORE YOU READ

How much is too much when it comes to talking about your personal life online? How do you feel about people who use social media sites as their private diaries? Are they a nuisance or an inevitable part of a more connected world?

WORDS TO LEARN

gulag (para. 2): a Russian prison camp (noun).

tiff (para. 2): a minor fight (noun).

heretofore (para. 3): until now (adverb).

exponentially (para. 3): at a rapidly increasing speed (adverb).

detractors (para. 3): opponents (noun).

scrutiny (para. 3): examination (noun).

spurn (para. 3): hatefully reject (verb).

pictorial (para. 4): a series of related photos (noun).

As a staff writer, Mary Katharine Ham contributes regularly to The Weekly Standard. *She is also a frequent guest on* The O'Reilly Factor. *A journalist and video blogger (see* HamNation*), she is a 2002 graduate of the University of Georgia.*

prowess (para. 4): ability (noun).

banality (para. 5): boringness (noun).

erosion (para. 5): the destruction of something over time (noun).

quintessentially (para. 7): exactly, as the perfect example of (adverb).

cultivate (para. 9): acquire and develop (verb).

ponder (para. 9): consider deeply (verb).

dissidents (para. 10): people who oppose an established political system, religion, organization, etc. (noun).

A llison is "furious. They think they'll break me, but they will only make me fight harder in the end."   1

Either I've got a friend in a gulag somewhere or I've got one who's tripped over one of the potholes of modern life — the overshare. Given that her message didn't arrive via waterborne bottle or scribbled in the margins of a dusty Russian novel, but via her Facebook update, I think it's safe to say that her little tiff at work hasn't placed her in physical danger.   2

It has, however, caused her to illustrate the dangers of living a life online. As millions of us have taken to MySpace, Facebook, and Twitter to connect with friends, share stories, and post pictures at a speed and volume heretofore unknown, we've also exponentially multiplied ways to humiliate ourselves. It's perhaps understandable then that the online life has its detractors. Facebook has been dubbed "mind-numbingly dull" and Twitter a service for "people who need to expose as much of their lives to public scrutiny as possible." As an enthusiastic user of both, I concede that these statements are true. Yet I cannot spurn the new social media. As a result, my online life is a balancing act.   3

Sure, I could settle for a routine in which only traditional social skills are required, but where's the fun in that? I long ago mastered not talking with my mouth full and placing a napkin in my lap, and still felt the world needed people like me — pioneers of electronic propriety — to make tough choices. Is my personal hygiene regimen or lack thereof fit for public consumption? Probably not. What about a pictorial on the proper position for a keg stand? Not a good idea, regardless of my prowess. Does my social circle need to know that the sour cream at Chipotle[1] tastes "a little off"? Tough call. Could be a public health issue.   4

> Sure, I could settle for a routine in which only traditional social skills are required, but where's the fun in that?

---

[1] Chipotle (para. 4): A popular Mexican fast-food chain.

It's a daily game of public Frogger,[2] hopping frantically to avoid   5
being crushed under the weight of your own narcissism, banality, and
plain old stupidity. Just as it took Alexander Graham Bell[3] a couple of
tries on the telephone to realize that "Hoy! Hoy!" simply wasn't going
to work as the standard greeting, so it took a brave South African man
to discover that calling your boss a "serial masturbator" on Facebook
will get you fired. There are thousands oversharing online as I write,
paying the price with a gradual erosion of their dignity, so you don't
have to.

Ironically, the antidote I've found for my own tendency to overshare   6
online is more sharing online. Everything on my Facebook and Twitter pages is openly available. It's amazing how reasonably you act when
everyone you know (and many you don't) is watching you.

I make a conscious decision to broadcast my life every day, and I   7
accept the consequences. In a way it's a quintessentially conservative
formula: The extent to which you take personal responsibility for your
actions dictates the risks and benefits of your online existence.

For me, the weird ("Will you send me a picture of your feet?") and   8
embarrassing (thank you to whoever uploaded the middle-school band
photos) is outweighed by the rewarding (getting to see my cousins more
than once a year). Facebook is such a natural extension of my daily life
that it became a fitting public place to memorialize my grandmother
with a simple picture when she passed away. What others would do at a
gravesite, I did on Facebook.

There's another attitude I've resolved to cultivate. Even though the   9
new social technologies are built to feel like they're all about you, it helps
to remember they're not. When pondering another photo shoot for my
profile picture the other day, I couldn't help recalling the Facebook users
who raised $800,000 for St. Jude Children's Research Hospital only
last week.

Similarly, when I'm tempted to post self-pitying status updates that   10
sound like I'm in prison instead of my condo, it occurs to me that
Twitter and Facebook also host actual dissidents. Their status updates
were a frightening enough breath of freedom that Iran blocked Facebook

---

[2] Frogger (para. 5): A popular arcade video game from the early 1980s, in which a
player must direct frogs to hop out of the way of oncoming traffic.

---

[3] Alexander Graham Bell (para. 5): (1847–1922) The inventor of the telephone.
He originally planned "Hoy! Hoy!" as the proper greeting when picking up the
phone, but it was quickly replaced by "Hello."

last week, only to lift the ban days later as Ahmadinejad[4] distanced himself from the unpopular crackdown. Every new technology needs its pioneers. Many are banal, but some are truly brave.

They make me think of other pioneers. The historian Donald Jackson 11 recounts that Lewis and Clark[5] "wrote constantly and abundantly, . . . legibly and illegibly, and always with an urgent sense of purpose." So do I, and almost always in 140 characters or less.[6]

VOCABULARY/USING A DICTIONARY

1. Ham describes oversharers as "being crushed under the weight of [their] own narcissism, banality, and plain old stupidity" (para. 5). What is a *narcissist*? What are the origins of the word?

2. What does it mean to *broadcast* one's life, in the sense that Ham uses it when she says she makes a "conscious decision to broadcast" (para. 7) her life every day? From what field does the word come?

3. What does Ham mean when she says she plans to "cultivate" an attitude (para. 9)? What does *cultivate* mean, and what is its origin?

RESPONDING TO WORDS IN CONTEXT

1. Look up the literal meaning of the word *erosion*. In what sense is Ham using it in paragraph 5 of her essay?

2. Ham writes that more online sharing is, "ironically, the antidote I've found for my own tendency to overshare online" (para. 6). What does *antidote* mean, literally? How is Ham using it here? What does its use imply about oversharing?

3. What are the connotations of the word *pioneer* (para. 10) as Ham uses it?

DISCUSSING MAIN POINT AND MEANING

1. Why does Ham say her Facebook and Twitter pages are highly public (para. 6)? What effect does this have on the way she uses them? What is

---

[4] Ahmadinejad (para. 10): Mahmoud Ahmadinejad, the president of Iran as of 2010, considered by many in the West to be a corrupt dictator. In the summer of 2009, the Iranian government cracked down on protesters, who kept their message alive on Twitter and other social media sites.

---

[5] Lewis and Clark (para. 11): The team of explorers who surveyed the vast Louisiana Purchase in the early nineteenth century, making careful records and maps along the way.

---

[6] 140 characters or less (para. 11): The maximum length of a post (or "tweet") on Twitter.

she implying she might do if she had a smaller audience reading her contributions to social media?

2. What are the advantages of social media and social networking as Ham describes them? What specific examples does she give, and how does this add to her main idea that the danger of these media is overuse?

3. What is the relationship between Ham's general point about the narcissism of oversharers online and her example of the Twitter revolution in Iran? How does she transition between these two points, and how does the organization of her essay accommodate both a slightly playful and a serious argument?

EXAMINING SENTENCES, PARAGRAPHS, AND ORGANIZATION

1. What is the significance of the title of Ham's essay? (Hint: Look up "We Shall Overcome" online.) How does this playful title add to the humor and irony of the essay?

2. Why does Ham start with an example? What is particularly effective about the example she chooses? What does Ham mean by her opening remark ("Either I've got a friend in a gulag somewhere ...") and how does it combine with paragraph 1 to set the tone for the essay?

3. Discuss the use of juxtaposition—putting together two dissimilar things—in Ham's essay. How does she juxtapose the present use of social media and the ways people communicated in the past? What is the meaning of her sentence comparing Alexander Graham Bell and the unfortunate South African in paragraph 5?

THINKING CRITICALLY

1. Do you agree that the example Ham gives in paragraph 1 is automatically an overshare? Does context matter, or is the category of tweet she is highlighting always a bit ludicrous? Where is the line between sharing something important and serious, and offering too much information?

2. What are the major positive uses of Facebook and Twitter? Give two examples besides those Ham offers.

3. Can social-networking sites really have the sort of political impact Ham describes in paragraph 10? Does hosting dissidents mean that dissent will be more meaningful or effective? Why or why not?

IN-CLASS WRITING ACTIVITIES

1. Look up *The Weekly Standard*—what kind of magazine is it and what are its politics? How does Ham claim her argument fits into *The Weekly Standard*'s mission? (See paragraph 7.) Do you agree? Is there a political dimension to the use of social-networking sites?

2. Give a few examples of oversharing online, either from your experience or your imagination. They might be from Twitter, Facebook, a blog, or any other depository of emotions and narratives you've run into on the Internet. How does oversharing make you feel? Do you greet it as silly but harmless, or do you think it's a real problem? Why?

3. Explain the analogy Ham draws between Twitter users like herself and Lewis and Clark (para 11). Look up more information on the explorers if necessary. To what extent is she being sincere about the analogy and to what extent facetious? Do you think Lewis and Clark might have been oversharers?

Brent Baughman (student essay)

Growing Older in the Digital Age: An Exercise in Egotism

[*The Berkeley Beacon*, Emerson College, February 25, 2010]

BEFORE YOU READ

Is Facebook making us all more egotistical? Are increased opportunities for advertising ourselves making us self-obsessed? How do you react to birthday invitations on Facebook and Twitter? Are they over-the-top?

WORDS TO LEARN

festers (para. 2): becomes worse, like a sore (verb).

collective (para. 2): belonging to all the people in a group (adjective).

interface (para. 4): the computer system a user uses (noun).

mitigate (para. 5): make less bad (verb).

codependence (para. 5): mutual reliance between people (noun).

antique (para. 6): an object held over from a previous age (noun).

Brent Baughman graduated from Emerson College in 2010. He now lives in Washington, D.C., where he works for National Public Radio.

I turned 22 last week. Someone told me it's like Bode Miller[1] from here on out: all downhill. And it might be true. Twenty-two is the last birthday most of us will see in college. The only milestone left to look forward to is qualifying for Social Security, and even that won't exist by the time I'm 65, unless Bill and Melinda Gates[2] get seriously bored.

1

Twenty-one: Now there's a milestone. There's a mischief to turning 21. Everyone makes twinkle-eyed jokes about getting drunk and hitting bars, where all the city's sexual energy apparently festers. There's a cultural connotation, a collective unspoken smirk, that to be a freshly knighted 21-year-old means you can finally be out scoring. It's magnetic, this idea. We pay attention to people turning 21. We wonder what they're doing, where they're going, how they'll celebrate.

2

That sort of attention, however deviant, is what the modern birthday is all about. But with technology in the mix, we're seeking 21-level attention at 22 and beyond. Too far beyond. The modern birthday is a fantasy of attention. On a single day, all the sacred technology we turn to for deliverance from solitude finally makes good on its promises. Birthdays are the one day of the year when compulsive e-mail checking finally pays off — every five minutes the latest note, e-card, or jotting of affection is waiting there in Gmail bold.[3] We never love technology like we do when we see that bold type. It's like being one of those Japanese men who date robots and take them to movies.[4]

3

> Birthdays are the one day of the year when compulsive e-mail checking finally pays off.

And Facebook. Oh, Facebook! The trick is setting Facebook updates to arrive in your e-mail. Here's the beauty of it: Your inbox becomes an Eden of wall updates and messages from Zuckerbergland.[5] You click in and out of these messages like candy, each one sweet in its own way. And

4

---

[1] Bode Miller (para. 1): An American Olympic alpine ski racer.

[2] Bill and Melinda Gates (para. 1): A famous American husband and wife team of philanthropists; Bill cofounded Microsoft in 1975.

[3] Gmail bold (para. 3): New messages in Google's popular e-mail service appear in bold type.

[4] Japanese men . . . movies (para. 3): A recent trend reported in Japan saw men "dating" robotic dolls.

[5] Zuckerbergland (para. 4): Mark Zuckerberg (b. 1984) founded Facebook in 2004.

then — even after you've exhausted your supply of that magic bold — you can still read the same messages on Facebook. It's here they become new again, where all those tokens of affection — even the most impersonal comma-free "Happy Birthday Brent!"'s — glisten with new promise in Facebook's interface.

Twitter, on the other hand, presents a challenge. It's more difficult to mask a call for attention in 140 characters. Maybe you mitigate by narrating plans instead of announcing your birthday outright: *Ducking homework. Duck confit and great friends for birthday dinner at Chez Henri.* See? I've publicized my birthday, but I'm not explicitly asking you to acknowledge it. Twitter is cute this way — it lets us project an image of independence upon a screen of codependence. The Twitterverse requires both Tweeters and Followers, but none of the former want to be seen as desperate for the latter.

We usually let birthday calls roll into voicemail because the phone call is an antique that violates the virtues of our favorite medium, the text message. It's our modern letter. It allows us to remain sovereign in our own world, while still achieving a degree of connection with someone else. Not too close, not too far, but just right. The joy we feel when our phones light up with the receipt of a new message is a micro-burst of the joy we feel when we open the mailbox to discover we've received a letter. It's a joy of ego.

But there's a problem with all this egotism. And no, it's not that we'll drive ourselves to self-worship, into a fire hydrant, and then to sex rehab. It's just generally lame for the people around us who are more than digital strangers. The birthdays we remember are ones that were made special by surprise parties or a perfect gift or a real show of love or friendship. We're missing the point if the first thing we look forward to on our birthday is an over-flowing inbox.

But if technology is your biggest priority on your birthday, I have the perfect gift for you. It'll take about two weeks to get here. I'll have to order it from Japan.

VOCABULARY/USING A DICTIONARY

1. Look up *interface* (para. 4) and provide a thorough definition. Give an example of an interface.
2. What does *mitigate* mean (para. 5)? What is the origin of the word?
3. Define *egotism* as Baughman uses it in paragraph 7 of his essay. What language does it come from, and what is the meaning of its root?

RESPONDING TO WORDS IN CONTEXT

1. What is a *smirk*? How is it different connotatively from similar expressions? What does Baughman mean when he refers to "a collective unspoken smirk" (para. 2)?

2. What is the literal meaning of the word *fester*? How is Baughman using it when he says that the "city's sexual energy . . . festers" (para. 2)?

3. What does Baughman mean when he calls the modern birthday a "fantasy of attention" (para. 3)? What are two possible meanings of *fantasy* here?

DISCUSSING MAIN POINT AND MEANING

1. Why does Baughman think that twenty-first birthdays are automatically fun and exciting? What does he argue Facebook has done to the practice of celebrating birthdays?

2. What differences does Baughman point to between the ways and conventions of advertising a birthday on various sites? What, however, does he maintain all these sites ultimately have in common?

3. What does Baughman feel is supposed to be really special about celebrating a birthday? What do people look forward to today, according to the essay?

EXAMINING SENTENCES, PARAGRAPHS, AND ORGANIZATION

1. How does Baughman establish that he is just as much a part of the problem he's describing as anyone else? Why is this important to his essay? Give examples from the text of points where he sympathizes with, rather than directly condemning, the foibles of the Digital Era.

2. What gift is Baughman referring to when he says he'll "have to order it from Japan" (para. 8)? How does this joke tie the essay together, and what is he implying about people who rely too much on technology?

THINKING CRITICALLY

1. How does Baughman use humor to advance a serious argument in this essay? Give three examples of jokes from the essay. Do you find them funny? Does the argument rely on the jokes working in order to be effective, or are they simply a way of dressing it up?

2. Do you agree with the spirit of Baughman's piece—that we've become addicted to the machines that are supposed to be making our real lives richer, instead of living those lives? Why or why not? Give specific examples to support your argument.

IN-CLASS WRITING ACTIVITIES

1. Give three concrete examples, besides the birthday invitation, of ways Facebook and Twitter are changing the way you and your friends socialize. What effect do you think these changes are having? Is your generation in fact becoming more self-involved, or are you more conscious of others? Or is it somewhere in between?

2. Try writing an invitation to your birthday party on four media: Facebook, Twitter, e-mail, and—if you can imagine it—a printed, snail-mail letter. What factors affect the content and tone of your message? How are you conscious of the size of your audience, who is seeing it and when, and what kind of atmosphere you want to convey?

Organizing an Essay by Division

One common way to organize the parts of your essay is to break your topic down into categories. For example, someone writing about the dating scene on campus might want to consider several different types of dates and then list each kind with a brief description. Note how Emerson College student Brent Baughman divides his topic into several categories as he proceeds to describe the different ways people receive birthday greetings within our new technology. Observe how in the body of his paper he discusses birthday messages as they are expressed in different media — e-mail, Facebook, Twitter, voicemail, and texting.

1

Baughman divides his essay into five different types of messages

Birthdays are the one day of the year when <u>compulsive e-mail checking</u> finally pays off—every five minutes the latest note, e-card, or jotting of affection is waiting there in Gmail bold. . . .

And <u>Facebook. Oh, Facebook</u>! The trick is setting Facebook updates to arrive in your e-mail. . . .

<u>Twitter, on the other hand,</u> presents a challenge. . . .

We usually let birthday calls roll into <u>voicemail because the phone call</u> is an antique that violates the virtues of <u>our favorite medium, the text message.</u>

STUDENT WRITER AT WORK
Brent Baughman

On Writing "Growing Older in the Digital Age:
An Exercise in Egotism"

RA. What was your main purpose in writing this piece?

BB. To highlight an aspect of life I think is under-thought-about by people my age. There's an argument that technology is warping our ability to communicate intimately with each other, and I hope it's clear that I don't agree with that. But I do think it distracts from certain ways we interact socially, and that we need to be conscious about it so we can lessen those distractions before our frontal lobes fuse to the microprocessors in our iPhones. So there's a constant struggle for balance we all face.

RA. Have you read or seen other work on this topic that has interested you?

BB. There's a lot of talk now about how technology is affecting our cranial motherboards. Nicholas Carr wrote an article last summer for *The Atlantic* called "Is Google Making Us Stupid?" that set off more of a mainsteam discussion about things, and he's coming out with a book about the same subject matter. I'm interested and pay attention to this sort of thing as well as I can. People seem to be considering it more thoughtfully as we become more wired, and I find that encouraging.

RA. How long did it take for you to write this piece? Did you revise your work? What were your goals as you revised?

BB. Like most of my columns, I wrote this over the course of a few days. During that time I'd revisit the text, make changes, insert ideas or revisions I'd thought of during off-hours. During revisions I'm looking mostly to make arguments clear, pace my sentences, and be super critical about whether I'm just spewing nonsense. I'd write a sentence and then imagine I was reading it in the paper myself and that I'd never heard of the writer. If it didn't feel true, I'd revise it.

RA. What topics most interest you as a writer?

BB. The way our social brains work, issues of science and technology, literature, and relationships. We'd probably have to sit down for coffee to parse out the Freudian foundation for my interest in these topics.

RA. Are you pursuing a career in which writing will be a component?

BB. I've recently started working at National Public Radio in Washington, D.C. Public radio is really a combination of journalism and creative writing, because they broadcast stories that often require a keen sense of pacing, language, voice, character, and plot. I'll be doing a lot of writing, yes, so I'm thankful for the practice I got in college.

RA: What advice do you have for other student writers?

BB: Actually, I find kind of it comforting to believe that most of us, at this age, are going to be not-very-good for quite a while, and that it just takes patience and practice to become kind-of-good. During my freshman year, I had a fiction professor say something like, "The guy who can lock himself in a room alone for the longest will be the best writer." Trying to emulate the writers you most admire can also work the necessary muscles, I think.

Elizabeth Stone

Grief in the Age of Facebook

[*The Chronicle Review,* March 5, 2010]

BEFORE YOU READ

How have Facebook and other social-networking sites changed the way we mourn when we lose a friend or loved one? It seems beyond argument that these sites will have a lasting effect on the way we communicate—will they (and should they) also change the way we grieve?

WORDS TO LEARN

dogged (para. 1): highly determined (adjective).

whimsical (para. 1): full of imagination (adjective).

markedly (para. 5): with clear indications (adverb).

solace (para. 5): comfort after a loss (noun).

spontaneous (para. 6): sudden and without a direct cause (adjective).

equestrian (para. 8): related to horse-back-riding (adjective).

penchant (para. 8): tendency (noun).

uncharted (para. 9): not on a map (adjective).

via (para. 9): through (preposition).

exuberance (para. 9): intense happiness (noun).

prescription (para. 11): piece of advice (noun).

reverberates (para. 12): echoes (verb).

A professor of English, communications, and media studies at Fordham University, Elizabeth Stone is the author of a memoir, A Boy I Once Knew: What a Teacher Learned from Her Student *(2002).*

On July 17 last year, one of my most promising students died. 1
Her name was Casey Feldman, and she was crossing a street in
a New Jersey resort town on her way to work when a van went
barreling through a stop sign. Her death was a terrible loss for everyone
who knew her. Smart and dogged, whimsical and kind, Casey was the
news editor of the *The Observer*, the campus paper I advise, and she was
going places. She was a finalist for a national college reporting award and
had just been chosen for a prestigious television internship for the fall, a
fact she conveyed to me in a midnight text message, entirely consistent
with her all-news-all-the-time mind-set. Two days later her life ended.

I found out about Casey's death the old-fashioned way: in a phone 2
conversation with Kelsey, the layout editor and Casey's roommate. She'd
left a neutral-sounding voice mail the night before, asking me to call
when I got her message, adding, "It's OK if it's late." I didn't retrieve the
message till midnight, so I called the next morning, realizing only later
what an extraordinary effort she had made to keep her voice calm. But
my students almost never make phone calls if they can help it, so Kelsey's
message alone should have raised my antenna. She blogs, she tweets, she
texts, and she pings. But voice mail? No.

Paradoxically it was Kelsey's understanding of the viral nature of 3
her generation's communication preferences that sent her rushing to the
phone, and not just to call boomers[1] like me. She didn't want anyone
to learn of Casey's death through Facebook. It was summer, and their
friends were scattered, but Kelsey knew that if even one of Casey's 801
Facebook friends posted the news, it would immediately spread.

So as Kelsey and her roommates made calls through the night, they 4
monitored Facebook. Within an hour of Casey's death, the first mourner
posted her respects on Casey's Facebook wall, a post that any of Casey's
friends could have seen. By the next morning, Kelsey, in New Jersey, had
reached *The Observer*'s editor in chief in Virginia, and by that evening, the
two had reached fellow editors in California, Missouri, Massachusetts,
Texas, and elsewhere — and somehow none of them already knew.

In the months that followed, I've seen how markedly technology 5
has influenced the conventions of grieving among my students, offering them solace but also uncertainty. The day after Casey's death, several editorial-board members changed their individual Facebook profile
pictures. Where there had been photos of Brent, of Kelsey, of Kate, now
there were photos of Casey and Brent, Casey and Kelsey, Casey and Kate.

---

[1] boomers (para. 3): Short for Baby Boomers, a term for the generation born
right after World War II.

Now that Casey was gone, she was virtually everywhere. I asked one   6
of my students why she'd changed her profile photo. "It was spontaneous," she said. "Once one person did it, we all joined in." Another student, who had friends at Virginia Tech when, in 2007, a gunman killed
32 people, said that's when she first saw the practice of posting Facebook
profile photos of oneself with the person being mourned.

Within several days of Casey's death, a Facebook group was cre-   7
ated called "In Loving Memory of Casey Feldman," which ran parallel
to the wake and funeral planned by Casey's family. Dozens wrote on that
group's wall, but Casey's own wall was the more natural gathering place,
where the comments were more colloquial and addressed to her: "casey
im speechless for words right now," wrote one friend. " i cant believe that
just yest i txted you and now your gone . . . i miss you soo much rest in
peace."

Though we all live atomized lives, memorial services let us know the   8
dead with more dimension than we may have known them during their
lifetimes. In the responses of her friends, I was struck by how much I
hadn't known about Casey — her equestrian skill, her love of animals,
her interest in photography, her acting talent, her penchant for creating
her own slang ("Don't be a cow"), and her curiosity — so intense that
her friends affectionately called her a "stalker."

> This new,
> uncharted form
> of grieving raises
> new questions.

This new, uncharted form of grieving   9
raises new questions. Traditional mourning
is governed by conventions. But in the age
of Facebook, with selfhood publicly represented via comments and uploaded photos,
was it OK for her friends to display joy or
exuberance online? Some weren't sure. Six
weeks after Casey's death, one student who had posted a shot of herself with Casey wondered aloud when it was all right to post a different
photo. Was there a right time? There were no conventions to help her.
And would she be judged if she removed her mourning photo before
most others did?

As it turns out, Facebook has a "memorializing" policy in regard to   10
the pages of those who have died. That policy came into being in 2005,
when a good friend and co-worker of Max Kelly, a Facebook employee,
was killed in a bicycle accident. As Kelly wrote in a Facebook blog post
last October, "The question soon came up: What do we do about his
Facebook profile? We had never really thought about this before in such
a personal way. How do you deal with an interaction with someone who
is no longer able to log on? When someone leaves us, they don't leave
our memories or our social network. To reflect that reality, we created

the idea of 'memorialized' profiles as a place where people can save and share their memories of those who've passed."

Casey's Facebook page is now memorialized. Her own postings and lists of interests have been removed, and the page is visible only to her Facebook friends. (I thank Kelsey Butler for making it possible for me to gain access to it.) Eight months after her death, her friends are still posting on her wall, not to "share their memories" but to write to her, acknowledging her absence but maintaining their ties to her — exactly the stance that contemporary grief theorists recommend. To me, that seems preferable to Freud's prescription, in "Mourning and Melancholia," that we should detach from the dead. Quite a few of Casey's friends wished her a merry Christmas, and on the 17th of every month so far, the postings spike. Some share dreams they've had about her, or post a detail of interest. "I had juice box wine recently," wrote one. "I thought of you the whole time :(Miss you girl!" From another: "i miss you. the new lady gaga cd came out, and if i had one wish in the world it would be that you could be singing (more like screaming) along with me in my passenger seat like old times." 11

It was against the natural order for Casey to die at 21, and her death still reverberates among her roommates and fellow editors. I was privileged to know Casey, and though I knew her deeply in certain ways, I wonder — I'm not sure, but I wonder — if I should have known her better. I do know, however, that she would have done a terrific trend piece on "Grief in the Age of Facebook." 12

VOCABULARY/USING A DICTIONARY

1. What is the meaning of *paradoxically* (para. 3)? What part of speech is it? To what word is it related, and what does that word mean?
2. Stone says that with Casey gone, she was "virtually everywhere" (para. 6). What are two meanings of the word *virtually*? Which meaning is Stone using here? (Or could she be using both?)
3. Define *atomized* (para. 8). What is the origin of this word?

RESPONDING TO WORDS IN CONTEXT

1. Stone writes that Kelsey's "understanding of the viral nature of her generation's communications preferences" caused her to call her professor rather than e-mail or text (para. 3). What does *viral* mean in this context? Where does the word come from, and what has it come to mean in communications?
2. Define *colloquial* as Stone uses it in paragraph 7 of the essay. What is a possible antonym of *colloquial*? Give an example of something colloquial and its opposite.

3. What does Stone mean when she refers to an *"uncharted* form of grieving" (para. 9)? What is the origin of the word *uncharted,* and how is it
used here?

DISCUSSING MAIN POINT AND MEANING

1. Stone does not come out and say whether she thinks Facebook grieving is
a good or bad thing. Which way do you think the essay leans? What is its
tone? Give examples from the text.
2. What are two dangers to Facebook mourning that Stone mentions?
3. How did Stone get to know Casey after her death in a way that might not
have been possible in another era?

EXAMINING SENTENCES, PARAGRAPHS, AND ORGANIZATION

1. Why does Stone mention Casey's "all-news-all-the-time mind-set" in
paragraph 1 of the essay? What is the importance of this detail to the
essay as a whole?
2. What is the effect of reproducing Casey's friend's "colloquial" wall post
exactly as the friend wrote it in paragraph 7? Why does Stone go to the
trouble to preserve the poster's syntax and spelling?
3. How is Stone's essay organized? Is it more of an argument or a narrative?
Why did she arrange it this way?

THINKING CRITICALLY

1. What does Stone say Freud's "prescription" for grief was, and what kind
of grief does she suggest Facebook mourners are evincing? What do
you think is the better, healthier way to express sorrow after a loss —
remembrance, detachment, or some combination of the two?
2. How do you feel about Facebook's policy of maintaining the pages of
members who pass away as memorials? Does it cheapen the mourning
process to do it online, or do Facebook and other sites allow wider access
to memorials and expand opportunities to express grief?
3. Discuss the way the essay ends. What is a "trend piece," and why does
Stone feel Casey would have written a good one with the same title as
her own essay?

IN-CLASS WRITING ACTIVITIES

1. Have you ever witnessed the phenomenon Stone describes? Have you
known someone who died whose friends set up a memorial online? If
so, describe what it was like. Did the use of the Internet and social media
make you feel closer to the person you lost, or give you any sense of
closure? If you haven't had the experience, imagine what it might
be like.

2. One of the issues the essay highlights is the relationship between students and teachers on social media. Are you friends with your professors on Facebook or other social-networking sites? Why or why not?

3. The essay is in large part about a bond between a teacher and a student, albeit one that occurred after the student's death. Indeed, one of the recurring themes in Stone's writing is what she has learned from her own students. Write about a close relationship you have had with one of your teachers, focusing on what you may have taught the teacher.

Discussing the Unit

SUGGESTED TOPIC FOR DISCUSSION

What will be the lasting impact of social networking on the way we communicate and relate to one another?

PREPARING FOR CLASS DISCUSSION

1. Garry Trudeau implies that Facebook is "ruining" our lives, and Mary Katharine Ham credits it with a near-revolution in Iran. But none of the authors in this chapter considers the possibility that the influence of social-networking sites is overblown. Is this a possibility? Could Facebook and Twitter be nothing more than a passing fad, or are they definitely here to stay for better or worse? Why?

2. The essays in this chapter focus on the impact of social networking on our schedules and our images of ourselves, but don't touch on one of the other major concerns critics have about social networks—their lack of privacy. Are you worried that you have less control over your privacy than you did before the advent of social networks? If so, why? Is your concern based on actual events, anecdotes, or just a lingering fear? If not, explain the concerns some people have about privacy online and why you think those concerns are overblown.

FROM DISCUSSION TO WRITING

1. Imagine a world without social networking: Facebook, MySpace, Bebo, Twitter, and all the rest suddenly disappear tomorrow. What would happen? How would it affect your social life? Would you even have one anymore? Write a short description of the networking apocalypse—do the stock markets crash and millions wander the streets aimlessly? Or does it instantaneously improve everyone's life?

2. Consider Stone's essay "Grief in the Age of Facebook" and write your own "In the Age of Facebook" essay in her style. Consider any aspect of life

Facebook has touched, and compare and contrast it before and after the social-networking revolution. Try to consider both the good and the bad that Facebook has wrought on your area of focus.

TOPICS FOR CROSS-CULTURAL DISCUSSION

1. Ham highlights the effects of Twitter overseas, where she contrasts online heroism with American narcissism and overindulgence. What do you think of this equation? Do you think social media is used more gainfully overseas than it is in the United States? Why or why not? In your experience, how do people from other cultures use sites like Facebook differently than you do?

2. Why do you think some social networks have been banned in several countries, like Syria and the United Arab Emirates? Are these countries paranoid? Are they simply totalitarian? Or are they expressing real concerns for safety and security?

11

Saving the Planet:
Is It Too Late?

For at least three decades, leading scientific opinion has held that the earth is getting hotter and that human activity, mostly in the form of carbon emissions, is to blame. But a chorus of skeptics has recently challenged the mainstream view, arguing either that the science behind global warming is faulty or that the threat is overblown. The skeptics were armed with new ammunition in their attack on the mainstream scientists in November 2009, when a hacker uncovered e-mail messages from a number of climate scientists that suggested data had been manipulated.

The chapter opens with one of America's leading environmental authors, Bill McKibben, who cites numerous alarming facts in his essay, "Waste Not Want Not." Concerned by the sheer amount of waste produced by our hyperconsuming nation—"A hundred million trees are cut every year just to satisfy the junk-mail industry"—McKibben persuasively reflects on the way we have constructed an economy that depends on waste. McKibben is not overly optimistic we can recover: "We may have waited too long," he concludes, "we may have wasted our last good chance. It's possible the planet will keep warming and the economy keep sinking no matter what."

McKibben's gloomy statistics and scenarios are confirmed by another influential environmental author, Jeff Goodell. In "Warming Gets Worse," Goodell reports on the speed at which the Arctic is melting and the catastrophe that can result. "The Arctic," he writes, "is melting so quickly that even top ice experts are stunned. Just a few years ago, scientists were assuring us that we wouldn't have an ice-free Arctic until 2100. Now the data suggests that, within a decade or two, there will be sailboats at the North Pole during the summer." But, as is common within the climate change debate, not everyone agrees on the speed or the science. In "Sinking 'Climate Change,'" the prominent conservative columnist Cal Thomas claims (and cites evidence to prove it) that global warming is a myth: "After spending years promoting 'global warming,'" Thomas argues, "the media are beginning to turn in the face of growing evidence that they have been wrong."

University of Massachusetts student Yevgeniya Lomakina has no doubts about the scientific reality of global warming, but she introduces a special twist into the climate change debate. In "'Going Green' Misses the Point," Lomakina objects to the way the environmentalist agenda has actually furthered consumerism. "While saving the planet is a good cause," she says, "carbon dioxide emissions will not decline if one invests in a 'Love planet Earth' T-shirt."

The chapter concludes with a prophetic 1985 warning about climate change from the late Carl Sagan, perhaps America's most popular scientist of his day. At that time, Sagan felt the situation, though real, was not urgent: "Fortunately," he said then, "we have a little time. A great deal can be done in decades." Sagan, it should be noted, believed in the potential of "commercial nuclear fusion power."

Bill McKibben

Waste Not Want Not

[*Mother Jones*, May/June 2009]

BEFORE YOU READ

Do we live in a wasteful society? How much do you waste, and how much waste do you witness in America? Is there anything that can be done about the waste problem?

WORDS TO LEARN

generates (para. 2): creates (verb).
sooty (para. 4): covered in ash (adjective).
exemplifies (para. 5): provides an example of (verb).
manifestly (para. 6): clearly (adverb).
cascade (para. 6): flood (noun).
torque (para. 7): the twisting force involved in car acceleration (noun).
laureate (para. 9): outstanding (adjective).
proximity (para. 9): closeness (noun).
assemblage (para. 11): gathering (noun).
boondoggle (para. 12): wasteful activity (noun).

profligacy (para. 13): wastefulness (noun).
topsoil (para. 14): the top layer of soil, where plants grow (noun).
buffer (para. 14): moderate, hold back (verb).
carnage (para. 15): bloodshed (noun).
commode (para. 15): toilet (noun).
frippery (para. 16): unnecessary showiness (noun).
transfixing (para. 18): holding down (verb).
doldrums (para. 18): depression (noun).

Once a year or so, it's my turn to run recycling day for our tiny town. Saturday morning, 9 to 12, a steady stream of people show up to sort out their plastics (No. 1, No. 2, etc.), their corrugated cardboard (flattened, please), their glass (and their returnable glass, which goes to benefit the elementary school), their Styrofoam peanuts, their paper, their cans. It's quite satisfying — everything in its place.

1

Bill McKibben is one of the nation's best-known environmental writers and activists. A former staff writer for The New Yorker, *he publishes regularly in a wide variety of leading periodicals.*

But it's also kind of disturbing, this waste stream. For one, a town of 2
550 sure generates a lot—a trailer load every couple of weeks. Sometimes you have to put a kid into the bin and tell her to jump up and down so the lid can close.

More than that, though, so much of it seems utterly unneces- 3
sary. Not just waste, but wasteful. Plastic water bottles, one after another—80 million of them get tossed every day. The ones I'm stomping down are being "recycled," but so what? In a country where almost everyone has access to clean drinking water, they define waste to begin with. I mean, you don't have a mug? In fact, once you start thinking about it, the category of "waste" begins to expand, until it includes an alarming percentage of our economy. Let's do some intellectual sorting:

There's old-fashioned waste, the dangerous, sooty kind. You're making 4
something useful, but you're not using the latest technology, and so you're spewing: particulates into the air, or maybe sewage into the water. You wish to keep doing it, because it's cheap, and you block any regulation that might interfere with your right to spew. This is the kind of waste that's easy to attack; it's obvious and obnoxious and a lot of it falls under the Clean Air Act and Clean Water Act[1] and so on. There's actually less of this kind of waste than there used to be—that's why we can swim in most of our rivers again.

There's waste that comes from everything operating as it should, only 5
too much so. If carbon monoxide (carbon with one oxygen atom) exemplifies pollution of the first type, then carbon dioxide (carbon with two oxygen atoms) typifies the second. Carbon monoxide poisons you in your garage and turns Beijing's[2] air brown, but if you put a catalytic converter[3] on your tailpipe it all but disappears. Carbon dioxide doesn't do anything to you directly—a clean-burning engine used to be defined as one that released only CO_2 and water vapor—but in sufficient quantity it melts the ice caps, converts grassland into desert, and turns every coastal city into New Orleans.

---

[1] Clean Air Act and Clean Water Act (para. 4): Two landmark pieces of environmental legislation in the United States.

---

[2] Beijing (para. 5): The capital of China, and one of the smoggiest cities in the world.

---

[3] catalytic converter (para. 5): A device used to reduce the toxicity of emissions from modern car engines.

There's waste that comes from doing something that manifestly doesn't   6
need doing. A hundred million trees are cut every year just to satisfy the
junk-mail industry. You can argue about cutting trees for newspapers, or
magazines, or Bibles, or symphony scores — but the cascade of stuff-porn
that arrives daily in our mailboxes? It wastes forests, and also our time.
Which, actually, is precious — we each get about 30,000 days, and it makes
one a little sick to calculate how many of them have been spent opening
credit card offers.

Or think about what we've done with cars. From 1975 to 1985, fuel   7
efficiency for the average new car improved from 14 to 28 miles per
gallon. Then we stopped worrying about oil and put all that engineering
talent to work on torque. In the mid-1980s, the typical car accelerated
from 0 to 60 mph in 14.5 seconds. Today's average (even though vehicles
are much heavier) is 9.5 seconds. But it's barely legal to accelerate like
that, and it makes you look like an idiot, or a teenager.

Then there's the waste that comes with doing something maybe per-   8
haps vaguely useful when you could be doing something actually useful instead. For instance: Congress is being lobbied really, really hard to
fork over billions of dollars to the nuclear industry, on the premise that it
will fight global warming. There is, of course, that little matter of nuclear
waste — but lay that aside (in Nevada[4] or someplace). The greater problem
is the wasted opportunity: That money could go to improving efficiency,
which can produce the same carbon reductions for about a fifth of the price.

Our wasteful habits wouldn't matter much if there were just a few of   9
us — a Neanderthal hunting band could have discarded six plastic water
bottles apiece every day with no real effect except someday puzzling
anthropologists. But the volumes we manage are something else. Chris
Jordan is the photographer laureate of waste — his most recent project,
"Running the Numbers," uses exquisite images to show the 106,000 aluminum cans Americans toss every 30 seconds, or the 1 million plastic cups
distributed on US airline flights every 6 hours, or the 2 million plastic bev-
erage bottles we run through every 5 minutes, or the 426,000 cell phones
we discard every day, or the 1.14 million brown paper supermarket bags
we use each hour, or the 60,000 plastic bags we use every 5 seconds, or the
15 million sheets of office paper we use every 5 minutes, or the 170,000
Energizer batteries produced every 15 minutes. The simple amount of stuff
it takes — energy especially — to manage this kind of throughput makes
it daunting to even think about our waste problem. (Meanwhile, the next

---

[4] Nevada (para. 8): The site of Yucca Mountain, a notorious nuclear waste
depository.

"Light Bulbs 2008" by artist Chris Jordan.
Depicts 320,000 light bulbs, equal to the number of kilowatt hours of electricity wasted in the United States every minute from inefficient electricity use.

time someone tells you that population is at the root of our troubles, remind them that the average American uses more energy between the stroke of midnight on New Year's Eve and dinner on January 2 than the average, say, Tanzanian consumes in a year. Population matters, but it *really* matters when you multiply it by proximity to Costco.)

Would you like me to go on? Americans discard enough aluminum   10
to rebuild our entire commercial air fleet every three months — and aluminum represents less than 1 percent of our solid waste stream. We toss 14 percent of the food we buy at the store. More than 46,000 pieces of plastic debris float on each square mile of ocean. And — oh, forget it.

These kinds of numbers get in the way of figuring out how much we   11
really waste. In recent years, for instance, 40 percent of Harvard graduates have gone into finance, consulting, and business. They had just spent four years with the world's greatest library, some of its finest museum collections, an unparalleled assemblage of Nobel-quality scholars, and all they wanted to do was go to lower Manhattan and stare into computer screens. What a waste! And when they got to Wall Street, of course, they figured out extravagant ways to waste the life savings of millions of Americans,

which in turn required the waste of taxpayer dollars to bail them out, money that could have been spent on completely useful things: trains to get us where we want to go — say, new national parks.

Perhaps the only kind of waste we've gotten good at cutting is the 12 kind we least needed to eliminate: An entire industry of consultants survives on telling companies how to get rid of inefficiencies — which generally means people. And an entire class of politicians survives by railing about government waste, which also ends up meaning programs for people: Health care for poor children, what a boondoggle.

Want to talk about government waste? We're going to end up spend- 13 ing north of a trillion dollars on the war in Iraq, which will go down as one of the larger wastes of money — and lives — in our history. But we spend more than half a trillion a year on the military anyway, more than the next 10 nations combined. That almost defines profligacy.

We've gotten away with all of this for a long time because we had 14 margin, all kinds of margin. Money, for sure — we were the richest nation on Earth, and when we wanted more we just borrowed it from China. But margin in other ways as well: We landed on a continent with topsoil more than a foot thick across its vast interior, so the fact that we immediately started to waste it with inefficient plowing hardly mattered. We inherited an atmosphere that could buffer our emissions for the first 150 years of the Industrial Revolution. We somehow got away with wasting the talents of black people and women and gay folks.

But our margin is gone. We're out of cash, we're out of atmosphere, we're out of luck. The current economic carnage is what happens when you waste — when the CEO of Merrill Lynch thinks he needs a $35,000 commode, when the CEO of Tyco[5] thinks it would be fun to spend a million dollars on his wife's birthday party, complete with an ice sculpture of Michelangelo's *David* peeing vodka. The melted Arctic ice cap is what you get when everyone in America thinks he requires the kind of vehicle that might make sense for a forest ranger. 15

> The melted Arctic ice cap is what you get when everyone in America thinks he requires the kind of vehicle that might make sense for a forest ranger.

Getting out of the fix we're in — if it's still possible — requires 16 in part that we relearn some very old lessons. We were once famously thrifty: Yankee frugality, straightening bent nails, saving string. We used

---

[5] Tyco (para. 15): An electronics company whose CEO, Dennis Kozlowski, was sentenced to prison for corrupt practices in 2007.

to have a holiday, Thrift Week, which began on Ben Franklin's birthday: "Beware of little expenses; a small leak will sink a great ship," said he. We disapproved of frippery, couldn't imagine wasting money on ourselves, made do or did without. It took a mighty effort to make us what we are today — in fact, it took a mighty industry, advertising, which soaks up plenty more of those Harvard grads and represents an almost total waste.

In the end, we built an economy that depended on waste, and bound-   17
less waste is what it has produced. And the really sad part is, it felt that way, too. Making enough money to build houses with rooms we never used, and cars with engines we had no need of, meant wasting endless hours at work. Which meant that we had, on average, one-third fewer friends than our parents' generation. What waste that! "Getting and spending, we lay waste our powers," wrote Wordsworth.[6] We can't say we weren't warned.

The economic mess now transfixing us will mean some kind of   18
change. We can try to hang on to the status quo — living a Wal-Mart life so we can buy cheaply enough to keep the stream of stuff coming. Or we can say uncle. There are all kinds of experiments in postwaste living springing up: Freecycling,[7] and Craigslisting,[8] and dumpster diving, and car sharing (those unoccupied seats in your vehicle — what a waste!), and open sourcing. We're sharing buses, and going to the library in greater numbers. Economists keep hoping we'll figure out a way to revert — that we'll waste a little more, and pull us out of the economic doldrums. But the psychological tide suddenly runs the other way.

We may have waited too long — we may have wasted our last good   19
chance. It's possible the planet will keep warming and the economy keep sinking no matter what. But perhaps not — and we seem ready to shoot for something nobler than the hyperconsumerism that's wasted so much of the last few decades. Barack Obama said he would "call out" the nation's mayors if they wasted their stimulus[9] money. That's the mood we're in, and it's about time.

---

[6] Wordsworth (para. 17): (William, 1770–1850) A major English poet. The quotation is from his sonnet "The World Is Too Much with Us."

---

[7] Freecycling (para. 18): The practice of giving away used consumer items instead of throwing them out.

---

[8] Craigslisting (para. 18): Using the Web site Craigslist, which allows users to post and respond to ads, often to sell or give away used stuff.

---

[9] stimulus (para. 19): The 2009 economic stimulus package passed by President Obama to create jobs by giving funds to state and local governments for needed projects.

VOCABULARY/USING A DICTIONARY

1. McKibben refers several times to *hyperconsuming* and *hyperconsumerism* (para. 19). What do these terms refer to? What does the prefix *hyper-* mean?
2. What are *particulates* (para. 4)? To what other words is this one related? What is the difference between *particulates* and *particles*?
3. Explain what McKibben means by *throughput* (para. 9). What more common word is this one related to?

RESPONDING TO WORDS IN CONTEXT

1. What are the various meanings of the word *obnoxious*? How exactly would you characterize the meaning of the word as McKibben uses it in paragraph 4?
2. What does McKibben mean when he says (in paragraph 14) that we've "gotten away with all of this for a long time because we had margin"? What does *margin* mean in this context? How is it related to other meanings of the word in the dictionary?
3. From context, what do the words *thrifty* and *frugality* (para. 16) mean?

DISCUSSING MAIN POINT AND MEANING

1. What is McKibben's answer to critics who say that our expanding population is at the root of our wastefulness? What does he mean when he says, "Population matters, but it *really* matters when you multiply it by proximity to Costco" (para. 9)?
2. What does McKibben say is the only kind of waste we are good at getting rid of? What is he referring to when he makes this point? Does he really believe that this is waste, or is he quoting someone else? If so, whom?
3. How does McKibben feel we're wasting our "Harvard graduates" (para. 11), and who more generally does he mean by that phrase? What would he rather the "Harvard grads" be doing?

EXAMINING SENTENCES, PARAGRAPHS, AND ORGANIZATION

1. What does McKibben mean by "stuff-porn" (para. 6)? How does phrasing it in this way help advance the argument he's making?
2. What is the combined effect of the first and last sentences of paragraph 10? What tone is McKibben trying to set when he asks, "Would you like me to go on?" and ends, "oh, forget it"?
3. Analyze the pattern McKibben employs in his examples of waste. Does he start with one particular kind of example and progress to another kind? How is his organization effective in getting his point across—or how could it be more effective?

THINKING CRITICALLY

1. Do we live in a wasteful society? Does McKibben point out a pattern indicative of some real problems in America, or is his argument over-blown? Can anything be done about waste as an epidemic problem, or is some amount of it inevitable?

2. McKibben uses humor throughout his essay. Do you think humor is appropriate for a subject as serious as the one he's broaching? Why or why not? What effect do jokes have in the essay? Pick out two jokes and analyze them — how are they integrated into the essay, what is their function, and how well do they work?

3. What do you think of McKibben's specific examples of American waste? Are they all right on, or are any of them stretches? Pick out one example and provide a counterargument — argue that what McKibben calls waste is necessary, that it can't be helped, or that it doesn't really provide any real peril to our civilization and our environment. Do you think his argument as a whole still stands?

IN-CLASS WRITING ACTIVITIES

1. Write a proposal for eliminating some kind of waste in America. It can be one of the forms of waste McKibben describes or one that you've noticed independently. How can we go about ending the way we misuse resources in the area you choose? Is it even possible? Why or why not? What will it take: individual action, a group effort, government intervention, or some combination of the three?

2. What are McKibben's politics? Where does he fall on the liberal-conservative spectrum? Give some evidence from the text. What effect do his politics have on his view of American waste? Is waste, as McKibben discusses it, a political issue? Or should people on both sides of the left-right debate in America be conscious of what resources we're wasting and be determined to preserve them?

3. McKibben mentions some of the "experiments in postwaste living spring-ing up" (para. 18) and lists Freecycling, Craigslisting, dumpster diving, and car sharing. Research some of these movements and offer an assessment of them. Do any of them have the potential to make a real impact on the way we live? Why or why not?

Jeff Goodell

Warming Gets Worse

[*Rolling Stone*, November 12, 2009]

BEFORE YOU READ

Are you concerned about global warming? Are you ever concerned you might not be concerned enough?

WORDS TO LEARN

fuse (para. 2): the material a flame moves along to explode a bomb (noun).

slab (para. 3): a large, thick, flat stone or piece of material (noun).

organic (para. 3): related to living things (adjective).

amplifying (para. 5): making larger or louder (adjective).

A s negotiators prepare to gather in Copenhagen[1] next month to try and reach an agreement to halt climate change, the world's leading scientists have come to an alarming conclusion: Global warming is happening even faster than they thought.   1

The Arctic, it turns out, is melting so quickly that even top ice experts are stunned. Just a few years ago, scientists were assuring us that we wouldn't have an ice-free Arctic until 2100. Now the data suggests that, within a decade or two, there will be sailboats at the North Pole during the summer. The melting Arctic is a ticking time bomb for the Earth's climate — and thanks to our failure to reduce greenhouse-gas pollution, the fuse has already been lit. "It's like man is taking the lid off the northern part of the planet," said Peter Wadhams, an ice expert at the University of Cambridge in England.   2

---

[1] Copenhagen (para. 1): Danish capital where the UN held a major climate-change conference in 2009; it was widely seen as failing to bring any real, effective resolutions.

A contributing editor to Rolling Stone *magazine, Jeff Goodell writes frequently on energy and the environment. He is the author most recently of* Big Coal: The Dirty Secret behind America's Energy Future *(2006) and* How to Cool the Planet: Geoengineering and the Audacious Quest to Fix Earth's Climate *(2010).*

The Arctic is more than just a frozen block of ice — it's more like a   3
frozen block of carbon. Beneath the ice, the region is covered with a slab
of permafrost — more than 1,000 feet thick in some places — composed
of partially decomposed trees, plants, woolly mammoths and other
organic matter that lived in the region thousands of years ago. As it thaws,
all that rotting debris sends carbon dioxide into the atmosphere. Worse,
the debris is a feast for microscopic bugs that transform it into methane,
a greenhouse gas at least 20 times more potent than CO_2. All told, there
are some 1 trillion metric tons of carbon
buried in the Arctic — the equivalent of

Melting the Arctic
is like firing up the
world's largest
furnace.

the oil, gas and coal reserves on the entire
planet. From a planetary perspective, melting the Arctic is like firing up the world's
largest furnace — one that will belch catastrophic levels of greenhouse gases into the
atmosphere.

But that's not the worst of it. A similarly huge amount of methane   4
is frozen in the floor of the shallow seas surrounding the Arctic. As the
water warms, these blocks of methane ice can bubble to the surface and
release millions of tons of methane — more or less cooking the planet
overnight. "If that happens," says Jim White, head of the Institute of Arctic and Alpine Research at the University of Colorado, "we are hosed."

Even without a sudden release of methane, what's happening in the   5
Arctic has created an ever-accelerating feedback loop that is already speeding up the rate of climate change. As the ice melts, it creates more open
water, which absorbs heat faster, which melts ice faster, which warms the
water more — and on and on. "One of the biggest questions in climate science is how fast these amplifying feedback loops accelerate," says Ken Cal-
deira, a climate modeler at the Carnegie Institution. One study found that
during periods of rapid sea-ice loss, the land warms three times faster than
average, amplifying the feedback loop and further accelerating warming.

A warmer Arctic is likely to have a major impact on our weather;   6
some scientists argue that the loss of summer sea ice is already partly
responsible for freakish weather events, such as the recent snowstorm
in Baghdad. "The Arctic is the global refrigerator for the northern hemisphere," says Mark Serreze, a scientist at the National Snow and Ice Data
Center in Colorado. "If you change it, you're likely to see a variety of
effects, including drier summers in the southwest United States and wet-
ter winters in the Mediterranean."

Even more alarming, rising temperatures in the Arctic threaten to   7
melt the Greenland ice sheets faster than expected. Only two years ago,
a United Nations climate report predicted that the seas would likely rise

by no more than 23 inches by 2100. Now, thanks largely to the radical changes in the Arctic in the past few years, scientists believe that even if we take drastic action and cut emissions quickly, we're still likely to see sea levels rise by as much as three feet. And if we don't take action, warns NASA's James Hansen, America's most respected climate scientist, sea levels could rise by as much as nine feet by the end of the century. Such a rise would be catastrophic for many of the world's major cities, including New Orleans, London and Shanghai, as well as the 40 million or so people who live in low-lying areas in poor nations like Bangladesh.

The big question is, is it too late to avert catastrophe? No one knows. 8 "We do not yet have a clear signal of significant methane release from the permafrost," says Ed Dlugokencky, a methane expert with the National Oceanic and Atmospheric Administration. "But we know that as the region heats up, it is inevitable." Once the Arctic is gone, it won't be coming back anytime soon — which is why cutting greenhouse-gas pollution now is so important. As Lonnie Thompson, a glacier expert at Ohio State University, has put it, "Mother Nature is the timekeeper — and nobody can see the clock."

VOCABULARY/USING A DICTIONARY

1. What exactly is *permafrost* (para. 3)? Where does it occur? What is the origin of the word?
2. What are the roots of the word *microscopic* (para. 3)? What does the word mean?
3. What is a *glacier* (para. 8)? What part of speech is it? What does the word *glacial* mean?

RESPONDING TO WORDS IN CONTEXT

1. Goodell warns us that melting the Arctic will release whole new levels of *greenhouse gases* (para. 3) into the atmosphere. What are greenhouse gases, and why are they so worrisome?
2. Based on context, what does Jim White's slang term *hosed* (para. 4) mean?
3. Look up *feedback loop* (para. 5), and provide a thorough definition of it. How is what Goodell is describing in the Arctic an example of a feedback loop? Can you name another example?

DISCUSSING MAIN POINT AND MEANING

1. How does a furnace work, and how, according to Goodell, is melting the Arctic like "firing up the world's largest furnace" (para. 3)?
2. Why would a nine-foot rise in sea level, if it happened, be "catastrophic" for cities like New Orleans and regions like Bangladesh (para. 7)? Why does Goodell single out poor nations like the latter?

3. How do you imagine Goodell would answer skeptics of global warming who say that the current data does not show the earth getting significantly hotter, or that it does not show that any rise in temperature over the next few decades is likely to cause a problem?

EXAMINING SENTENCES, PARAGRAPHS, AND ORGANIZATION

1. Goodell writes that "within a decade or two, there will be sailboats at the North Pole druing the summer" (para. 2). What does he mean by this? Should we take the statement literally?
2. Goodell and the sources he quotes use a number of metaphors—familiar concepts used to illustrate more complicated ones. List all the metaphors you can find in the essay. How do they help a reader understand the complexities of the kind of warming Goodell is explaining?
3. How would you characterize the tone of this short essay? Is Goodell attempting to sound wildly opinionated or precise and factual? Is he optimistic or pessimistic about the future of the Earth's environment?

THINKING CRITICALLY

1. What is the effect of the first sentence of this essay? How does the mention of negotiators gathering at Copenhagen contrast with the new data Goodell will go on to cite about the effects of global warming? How does this contrast help move forward the main point Goodell will be making throughout the essay? Look up a little information on the 2009 Copenhagen conference. Does it sound to you like it was a success?
2. One of the major issues in the climate-change debate is whether any change in the earth's temperature is *anthropogenic*—that is, caused by humans. Where does Goodell fall on this question? Give evidence from the text. Does he argue a case for man-made climate change, or does he appear to assume that his audience accepts it?
3. Goodell asks if it is "too late to avert a catastrophe" such as the one he outlines in the essay (para. 8), but does not explain how we might go about avoiding it. What is Goodell implying humans would need to do in order to stop the vicious cycle of melting in the Arctic? Why might it be too late?

IN-CLASS WRITING ACTIVITIES

1. Are you troubled by reports like this one about the effects of greenhouse gases and climate change? Why or why not? Do you think you'll see the "catastrophic" effects of warming Goodell hints at in your lifetime? Or are numbers and statistics like the ones Goodell lists too vague for you to worry about directly? If you are worried, what, if anything, are you doing about it? If you're not worried, why not?

2. A number of skeptics, including Cal Thomas in the next selection, challenge statistics and conclusions like the ones Goodell presents here. Research some of the specific answers skeptics have to the rapid melting of the Arctic. Why do they think the threat is overblown? Give specifics. Whose evidence do you find more convincing, and why?
3. Goodell uses the terms "global warming" and "climate change" almost interchangeably throughout this essay. What is the difference? Do some research into the history of these terms. Why have scientists and science journalists begun shifting from *global warming* to *climate change* over the last few years? Which term gives the public a more accurate picture of what is happening to the Earth's temperature?

Cal Thomas

Sinking "Climate Change"

[*Townhall.com*, June 3, 2010]

BEFORE YOU READ

Is global climate change really happening? Or is it possible certain forces in government and society just want you to think so?

WORDS TO LEARN

transparent (para. 1): doing things out in the open (adjective).
bickering (para. 4): fighting back and forth (verb).
designation (para. 5): specially declared status (noun).
lamented (para. 6): mourned (noun).

bamboozled (para. 6): tricked (verb).
inhibited (para. 10): stopped from growing (verb).
diversifying (para. 11): making more varied (verb).
underwrite (para. 11): provide financial support for (verb).

Three modern myths have been sold to the American people: the promise of a transparent administration (President Obama); the promise of a more ethical Congress (Speaker Pelosi); and the myth of "global warming," or climate change.

1

Cal Thomas is one of the leading conservative columnists in America. His widely syndicated column appears in over 550 U.S. newspapers and is over 25 years old. Thomas is also a regular presence on radio and television.

The first two are daily proving suspect and now the third is sinking   2
with greater force than melting icebergs — if they were melting, which
many believe they are not.

After spending years promoting "global warming," the media are   3
beginning to turn in the face of growing evidence that they have been
wrong. The *London Times* recently reported: "Britain's premier scientific
institution is being forced to review its statements on climate change
after a rebellion by members who question mankind's contribution to
rising temperatures."

It gets worse, or better, depending on your perspective. *Newsweek*   4
magazine, which more than 30 years ago promoted global cooling and
a new ice age — and more recently has been drinking the global warming Kool-Aid[1] — headlined a story, "Uncertain Science: Bickering and
Defensive, Climate Researchers Have Lost the Public's Trust." *Newsweek*
does its best to cling to its increasingly discredited doctrine, but the
growing body of contrary evidence only adds to the public's disbelief.

In Canada, the polar bear — which has been used by global warming   5
promoters to put a cuddly face on the issue — is in danger of not being
endangered any longer. *CBC News* reported that the polar bear's designation as a "species of special concern" has been suspended "while the
government reviews the polar bear's status and decides whether to renew
the classification or change it."

The *New York Times* recently lamented "global warmism's loss of   6
credibility" in a story about hundreds of "environmental activists who met
to ponder this question: 'If the scientific consensus on climate change
has not changed, why have so many people
turned away from the idea that human activity is warming the planet?' " The "consensus" never was a consensus. Most of us may
not have gotten an "A" in science, but we can
sense when we are being bamboozled.

> The "consensus"
> never was a
> consensus.

The German online news magazine *Focus* recently carried a   7
story, "Warm Times Will Soon Be Over!" Commenting on the
"new NASA high temperature record," which may be set, the magazine blames it on El Niño.[2] Meteorologists, like Joe D'Aleo of The

---

[1] drinking . . . the Kool-Aid (para. 4): An expression for accepting an idea blindly,
derived from the poisoned Kool-Aid drunk by cult members in the 1978 Jones-
town massacre.

---

[2] El Niño: A complex weather pattern occurring irregularly in the Pacific Ocean
and having a widespread effect; La Niña is its "sister system."

Weather Channel, are publicly distancing themselves from the false doctrine of global warming. D'Aleo says, "We'll have La Niña conditions before the summer is over, and it will intensify further through the fall and winter. Thus we'll have cooler temperatures for the next couple of years."

Remember the scare ignited in 2007 by supposed melting Arctic ice caps? The *Star Canada* says a new analysis shows that the apparent change was the result of "shifting winds," while an expedition last year to the North Pole discovered the ice "100 percent thicker than expected."   8

Much of this information — and more — is available at the useful Web site www.climatedepot.com.   9

It is a given that America needs new sources of energy. Environmentalists have inhibited efforts at exploration by supporting policies that have forced some domestic exploration too far offshore (thus increasing chances of an ecological disaster as is occurring in the Gulf of Mexico).[3]   10

Instead of trying to sell us a dubious doctrine at an estimated cost of $100 billion a year worldwide (so far), environmentalists would have done themselves and the world more good had they chosen a different strategy, such as not sending oil money to countries that want to destroy us. This would have increased our patriotic spirit and had the additional benefit of not only diversifying our energy supply, but also depriving our enemies of money they use to underwrite terrorism.   11

Watch for the hardcore "global warming" cultists to continue clinging to their beliefs; but also watch increasing numbers of scientists and eventually politicians to abandon this once "certain" faith and to look for other ways to control our lives. In that pursuit, the left never quits. Rather than acknowledge their error, they will go on to make new mistakes, knowing they will never be held accountable.   12

VOCABULARY/USING A DICTIONARY

1. What is a *consensus*? Why does Thomas put the word in quotation marks when he uses it in paragraph 6?
2. To what does *domestic exploration* (para. 10) refer? What is the opposite of *domestic*?
3. What does *dubious* (para. 11) mean? What part of speech is it?

---

[3] Gulf of Mexico: A reference to the 2010 BP oil spill, the worst ecological disaster in history.

RESPONDING TO WORDS IN CONTEXT

1. Thomas uses the word *myth* throughout the essay. What is the origin of the word? How is it most traditionally used, and what is the precise meaning of the word as he uses it?
2. What does Thomas mean when he says that the polar bear has been used to "put a cuddly face on the issue" (para. 5)? What does *cuddly* mean in this context, and what does its use imply about the way Thomas believes climate change is discussed?
3. What is a *cultist* (para. 12)? From where does that word derive? How does Thomas characterize believers in climate change by calling them cultists?

DISCUSSING MAIN POINT AND MEANING

1. Why does Thomas mention that *Newsweek* magazine "more than 30 years ago promoted global cooling and a new ice age" (para. 4)? Why is *Newsweek*'s history important to Thomas's argument?
2. Thomas says it's "a given that America needs new sources of energy" (para. 10). What do sources of energy have to do with the climate?
3. What strategy does Thomas think environmentalists should have pushed for? What benefits, besides being good for the environment, does he say this strategy would have had?

EXAMINING SENTENCES, PARAGRAPHS, AND ORGANIZATION

1. Explain the joke Thomas makes in his title. Why is it ironic to "sink" climate change?
2. Why does Thomas begin with his other two myths? How are these related to what he considers the "myth" of climate change?
3. What is the function of paragraph 7 in the essay as a whole? How do the conclusions of the German online newsmagazine fit into Thomas's argument?

THINKING CRITICALLY

1. Thomas says that liberals who promote climate change will eventually have to give up their claims and "look for other ways to control our lives." What does he think climate change believers have to gain from their fabrications? Why do they continue to push for changes, in Thomas's mind, when they've been proven wrong on so many things? What is their real agenda?
2. Discuss Thomas's characterization of the media in the essay. Does he consider the media honest and objective? What role does he believe the media play in selling climate change to the public, and why?
3. Take a look at the Web site Thomas recommends, www.climatedepot.com. Does the site look like a useful, objective repository of statistics, as Thomas claims it to be? Or does it have an agenda? If so, what? Do you find its arguments compelling? Why or why not?

IN-CLASS WRITING ACTIVITIES

1. Thomas is writing for *Townhall.com*, a conservative Web site. Why have political conservatives taken up the issue of climate change with such skepticism? Why do liberals promote it? Should climate change be a political issue, or is it something we should approach as a society without politics intruding? Is that possible anymore? Why or why not?

2. Do you believe that climate change is real? Do you feel confident in your answer? How much do you accept your position blindly, and how much of your belief is based on research and evidence? If you are a believer, how do you respond to Thomas's arguments? If you're a skeptic, what would you add to or subtract from Thomas's essay?

3. Thomas writes of climate change believers that "rather than acknowledge their error, they will go on to make new mistakes, knowing they will never be held accountable." Thomas points out a problem that confounds many areas of public life. Give another example of a mistake policy makers cling to even when proven wrong. Why do people persist in errors? What forces keep them going? What does it take to break their resolve?

Yevgeniya Lomakina (student essay)

"Going Green" Misses the Point

[*The Daily Collegian*, University of Massachusetts, April 22, 2010]

BEFORE YOU READ

What can individuals do to curb climate change and fix the environment? Is the burden on big corporations, on governments, or on people like you?

WORDS TO LEARN

amplifies (para. 1): makes louder or more noticeable (verb).
emitting (para. 3): letting out (verb).

suppressed (para. 4): kept quiet (adjective).
spheres (para. 4): areas (noun).
embarked (para. 4): set out (verb).

Yevgeniya Lomakina is a student at the University of Massachusetts.

W hat is one catchphrase that has recently become more and more popular? The arrival of spring and Earth Day only amplifies its emergence. Occasionally against their will, numerous times a day, unsuspecting consumers are faced with various "Earth-friendly" slogans. 1

Words of affection toward the planet appear on bags, mugs, shirts, pants, cars, buses, buildings and the list can go on. The "green living" movement is here to stay. TV programs encourage viewers to buy Earth-friendly products. Campuses and job facilities boast about their green initiatives. A new market for specifically "green" jobs is on the rise. All these actions are aimed at doing "a little part" at saving the planet from global warming. With such a noble cause in mind, it seems that no price is too high. 2

It can no longer be denied: The Earth is affected by global climate change, which was initiated by humans' misuse of natural resources. The statistics have forced the public to finally acknowledge the problem. In 2002, Colorado and Arizona had their worst wildfire seasons. Extreme heat waves in 2003 caused numerous deaths in Europe and more around the globe. The United States is said to lead the world in pollution, emitting more carbon dioxide than China, India, and Japan combined. Based upon such statistics, it is apparent that action against global climate change was long overdue. 3

While saving the planet is a good cause, carbon dioxide emissions will not decline if one invests in a "Love planet Earth" T-shirt. However, the media create a strong argument for the positive impact of "going" green, at any cost. Those who consent to help "save the environment" are perceived as "Earth-conscious" and their opponents are suppressed. It seems as if suddenly, all spheres of society, from factory owners to private individuals, have embarked upon a massive race for who can be the most green. 4

> Green initiatives are as diverse as the people who embrace them.

Green initiatives are as diverse as the people who embrace them. If the planet could be saved based on what kind of cereal a consumer bought, evidently, there would be no problem. The question, however, lies much deeper. 5

Did advertising and popular culture turn a genuine concern for the environment into an easily solvable problem? It seems that the answer to saving the Earth is only one purchase away. Do you want to live green? Buy a mug. Do you want to live greener? Buy a hybrid car. Choosing an environmentally safe product may simply allow the consumer to have a guilt-free conscience, but, in reality, will cost more for the environment. 6

Costs for transportation, packaging, and the novelty of green products must all be taken into account. It is better to spend a lesser amount of money on a regular product, or even better, not to buy any product at all. Some Earth-friendly initiatives require no spending on the part of the consumer. Instead of buying a hybrid car, a better choice would be taking better care of the currently owned model. To save gas, carpool. Instead of buying newer "green" household electric products, once again, take good care of the ones you already own. Instead of buying organic vegetables at Whole Foods, choose to buy them at a local farm stand. However, these simple ways to reduce carbon emissions and spending do not seem to be "popular" enough. It is assumed that if one's initiatives to be green are not publicly seen, they are not present. 7

It is interesting to note that criticisms of green consumption have only come from individual activists, and not large environmental groups, such as Sierra Club, or Rainforest Action Network.[1] 8

Globalization is on the rise, and more and more countries now produce in surplus quantities and export their products all over the globe. In order to "stop" global warming with any significant rate, every country on the planet needs to play its part in reducing carbon emissions. However, countries outside the United States may not be as easily persuaded to join the green movement, partly due to the common belief that the United States is responsible for global warming. Al Gore expresses it best in his documentary *An Inconvenient Truth* when he says that in order to reduce global warming, every nation needs to contribute its part. Otherwise, individual efforts are meaningless on a worldwide scale. 9

It is only when buyers begin to diminish their consumerist desires that any change will start to take place. If one truly wants to go green, it can be done without expensive purchases. Meanwhile, if the voice of the media remains above the voice of reason, the global warming situation will remain unchanged. 10

VOCABULARY/USING A DICTIONARY

1. Give an example of a *green initiative* (para. 2). Look up the term online if necessary. What does the word *initiative* mean? Where does the word come from?

2. What does *novelty* (para. 6) mean? What is the origin of the word, and what are some other words to which it's related?

---

[1] Sierra Club, Rainforest Action Network (para. 8): Two large nonprofit public-interest environmental groups.

3. Several essays in this chapter refer to *carbon emissions* (paras. 4, 7, and 9). What does the word *emission* mean? What part of speech is it? What are related parts of speech, and what is the word's origin?

RESPONDING TO WORDS IN CONTEXT

1. What is a *catchphrase* (para. 1)? Give an example of a catchphrase besides the one Lomakina gives. What are the connotations of the word, and how does her use of it help to advance her argument?

2. What are *organic* vegetables (para. 7)? Why are they considered an aspect of the environmental movement?

3. What does Lomakina mean when she refers to *consumerist desires* (para. 10)? What is *consumerism*, and what does it mean for something to be *consumerist*?

DISCUSSING MAIN POINT AND MEANING

1. To back her claim that climate change is real, Lomakina writes that the United States emits "more carbon dioxide than China, India, and Japan combined" (para. 3). Explain how the emission of carbon dioxide affects the environment and how scientists say it causes the climate to change.

2. What does Lomakina mean when she writes, sarcastically, that "it seems that the answer to saving the Earth is only one purchase away" (para. 6)? Explain the cultural phenomenon she's criticizing with this assertion.

3. Give a few examples, besides those Lomakina offers, of the types of changes she is encouraging people to make. How do these differ from the behaviors typically encouraged by the "green" movement?

EXAMINING SENTENCES, PARAGRAPHS, AND ORGANIZATION

1. What is the tone of the phrase "words of affection toward the planet" (para. 2)? What is Lomakina implying by using this phrase?

2. Analyze the comparisons and contrasts Lomakina uses in paragraphs 6 and 7. How does the author use rhetorical questions and parallel structures to compare what she considers ineffective and effective ways of saving the planet?

3. What is the function of paragraph 8 in the context of the essay as a whole? Why does Lomakina condemn the groups she mentions in that paragraph by contrasting their behavior with the information she provides in the previous paragraphs?

THINKING CRITICALLY

1. One commenter on the online edition of the *Daily Collegian* writes that he doesn't think the green movement's popularity "necessarily excludes the potential to help the environment. Hey, if the yuppies get on board because their neighbors do, everybody's happy." One could argue that Lomakina is attacking people's motives for environmentally friendly action in this article, not the actions themselves. Do you agree? If a movement is going in the right direction, does it matter why people join it?

2. Do you agree with Lomakina that the best and most effective methods of saving the environment are the ones that are not "publicly seen" (para. 7)? Are there any possible advantages of public displays of environmental consciousness Lomakina fails to consider?

3. Lomakina writes that "countries outside the United States may not be as easily persuaded to join the green movement, partly due to the common belief that the United States is responsible for global warming" (para. 9). Do you agree that the United States is more responsible for global warming than other countries are? Look up some facts to back your opinion if necessary. Would that matter anyway to the balance of worldwide responsibility for fixing the problem or, as Lomakina asserts, are we all in it together no matter who's at fault?

IN-CLASS WRITING ACTIVITIES

1. Write your own manifesto for how an individual can make a difference in the environment. Is there anything one person can do to save the earth and, if so, what is it? Or do you think, like Lomakina, that it takes large collective action that can't be reduced to a simple set of slogans and pat-yourself-on-the-back actions? Why?

2. One of the themes of Lomakina's essay is that the media has lulled Americans into a sense of complacency about the environment by making them feel that "going green" is really making a difference. Do you agree? Give examples of cases in which the media encourages the view that the environmental crisis is, in Lomakina's words, "an easily solvable problem" (para. 6). Do you think television, the press, and the Internet have had a positive or a negative effect on the way people see environmental issues? Why?

3. Pretend you're organizing a new media campaign to replace the current "green" movement—your job is to educate the public on what it can do locally to save the earth. What, if anything, would you change? How would you get your message across? Write a sample press release detailing three things individuals can do to help curb global warming.

Effective Persuasion: Recommending a Course of Action

The primary purpose of a persuasive essay is to change someone's attitude or course of action. On Election Day, a newspaper editorial will encourage its readers to vote for a particular candidate; in the same paper, a film review may discourage moviegoers from attending a certain film the reviewer finds "pointless, trivial, and embarrassingly dumb." And an opinion column in that paper may try to persuade parents to avoid buying fast food meals for their children. All of these pieces may offer reasons for their views, but they will also urge readers to take some form of action. In "'Going Green' Misses the Point," University of Massachusetts student Yevgeniya Lomakina wants her readers to realize that if they purchase certain items simply because they are advertised or promoted as "green," they may be wasting their time and money. "If one truly wants to go green," she says, "it can be done without expensive purchases." Note how she moves her argument into recommending a course of action by first showing in one paragraph how such "green" purchases defeat their purpose and then in the next paragraph showing what people can do "instead" that would be more effective and cost less or nothing.

1
Lomakina claims that "green" purchases may be environmentally useless

Did advertising and popular culture turn a genuine concern for the environment into an easily solvable problem? It seems that the answer to saving the Earth is only one purchase away. Do you want to live green? Buy a mug. Do you want to live greener? Buy a hybrid car. Choosing an environmentally safe product may simply allow the consumer to have a guilt-free conscience, but, in reality, will cost more for the environment. Costs for transportation, packaging, and the novelty of green products must all be taken into account. It is better to spend a lesser amount of money on a regular product, or even better, not to buy any product at all. (1)

2
She then suggests more effective options that may cost nothing

Some Earth-friendly initiatives require no spending on the part of the consumer. Instead of buying a hybrid car, a better choice would be taking better care of the currently owned model. To save gas, carpool. Instead of buying newer "green" household electric products, once again, take good care of the ones you already own. Instead of buying organic vegetables at Whole Foods, choose to buy them at a local farm stand. (2) However, these simple ways to reduce carbon emissions and spending do not seem to be "popular" enough. It is assumed that if one's initiatives to be green are not publicly seen, they are not present.

AMERICA THEN . . . 1985

The Warming of the World

In a famous short poem in 1920, Robert Frost wondered whether the earth would end in fire or ice — melted by overheating or turned completely into a frozen wasteland. At the time, it appeared that the future climate of the earth could go in either direction. Many doomsday scenarios, in fact, pictured another Ice Age, with the earth becoming uninhabitable as glaciers expanded and rivers and seas froze over. In the mid-1970s, such predictions grew popular, and they found scientific support in 1981 when a prominent British astronomer, Sir Frederick Hoyle, published his forecast of a new ice age, *Ice: The Ultimate Human Catastrophe.*

But by this time, many scientists were also gathering evidence for an opposing worst-case scenario: The earth was seriously overheating as a result of what was called a "greenhouse effect." The crisis was man-made and attributable to the ever-increasing use of fossil fuels (coal, gas, and oil). In 1985, one of America's leading scientists and a prolific

Astronomer Carl Sagan, 1981. Carl Sagan (1934–1996) was for years one of America's best-known scientists, largely because of such popular books as *The Dragons of Eden: Speculations on the Evolution of Human Intelligence* (1977), *Broca's Brain: Reflections on the Romance of Science* (1979), and the enormously successful TV series he hosted, *Cosmos.* Part of his popularity can be attributed to his respect for the general public he was writing for and speaking to. He once said, "The public is a lot brighter and more interested in science than they're given credit for. . . . They're not numbskulls. Thinking scientifically is as natural as breathing."

scientific writer, Carl Sagan, published a warning in the popular Sunday magazine *Parade*. In "The Warming of the World," Sagan — like Hoyle, an astronomer — explained to his readers how fossil fuels produced dangerous levels of carbon dioxide (CO_2) that were "irreversible." Since the industrial revolution, Sagan wrote, the amount of CO_2 in the atmosphere has been steadily increasing and, unless nothing changes, the surface temperature of the earth will also increase.

One of the earliest proponents of global warming (a term that was first used in 1969), Sagan asked in his *Parade* essay the key questions: At our present rate of fuel consumption, how long will it take before our climate becomes dangerously warmer? And what would be the consequences of a perceptibly warmer earth? But despite the alarming evidence even then, Sagan never sounded panic-stricken and he was optimistic that solutions would be discovered in time. Had this great scientist lived into his late seventies, it would be interesting to see what his attitude towards climate change would be today.

Discussing the Unit

SUGGESTED TOPIC FOR DISCUSSION
How can an issue based in hard science—whether the earth is getting warmer, whether humans are the cause, and how dangerous the effects will be—engender a debate like this one? How did politics get involved in the issue of climate change, and will it finally make real discussion of the issue impossible?

PREPARING FOR CLASS DISCUSSION
1. Bill McKibben's essay, which takes for granted that climate change is real, comes from a liberal magazine; Cal Thomas's, which argues that climate change is invented, comes from a conservative blog. Explain the political side of the global warming debate in concrete terms. Why has this issue become polarized?
2. Could it in fact be too late to do anything about climate change? Or are there always solutions?

FROM DISCUSSION TO WRITING
1. Assuming climate change is a real problem, where will the solution come from? Will it be individual action, the private sector, or massive government intervention? Take the authors in this chapter who believe climate

change is real and truly dangerous, and assess where they think the solution—if there even is a solution—will finally lie.

2. None of the essays in this chapter was written by a scientist. Why has the debate been dominated by pundits, rather than the people who hold the actual data? Does a similar rift exist among scientists? Are their conclusions too complex to relay to the public, or are they just too muddy for a readership that likes clear, easy answers?

TOPICS FOR CROSS-CULTURAL DISCUSSION

1. What countries will be hardest hit by the climate crisis, if it's in fact real, and which countries should be the most responsible for fixing it? Why?

2. America remains the country with the most climate-change skeptics, as well as the loudest. Why is this? Why are other countries sold so much more easily on the idea than the United States is? Is it a reflection of boundless American optimism or foolhardy ignorance?

12

Immigration: Who Is an American?

In April 2010, Arizona's governor signed the strictest anti-illegal immigration law any state has passed in decades. Claiming the federal government had dropped the ball in protecting Arizona's border with Mexico and enforcing its own immigration laws, Arizona authorized local law enforcement to uphold the federal laws. But some provisions gave many both inside and outside Arizona pause: SB 1070—its moniker was soon famous—made it a misdemeanor for any immigrant to be in public without documentation and allowed law enforcement to ask immigrants for their papers. Critics immediately alleged that the law sanctioned racial profiling and the wholesale harassment of the one minority group it seemed tacitly aimed at: Latin Americans.

Immigration has been and will continue to be one of the most divisive issues facing the nation. The debate can be seen and heard daily on television and radio talk shows and is a regular feature of newspapers and magazines. An example of the debate in miniature appears in "Does Immigration Increase the Virtues of Hard Work and Fortitude in the United States?" The debate, sponsored by *In Character* magazine, features two specialists on the topic of immigration who take opposite sides on the general issue of what immigrants contribute to the United States. The president of Immigration Works USA, Tamar Jacoby, argues affirmatively that new immigrants work harder than native Americans and tend to "rely less on government benefits." But the executive director of the Center for Immigration Studies, Mark Krikorian, sees things differently and points out the high percentage of immigrants receiving welfare. He argues also that in the past, because of the enormous hardship of transportation and relocation, immigrants may have been a more "enterprising" group of people, but that today with the relative ease of travel and communication this is no longer the case.

One wonders how the author of the next selection would feel about Krikorian's assessment that transportation and relocation make immigration today so much easier than in the past. For many undocumented workers who try to enter the United States in the hopes of finding employment, the journey can be difficult, long, expensive, and dangerous. In "The Crossing," Vicente Martinez (the name is fictitious) offers a detailed description of what it was like to get across the Mexican border into California and eventually on to Portland, Oregon, where he felt confident — largely because of his English language skills — that he could find work.

For most people who decide to come to the United States — whether documented or not — one of the greatest obstacles is language. This was especially true for immigrants who, at any time in our history, arrived speaking only their native languages, but it also affected their children who were born in the United States. A large part of the American immigrant narrative is the story of young Americans who grew up trying to learn English in a family where parents only spoke Spanish, Italian, Arabic, Chinese, or any other foreign language. Because of the demands of work and education, quite a few young people eventually lose fluency in the language heard at home; some caught in the conflict of "English Only" standards never reach proficiency in either language. In "Slurring Spanish," noted author Luis J. Rodríguez wonders why in a nation that is the "fifth-largest Spanish-speaking country in the world," speaking Spanish remains a problem.

The daily news shows may make it appear that immigration is an issue only along America's Mexican border, but the problem is much bigger, as the next two selections demonstrate. In "Uniting Families," Tulane University student Elyse Toplin covers pending legislation in

Congress known as the Uniting Americans Family Act that would allow partners of LGBT (lesbian, gay, bisexual, transgender) Americans the same path to citizenship that heterosexual couples enjoy.

Immigration issues also affect our concepts of racial and ethnic identity. This has been especially the case in the African American community, which in the past several decades has experienced unprecedented migrations of people from African nations, the Caribbean, and the Pacific. How has this influx of foreign-born black populations affected the identity of native-born African Americans? In "Migrations Forced and Free," the prominent historian Ira Berlin considers this difficult topic and concludes that all the diverse groups of black Americans share a common experience, "for the migrations that are currently transforming African-American life are directly connected to those that have transformed black life in the past."

The chapter concludes with a 1999 advertisement that views United States immigration policies as a threat to a sustainable future.

Tamar Jacoby

Does Immigration Increase the Virtues of Hard Work and Fortitude in the United States? Yes

[*In Character*, Spring 2009]

BEFORE YOU READ

What effect do illegal immigrants have on the United States? Do they take up resources or provide valuable services? Do we even notice them?

WORDS TO LEARN

fortitude (title): bravery, courage (noun).

pluck (para. 2): spirit of courage (noun).

avail (para. 4): make use of (verb).

assimilate (para. 6): become part of something (verb).

M ost migrants make the trip for the opportunity to work. The decision is an economic, not moral one. And like any group, today's newcomers are a mixed bunch, with good and bad apples among them.

But migration is also a winnowing experience. Those who end up staying in the U.S. despite the hardships are a self-selecting few. Among the qualities that distinguish them are their pluck and determination.

Immigrants work harder than native-born Americans. In 2006, before the economic downturn, when 66 percent of native-born men were working or actively looking for work, the rate for males from Mexico was 88 percent, and that for Mexican men in the U.S. illegally

1

2

3

The president of Immigration Works USA, Tamar Jacoby is a widely published writer on the topic of immigration. A 1976 graduate of Yale University, she is the author of Someone Else's House: America's Unfinished Struggle for Integration *(1998) and editor of the anthology* Reinventing the Melting Pot: The New Immigrants and What it Means to Be American *(2004).*

was 94 percent. Immigrants also worked longer hours: At the height of the boom, a typical low-skilled immigrant's work week was a stunning 56 percent longer than a typical low-skilled native's.

Newcomers rely less on government benefits. Not even legal immi- 4 grants are eligible for federal welfare programs in their first five years in the U.S., and illegal immigrants are ineligible for handouts of any kind. Even when U.S.-born children qualify families for the program most people think of as welfare, Temporary Assistance for Needy Families, only 1 percent of immigrant-headed households avail themselves, compared to 5 percent of households headed by U.S. citizens.

Migrants are risk-takers by definition, and uprooted, hungry people 5 are always going to be scrappier than settled folks. Remember the immigrant workers rushing to New Orleans in the wake of Katrina for cleanup and construction jobs. We shouldn't be romantic about this: The jobs immigrants do are often dirty and dangerous, and their eagerness to work under any conditions makes it all too easy for some employers to exploit them. But their drive pays off, both for them and for us, and at both the low and high ends of the economic ladder.

> Their drive pays off, both for them and for us.

By the third generation, ironically, this determination falls off as 6 immigrant families assimilate to America's far less driven norms. So it has always been, since Ellis Island[1] and before. The good news: By the time the drive gives out, there is another wave of newcomers waiting in the wings, attracted by the beacon that is America and ready to test their spirit in a country they don't know.

VOCABULARY/USING A DICTIONARY

1. What are the various meanings of the verb *winnow* (para. 2), and how has it come to have the meaning Jacoby deploys in her essay?
2. What are *norms* (para. 6)? Give a few examples of America's norms.

RESPONDING TO WORDS IN CONTEXT

1. How would you define *scrappier* as it's used in paragraph 5? How does this word characterize the immigrants Jacoby is talking about?
2. What is a *beacon* (para. 6)? How is Jacoby using the word in this context? Is it meant literally?

---

[1] Ellis Island (para. 6): The immigration center in New York famous for processing many European immigrants in the nineteenth and twentieth centuries.

DISCUSSING MAIN POINT AND MEANING

1. What does Jacoby mean when she writes that the decision to come to America is "an economic, not moral one" (para. 1)? What view is she trying to dispel? How does casting the decision as an economic one support Jacoby's general argument and position?

2. What sorts of jobs is Jacoby referring to when she writes that "the jobs immigrants do are often dirty and dangerous" (para. 5)? Give a few examples. Why does Jacoby dwell on these jobs? You will note in the following selection that Krikorian doesn't mention the sorts of jobs immigrants do at all.

EXAMINING SENTENCES, PARAGRAPHS, AND ORGANIZATION

1. Which of Jacoby's six paragraphs contain statistics? Which do not? How is the pattern of general assertion and hard facts effective in this essay? (Or what could Jacoby have done to make it more effective?)

2. Jacoby writes, "By the third generation, ironically, this determination falls off as immigrant families assimilate to America's far less driven norms" (para. 6). Explain Jacoby's use of the word *ironically* here. How is the diminished work ethic of the grandchildren of immigrants ironic? Do you agree that it is?

THINKING CRITICALLY

1. What exactly does Jacoby mean when she calls migration "a winnowing experience" (para. 2)? What process is she describing? Is her assertion accurate? Does it take "pluck and determination" to make it as a migrant?

2. Central to Jacoby's claim is that immigrants' drive "pays off, both for them and for us" (para. 5). Describe how the drive pays off for them and how it pays off for us, in Jacoby's estimation. Do you agree with either or with both of these claims? Why or why not?

IN-CLASS WRITING ACTIVITIES

1. Do you think Jacoby's assertion that the work ethic of immigrant communities dies off by the third generation is accurate? If so, write a brief essay explaining why exactly you think this happens. If not, how do you think a work ethic is actually apportioned among the generations, and why?

2. Write a short, descriptive essay about what comes to your mind when you hear the word *immigrant*. What country is the person from? What motivates him or her? How does it relate to your views on the political dimension of the issue?

DEBATE

Mark Krikorian

Does Immigration Increase the Virtues of Hard Work and Fortitude in the United States? No

[*In Character*, Spring 2009]

BEFORE YOU READ

Should we tolerate any amount of illegal immigration into the country? How much of your opinion is based on the value you believe immigrants add or subtract from society, and how much is based on ideas of fairness, compassion, or rule of law?

WORDS TO LEARN

enterprising (para. 1): clever and creative in solving problems (adjective).

psychic (para. 1): psychological (adjective).

debunks (para. 2): exposes as false (verb).

succumb (para. 4): give in (verb).

degenerate (para. 4): completely fallen and immoral (adjective).

miasma (para. 5): a very bad atmosphere (noun).

P erhaps in the past there was some self-selection among immi-   1
grants; only the most enterprising would dare undertake the long and dangerous journey. But even if that were so, modern transportation and communications technologies have changed things permanently. There is no longer a weeks-long trip in steerage[1] to scare

---

[1] steerage (para. 1): The bottom of a ship, reserved for passengers with the cheapest tickets or with no tickets at all; brings to mind immigrants to America in previous centuries.

The executive director of the Center for Immigration Studies, Mark Krikorian is an advocate for a stricter immigration policy and tougher enforcement of immigration laws. A graduate of Georgetown University, he received a master's degree from the Fletcher School of Law and Diplomacy at Tufts University. A regular contributor to The National Review, *he is the author of* The New Case against Immigration, Both Legal and Illegal *(2008).*

off the weak-willed, nor the prospect of being permanently cut off from contact with home. In fact, in modern conditions, we see the development of transnationalism, where people are essentially able to live in two countries at the same time. This dramatically reduces the psychic and emotional price of departing for America, and is thus less likely to weed out the less "gritty" among potential immigrants.

> People are essentially able to live in two countries at the same time.

Welfare use among immigrants debunks the fable of the grit-bearing newcomer. While in 2007 19 percent of households headed by a native-born American used at least one major welfare program (a pretty alarming figure in itself), the number for immigrants was 33 percent. For immigrants who'd lived here twelve years or more, it was 34 percent. And for Mexicans, whose number is equal to the next ten immigrant groups combined, the welfare use rate was more than 50 percent. 2

Not much here to deliver us from our decadence. 3

In trying to understand why the myth of immigrant superiority is false, it's important not to succumb to its flip side, the myth of the "degenerate immigrant," which sees the new arrival as a parasite determined to live off the taxpayer. Instead, immigrants are people like any other, subject to the same temptations and weaknesses, but with an added disadvantage. Immigrants generally come here from pre-industrial societies, with low levels of skill and education, a lot like many of our ancestors a century ago. But unlike our ancestors, these characteristics do not prepare them for life in the America they are entering. 4

This mismatch renders their labor of relatively little worth and plunges them and their children into a moral miasma that we, at least, have had many years to adjust to and evolve with. 5

VOCABULARY/USING A DICTIONARY

1. What do *gritty* (para. 1) and *grit* (para. 2) mean? What is the literal meaning of the noun? Why does Krikorian put the adjective in quotation marks?
2. Explain the word *transnationalism* as Krikorian uses it in paragraph 1. How does your dictionary define it? What does the prefix *trans-* mean in the word? Give another example of this prefix at use in the essay.

RESPONDING TO WORDS IN CONTEXT

1. What does Krikorian mean by our *decadence* in paragraph 3? What is the dictionary definition of the word, and how is it used here?
2. What are the various meanings of the word *parasite* (para. 4)? Which meaning is at work in Krikorian's piece?

DISCUSSING MAIN POINT AND MEANING

1. Why, according to Krikorian, is the labor of recent immigrants "of relatively little worth" (para. 5)? How does Jacoby's position differ?

2. What is the "moral miasma" to which Krikorian refers in paragraph 5? Why are new immigrants unique in having to deal with it?

EXAMINING SENTENCES, PARAGRAPHS, AND ORGANIZATION

1. How does Krikorian tie the end of his essay to its beginning by referencing "our ancestors a century ago" (para. 4)? How do these ancestors provide a thematic backdrop to the entire essay?

2. Why is paragraph 3 so much shorter than the other paragraphs in this brief essay? What effect is Krikorian going for, and why did he select that paragraph to deploy it?

THINKING CRITICALLY

1. Discuss the ways Krikorian's statistics clash with Jacoby's. What is the major issue on which their respective numbers disagree? Whose are you more inclined to believe? Why?

2. Do you think Krikorian's characterization of the societies immigrants are coming from as "pre-industrial" (para. 4) is accurate? Or is it an exaggeration? What exactly does the word mean? (Look it up online if you're not sure.) Which societies does he have in mind? How reliant is his argument on the premise that these societies are in fact pre-industrial?

IN-CLASS WRITING ACTIVITIES

1. Notice that Krikorian's essay uses the word "we" (para. 5) to mean non-immigrants—he assumes there are no migrant workers or undocumented aliens reading his argument. Do you think this is a reasonable assumption? Is it a fair one? How do you think his essay, and Jacoby's, would be different if they were writing directly for the immigrants they are writing about?

2. Weigh in on the debate yourself. Do immigrants work harder than native-born citizens in this country? Do they add to or subtract from the nation's total work ethic and output? Is your opinion based on facts, anecdotes, impressions, or some combination? Do you even feel qualified to give a definite answer? Why or why not?

Vicente Martinez

The Crossing

[*Oregon Humanities*, Fall/Winter 2009]

BEFORE YOU READ
Does the often atrocious experience of crossing the border illegally change the way you feel about illegal immigration?

WORDS TO LEARN

inconspicuous (para. 12): not very visible (adjective).

verified (para. 16): made sure (verb).

vulnerable (para. 19): easy to harm (adjective).

traversing (para. 23): traveling across (verb).

hunched (para. 25): crouched with shoulders up (verb).

inclement (para. 29): unpleasant (adjective).

dire (para. 30): serious (adjective).

initially (para. 34): at first (adverb).

potable (para. 35): drinkable (adjective).

wiring (para. 38): sending by telegraph (verb).

On Wednesday, February 4, 2009, I said goodbye to my family. 1
I didn't want to leave, but the thought of getting sick was often on my mind.

I'd been looking for work since arriving in Las Calandrias in October. 2
But the economy was in terrible shape, and I wasn't an ideal job candidate. I couldn't do hard labor with my health condition, and I was too old to be considered for most jobs; the cut-off was typically forty, and I was forty-one. I hoped my English language skills might help me find a job with a company that needed bilingual people in Guadalajara — the capital of Jalisco state, where my family lives — but my application was turned down. Ironically, it was far easier for me to find work as an undocumented worker in Portland than as a legal citizen in Mexico.

According to Oregon Humanities: *"This essay, adapted from a longer unpublished work, chronicles the fifth border crossing to the United States by Vicente Martinez (a pseudonym).* Oregon Humanities *magazine editorial advisory board member Camela Raymond worked with Martinez on editing this essay for publication. Some names and details have been changed."*

To control my HIV, I needed a regular supply of medicine and peri-   3
odic blood tests. I could get these for free at a clinic in Portland, but here
in Mexico, although I could get my medicine free of charge at a local hos-
pital, I had to pay for my own lab work — 500 pesos every three months.
Even if I found a full-time job, which seemed increasingly unlikely, this
would be difficult to afford. Minimum wage was 700 pesos a week, barely
enough to get by.

That Wednesday around noon, I found my mother sitting on her   4
bed. I told her I was going to leave, and she began to cry. The sight of her
tears broke my heart. We'd last seen each other almost eighteen years
ago, and this recent reunion had lasted only three and a half months.
I couldn't tell her the real reason I was leaving. I'd never told my parents I
had HIV. I didn't want them to worry. If they knew, they would assume
I was suffering; they wouldn't understand that the medicine I was taking
would keep me healthy for some time.

I kissed my mother, and she kissed me. I assured her that my trip   5
across the border would be easier than it was the first time, when I was
twenty-four and walked for days without food. Then I said goodbye to
my eighty-one-year-old father, who was also very close to crying. It hurt
me to leave him, alone and sad.

To pay the *coyote*,[1] I'd sold the truck I'd driven from Portland   6
(I'd hoped to give it to my parents, who were one of the few families in
Las Calandrias that didn't have a car). So my younger brother Andres
drove me to the bus stop about ten miles away in Santa Cruz in our
brother Manuel's old car, which broke down all the time. Also with us
was Felipe, a young guy in his late twenties, also from Las Calandrias,
who was going to cross with me. On the highway at the edge of Santa
Cruz, I said goodbye to Andres and told him to behave.

Friday morning, after nearly two days on the road, Felipe and I   7
arrived at the Tijuana bus station. I found a pay phone and called Pedro,
the *coyote* I'd met in Las Calandrias. About thirty minutes later Pedro
pulled up in a white van and took us to his house, which was in a different
part of town, on a hill near some railroad tracks. Three dogs guarded the
front door from inside a small, walled patio.

The house was old, but in decent shape. One guy was sleeping on the   8
living room sofa, another in one of the two bedrooms. Counting Felipe
and me, that made four *pollos*[2]— chickens waiting for the *coyote* to take
us across.

---

[1] *coyote* (para. 6): A smuggler who ferries immigrants across the border from
Mexico illegally, usually for a large fee.

---

[2] *pollos* (para. 8): Spanish for "chickens."

I called my cousin Luis in Escondido, California. His wife, Sofia, a U.S. citizen, agreed to drive down to Tijuana and meet me later that night. She'd take the $2,500 I'd set aside to pay the *coyote*, along with my Oregon driver's license and some other important documents, and hold everything in Escondido until I was safely across. 9

Pedro left for a couple of hours and came back loaded with food. He had to attend a funeral in his hometown, he said, and would be gone for two days. Meantime, the four of us would have plenty to eat and were free to do whatever we wanted. This was unfortunate news, but I wasn't too worried; it felt safe at Pedro's house, and I trusted he'd be back. 10

Pedro was supposed to be back on Sunday. On Monday, he still hadn't returned. On Tuesday evening, an associate of Pedro's in his early fifties arrived at the house. He didn't introduce himself, but the dogs knew him; later I found out he was Pedro's stepfather. He told us to get our things. It was time to cross over. 11

Twenty minutes later we arrived at a residential street, not far from the main gate. Pedro's stepfather led us to an inconspicuous spot between two houses. The plan was to cross the border through an underground sewer tunnel; the entrance to the tunnel was being guarded by several border control cars, visible in the near distance. We were to wait here until they moved. 12

Hours went by, and the cars didn't move — unsurprising, I thought. Finally, at about ten-thirty at night, Pedro's stepfather let us have a break. He led us to an abandoned house a few blocks away, gave us a blanket (one for all four of us), and said he'd be back the following morning with food. He left a dog guarding the entrance. 13

I slept for a few hours. It was cold, and there was no working toilet or any running water in the house. In the morning, before Pedro's stepfather returned, I convinced the others to leave. Using some pieces of metal and wood lying in the yard, I trapped the dog against the house. We walked a few blocks to a commercial area, hailed a taxi, and drove back to Pedro's house. His stepfather showed up later, surprised we'd escaped. 14

By Thursday, we had been at Pedro's house for almost a week. Though it felt safe there, it was becoming apparent we were wasting our time. Reluctantly, we decided to go downtown and look for another *coyote*. Within a couple of hours, we found one near the main gate — a tall, chubby guy who called himself Sonora, after the Mexican state. His price was US$1,800, cheaper than Pedro. 15

Sonora's operation moved quickly. Once we got to his house, the *coyotes* (there were two, including Sonora, who appeared to be the big bosses) immediately asked for the phone numbers of our contacts in the 16

United States and verified they'd pick us up and pay our crossing fees. A little later they brought us three blankets to share, roasted chicken for lunch, and more food to take on the road: for each person, two cans of tuna, a loaf of bread, some refried beans, and two bottles of water.

That night, we were taken in a pickup truck to a street corner in   17 Tijuana, where five more *pollos* joined us. An hour or so later, a first-class bus, with a sign that read "Bienvenidos" and flashing lights, arrived. All nine of us, plus a guide, boarded. Soon we arrived at an isolated stretch of highway just east of the city of Tecate, where the driver pulled over.

The guide led us across the highway. We walked in single file, car-   18 rying no flashlights, which would attract attention, just knapsacks holding our food and blankets. We passed a small village, went through some bushes, and climbed over a five-foot chicken-wire fence. Mostly, though, the terrain was flat and empty. After about four hours, the guide stopped, and we all lay down on the ground and attempted to sleep.

Moments later it got very cold, and before long, we were all shaking.   19 Four of us shared three blankets, but the remaining guys had nothing to keep them warm. One of them asked if we'd share ours, but I said no. Though I felt bad refusing him, he was young and healthy; I was older and more vulnerable to getting sick.

My body became so cold that night that I thought I wouldn't make it to morning. I   20 spent the hours praying to God, telling Him that if it was my turn to go, He should go ahead and take me. But at the same time, I asked Him to spare me: I had promised my mother I would survive the trip without harm, and the thought that I might die that night filled me with sadness.

> My body became so cold that night that I thought I wouldn't make it to morning.

Sometime in the middle of the night, the guide stood up and said   21 it was time to get moving again. Before we started walking, though, he asked us to hand over our blankets. With a knife, he cut the three blankets into nine pieces, handing one to each of us.

It felt better once we started walking and my body grew warm again.   22 The going was quite easy for a while, with flat ground dotted sparsely with tall bushes. But soon we came to a sign warning of an approaching decline, and we descended into a canyon. At the bottom, the guide told us to wait while he climbed the slope on the other side. He stood at the top of the canyon for at least a half hour, scanning the hills ahead for signs of border patrol — and, perhaps, for *bajadores*, the Mexican bandits who often rob border crossers. Beyond the hills, in the far distance, I could see vehicle lights flashing.

After crossing the canyon, we came to a dirt road. The guide asked   23
for our blankets and laid them down on the road so that we wouldn't
leave footprints. Then we continued on unmarked terrain, traversing a
hill and another canyon. When dawn broke, the guide pointed to some
large boulders atop a nearby hill. He was going to go on some unexplained mission. We were to hide among the boulders until he returned.

Some hours later the wind began to blow, and I started to shiver   24
again. I pulled a big plastic garbage bag, which the guide had given
me, over my entire body, but the wind kept seeping through. Morning
passed, then afternoon, and we didn't move except in order to urinate
near the edge of the rocks. Some of the others were able to fall asleep,
but I couldn't.

The guide had given us a code word, and at dusk, we heard him yell-   25
ing it, and we swiftly packed up our things. Then we continued to walk.
We passed over a couple of hills, heading toward the lights of a small
town. Suddenly the guide stopped, turned around, and led us back to the
top of the nearest hill. We hunched down. I could see people with flashlights, INS[3] agents, combing an area below us. Moments later it started
to rain, and we all got inside our plastic bags. After a while the agents left,
and we started walking again.

We passed straight through the town, avoiding the streets and walk-   26
ing instead through people's yards, climbing over several fences, until we
reached a highway marked State Route 94. This indicated not only that
we were in U.S. territory, but also that we were nearing the road, Highway 8, where we'd be picked up and delivered to safety.

We continued climbing the hills, very high hills this time. My legs   27
almost gave out, but I kept moving. At dawn of the second day we
stopped near another large rock. Thankfully, on this day the sun came
out. We spent the whole warm, bright day in the shade of the big rock,
dozing fitfully, drying out our socks, and eating a little of the remaining
food we'd brought.

At dusk we started walking again. About four hours later, in the mid-   28
dle of the night, we finally reached Highway 8. We crossed beneath the
above-grade roadway through a large drainage tunnel, and as we headed
for a grassy shoulder on the other side, the guide ordered the guy at the
back of the line to use his piece of blanket to erase the footprints we
were leaving in the dirt. Then we proceeded west alongside the freeway,
crouching down every time a car passed, until we reached a road sign that
marked the place the *coyotes* were supposed to pick us up.

---

[3] INS (para. 25): Immigration and Naturalization Services, the federal agency in
charge of border patrol.

The guide had already called them on his cell phone. Within   29
moments, a pickup truck arrived. Instead of taking us away in his truck,
however, the driver only dropped off some food. We wouldn't be picked
up until it rained, our guide explained. According to him, there was an
INS checkpoint on the freeway that we had to pass through, and it would
probably shut down in inclement weather.

We spent the night very close to the freeway. Since the road was built   30
on a high concrete foundation, we weren't visible to the passing cars.
Still, there was nothing, not even a rock or a tree, to provide shelter from
the cold, and the temperature dropped so low that, once again, all of us
shivered badly. The cold made me extremely thirsty, but I had less than a
medium-size bottle of water left, and the pickup driver had dropped off
only one additional gallon of water for all of us. Sometime in the middle
of the night, I took a sip from my bottle, and pieces of ice hit my tongue.
I thought I might die from cold again that night; I even planned out how
I'd run to the freeway and ask for help if things became truly dire.

Before dawn, we moved slightly away from the freeway and lay down   31
under a big tree. Later we moved farther away, hiding in some bushes.
There we spent the day, eating a bit of the food left over from what the
driver had dropped.

Night came, and still we were stranded. Once the rain started, the   32
driver would come, the guide repeated.

We were all becoming angry. "What if it doesn't rain for a week?" we   33
said to each other. "Are we going to be stuck here in the cold the whole
time, with no food and water?"

The *coyotes* had initially told us the entire trip would require only six   34
hours of walking. This estimate wasn't ridiculously far off — we'd spent
no more than about ten hours on our feet — but it didn't account for the
fact that we'd be walking over a period of three days, and that during that
time we wouldn't have enough food, water, and warm clothing. If we died
of hypothermia, the *coyotes* wouldn't care, though. They'd just be out a
few cans of tuna. The guide was the only one working for his money, and
he was clueless; in fact, he was smoking weed day and night.

The following day, just before dawn, the guide took our empty bottles   35
and asked one of the other *pollos* to help him fetch some water. When
they returned, we drank greedily. We weren't sure where the water came
from — presumably some nearby stream — or whether it was potable,
but at least it quenched our thirst.

Suddenly, a light rain began to fall, and within moments, the guide   36
received a call alerting us that we'd soon be picked up. Once a second call
came through, we moved right up beside the freeway, a tall cyclone fence

between us and the pavement. When the pickup truck arrived, the same one that had dropped the food the night before, we all jumped the fence and scrambled in. A couple of guys took seats in the cab, and the rest of us lay flat in the open bed. The driver took off speeding.

Within about thirty minutes, we arrived at a house in San Diego. The   37
house was full of people — a group of ten additional border crossers had just arrived; they'd used a route farther east, braving tall hills and snow to avoid the INS checkpoint. The nine from our group were put in the garage. The coyotes brought us plates of warm food — rice, beans, eggs, and tortillas — and immediately began calling our contacts to make arrangements to drop us off. Meantime, they made sure we didn't escape before paying; whenever we used the bathroom, we had to remove our shoes, so as not to be tempted to leave the house through the small bathroom window.

It was agreed that instead of wiring my payment, my cousin Luis   38
would pay the *coyotes* in cash once they dropped me at his apartment in Escondido thirty minutes away; I wanted to make sure the *coyotes* really got me all the way there. Before long only four other guys and I were left, and the pickup truck returned for us. Since it was dark, we were allowed to sit upright in the truck bed, but we had to cover our heads with a blanket until we reached the freeway; this, I think, was to prevent us from learning precisely where the *coyotes* lived.

We arrived in Escondido, Luis handed over my $1,800, and I was   39
free. Sofia made us a nice, big dinner. It felt good to be with them; Luis was the son of my father's departed sister, and Sofia and I had always been naturally fond of each other.

That was Monday night, and I needed to be in Huron, about three   40
hundred miles away, by Wednesday. From there, another cousin would drive me to the Sacramento bus station, where I'd catch a Greyhound to Portland.

Tuesday night, Luis and I started out for Huron. The INS checkpoint   41
on Highway 15 didn't ordinarily inspect vehicles, but the traffic started slowing down as we approached the station. We had already passed a couple of INS cars stopped by the side of the road, and Luis, not wishing to take any chances, turned back home. But we immediately returned to the same route, this time with Sofia driving about a mile ahead. Once she passed the checkpoint, she called and reported that it was clear, and Luis and I drove on.

That night I stayed with Luis's sister in Huron, and the following   42
evening, my nineteen-year-old nephew Marcos drove me to Sacramento, where yet another cousin gave me a ride to the bus station.

The ticket clerks were checking everyone's ID, but when I got to   43
the front of the line, the woman behind the counter noted my Mexican

appearance and turned to another female employee. "Do I sell him a ticket?" she asked. "Go ahead," the other woman replied. It was a kind favor, though I had a valid Oregon driver's license in my wallet.

I arrived in the beautiful city of Portland, Oregon, on Thursday afternoon, February 19, 2009. I felt like I was home.   44

VOCABULARY/USING A DICTIONARY

1. What is the meaning of the word *isolated* (para. 17)? What language does the word come from, and what does its root word mean in that language?
2. Define *seep* (para. 24). What part of speech is it, and what is its origin? What is usually described as "seeping"?
3. What is the origin of the word *hypothermia* (para. 34)? What does the prefix *hypo-* mean?

RESPONDING TO WORDS IN CONTEXT

1. What is a *commercial* area (para. 14)? What does the word *commercial* mean, and what does this usage contrast the area with? How is this meaning related to other senses of the word you're familiar with?
2. What exactly does *terrain* mean as Martinez uses it in paragraph 18? How does its meaning differ from *land* or *earth*?
3. What is the meaning of the word *shoulder* in paragraph 28?

DISCUSSING MAIN POINT AND MEANING

1. What specific factors does Martinez mention that make his story especially moving? List three things that made the crossing harder for him than it would be for the typical immigrant.
2. How does Martinez characterize the *coyotes* throughout the essay? What is the picture of these men and their motives you get when Martinez writes "they'd just be out a few cans of tuna" (para. 34)? What other scenes reinforce this characterization?
3. Why was Martinez's head covered with a blanket on the last leg of his journey? Why is this detail important?

EXAMINING SENTENCES, PARAGRAPHS, AND ORGANIZATION

1. Martinez describes much of the landscape of his trip in great detail, as in paragraph 22: "The going was quite easy for a while, with flat ground dotted sparsely with tall bushes." Why does he attempt to paint such a vivid picture of the physical environment he crossed? What effect is this intended to have on the reader?
2. Martinez never breaks from the narrative form in this essay—he never once mentions his opinion on immigration reform, for instance, or

describes what he thinks should be done to improve the condition of undocumented people in the United States. Why is the narrative form of his essay important? Do you think it would be more or less effective if he advanced an argument or used more varied rhetorical forms? Why?

THINKING CRITICALLY

1. Martinez refers to himself as an "undocumented worker" (para. 2), a term used as an alternative to "illegal immigrant." What does each term imply, and why do you think Martinez prefers the first? Which one do you think should be used in most cases, and why?

2. Discuss the activity of the INS as depicted in Martinez's story. How is he trying to characterize their activity? What do you think of the checkpoints they set up on the highway? Do you think that they effectively police the community and enforce the law, or might their presence lead to something more sinister?

3. How does Martinez paint the immigrant community along the Pacific Coast? How does this image fit with your preconceptions of communities of Latin American immigrants in the United States?

IN-CLASS WRITING ACTIVITIES

1. Analyze Martinez's writing style. Is it flowery or plain? Does he attempt to set a visual scene or to make you think about the internal lives of his characters? Pick out an episode or a detail that you especially liked and analyze why it was so effective.

2. Tell another story of crossing over into America — it can be your ancestors', your parents', a friend's, or your own. Take a cue from Martinez and be vivid in your details, even if you're relying on your imagination. Consider as you write what's different about your story and what similarities all immigrant tales have in common.

3. Did reading Martinez's story change the way you think about illegal immigration and migrant workers at all? If so, explain in a brief essay how so. If not, explain your thoughts on undocumented workers and why they held firm against (or with) Martinez's narrative.

Luis J. Rodríguez
Slurring Spanish

[*The Progressive*, March 2010]

BEFORE YOU READ

What do you think of bilingual education? Should students in American schools who speak another language be encouraged to learn English, to grow in their native language, or both?

WORDS TO LEARN

deficit (para. 2): something that is insufficient; a disadvantage (noun).
marginalized (para. 5): made to feel or seem unimportant (adjective).
phenomenon (para. 6): situation or set of events (noun).
barrios (para. 6): Latin American neighborhoods (noun).

fluent (para. 11): able to speak a language with ease and perfect accuracy (adjective).
citing (para. 11): using as evidence (verb).
rescinded (para. 11): took back (verb).
garnered (para. 16): gained (verb).

In 1960, I entered first grade at 109th Street School in Watts[1] speaking only Spanish. I was pushed from one classroom to another. When I finally found a teacher to accept me, I was placed in a corner and told to play with blocks. This lasted for a year. Whenever I spoke Spanish in the classroom or playground, I was yelled at and sometimes swatted. 1

Speaking Spanish, which could have been a valuable tool in my learning, in grasping a new language, in having a healthy social life, instead became a handicap, a social burden, one of the many "deficits" I encountered in my school life during the 1960s and early 1970s. 2

You would think that after years of activism around the country, which secured bilingual education, multicultural curriculums, and a 3

---

[1] Watts (para. 1): A neighborhood of Los Angeles.

An award-winning poet, novelist, and journalist, Luis J. Rodríguez is a regular contributor to The Progressive, *where "Slurring Spanish" first appeared. An active gang member in his youth, he published his memoir* Always Running: La Vida Loca: Gang Days in L.A. *in 1993. He is also well-known for his successful writing workshops.*

semblance of cultural and racial equity, that this kind of thing wouldn't happen anymore.

But it does.   4

Today, Spanish speakers still remain highly marginalized in most   5
U.S. schools.

Mayra Zaragoza is a nineteen-year-old recent high school graduate. Although   6
Mayra was born in the United States, both her parents spoke only Spanish.
Mayra didn't learn English until later, a phenomenon quite common in bar-
rios such as Pacoima in the San Fernando Valley,[2] where she grew up.

"I suffered a lot, and I still suffer now, from starting school with   7
Spanish as my first language," Mayra says. "Spelling and grammar are
my biggest weaknesses. At one point, all I wanted to speak was English
because I was told in school 'If you only
speak English, you will get better at it.'"

> Speaking Spanish does not have to be a crisis in the United States.

This made Mayra see Spanish as some-   8
thing bad, something inferior, something
that labeled her as a problem student.

In my travels and talks in schools all   9
over the country, Spanish-speaking children
are often seen as trouble. Many are forced into speaking English as quickly
as possible, often by threat of punishment. Under these kinds of pressures,
however, most students don't get good at Spanish or English.

"It's wrong to target Spanish-speaking kids as 'at-risk' only because   10
of their language," Mayra says. "It first happened to me in my English
class where I was told to speak only English."

Zach Rubio, sixteen, was suspended in 2005 from a Kansas City school   11
for speaking Spanish. Rubio, a fluent English speaker, apparently said "*no
problema*"[3] (often used by English speakers as slang) after a friend asked to
borrow money between classes. The school principal promptly suspended
Rubio, citing a policy she instituted to outlaw Spanish in the school. The
school district, however, rescinded the suspension and the policy, stating
that speaking a foreign language was no grounds for suspension, especially
outside a classroom.

But I've heard from other students that such punishments continue in   12
their schools.

Speaking Spanish does not have to be a crisis in the United States,   13
which is already the fifth-largest Spanish-speaking country in the world,

---

[2] San Fernando Valley (para. 6): Part of Southern California made up chiefly of
Los Angeles.

---

[3] *no problema* (para. 11): No problem.

with about forty million speakers. Spanish-language speakers can learn English and still maintain their Spanish, a process that favors both languages. But with "English Only" laws, school suspensions, and the derailment of bilingual education programs, Spanish is again being devalued and people who speak it discriminated against.

The ramifications are that millions of school-age children in this country think something is wrong with them for speaking Spanish — the way I felt around fifty years ago. 14

"Culture and roots are important to teach in our schools," Mayra says. "When a Spanish-speaking teenager falls into becoming a social statistic this is mainly due to not having a positive self-identity, of not knowing what their true selves really are. The end result is often drugs, gangs, or violence." 15

With great effort, and despite what schools did to me in my youth, I spent most of my adult life dominating English as well as improving my Spanish. Since then my language skills have garnered me fourteen books in poetry, children's literature, fiction, and nonfiction. I've worked for newspapers and radio. And I'm a regularly requested speaker on campuses, conferences, events, and more. Although the vast majority of my writing and talks are in English, I speak Spanish whenever possible. 16

Today, I wish I could show my books and other recognition to the many teachers I had growing up who told me far too often that I'd "never amount to anything." 17

Again I defer to the wisdom of Mayra Zaragoza. 18

"A bilingual society is needed because we now have more people that speak different languages in this country than ever before — and we all deserve the same opportunity and support as English-only speakers," she declares. "I say we should give more support to classes and workshops that help with bettering our English as well as allowing us to master Spanish." 19

Many countries around the world place great importance on the skill of speaking more than one language. Why shouldn't this be true of the United States, as well? 20

To speak two or more languages. . . . *No problema!* 21

VOCABULARY/USING A DICTIONARY

1. What is the origin of the word *curriculum* (para. 3)? What has the word come to mean today?
2. What does the prefix in the word *bilingual* (para. 3) mean? Find two other words that share this prefix and define them.
3. Define the word *ramifications* (para. 14). What part of speech is it? What verb is it related to?

RESPONDING TO WORDS IN CONTEXT

1. Define the word *multicultural* (para. 3) and explain its origin. Based on the way Rodríguez uses the word, do you think he regards it as a good or a bad way to describe something?
2. What does the word *derailment* mean as Rodríguez uses it in paragraph 13? Where does the term come from, and what process is he referring to here?
3. What does Mayra mean when she refers to "becoming a social statistic" (para. 15)? What exactly does the word *statistic* mean and imply here?

DISCUSSING MAIN POINT AND MEANING

1. What general disciplinary practice does Rodríguez criticize as deeply flawed though widespread in America's schools? What does he say is wrong with it?
2. What attitude does Rodríguez think the American school system instills in students? Why? What does he argue can be done about this?
3. What argument does Rodríguez offer that suggests he believes bilingual education would benefit English as well as Spanish speakers?

EXAMINING SENTENCES, PARAGRAPHS, AND ORGANIZATION

1. The first two sections of the essay begin with narratives, the first Rodríguez's own story, the second that of Mayra Zaragoza. Why does the author structure the opening of his essay in this way? What larger point is he trying to get across by placing these two stories together?
2. Four paragraphs in this essay are almost completely made up of quotations from Mayra. Identify these paragraphs. Why does Rodríguez put so much of the essay directly in Mayra's voice?
3. What is the impact of ending with the phrase *no problema*? How does it tie the essay together, and what effect does it have on the overall tone of the essay?

THINKING CRITICALLY

1. Do you agree that schools should encourage students who speak primarily Spanish — or any other language, for that matter — to grow in their knowledge of their native language and culture? Why or why not?
2. What evidence does Rodríguez give of his own success, despite the school system he was raised in? What do you think of Rodríguez's measure of success? Does he mean to hold himself up as an example of something every Spanish-speaking student in the United States should strive for? How would you judge the ultimate success of an immigrant who comes

to his or her adopted country without knowing the language? Should the standard of success be lower than that for native speakers and citizens? Why or why not?

3. Rodríguez mentions that other countries "place great importance on the skill of speaking more than one language" (para. 20). Look up an example of a country that does so. What factors, if any, are present in that country that make it more conducive to using multiple languages than in America? Could the United States ever really be a multilingual country? Why or why not?

IN-CLASS WRITING ACTIVITIES

1. What are the major arguments *against* bilingual education? Research them online if you need to. List three arguments that proponents of English-only education in American schools might offer, and explain how Rodríguez would likely answer each one.

2. Rodríguez writes poignantly that "speaking Spanish, which could have been a valuable tool in my learning, in grasping a new language, in having a healthy social life, instead became a handicap, a social burden, one of the many 'deficits' I encountered in my school life" (para. 2). Think of another example—not involving language—in which something that should have been an advantage became a social burden to you or someone you knew. Describe what happened and how it felt.

3. Look into some of the "English Only" laws Rodríguez references in paragraph 13. What motivates these laws? Are they sincerely set up to improve the efficiency of society, or is there perhaps a hidden racial element behind them? Write a short essay defending or attacking a hypothetically proposed "English Only" law in your community.

Elyse Toplin (student essay)

Uniting Families

[*The Hullabaloo,* Tulane University, January 29, 2010]

BEFORE YOU READ
Should citizenship be automatically extended to the partners of LGBT citizens? What about to the straight ones?

WORDS TO LEARN
visa (para. 2): a temporary allowance for an immigrant to live or work in a country legally (noun).
contingent (para. 5): depending on (adjective).

unfounded (para. 7): without any reason (adjective).
comprehensive (para. 9): complete (adjective).

I n his State of the Union address Wednesday night [January 27, 2010], President Barack Obama said, "We should continue the work of fixing our broken immigration system . . . and ensure that everyone who plays by the rules can contribute to our economy and enrich our nation." A problem in the LGBT [lesbian, gay, bisexual, and transgender] community is a great example of where we can start. Under current laws, gay citizens aren't allowed to transfer citizenship to immigrant spouses like straight couples. This is an example of "our broken immigration system" and the passage of the Uniting American Families Act would be a great first step to fix it.

Meet Gordon Stewart. Stewart is an American citizen who currently lives in the United Kingdom with his partner of more than nine years, Renato. Renato lived with Stewart in 2003 while he was studying in the United States, but had to return to his home in Brazil when his visa expired. He was unable to get it renewed, and Stewart could not sponsor his partner because they were not married or otherwise related.

After years of continuing their relationship on two continents, the couple decided to move to the United Kingdom, where they could live

1

2

3

Elyse Toplin is a junior at Tulane University. At The Hullabaloo *she is a member of the managing editorial board and serves as the chief copyeditor of the paper.*

together. However, in his testimony before Congress in June, Stewart (who traveled to testify alone because Renato is still unable to get so much as a tourist visa to the United States) explained the reality of this situation.

"I am furious that we can not visit or live together in the U.S.," Stewart said. "Despite the fact that I am a tax-paying, law-abiding and voting citizen, I feel discrimination from my government. . . . I would like to be able to come home; I should have the right to come with my partner to visit or to live; but we can't."

Sadly, Stewart's story is not unique. Shirley Tan, whose stay in the United States is currently contingent on the existence of a private bill by Senators Dianne Feinstein and Barbara Boxer, is dealing with the same situation, and faces deportation to the Philippines if the Uniting American Families Act does not pass while the 111th Congress is in session. Tan has lived in the United States for more than two decades, and she and her partner [Jay Mercado] have two sons. The family goes to church, the parents are involved in the school, and the kids get good grades. Essentially, they are exactly the type of person that most Americans would want in this country. However, because Tan and Mercado cannot get married, Mercado cannot sponsor Tan for citizenship.

4

"Despite the fact that I am a tax-paying, law-abiding and voting citizen, I feel discrimination from my government."

5

The Uniting American Families Act would right these injustices, as well as rescue the lives of thousands of Americans who risk deportation because they cannot get married. UAFA would change the wording of the Immigration and Nationality Act, adding the words "permanent partner" and "permanent partnership" after the words "spouse" and "marriage" to relevant parts of the bill. This would allow immigrants who are in long-term committed relationships to have a pathway to citizenship in the same way that heterosexual couples can, and those who violate the law would face the same penalties as their heterosexual counterparts, including up to five years imprisonment or a fine of $250,000.

6

Though some may think that fraud would increase with the passage of UAFA, it is not unfounded to believe that many homosexual couples could prove — just as their heterosexual counterparts can — that they are part of a committed, long-term relationship. After Renato was denied entry to the United States, for example, Stewart commuted to Brazil from New York every other weekend for more than a year. When the financial burden of this task became too much to bear, the couple moved to England, where they could still be together. Though most heterosexual

7

couples are never asked to do things this extreme, the strength of their commitment is never questioned.

The United States would not be unique in providing immigration rights for homosexuals with the passage of UAFA. Eighteen countries have similar laws, and these countries include Australia, Canada, Israel, the United Kingdom, Spain, South Africa, Germany, and France.   8

UAFA has been introduced in every Congress since 2000, and has never made it out of the Senate Judiciary Committee.[1] This bill affects far too many people for it to fail again, and must either pass on its own or be included in any comprehensive immigration reforms considered by the 111th Congress.   9

Gordon Stewart is an American citizen. He votes in elections, abides by laws, and pays taxes from abroad. As such, he is guaranteed the unalienable rights of life, liberty, and the pursuit of happiness. So is Jay Mercado, Shirley Tan's partner of over twenty years. Neither of them, however, will have the right to the pursuit of happiness until the passage of the Uniting American Families Act.   10

VOCABULARY/USING A DICTIONARY
1. What is the origin of the word *deportation* (para. 6)?
2. What do the prefixes *homo-* and *hetero-* mean in *homosexual* and *heterosexual*? Give another example of a pair of English words with these prefixes.

RESPONDING TO WORDS IN CONTEXT
1. Explain the meaning of *introduced* as Toplin uses it in paragraph 9. What kind of context is it used in, and what does it mean in that context?
2. To what is Toplin alluding when she refers to the couples' "unalienable rights of life, liberty, and the pursuit of happiness" (para. 10)? Look up the phrase if it's not familiar. How does this reference strengthen her point?

DISCUSSING MAIN POINT AND MEANING
1. Explain what Toplin means by "fraud" in paragraph 7. How might some people use legislation such as UAFA to perpetrate fraud?
2. What is the point of listing countries with similar laws in paragraph 8? How does this list add to Toplin's argument?

---

[1] Senate Judiciary Committee (para. 9): A standing committee, or special group, of U.S. senators that considers bills related to judicial matters; to "make it out" of the committee means a proposal gets a vote in the full Senate.

EXAMINING SENTENCES, PARAGRAPHS, AND ORGANIZATION

1. Discuss the transition between the first two paragraphs. What is the function of the first sentence of paragraph 2, and how does it shift the focus and strategy of the essay? Do you think it's an effective way to begin the essay?

2. Why does Toplin mention, of Shirley Tan's family, that "the family goes to church, the parents are involved in the school, and the kids get good grades" (para. 5)? What does she mean to communicate about the family with this sentence?

3. Identify a point in the essay in which Toplin brings up a counterargument and answers it. What case does she anticipate opponents of UAFA will bring up? How does she respond? How does bringing the issue up improve the argumentative force of her essay?

THINKING CRITICALLY

1. Toplin appeals to our sense of equal rights for gay and lesbian couples, but never questions the fundamental idea that the partner of a citizen should get citizenship rights. Do you think this widely accepted notion is right? What are some possible arguments against extending citizenship to any foreign spouses of citizens—gay or straight? How do you come down on these arguments, and why?

2. How does Toplin characterize the various gay couples she mentions (like Gordon Stewart and Renato)? What image do you have of these couples? Why is this image important to Toplin's essay?

3. Does Toplin's argument presume that gay marriage should be legal? Are you for or against gay marriage? Why? Do you think it's possible to accept Toplin's premise that gay couples deserve the same protections straight couples get when it comes to immigration without believing in gay marriage? Why or why not?

IN-CLASS WRITING ACTIVITIES

1. One of the problems this essay touches on is how immigration authorities can separate couples in "long-term committed relationships" (para. 6) from those attempting to defraud the system and gain citizenship with a phony relationship. Write an essay describing some of the problems you imagine authorities have making this distinction. What solution, or set of solutions, would you propose to the challenges?

2. Toplin introduces the UAFA as a "great example of where we can start" fixing the immigration system (para. 1). What else do you think President Obama means when he says he wants to give everyone who is law-abiding a chance to "contribute to our economy and enrich our nation"? Give a few examples of immigration reforms you think would improve our system and our economy.

The Art of Argument — Anticipating Opposition

When you take a position you think will be unpopular or controversial, an effective strategy is to anticipate the opposition you may receive. In this way, you indicate that you have thought carefully about your position, and you make it more difficult for those who resist your argument to reject your claims outright. In nearly all effective argument and debate, the writer or speaker will attempt to preempt arguments likely to be made by the other side by dealing with them first. This doesn't mean, of course, that you have answered those opposing arguments satisfactorily, but it does mean that the opposing side will need to take into account your awareness of its position.

In "Uniting Families," Tulane University student Elyse Toplin realizes that one objection readers may have to her position on the Uniting American Families Act is that the legislation, if passed, could open the door to fraud — that is, people might lie about the strength of a relationship to gain citizenship. That is why she acknowledges this possibility directly in paragraph 7. By mentioning that "some may think that fraud would increase with the passage of UAFA," she shows she is aware of this opposing argument. She then answers the objection by saying that same-sex relationships can be as committed as those of heterosexuals and uses her earlier example of such a relationship to reinforce her point.

1

Toplin anticipates the argument that opponents of her position may make

Though some may think that fraud would increase with the passage of UAFA, it is not unfounded to believe that many homosexual couples could prove — just as their heterosexual counterparts can — that they are part of a committed, long-term relationship. (1) After Renato was denied entry to the United States, for example, Stewart commuted to Brazil from New York every other weekend for more than a year. When the financial burden of this task became too much to bear, the couple moved to England, where they could still be together. Though most heterosexual couples are never asked to do things this extreme, the strength of their commitment is never questioned.

STUDENT WRITER AT WORK
Elyse Toplin

On Writing "Uniting Families"

RA. What inspired you to write this essay? And publish it in your campus paper?

ET. I was inspired to write this essay after attending a hearing on UAFA for my summer internship at the Hebrew Immigrant Aid Society in 2009. The hearing, where I heard testimony from Shirley Tan and Gordon Stewart, made me aware of the challenges faced by LGBT couples as they navigate our complicated immigration system. Publication in the campus newspaper was almost by accident. I had written the essay for a class and then showed it to one of my friends on the newspaper, who then showed it to an editor, and he decided to publish it that week.

RA. What response have you received to this piece? Has the feedback you have received affected your views on the topic you wrote about?

ET. I received many positive responses after the article was published online. I was told that it was the only "Views" article that the *Hullabaloo* has ever run that received only positive feedback. The article was also picked up by several blogs, and many people responded to the article with their own stories. The feedback strengthened my opinion that the United States has a flawed immigration policy that needs to be changed.

RA. How long did it take for you to write this piece? Did you revise your work? What were your goals as you revised?

ET. I wrote the original essay for my class in a few hours, and then I revised it to make the point stronger and to adhere to the 750-word limit that my professor had included in the assignment. Once we decided to include the article in the paper, I revised it again and rewrote the introduction, and then the article was further revised before the newspaper was published. My goals while revising were to make my point stronger and more coherent, and I rewrote the introduction to make it more relevant to the student readers. I did this by tying in the recent State of the Union address.

RA. What magazines and newspapers do you like to read?

ET. The magazines and newspapers I read the most frequently are *The Washington Post, Express by the Washington Post, BBC News Online, Time* magazine, and *People*. I also read a lot of magazines related to health and fitness, including *Shape, Self,* and *Runner's World*.

RA. Are you pursuing a career in which writing will be a component?

ET. I definitely plan to have writing play a key role in any career I choose; however, I don't know what I want to be when I grow up and therefore I don't know what exactly that role will be.

RA. What advice do you have for other student writers?

ET. My best advice for other student writers is to read a lot, and become informed about topics that interest you. This will help to form opinions about issues that you are passionate about, and writing about those issues is far easier than writing about issues that you aren't interested in. Also, never stop writing, because if you constantly write and get feedback you will become a more confident writer and then a better writer by being responsive to constructive criticism.

Ira Berlin

Migrations Forced and Free

[*Smithsonian*, February 2010]

BEFORE YOU READ
Does being black in America mean only sharing a part of the history of slavery and segregation, or are recent immigrants from Africa and the Caribbean part of the African American community?

WORDS TO LEARN
interplay (para. 1): the effect two things have on each other (noun).

abolitionist (para. 1): opposing slavery (adjective).

emancipation (para. 1): freeing, especially of a slave (noun).

articulated (para. 3): stated (adjective).

turmoil (para. 3): trouble (noun).

warrant (para. 4): make necessary (verb).

One of the leading historians of the African American experience, Ira Berlin is a distinguished professor at the University of Maryland and the author of numerous books, including Many Thousands Gone: The First Two Centuries of Slavery in North America *(1998), which received the prestigious Bancroft Prize, and the prize-winning* Generations of Captivity: A History of African American Slaves *(2003).*

S ome years ago, I was interviewed on public radio about the mean- 1
ing of the Emancipation Proclamation.[1] I addressed the familiar
themes of the origins of that great document: the changing nature
of the Civil War, the Union army's growing dependence on black labor,
the intensifying opposition to slavery in the North and the interplay of
military necessity and abolitionist idealism. I recalled the longstanding
debate over the role of Abraham Lincoln, the Radicals in Congress, abo-
litionists in the North, the Union army in the field and slaves on the plantations of the South in the destruction of slavery and in the authorship
of legal freedom. And I stated my long-held position that slaves played a
critical role in securing their own freedom. The controversy over what
was sometimes called "self-emancipation" had generated great heat
among historians, and it still had life.

As I left the broadcast booth, a knot of black men and women — most 2
of them technicians at the station — were talking about emancipation
and its meaning. Once I was drawn into their discussion, I was surprised
to learn that no one in the group was descended from anyone who had
been freed by the proclamation or any other Civil War measure. Two
had been born in Haiti, one in Jamaica, one in Britain, two in Ghana, and
one, I believe, in Somalia. Others may have been the children of immigrants. While they seemed impressed — but not surprised — that slaves
had played a part in breaking their own chains, and were interested in
the events that had brought Lincoln to his decision during the summer
of 1862, they insisted it had nothing to do with them. Simply put, it was
not their history.

The conversation weighed upon me as I left the studio, and it has 3
since. Much of the collective consciousness of black people in mainland North America — the belief of individual men and women that
their own fate was linked to that of the group — has long been articulated through a common history, indeed a particular history: centuries
of enslavement, freedom in the course of the Civil War, a great promise
made amid the political turmoil of Reconstruction and a great promise
broken, followed by disfranchisement, segregation and, finally, the long
struggle for equality.

In commemorating this history—whether on Martin Luther 4
King Jr.'s birthday, during Black History Month or as current events
warrant — African-Americans have rightly laid claim to a unique identity.
Such celebrations—their memorialization of the past — are no different

---

[1] The Emancipation Proclamation (para. 1): The document President Abraham
Lincoln wrote in 1862 and issued in 1863, freeing most of the slaves in the
United States.

from those attached to the rituals of Vietnamese Tet[2] celebrations or the Eastern Orthodox Nativity Fast,[3] or the celebration of the birthdays of Christopher Columbus or Casimir Pulaski;[4] social identity is ever rooted in history. But for African-Americans, their history has always been especially important because they were long denied a past.

And so the "not my history" disclaimer by people of African descent seemed particularly pointed — enough to compel me to look closely at how previous waves of black immigrants had addressed the connections between the history they carried from the Old World and the history they inherited in the New.   5

In 1965, Congress passed the Voting Rights Act, which became a critical marker in African-American history. Given opportunity, black Americans voted and stood for office in numbers not seen since the collapse of Reconstruction almost 100 years earlier. They soon occupied positions that had been the exclusive preserve of white men for more than half a century. By the beginning of the twenty-first century, black men and women had taken seats in the United States Senate and House of Representatives, as well as in state houses and municipalities throughout the nation. In 2009, a black man assumed the presidency of the United States. African-American life had been transformed.   6

Within months of passing the Voting Rights Act, Congress passed a new immigration law, replacing the Johnson-Reed Act of 1924, which had favored the admission of northern Europeans, with the Immigration and Nationality Act. The new law scrapped the rule of national origins and enshrined a first-come, first-served principle that made allowances for the recruitment of needed skills and the unification of divided families.   7

This was a radical change in policy, but few people expected it to have much practical effect. It "is not a revolutionary bill," President Lyndon Johnson intoned. "It does not affect the lives of millions. It will not reshape the structure of our daily lives."   8

But it has had a profound impact on American life. At the time it was passed, the foreign-born proportion of the American population had fallen to historic lows — about 5 percent — in large measure because of   9

---

[2] Tet (para. 4): The Vietnamese New Year festival.

---

[3] Eastern Orthodox Nativity (para. 4): The holiday celebrating Jesus' birth in the Eastern Orthodox Church, a branch of Christianity centered in Eastern Europe and Asia.

---

[4] Casimir Pulaski (para. 4): A Polish-American cavalry officer (1745–1779) during the time of the Revolutionary War who saved George Washington's life; he is honored by Polish-Americans, particularly in Illinois, on Casimir Pulaski Day.

the old immigration restrictions. Not since the 1830s had the foreign-born made up such a tiny proportion of the American people. By 1965, the United States was no longer a nation of immigrants.

During the next four decades, forces set in motion by the Immigra-   10
tion and Nationality Act changed that. The number of immigrants entering the United States legally rose sharply, from some 3.3 million in the
1960s to 4.5 million in the 1970s. During the 1980s, a record 7.3 million
people of foreign birth came legally to the United States to live. In the last
third of the 20th century, America's legally recognized foreign-born population tripled in size, equal to more than one American in ten. By the
beginning of the twenty-first century, the United States was accepting
foreign-born people at rates higher than at any time since the 1850s. The
number of illegal immigrants added yet more to the total, as the United
States was transformed into an immigrant society once again.

Black America was similarly transformed. Before 1965, black peo-   11
ple of foreign birth residing in the United States were nearly invisible.
According to the 1960 census, their percentage of the population was to
the right of the decimal point. But after 1965, men and women of African
descent entered the United States in ever-increasing numbers. During
the 1990s, some 900,000 black immigrants came from the Caribbean;
another 400,000 came from Africa; still others came from Europe and
the Pacific rim. By the beginning of the twenty-first century, more people
had come from Africa to live in the United States than during the centuries of the slave trade. At that point, nearly one in ten black Americans
was an immigrant or the child of an immigrant.

African-American society has begun to reflect this change. In New   12
York, the Roman Catholic diocese has added masses in Ashanti and
Fante, while black men and women from various Caribbean islands
march in the West Indian-American Carnival and the Dominican Day
Parade. In Chicago, Cameroonians celebrate their nation's independence
day, while the DuSable Museum of African American History hosts a
Nigerian Festival. Black immigrants have joined groups such as the Egbe
Omo Yoruba (National Association of Yoruba Descendants in North
America), the Association des Sénégalais d'Amérique and the Fédéra-
tion des Associations Régionales Haïtiennes à l'Étranger rather than the
NAACP or the Urban League.

To many of these men and women, Juneteenth celebrations — the   13
commemoration of the end of slavery in the United States — are at
best an afterthought. The new arrivals frequently echo the words of
the men and women I met outside the radio broadcast booth. Some
have struggled over the very appellation "African-American," either
shunning it — declaring themselves, for instance, Jamaican-Americans

or Nigerian-Americans — or denying native black Americans' claim to it on the ground that most of them had never been to Africa. At the same time, some old-time black residents refuse to recognize the new arrivals as true African-Americans. "I am African and I am an American citizen; am I not African-American?" a dark-skinned, Ethiopian-born Abdulaziz Kamus asked at a community meeting in suburban Maryland in 2004. To his surprise and dismay, the overwhelmingly black audience responded no. Such discord over the meaning of the African-American experience and who is (and isn't) part of it is not new, but of late has grown more intense.

> African-American history might best be viewed as a series of great migrations.

After devoting more than 30 years 14 of my career as a historian to the study of the American past, I've concluded that African-American history might best be viewed as a series of great migrations, during which immigrants — at first forced and then free — transformed an alien place into a home, becoming deeply rooted in a land that once was foreign, even despised. After each migration, the newcomers created new understandings of the African-American experience and new definitions of blackness. Given the numbers of black immigrants arriving after 1965, and the diversity of their origins, it should be no surprise that the overarching narrative of African-American history has become a subject of contention.

That narrative, encapsulated in the title of John Hope Franklin's clas- 15 sic text *From Slavery to Freedom*, has been reflected in everything from spirituals to sermons, from folk tales to TV docudramas. Like Booker T. Washington's *Up from Slavery*, Alex Haley's *Roots* and Martin Luther King Jr.'s "I Have a Dream" speech, it retells the nightmare of enslavement, the exhilaration of emancipation, the betrayal of Reconstruction, the ordeal of disfranchisement and segregation, and the pervasive, omnipresent discrimination, along with the heroic and ultimately triumphant struggle against second-class citizenship.

This narrative retains incalculable value. It reminds men and 16 women that a shared past binds them together, even when distance and different circumstances and experiences create diverse interests. It also integrates black people's history into an American story of seemingly inevitable progress. While recognizing the realities of black poverty and inequality, it nevertheless depicts the trajectory of black life moving along what Dr. King referred to as the "arc of justice," in which exploitation and coercion yield, reluctantly but inexorably, to fairness and freedom.

Yet this story has had less direct relevance for black immigrants. 17
Although new arrivals quickly discover the racial inequalities of American
life for themselves, many — fleeing from poverty of the sort rarely experienced even by the poorest of contemporary black Americans and tyranny
unknown to even the most oppressed — are quick to embrace a society that
offers them opportunities unknown in their homelands. While they have
subjected themselves to exploitation by working long hours for little com-
pensation and underconsuming to save for the future (just as their native-
born counterparts have done), they often ignore the connection between
their own travails and those of previous generations of African-Americans.
But those travails are connected, for the migrations that are currently
transforming African-American life are directly connected to those that
have transformed black life in the past. The trans-Atlantic passage to the
tobacco and rice plantations of the coastal South, the nineteenth-century
movement to the cotton and sugar plantations of the Southern interior,
the twentieth-century shift to the industrializing cities of the North and
the waves of arrivals after 1965 all reflect the changing demands of global
capitalism and its appetite for labor.

New circumstances, it seems, require a new narrative. But it need 18
not — and should not — deny or contradict the slavery-to-freedom
story. As the more recent arrivals add their own chapters, the themes
derived from these various migrations, both forced and free, grow in significance. They allow us to see the African-American experience afresh
and sharpen our awareness that African-American history is, in the end,
of one piece.

VOCABULARY/USING A DICTIONARY

1. What is *idealism* (para. 1)? Explain how it is related to the word *ideal*. To
   what does *abolitionist idealism* refer?
2. What exactly does the phrase *collective consciousness* mean as Berlin
   uses it in paragraph 3?
3. Define *disfranchisement* (para. 3). Explain its origin and the meaning of
   the related word *franchise*.

RESPONDING TO WORDS IN CONTEXT

1. What does Berlin mean by the word *authorship* in paragraph 1? How were
   slaves the *authors* of their legal freedom, literally and figuratively?
2. Berlin describes seeing a "knot of black men and women" (para. 2) in the
   radio station office. What does *knot* mean here? What image does the
   word give you?

3. Explain the use of the word *rooted* in paragraph 4. What does it mean for social identity to be "rooted in history"? What further connotation does the word have here?

DISCUSSING MAIN POINT AND MEANING

1. To what does Berlin's title, "Migrations Forced and Free," refer? What is a migration, and which are the forced and free ones in his essay? How does this title frame the themes of the short essay?
2. What exactly is it about the history and identity of black people in the United States that Berlin considers "unique" (para. 4)? Why does he argue that the consciousness of African Americans is different from that of other ethnic groups?
3. Explain, in your own words, why the conversation of the technicians at the station weighed on Berlin so much. How did their feelings about emancipation lead to Berlin's conclusion in the final paragraph of the essay?

EXAMINING SENTENCES, PARAGRAPHS, AND ORGANIZATION

1. What is the purpose of the examples listed in paragraph 4 ("Vietnamese Tet celebrations ... Casimir Pulaski")? What do these examples illustrate? What sort of examples has Berlin attempted to select?
2. Discuss the overall organization of this short essay. What modes of writing does Berlin start with, and how does he conclude? Do you think it's effective? Why or why not?

THINKING CRITICALLY

1. What does Berlin mean by his "long-held position that slaves played a critical role in securing their own freedom" (para. 1)? Why might this be considered a controversial position, and what evidence did Berlin offer in its defense on the public radio show? Based on your research and knowledge of American history, how — if at all — do you think slaves achieved freedom for themselves?
2. What makes someone black in America? Are immigrants from Ghana and the Caribbean who came to North America after the abolishment of slavery still part of the African American community and experience? Why or why not?
3. Berlin elevates celebrations rooted in ethnic heritage, like Black History Month. How do you feel about official celebrations that focus on the contributions and history of one group? Give specific examples. Why does Berlin feel these celebrations are so important? Do you agree? Or do you see them as divisive?

IN-CLASS WRITING ACTIVITIES

1. Discuss the relationship you have to your own ethnic heritage and identity. Was where your family came from an important part of how you were taught to define yourself? Why or why not? To what extent, if any, does your racial, ethnic, and national heritage define you? Why?

2. Berlin refers to "the collective consciousness of black people in mainland North America" (para. 3). Give a few examples of what a collective consciousness is and does. Do you believe the collective consciousness — whether of a society, a nation, a race, or even a family — is a real thing? Why or why not?

The Census Bureau projects that there will be 400 million people in the U.S. by 2050.

Remember when this was heavy traffic?

Ask any of your neighbors – things have changed over the past few years. Traffic has gotten worse and schools more crowded. Large developments, eight-lane highways and shopping centers have replaced open fields and wooded areas. Our suburban communities are overwhelmed by the demands of a larger population.

According to the Census Bureau, the U.S. population will grow from 273 million today to over 400 million within the next fifty years – with mass immigration accounting for over 60% of that growth. Every year, our outdated immigration policy brings over 1,000,000 people to the United States. If immigration and population growth continue at these unsustainable levels, a livable America will become a thing of the past.

– – – – – – – – – – – – – – – – – –

Yes, I want to help NPG work for environmentally sound national and global population policies. Here is my tax-deductible contribution.

❑ $30   ❑ $50   ❑ $100   ❑ Other

Name ....

Address ....

City .... State .... Zip ....

Please mail to: NR-180

Negative Population Growth
P.O. Box 53249 • Washington, DC 20009 • (202) 667-8950

For more information about immigration, population growth and the environment, please visit NPG's home on the internet at **www.npg.org**

Negative Population Growth (NPG) was founded in 1972. The national organization is committed to reducing America's population growth. One of the significant ways to do this, the organization proposes, is to drastically cut back on immigration. According to its Web page, the organization's goal is "to educate the American public and political leaders about the detrimental effects of overpopulation on our environment, resources, and quality of life. NPG advocates a smaller and truly sustainable United States population accomplished through smaller families and lower, more traditional immigration levels."

Recently, NPG commended the former director of the United Nation's Population Division and current research director at the Center for Migration Studies, Joseph Chamie, who has stated: "Contrary to popular thought, the dominant force fueling America's demographic growth is not natural increase, but immigration." NPG then goes on to say: "Statistics show that U.S. population growth would have stabilized in about 1970 if it were not for the tremendous number of immigrants entering our country after the passage of the Immigration Act of 1965. To make matters even worse, the U.S. Census Bureau estimates that the vast majority of our future population growth will be driven by immigration. In order to halt and eventually reverse our population growth, we absolutely must reduce our current immigration rates."

In 1999, NPG released the print advertisement shown here, which appeared in major magazines nationwide. The ad addresses the issue of overcrowding and what Americans can do about it.

Discussing the Unit

SUGGESTED TOPIC FOR DISCUSSION
What can be done about America's borders, particularly its border with Central America? Should we close it up and attempt to police it more tightly? Or do we need an immigration policy that addresses the root causes of immigration and that deals with the problems immigrants themselves face in the United States?

PREPARING FOR CLASS DISCUSSION
1. How does the debate between Tamar Jacoby and Mark Krikorian in this chapter summarize our immigration debate? Do you think it's the right one to be having? Should it even matter if immigrants are harder

working than native-born Americans? Or, as Luis Rodríguez suggests, is there an inherent value in populating a country with people of different values and traditions?

2. Consider why conservatives, who often believe in less government, and liberals, who traditionally advocate for more, switch sides on this issue. Liberals like Jacoby want less enforcement of the border and of immigration laws, while conservatives argue for a crackdown on what they term illegal immigrants. How does this line up with the rest of the left-right dichotomy in America now? Does your position on immigration match the rest of your politics in this way? Why or why not?

FROM DISCUSSION TO WRITING

1. Discuss the image of the immigrant as described by two of the authors in the chapter, and compare it with the first-person image Vicente Martinez portrays. How do native-born Americans portray immigrants, even when they're sympathetic to their plight? Is talking about a typical immigrant reductive, or even ethnocentric or racist?

2. Write out your own immigration policy to submit to President Obama. Who should get into America, who shouldn't, and how should those in the country illegally be managed? Cite at least two of the essays in this chapter as expert testimony.

TOPICS FOR CROSS-CULTURAL DISCUSSION

1. Four of the essays in this chapter deal with immigration from Latin America, but since 9/11, immigration from other nations around the world has become a national priority for security reasons. Describe the new immigration challenges the country faces as a result of the threat of terrorism. How are these challenges similar to the ones described in this chapter, and how are they different?

2. While our immigration problem seems daunting, America is hardly the only country facing the issue—it's been a headline topic in countries like Denmark, the Netherlands, and even Kuwait. Research another country's immigration debate. What does it have in common with America's? How is it different?

Continued from page ii

Brittany Bergstrom. "The Fighting Sioux: The End of a Legacy?" from *The Spectrum*, The University of North Dakota, September 29, 2009. Reprinted by permission of the author.

Ira Berlin. "Migrations Forced and Free" (*Smithsonian Magazine*, February 2010), from *The Making of African America* by Ira Berlin, copyright © 2010 by Ira Berlin. Used by permission of Viking Penguin, a division of Penguin Group (USA) Inc.

Liz Breslin. "Does a Family Need to Share a Surname? Yes." Reprinted from *Brain, Child,* Winter 2009, by permission of the author.

Chris Clarke. "How to Write an Incendiary Blog Post" from *Boston.com*, February 14, 2010. Reprinted by permission of the author.

Amy Domini. "Why Investing in Fast Food May Be a Good Thing" from *Ode Magazine*, Volume 7, Issue 2. Reprinted by permission of the publisher.

Kim Elsesser. "And the Gender-Neutral Oscar Goes To . . ." from *The New York Times,* March 4, 2010. Copyright © 2010 by The New York Times. All rights reserved. Used by permission and protected by the Copyright Laws of the United States. The printing, copying, redistribution, or retransmission of the material without express written permission is prohibited.

Barbara Fredrickson. Interview with Angela Winter, "The Science of Happiness" from *The Sun,* May 2009. Reprinted by permission of Angela Winter.

Ann Friedman. "Swagger Like Us" reprinted with permission from *The American Prospect,* March 2010. Volume 21, Issue 2. http://www.prospect.org. *The American Prospect,* 1710 Rhode Island Avenue, NW, 12th Floor, Washington, DC 20036. All rights reserved.

Daniel Gilbert. "What You Don't Know Makes You Nervous" from *The New York Times,* May 21, 2009. Copyright © 2009 by The New York Times. All rights reserved. Used by permission and protected by the Copyright Laws of the United States. The printing, copying, redistribution, or retransmission of the material without express written permission is prohibited.

Jeff Goodell. "Warming Gets Worse" from *In Character,* Spring 2009. Reprinted by permission of the John Templeton Foundation.

Jay Griffiths. "The Tips of Your Fingers" from *Orion,* January/February 2010. Reprinted by permission of the author.

Rob Haggart. "This Photo Is Lying to You" by Rob Haggart from *Outside,* September 2009. Reprinted by permission of the author.

Mary Katharine Ham. "We Shall Overshare" from *The Weekly Standard,* June 8, 2009. Reprinted by permission of the publisher.

Aprille Hanson. "Stop Relying on Bloggers for News" from *The Echo,* The University of Central Arkansas, April 7, 2010. Reprinted by permission of the author.

Christopher Hedges. "Celebrity Culture and the Obama Brand" reprinted by permission of International Creative Management, Inc. Copyright © 2010 by Christopher Hedges. First appeared in *Tikkun,* January/February 2010.

Tom Hewitt. "Learning From Tison" from *The Sun Star,* University of Alaska, Fairbanks, December 15, 2009. Reprinted by permission of the author.

Tom Jacobs. "Romance Novel Titles Reveal Readers' Desires," *Miller-McCune,* March 2, 2010. Reprinted by permission of the publisher.

Tamar Jacoby. "Does Immigration Increase the Virtues of Hard Work and Fortitude in the U.S.? Yes." From *In Character,* Spring 2009. Reprinted by permission of the John Templeton Foundation.

Mohammed Khan. "The Need for Safety Is Paramount" from *The Daily Evergreen,* Washington State University, January 13, 2010. Reprinted by permission of the author.

Mark Krikorian. "Does Immigration Increase the Virtues of Hard Work and Fortitude in the U.S.? No." From *In Character,* Spring 2009. Reprinted by permission of the John Templeton Foundation.

Cal Thomas. "Sinking 'Climate Change'" by Cal Thomas, *Townhall.com*, June 3, 2010. Reprinted by permission.

Clive Thompson. "The New Literacy" by Clive Thompson. First published in *Wired*, September 2009. Copyright © 2010 Clive Thompson. Reprinted by permission of Featurewell.com.

Elyse Toplin. "Uniting Families" from *The Hullabaloo*, Tulane University, January 29, 2010. Reprinted by permission of the author.

John Edgar Wideman. "Street Corner Dreamers" from *Essence*, January 2009. Reprinted by permission of the author.

Laura Williamson. "Does a Family Need to Share a Surname? No." Reprinted from *Brain, Child*, Winter 2009, by permission of the author.

Pearl Wong. "Obama— President For All" from *The Santa Clara*, Santa Clara University, February 25, 2010. Reprinted by permission of the author.

Erica Zucco. "Quit Living in Swine Fear" from *The Maneater*, University of Missouri, Columbia, September 4, 2009. Reprinted by permission of the publisher.

Index of Authors and Titles